THE SECRETS OF MOUNT SHASTA
AND
A DWELLER ON TWO PLANETS

Channeled by Phylos
From The Soul Of Atlantis

Edited, Modernized and Abridged by Sean Casteel
New Material by
Nick Redfern, Timothy Green Beckley
And Paul Dale Roberts

THE SECRETS OF MOUNT SHASTA
AND
A DWELLER ON TWO PLANETS

Channeled By Phylos (Frederick S. Oliver)

Edited, Modernized And Abridged By Sean Casteel
Includes Special Additional Material By:
Timothy Green Beckley
Nick Redfern
Paul Dale Roberts

Timothy Green Beckley—Editorial Director
Carol Rodriquez—Publisher's Assistant
Sean Casteel—Associate Editor
Tim Swartz—Editorial Assistant
Typesetting, Formatting and Cover Design: William Kern

Printed in the United States of America

For a Free catalog, write:
Global Communications
P. O. Box 753
New Brunswick, NJ 08903
Free subscription to Conspiracy Journal e-mail Newsletter
www.ConspircayJournal.com

Do UFOs "hide" within the strange cloud formations often sighted over Shasta?

CONTENTS

R.I.P. BLEU OCEAN – PASSED JUNE 29, 2011
THIS BOOK IS DEDICATED TO OUR LONG
TIME ASSOCIATE AND FRIEND

Our friendship goes back many years. Rooted in rock and roll music, — we first met at the famous Max's Kansas City club — our association with Bleu Ocean was many layered. He was not only our tech support when we knew little about computers, but he traveled with us to almost every conference and seminar we set up as our audio visual technician and general organizer.

As anyone can tell you who knew him, Bleu led a very colorful life.

He was a member of the Klamath Indian tribe, who was actually born in a teepee on Mount Shasta. When he was several weeks old his uncle left him a drum and when he was seventeen he flew to New York and auditioned for a back up band that backed up the Monkees. He was hired on the spot, playing behind a lowered curtain as the Monkees were not actually able to play their instruments at that time. Many years later he made music history when, in 1979, working with CBS on Pink Floyd's album, "The Wall," on the song "Bring The Boys Back Home," Bleu assembled 30 drummers to play together on the song.

But our main interest in dedicating this book to our friend Bleu has to do with his various perplexing encounters with the unknown on Mount Shasta while growing up. One day after returning home from school, at about 3500 feet on Mount Shasta he saw a strange interloper.

"It was around late October," as he related his experience to me. "I was there with my cousins. Visibility was medium, as it usually is dismal that time of year anyway. In the distance – about 20 feet at the most – we saw what appeared to be a 'hunched man' that seemed to be covered in hair all over his body. I remember he had slightly long arms. The creature, or whatever it was, was walking away from us. We tried to follow him and as we got closer to him we began to see prints in the snow that looked like a large animal's. We felt we might be in danger. We all had bows and arrows, so we stood in one of the tracks until he was out of sight.

Bleu says that when he was in his early teens, "At night we could hear something like wolves or other howling 'animals'; sounds that originated from the middle of the mountain at about 5,500 feet. It was like a surround sound and it was impossible to pinpoint the location.

"As we heard them, we often decided to pursue them. There were five or six of us teenage boys with bows and arrows.One day finally we found ourselves very close to the sound. When we looked up there were these midget-like 'men' who seemed to be walking on all fours but we couldn't say for sure as we were ourselves frightened and paralyzed. They seemed to be like a herd – 15 0r 20 of them – and beyond them were three to five larger 'men' who stood over seven feet tall with large staffs in their hands and amazingly long beards. They seemed to be coming out from inside Mount Shasta, from some kind of cave.

"And it seemed to us like these 'midgets' were protecting their 'masters' just like a dog would protect its owner. These men I will never forget. There was an illumination to their skin, like a fluorescent light was coming out of them. Later on, when I met Tim Beckley and did one of his UFO conferences, I was told by one of the people at the conference that there was a civilization inside the mountain and that I had not dreamed it up."

Bleu also told me once that he felt it was possible to contact the occupants of UFOs through the beating of drums, setting up a special rhythm that the "aliens" could relate to on a level of higher consciousness. Bleu felt that many of the ultra-terrestrials were friendly and their craft were sighted around Mount Shasta because they liked the vibrations of this majestic mountain.

Timothy Green Beckley, Publisher
mrufo8@hotmail.com

Are We All Not A Dweller On Two Planets?

By Timothy Green Beckley

I remember first picking up a copy of the book channeled by Phylos when I was a teenager. Though it was a tedious and ponderous read for someone my age, I was fascinated by the nature and content of the volume.

I had a little bookselling business going even in those days and so I added it to my list of New Age books by authors like Michael X and George King. There was little I could do to confirm the content of this wondrous volume that lay open before me, but I was intrigued by both the message and the method by which the text had been received. Like actress and former **"Rat Pack"** follower Shirley MacLaine, **"A Dweller On Two Planets"** was my first inkling that there was such a thing as channeling, and that entities could speak through the vocal cords of others, to bring forth messages of enlightenment that could be for the betterment of all of us. I was impressed, but saw no proof that this was either possible or happening right under our very noses. I am still skeptical to this day.

The Secrets Of Mount Shasta And A Dweller On Two Planets

But the story told by Phylos is an intriguing one, and, thanks to journalist Sean Casteel, it has been brought into the 21st Century with his editing and abridging skills. "A Dweller" was always "stiff" reading. Hard to get through. You would think that one of the Old Testament prophets had written it. But now we can look at the text in the light of a new day.

AND IT TRULY IS WONDROUS — more so than ever before. Plus, in addition, we find that Mount Shasta, where the epic was channeled, is a wondrous place in itself, a zone of pure enlightenment. People go to this incredible natural landmark not only to hike and sightsee but to meditate and have a spiritual experience. We welcome you to join us on this updated journey. For, after all, are we all not a dweller on two planets — the physical and the spiritual?

Timothy Green Beckley, Publisher

mrufo8@hotmail.com

Mount Shasta: The Most Magical
and Mysterious of all Mountains!

By Nick Redfern

Native American Lore and Legend

Situated on the southern tip of the vast and mountainous Cascade Range – which encompasses parts of British Columbia, California, Washington State, and Oregon - Mount Shasta is a huge, all-dominating peak that, at nearly fifteen thousand feet, is the fifth tallest mountain in the Golden State, and one that has been home to human civilization, in varying degrees, since around 5,000 B.C. It's also a mountain steeped in matters mysterious, unearthly, and deeply ancient.

On this latter point, Native American lore of the Klamath tribe tells of how, thousands of years ago, a mighty and turbulent battle was fought between Llao, the deity of the Underworld, and Skell, the Klamath's god of the skies. According to folklore, Llao found a way to exit the terrible world below via a portal in Mount Mazama – also on the Cascade Range – and succeeded in traveling to the stars, where Skell dwelled, provoking outright, hostile confrontation in the process. As a result, when Llao returned to Mazama, so Skell, too, descended from the heavens, to Mount Shasta, and a frightful war began. Such was the destructive and thunderous nature of the violent conflict between the gods that Mount Mazama erupted, leading to the creation of what is famously known today as Crater Lake. And, as punishment for daring to take on Skell in cosmic combat, and having been de-

3

feated, Llao was banished back to the darkest depths of the Underworld.

Moving on, but still on matters of a Native American nature, Hopi legend tells of a race of lizard-like people that built thirteen underground cities along the Pacific Coast thousands of years ago, one of which, it is claimed, exists deep within the cavernous bowels of Mount Shasta. Then there are the Miwok and Siskiyou Indians, both of whose folklore maintains that a race of invisible people, rather than lizard folk, roam the area – both above and underground.

Relative to issues of a spiritual and deity-driven nature, more than a century ago, Italian settlers – who had moved to the United States and worked in the fields of stonemasonry – laid the cornerstones of a soon-thriving Catholic community on Mount Shasta. And, in 1970, a Buddhist monastery, Shasta Abbey, was created by one Houn Jiyu - who held the title of Roshi, a Japanese term meaning Elder Master or Old Teacher – and which continues to offer visitors and disciples an abundance of data and teachings on all matters of a Buddhist nature.

The Native American Klamath tribe settled on Mount Shasta. Many tribal members — including our friend the late musician Bleu Ocean — reported numerous strange occurrences throughout the years.

The Secrets Of Mount Shasta And A Dweller On Two Planets

The Dwellers of Lemuria and the Book of Dzyan

As well as being a haven for a whole variety of religious teachings and beliefs, Mount Shasta is, as shall soon become clear, also the realm of Bigfoot and – widespread belief suggests – the last vestiges of a mighty, renowned race of legendary people that dominated the planet in the fog-shrouded past. They were known as the Lemurians and were said to have inhabited a now sunken land, possibly situated somewhere in either the Pacific or Indian Ocean. Although the people of Lemuria reportedly attained their peak millennia upon millennia ago, it was not until the late 19th Century, and through the middle years of the 20th Century, that they caught the public's attention on a large scale – and particularly so in relation to a certain connection with Mount Shasta. Truly, the story is a swirling cauldron of deep strangeness.

Madame Helena Blavatsky spoke of lost civilizations like the ones associated with Mount Shasta.

Back in the 1800s, Helena Blavatsky, the co-founder with William Quan Judge and Colonel Henry S. Olcott of the Theosophical Society - the original mandate of which was the study and elucidation of occultism - claimed to have been exposed to an ancient text of mysterious proportions that was said to have pre-dated the times and people of Atlantis. Its title was the *Book of Dzyan* and was guarded with near paranoid zeal by a brotherhood of powerful and ancient proportions. As a result of her reported exposure to the old and mighty tome, and while in Tibet studying esoteric lore, Blavatsky developed a remarkable framework concerning, and a belief in, the Lemurians that ultimately led to the very heart of Mount Shasta itself.

According to Blavatsky's findings, the Lemurians were the type of people for whom the phrase *once seen, never forgotten* might justifiably have been created. Around seven feet in height, they were egg-laying hermaphrodites that, while not overly mentally developed, were, spiritually-speaking, far more advanced than those who came before them. As Blavatsky described it, the Lemurians were the Third Root Race of a total of seven who were ultimately destroyed by appalled and angered gods after they, the people of Lemuria, turned to bestiality, and in doing so sealed their doom, around 12,500 B.C. But, the gods were not done with life on Earth: they soon embarked on the creation of a Fourth Root Race, the equally legendary Atlanteans. Little did the gods realize it when they set about the creation of a new race, some of the Lemurians escaped the destruction and made their secret way to - as you may by now have guessed – a certain mountain in the Cascades.

Frederick Spencer Oliver Enters the Scene

The revelations of Helena Blavatsky were elaborated on to a considerable degree by a British theosophist named William Scott-Elliot. He, in turn, had acquired his data from yet another theosophist, Charles Webster Leadbeater, who claimed clairvoyant communication with spiritually advanced, supernatural masters that imparted a wealth of data on both Lemuria and Atlantis. Also hot on the heels of Blavatsky, and only six years before the dawning of the 20th Century, a teenager named Frederick Spencer Oliver completed the writing of his book *A Dweller on Two Planets*. Published in 1905, six years after Oliver's untimely and very early death, the book caused a firestorm of controversy with its claims that the Lemurians shared a lineage with the Atlanteans, and that those Lemurians that escaped the pummeling wrath of the gods made their secret and collective way to Mount Shasta; just as Blavatsky had asserted. And they weren't just living *on* the mountain, but deep *within* it, too, in certain, secret, cavernous depths that Oliver claimed could be accessed if one only knew the specific and secret entrance points of old. If one should ever encounter a tall, white-robed figure on Mount Shasta, said Oliver, it was all but certain to be a Lemurian.

And how, exactly, did Oliver know all this? Well, he claimed to have been in contact with a being that called itself Phylos the Tibetan. Phylos, whose controversial data was imparted to Oliver by a mind to mind process known as channeling, was said to have lived a number of lives or incarnations; one as a Lemurian and another as an Atlantean. Phylos also claimed to have reincarnated as one Walter Pierson, a gold prospector who maintained he had seen a huge temple inside Mount Shasta. It was a structure that seemed to be practically constructed out of gold, silver, copper, precious ores and priceless stones, and one that, today, would surely provoke definitive *Raiders of the Lost Ark* style imagery and adventures of an Indiana Jones variety.

As controversial as the story of Pierson most certainly sounded, it was one that received support from yet another prospector, J.C. Brown, who reported seeing a very similar structure deep inside the mountain in 1904. But Brown had another revelation too. Strewn across the floor of the temple were the aged skeletons of numerous gigantic humanoids: nothing less than a race of ancient giants. Brown quickly departed, both amazed and scared, and said nothing to anyone about the temple or its astounding contents for years. Rather curiously, however, decades later, and after having become overwhelmingly obsessed by the hidden realm and gone public with his story, Brown vanished on the eve of what was to be his ultimate quest to once again locate the Aladdin's Cave of secrets. He was never seen again.

Other Examples of Ancient Temples and Cities under California

It's worth noting that the story of J.C Brown, above, is eerily paralleled by other tales – also from California – that suggest there are massive, ancient structures below California, ones built by highly advanced people now long gone. Located within California's Mojave Desert, Death Valley is a most apt name for a place that resembles the rugged surface of some far away, battle-scarred planet, and holds the dubious honor of being home to the highest recorded temperature in the western world. An incredible 136° Fahrenheit, it was noted on July 10, 1913, in the very appropriately named Furnace Creek. It is somewhat ironic that, although Death Valley got its memorable moniker during the famous Gold Rush of 1849, only one death among all of the prospectors eager to seek out gold was actually reported during that turbulent period. While the name of the valley may be relatively new, the history of the area is most definitely not. For more than a thousand years the Timbisha Native Americans have lived in the harsh environs of Death Valley. And, in times both past and present, so have a whole range of things undeniably weird.

One of the strangest of all sagas relative to the mysteries of Death Valley erupted in the summer of 1947, the very same period in which the era of the flying saucer took the entire world by storm. In early August of that year,

The Secrets Of Mount Shasta And A Dweller On Two Planets

Howard E. Hill, of Los Angeles, spoke before the city's Transportation Club and told a story of sensational proportions. It was an extravagant tale that described the work of a certain Dr. F. Bruce Russell, a retired Cincinnati, Ohio physician, who claimed to have discovered, in 1931, a series of complex tunnels deep below Death Valley.

Well, you may justifiably ask, so what? After all, caves, caverns and underground grottos exist pretty much all around the world, don't they? Yes, they most certainly do. But, there was something very special and unique about these particular tunnels beneath Death Valley. According to the story told to Hill by Russell, the caves contained the skeletons of several gigantic men, each in the region of around nine feet in height, which Russell stumbled upon with a colleague, Dr. Daniel S. Bovee, who Russell had worked with on archaeological excavations in Mexico several years earlier. And *stumbled upon* is highly apt terminology. Russell reportedly fell headlong into one of the caves when the surface soil gave way beneath him as he was in the middle of busily sinking a shaft for a mining claim.

Hill amazed and hushed the audience of the Transportation Club when he said that the huge figures were dressed in what resembled medium-length jackets and pants, but that seemed to be made out of the hides of animals of distinctly unknown origins. Upping the weird stakes even further still, Hill said that while deep underground Russell and Bovee apparently came across what they described as a huge hall, in which were found unspecified devices adorned with markings that befitted none other than the regalia of the Freemasons. More bizarrely, the long-dead remains of both tigers and elephants – or, as was later suggested, and which was certainly far more plausible, the remnants of ancient saber-tooth tigers and mammoths – were also found strewn across the floor of the huge hall.

As for this fantastic, below-surface realm, we're not talking about just a few, measly tunnels either. Hill revealed that then current estimates suggested there were at least thirty-two of them, and they ran for an amazing 180 square miles, covering whole swathes of Death Valley and certain parts of southern Nevada. As for the era in which the bodies originated, while no explanation was given as to how Russell had come up with such a figure, he estimated they extended back an incredible 80,000 years, if not even longer, Hill told the crowd.

Hardly surprisingly, the local media of the day scoffed, and loudly cited

The Secrets Of Mount Shasta And A Dweller On Two Planets

the comments of certain, unnamed professional archaeologists who openly laughed at such a story, assuring anyone and everyone who would listen that the tale simply had to be that and nothing else at all: a tall story of April Fools' Day proportions. Rather incredibly, but some might say predictably, no-one in the professional world of archaeology would even dare take up the challenge to see the incredible evidence for his or herself – possibly fearful of being viewed as gullible and lacking in credibility if they chose to do so. The result: it was left up to Howard E. Hill to continue to speak on behalf of Dr. Russell – which he certainly did, until the story died a mysterious and sudden death, and Hill, Russell and Bovee vanished into the shadows (or, perhaps, into the depths of those old caves), never, ever to return.

While many might be inclined to dismiss out of hand an undeniably controversial report of just such a type, very similar ones abound from the heart of Death Valley. One such story predated Howard Hill's revelations by a decade and a half. In 1932, only one year after Russell and Bovee reportedly came across that infamous network of underground tunnels, large hall, and a multitude of gigantic skeletons, a very similar story surfaced from Bourke Lee, a noted, early chronicler of Death Valley history and folklore. According to Lee, he got the story in the late 1920s, which would have placed it several years before the experience of Russell and Bovee, but it must be admitted that the parallels between both accounts are remarkably alike.

In the story told to Lee by Jack and Bill – which, given that Lee used first-names only, sound suspiciously like pseudonyms created by Lee to protect the real identities of his sources – the underground realm was discovered after they fell through the surface soil and inadvertently stumbled upon the amazing evidence, just like Russell reportedly did several years later. In this case, however, Jack and Bill plunged into the heart of a vast cavern that seemingly extended for around twenty miles, but which eventually opened up into what could only be described as a massive, spacious city of undeniably ancient origins and almost *Arabian Knights*-like appearance. And then there were the bodies. They weren't giant skeletons, however. Rather, they were the remains of several mummified men, all carefully positioned in upright fashion and holding gold-colored spears in their hands.

Just about everything in the old, huge city seemed to be constructed out of gold, Bourke was told: walls, tables, floors, huge pillars, and vast doors; it was a prospector's greatest dream come to full fruition. There was even some form of artificial lighting in evidence, too – it appeared to be ingeniously powered by a complex network of underground natural gas. Recognizing the clear importance of the secret world of the distant past they had inadvertently uncovered, Jack and Bill slowly and carefully retraced their steps, and finally managed to clamber their way back to the surface world that had so fortuitously given way beneath them. As to who, or what, the ancient creators of this historic and historical world may have been, Jack and Bill told Bourlto Loo they had no idea at all, but they had every intention of going back and finding out, once and for all. If they did succeed in penetrating the heart of that old city once again, they may very well have never lived to tell the tale. Despite intensive digging on his part, Lee heard no more from them. And, for that matter, neither did anyone else. Death Valley, perhaps, had no intention of giving up its mysterious secrets of civilizations long gone quite that easily.

Channeling and UFOs

As a brief aside – and just before we return to the many and varied paranormal mysteries of Mount Shasta – it's worth noting that channeling, of the very type described by Frederick Spencer Oliver in *A Dweller on Two Planets*, gained something of a major resurgence in the early 1950s, and in relation to the matter of nothing less than alien visitations.

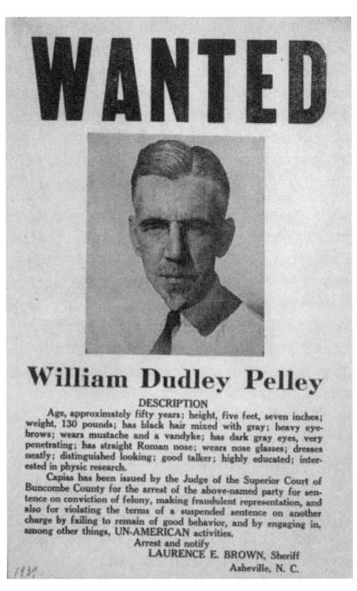

WANTED

William Dudley Pelley

DESCRIPTION

Age, approximately fifty years; height, five feet, seven inches; weight, 130 pounds; has black hair mixed with gray; heavy eyebrows; wears mustache and a vandyke; has dark gray eyes, very penetrating; has straight Roman nose; wears nose glasses; dresses neatly; distinguished looking; good talker; highly educated; interested in physic research.

Capias has been issued by the Judge of the Superior Court of Buncombe County for the arrest of the above-named party for sentence on conviction of felony, making fraudulent representation, and also for violating the terms of a suspended sentence on another charge by failing to remain of good behavior, and by engaging in, among other things, UN-AMERICAN activities.

Arrest and notify
LAURENCE E. BROWN, Sheriff
Asheville, N. C.

An arrest warrant was issued for the controversial channeler/neo-Nazi William Dudley Pelley, who was said to have made fraudulent claims regarding the arrival of the masters on Mount Shasta. Pelley at one time served eight years in prison for his wartime opposition to President Franklin Roosevelt.

The Secrets Of Mount Shasta And A Dweller On Two Planets

Also known as Michael d'Obrenovic and Brother Philip, George Hunt Williamson was born in Chicago, Illinois in 1926, became entranced by the occult in his teens, and evolved into a significant player on the saucer scene of the 1950s. In early 1951 Williamson was thrown out of the University of Arizona; however, having read, and been deeply influenced by, William Dudley Pelley's 1950 book *Star Guests*, he subsequently helped produce the group's monthly publication *Valor*.

At the time, Pelley had been recently released from prison after serving eight-years for his wartime opposition to President Roosevelt. The leader of a definitively fascist group known as the *Silver Shirts*, Pelley, just like Williamson, was fascinated by occult matters and compiled massive volumes of "automatic writing" on channeled contact with allegedly higher forms of intelligence. Pelley became a major influence on the life of Williamson – who ultimately combined his fascination with the occult and flying saucers by trying to contact extraterrestrial intelligences with a home-made Ouija board. Upon learning of some of the early assertions of the infamous "UFO Contactee" George Adamski, Williamson became a regular visitor to Adamski's commune in California.

In 1954, Williamson and a colleague and friend, Al Bailey, published their own saucer-dominated volume: *The Saucers Speak*, which focused upon Williamson's attempts to channel contact with extraterrestrials via the alternative mediums of short-wave radio and Ouija-boards. Actar of Mercury; Adu of Hatonn in Andromeda; Agfa Affa from the dark depths of Uranus; Ankar-22 of Jupiter; Artok of Pluto; and numerous others were among the motley alien crew with whom Williamson claimed to have communicated via the medium of channeling. In the late 1950s, Williamson changed his name, created a new fictitious academic and family background to accompany his latest moniker, and – as far as the Contactee issue

George Hunt Williamson

was concerned – largely vanished. Williamson died in 1986, a figure by then largely forgotten by, or completely unknown to, the UFO research community of the day. Adamski, meanwhile, was a player on the saucer scene right up until the time he took his very last breath.

On the matter of the relationship between Adamski and Williamson, researcher Colin Bennett states: "Adamski was not an educated man, and he used the better-educated Williamson as he used Desmond Leslie, that is as an extra cerebral lung. As such, George Hunt Williamson was the top of Adamski's multi-media head. As they used to say in those days, they both tripped one another out. The Mojave was certainly rich in ancient Indian legends concerning flying vehicles. This was one of the reasons why George Hunt Williamson and the Baileys accompanied Adamski to the desert.

"It is more than possible that the group wanted to conjure up something like the kind of presence that they thought they had contacted from their automatic writing, and at least Adamski got more than he bargained for. A combination of high intrigue, burgeoning exotic technology combined with the ancient desert and its prehistoric features was not to be trifled with, and a genie came right out of the alchemical bottle. All the best books on occultism contain the warning that the attempted raising of images is not to be taken lightly.

"It is important to understand that like Alan Ginsberg and Jack Kerouac, both Adamski and Williamson were fully inspired by the birth of this brave new world. It threaded through them as ivy threads through a house if it is not cut off; and neither Adamski nor Williamson were the kind of men to cut off any kind of speculative growth. Prototypal belief-systems sprouted almost from the top of their heads, and surreal conspiracies were the very breath of their being. Both were breathless Americans in the first nuclear age, and both were as excited as rich kids let loose in a big-city toyshop."

Guy Ballard and the I AM Activity

The next development of real significance in the strange saga of the Lemurians of Mount Shasta began in the 1930s when a man named Guy Warren Ballard, along with his wife, Edna, created what became known as the I AM Activity. Born in Iowa, and someone who served with the U.S. military during the First World War and later worked as a mining engineer, Ballard told a story that was as fascinating as it was undeniably controversial. As someone whose life and belief systems were steeped in both occult teachings and theosophy, Ballard claimed that while hiking on Mount Shasta in 1930 he encountered one Count of Saint Germain. An 18th Century alchemist who, it was claimed by many, had uncovered the secrets of nothing less than literal immortality, the count was variously described as being the so-called Wandering Jew that taunted Jesus Christ on the way to the Crucifix-ion; the son of Francis II Rakoczi, a prince of Transylvania; or the illegitimate son of the widow of Charles II of Spain, Maria Anna of Pfalz-Neuburg. Or:

maybe all of them! That, at the very time of his most fortunate en-counter, Ballard was on the mountain look-ing for what was de-scribed as an esoteric brotherhood – possi-bly, it was rumored, an offshoot of the very same brotherhood that guarded the Tibetan *Book of Dzyan* as de-scribed by Helena Blavatsky - only made matters even weirder.

Guy Ballard, seen here along with his wife, headed the million-strong I AM spiritual movement and is believed to be the first to talk about Lemurians living inside Mount Shasta. He also claimed to have encountered Count Saint Germain while wandering about the tree line.

It was during this experience on Mount Shasta that the enigmatic count reeled off to Ballard countless data on the future, positive role the United States would play in ushering in a new era for the people of Earth, as well as his personal knowledge of so-called As-cended Masters. The latter, the I AM Activity came to solidly accept, were once human people of both historical renown and major influence, includ-ing Jesus Christ and Maitreya. After their physical deaths, Ballard told his followers – which, by the dawning of the 1940s, were in excess of a highly impressive *one million* – the Ascended Masters existed in supernatural form, but would impart words of deep wisdom to certain people on Earth who had significant roles to play in the Earth's future, including, of course, Guy and Edna Ballard. And that Ballard claimed loudly to have been the re-embodi-ment of no less than George Washington only added further fuel to the con-troversial fire that forever seemed to surround him.

There was, needless to say, a great deal of debate concerning the I AM

The Secrets Of Mount Shasta And A Dweller On Two Planets

Activity and the Ballard family. Many within the local media of the day considered the whole thing to be nothing more than one big scam designed to ensure the pair a great deal of money from gullible souls willing to donate their hard earned wages and savings to the curious cause. And that many of the original members of the group were also members of a near-fascist organization called the Silver Legion added even more to the debate. The Silver Legion – whose members went by the title of Silver Shirts – was established in 1933 by the previously mentioned William Dudley Pelley, a racist, anti-Semitic character who had a deep admiration for Adolf Hitler and spiritualism. Guy Ballard, then, most certainly moved in controversial circles and not all of them were to be found on the slopes of Mount Shasta. And the controversy continued.

In 1942, three years after Guy Ballard's death, Edna and their son, Donald, were charged with no less than eighteen counts of mail fraud, as a result of the unproved data contained in a variety of their books and pamphlets relative to Ascended Masters, Lemuria, Mount Shasta, and much more of an interconnected nature. And although the pair was convicted on each count, in what ultimately turned out to be a landmark case when it came to what could or could not be said, or published, in the name of religion without offering any form of evidence in support of such claims, the convictions were finally, and somewhat dramatically, overturned. Demonstrating the allure of Ballard's teachings, more than eighty years after his alleged encounter with the Count of Saint Germain on Mount Shasta, devotees of his movement continue to hold an annual event on the mountain – called the *I AM Come!* pageant - which gives praise to the life and teachings of Jesus Christ. Guy Ballard still looms large at Mount Shasta, long after his physical passing.

Bigfoot: Mount Shasta's Resident Man-Beast

Like so many of the places we have examined in the pages of this book so far, Mount Shasta can also claim its very own resident Bigfoot. Its wild antics hit the local media on September 9, 1976, only a few days after the foul-smelling thing was seen near Cascade Gulch, which is located on the lower slopes of the legendary mount. The man that had the misfortune to cross paths with the monster was a logger from the town of Salmon: Virgil Larson.

In a subsequent interview with Sergeant Walt Bullington of the local police, the then forty-seven year old Larson explained how, at around 8.30

14

The Secrets Of Mount Shasta And A Dweller On Two Planets

a.m. only a few days earlier, he and a colleague, Pat Conway − both of the Columbia Helicopter Company - carefully negotiated the treacherous slope to their place of walk, having left their truck at a parking area adjacent to the road. It was while they were getting their breath back at the base of the hilly area in question − but now separated from each other by a few hundred feet, due to the rigors of the descent - that something occurred to Larson he most certainly was not anticipating in the slightest.

After a couple of minutes of taking a rest, Larsen's attention turned to the sound of loud, thumping footsteps coming down the hill. For a few moments he could see no-one, but quite naturally assumed it was yet another colleague from the U.S. Forest Service. It was not − that is, unless, the ser-

vice had some truly strange characters in its employ. Finally, at a distance of around fifty feet, Larsen could now see what, at first, looked like a darkly dressed man descending along a crude pathway through the trees that the logging company had created.

With thick bushes and trees dominating the entire scene, however, Larsen could only get the barest glimpses of the figure as it made its lumbering way down the hill; so, he called out, by way of wishing the character a good day. Bigfoot, evidently, is hardly one enamored by early morning, genial chatter. The dark form suddenly stopped, briefly turned its head in Larson's direction, then began walking again,

The legendary hairy beast Bigfoot has been seen on many occassions wandering the slopes of Mount Shasta, leaving many bold footprints behind.

at a noticeably increased speed – all without any form of reply to Larsen's greeting. Then, when the thing was barely fifteen feet away and no longer largely obliterated from view by the dense foliage, Larsen was at last able to see the enigmatic visitor in its fullest form. It was at this point that Larsen's mind became flooded by fear and panic: there was no man in his midst, after all. What *was* in his full midst for a second or several was a bulky, black-hair covered monstrosity that stunk like rotting meat and stood at around a towering seven and a half feet. Having got the disturbing impression that the creature was possibly sizing him up – whether as foe, food or even both – Larsen didn't wait around to get a better look and very wisely fled the area at high speed.

Having raced to where Pat Conway was also taking a break before beginning the day's activities, Larsen breathlessly related to his amazed partner what he had just seen. Thirty minutes later and armed with a couple of thick tree limbs for protection, the pair tentatively returned to the area and checked out the site. The creature was gone, but the terrible odor was still very much hanging around, while strange and somewhat indistinct tracks dominated the forest floor. It was now time, both men concluded, to bring in the sheriff.

Three Forest Service employees, Don Wopschal, Bob Gray and Rex Lebow, soon arrived with the previously referred to Sergeant Bullington. Interestingly, Larsen's encounter was taken most seriously by officialdom, which surely begs the inevitable and thought-provoking question of: was the seriousness prompted by other, earlier Bigfoot encounters in the area that had caught the attention of concerned authorities? Whatever the answer to that potentially important question, the positive response by the sheriff's office did not stop the authorities from ultimately trying to downplay the affair, however. A somewhat condescending suggestion was made that perhaps Larsen had been frightened by nothing stranger than a long-haired environmentalist that had a problem with loggers chopping down the old, mighty trees of Mount Shasta. Neither Larsen nor his wife was in any fashion satisfied by such a bizarre and unlikely theory. Larsen remained in a state of emotional turmoil for a number of days, while his wife stated that her husband was a man with three decades of experience working in the woods and one who had been frightened witless by his encounter. Mount Shasta had just become even weirder, if such a thing was even conceivably possible.

The Secrets Of Mount Shasta And A Dweller On Two Planets

The Kenneth Arnold Connection

Finally, it may not be without some significance that also contained in the huge Cascade Range is Mount Rainier. It was there, on June 24, 1947, that a pilot named Kenneth Arnold witnessed a veritable armada of strange, aerial vehicles that practically singlehandedly ushered in the era of the flying saucer. It was around 3.00 p.m. and Arnold was engaged in looking for an airplane that had crashed on the southwest side of Mount Rainier. "I hadn't flown more than two or three minutes on my course when a bright flash reflected on my airplane," said Arnold. "It startled me as I thought I was too close to some other aircraft. I looked every place in the sky and couldn't find where the reflection had come from until I looked to the left and the north of Mount Rainier, where I observed a chain of nine peculiar looking aircraft flying from north to south at approximately 9,500 feet elevation and going, seemingly, in a definite direction of about 170 degrees."

Arnold added that the mysterious craft were closing in rapidly on Mount Rainier, and that he was highly puzzled by their overall design: "I thought it was very peculiar that I couldn't find their tails but assumed they were some type of jet plane. The more I observed these objects, the more upset I became, as I am accustomed and familiar with most all objects flying whether I am close to the ground or at higher altitudes. The chain of these saucer-like objects [was] at least five miles long. I felt confident after I would land there would be some explanation of what I saw [sic]."

No firm conclusion for Arnold's encounter ever did surface; however, as the skies of the United States became populated with more and more fly-ing saucers during the heady summer of 1947, the U.S. military quickly realized that finding an answer to the mystery was an issue of paramount importance. If the military did uncover the startling truths behind the UFO conundrum, it has not elected to share those truths with the rest of us.

Mountains of mystery indeed!

The Secrets Of Mount Shasta And A Dweller On Two Planets

Sources:

"About Mount Shasta." http://www.siskiyous.edu/shasta/fol/lem/index.htm;

"Charles Webster Leadbeater, His Life, Writings and Theosophical Teachings."

http://blavatskyarchives.com/leadbeaterbib.htm.

Childress, David Hatcher. *Lost Cities of North and Central America*, Kempton, IL:

Adventures Unlimited Press, 1992.

Crawford, Lois, J. "Our Beloved Messenger: Guy W. Ballard." http://www.lcrawfords-

manymansions.com/Ascended%20Master%20Instruction/Guy%20Ballard/Guy%20

Ballard%202.htm.

"Creature spotted on Mt. Shasta." *Mount Shasta Herald*, September 9, 1976.

Death Valley National Park." *http://www.desertusa.com/dv/du_dvpmain.html.*

"Death Valley National Park." *http://www.nps.gov/deva/index.htm.*

Johanek, David. "Death Valley's Lost City."

http://home.rconnect.com/˜arcanaresearch/id6.html.

"Klamath Indian Legends." *http://oe.oregonexplorer.info/craterlake/history.html.*

Lee, Bourke, *Death Valley*, New York: Macmillan Co., 1930.

Lee, Bourke, *Death Valley Men*, New York: Macmillan Co., 1932.

"Mount Shasta Sighting, The." http://www.thecryptocrew.com/2012/01/mount-shasta-

sighting.html.

"Origin of the Lemurian Legend, The."

http://www.siskiyous.edu/shasta/fol/lem/index.htm.

The Secrets Of Mount Shasta And A Dweller On Two Planets

"Original 'I AM' Instruction: How it all Began." http://www.saintgermainfoundation.org/.

Redfern, Nick. *Contactees: A History of Alien-Human Interaction*. Pompton Plains, NJ:

New Page Books, 2009.

Saint Germain Foundation. *The History of the "I AM" Activity and Saint Germain*

Foundation. Schaumburg, IL: Saint Germain Press, 2003.

Scott-Elliot, W. *Lost Lemuria, The*. Charleston, SC: Forgotten Books, 2007.

"Stanzas of Dzyan, The." http://blavatskyarchives.com/dzyan.htm.

"Strange and Unexplained – Hollow Earth."

http://www.skygaze.com/content/strange/HollowEarth.shtml.

Winton, Ellis P. "Lemurian Encounter on Mount Shasta."

http://onelight.com/telos/wintonellis.htm.

Zanger, Michael. *Mt. Shasta: History, Legend, Lore*. Berkeley, CA: Celestial Arts, 1992.

About Nick Redfern

Nick Redfern works full time as an author, lecturer, and journalist. He writes about a wide range of unsolved mysteries, including Bigfoot, UFOs, the Loch Ness Monster, alien encounters, and government conspiracies. His books include *Monster Files*; *The World's Weirdest Places*; *Wildman!*; *Final Events*; *A Covert Agenda*; *The Pyramids and the Pentagon*; *There's something in the Woods*; *Keep Out!*; *Man-Monkey*; *The Real Men in Black*; *Cosmic Crashes*; *The NASA Conspiracies*; *Science Fiction Secrets*; *Contactees*; *The FBI Files*; and *Memoirs of a Monster Hunter*. He writes for many publications, including *UFO Magazine*, *Fate*, and *Fortean Times*. Nick has appeared on numerous television shows, including Fox News; The History Channel's *Ancient Aliens*, *Monster Quest*, and *UFO Hunters*; VH1's *Legend Hunters*; National Geographic Channel's *The Truth about UFOs* and *Paranatural*; BBC's *Out of this World*; MSNBC's *Countdown*; and SyFy Channel's *Proof Positive*. He can be contacted at *http://nickredfernfortean.blogspot.com*.

The Secrets Of Mount Shasta And A Dweller On Two Planets

Snow collects very easily at the base and on the many slopes of Mount Shasta well into the spring.

The Secrets Of Mount Shasta And A Dweller On Two Planets

We Uncover More Eerie Mount Shasta Paranormal Activities
by Paul Dale Roberts

PUBLISHERS NOTE: I like to call paranormal investigator Paul Dale Roberts the "King of Mount Shasta." Paul is always in the "fray" it seems, tracking down some of the strangest stories you are likely to encounter, and quite a few of them happen as close to Mount Shasta as you can possibly get without being up in the timber itself. Weed is the next town over and it's where you will find various metaphysical centers and occult book stores. My Native American friend Bleu Ocean grew up in Weed and in my previous MYSTERIES OF MOUNT SHASTA book both he and Mr. Roberts clued us in on the various sightings of Bigfoot and UFOs in the surrounding neighborhoods. But I guess Sasquatch isn't the only cryptid you're going to come across in these parts, as witnessed by the appearance of Batsquatch. And then get ready for a bit of ghost hunting Mount Shasta style, all courtesy of our friend Paul. After all, someone has to keep their eyes open and their ears to the ground.

Tim Beckley

Today is a gorgeous day and I am doing a little bit of yard work with "Let It Rock" by Kevin Rudolf w/Lil Wayne playing in the background, when all of a sudden my cell phone rings. The conversation goes like this:

Caller: "Are you the paranormal investigator?"

Paul: "Yes, I am with HPI (Haunted and Paranormal Investigations International). How can I help you?"

Caller: "Me and my friend were hiking around Mount Shasta and this big creature flew out of one of the crevices. I mean this thing was huge. It was as tall as a man, as stocky as Hulk Hogan and had leathery wings. I believe the wing span was at least 50 feet from one end to the other. I was holding up my camera, but was paralyzed with fear as this thing flew by. I didn't get a picture, sorry. What do you think this might be? Could it have been a pterodactyl? It was flying or gliding fast; it seemed to have a head of a bat. Thinking about it, it doesn'thave the head of a pterodactyl, I just saw a picture of a pterodactyl and the heads are not similar. I would think it had the head of a bat or maybe more like a fox. The damn thing finally flew into a clump of trees and vanished. I heard you guys might be going back to Mount Shasta. If you do, please look out for this thing. If you see it, you will xxxx all over yourself, I kid you not."

The closest thing to what the caller describes is a creature called the Batsquatch. Batsquatch is seen at Mount Saint Helens. Some people theorize that when Mount Saint Helens erupted it also opened up a dimensional portal, into which the Batsquatch entered. Just like the TNT factory at Point Pleasant may have caused a dimensional rift that brought in the Mothman. The Batsquatch has been around since 1980 and has been seen into present times.

Some small animals have been savagely slaughtered near and around Mount Saint Helens. Could this be the results of a feeding frenzy orchestrated by the Batsquatch? If so, then this cryptid creature would be carnivorous. Descriptions of the Batsquatch say that it has the head of a bat, red eyes, purple skin and wings of a pterodactyl. Mount Shasta has not erupted since possibly 1786 as observed by French Naval officer/explorer Jean-Francois de Galaup or maybe by some Spanish explorers. Could the sighting of a Batsquatch creature near Mount Shasta be the sign of a future eruption? There are so many strange and mysterious sightings thoughout our whole universe. Without actually seeing the creature that the caller describes, I can't determine what the caller may have seen with any surety. All I can do is tell the caller is that the next time I am back in Mount Shasta with my scouts, we will be looking for Lemurians, UFOs, Bigfoot, ghosts, Count Saint-Germaine and now.............................Batsquatch!

The Haunting of Black Butte Saloon – Near The Base of Mount Shasta

By Paul Dale Roberts, HPI Owner, Black Butte Tactical Squad

Dedicated to and In Memory of: Timothy Randall Schulz - April 20,

The Secrets Of Mount Shasta And A Dweller On Two Planets

1989 - November 6, 2012. May Timothy soar with the angels above. Special Note: On November 11, 2012 Sunday - the funeral was held at Lincoln United Methodist Church - 629 I Street, Lincoln. I tried to make the funeral, but returned too late from Black Butte Saloon. My thoughts were with Lori and her family on this day. God bless them all.

http://www.youtube.com/watch?v=k7kEwdJxIns&feature=youtu.beBlack Butte Saloon Part 1

http://www.youtube.com/watch?v=ZJwbiz92rRg&feature=youtu.beBlack Butte Saloon Part 2

http://www.youtube.com/watch?v=drcZW7VyJEY&feature=youtu.beBlack Butte Saloon Part 3 Mystical Mount Shasta

Note: We did a UFO Hunt - saw no UFOs in the night sky over Mount Shasta - the place where the last of the Lemurians are supposed to reside in the caverns. But we found that spirits definitely abound in this place. . . Many see Mount Shasta and the surrounding area as a vortex to other dimensions. This following case would seem to strengthen this claim.

INITIAL REPORT: Time to be there: Nov 10, 2012 Sat

Time to be there: 1600 Hours. Location: Black Butte Hotel: 261 Main Street, Weed, CA. Contact Person: Debbie 530 209 2890. Activity & History: This hotel rents out their rooms by the month - not on a nightly basis, so you cannot rent out a room, unless they have one available. Hotel built in 1917. They have a madam's office from their bordello days. Big curtains are seen spreading apart on their own, as if someone is looking out the window. A hooker back in the early 1900s was found dead in a closet; she still haunts the establishment. Entities call out employee's names. Renters see apparitions all the time. People run out of their rooms - a common occurrence. There is a bar and saloon at this place. The town of Weed can also be explored, has a lot of history and other haunted locations. People are heard humming in the hallways. Strange lights will manifest. Entities are heard constantly walking around. The place is ALL OURS to investigate. HPI General Manager/Case Manager Chantal Apodaca got us this case! Good work Chantal!

BLACK BUTTE TACTICAL SQUAD / ROLL CALL: HPI Investigators/ Black Butte Tactical Squad Present: Paul Dale Roberts - HPI Owner; Breanna 'Bree' Apodaca/Psychic; Deanna Bailey - Lead Investigator/Driver; Chantal

The Secrets Of Mount Shasta And A Dweller On Two Planets

Apodaca/HPI General Manager/ Case Manager/Psychic; Shari Aresta - Lead Investigator.

Deborah Hart w/ Stephanie Shaver

INTERVIEW WITH STEPHANIE SHAVER

Stephanie Shaver Tells Her Story at the Black Butte Saloon: Stephanie is the CEO of the Black Butte Saloon LLC dba Historic Black Butte, an Event Hall in Downtown Weed."I have frequented the Black Butte since I first arrived in Weed, CA. I began coordinating events with other business owners in the building over the years, and now have been so lucky to run the business myself with my husband Billy Shaver. I have experienced an overwhelming welcoming feeling since the first moment I walked into the building. I am almost embarrassed by my comfy feeling in an old brothel, saloon, and mad house. Haha… Nonetheless I have felt the presence of the original Madame, Georgia Clark, her support of me and events, clientele and everything I am doing has been non stop. I feel her whisper, "You got this Girl." I know that sounds hokey, but I feel completely welcomed and wanted by the "spirits." One day I had my 7 year old son in the building with me helping clean and sweep and shoot pool with me, when he says to me, "I've been here before." I ask him, "How so? This is your first time in." He says, "I've been here a hundred times." He looked just as confident and confused as I was…. I thought to myself… what the hell was my son doing in a saloon in his last life? Then I laugh and think… Well, hmmm, what was I doing here? My experiences haven't been scary, or visual, or anything of the spooky sort… just plain and simple, welcoming and wanted."

INTERVIEW WITH VAUNE DILLMAN, LOCAL HISTORIAN:

Vaune Dillman, previous owner of the Black Butte Saloon, tells me that a Vietnamese lady that could not adapt to living in Weed was killed by a man in the hallways of the Black Butte Saloon. Vaune tells me the significant stories of the Black Butte Hotel. They are: 1. Some guy fell in the back stairs and broke his neck. Note: We investigated this area and captured an EVP that says 'no,' when I asked, "Did someone push you down the stairs?" This entity is identified as Levi Morgan. 2. There was a guy that when tying up his horse at the 'pit' fell off the railing and died. 3. Choc Sbarabaro and his wife Helen were colorful previous owners of this establishment. 4. Characters like Joe Bananas, an African American baseball player for the team called 'Weed Sons Baseball Team,' frequented this former hotel, now a saloon. A guy named 'Red' that worked at the lumber mill frequented this hotel. Note: The town of Weed is named after Senator Abner Weed. 5. When Black Butte Saloon was a hotel, it was known as Sodom and Gomorrah. The town of Weed boasted 13 saloons and 17 cathouses. When the passing train would see red lights on top of various homes, this indicated that the whores were out. Dorothy Manning and Georgia Clark were the most prominent madams of the Black Butte Saloon. In fact Vaune discovered a wall that Georgia Clark etched her name in and he cut out a piece of the wall and kept it. 6. A character of this former hotel named Borgnis would tell everyone that if the beds could talk, they could tell some stories; this is when the hotel was being used as a bordello.

DEACON FATLIP SMITH

One customer who does not want to be identified says that an outlaw from New Mexico named Deacon Fatlip Smith would also frequent this hotel during the time it was a bordello. Deacon boasted of killing three men in a gun fight in Tombstone, Arizona. Deacon made the claim that he was friends with Wyatt Earp and missed the OK Corral shoot out by three days.

Lorena Starzer & Patience Rossi

INTERVIEW WITH PATIENCE ROSSI/ LORENA STARZER

Interview with Residents Patience Rossi and Lorena Starzer in Room #15. Patience and Lorena tell me that Patience's room (#15) is haunted and I did get an EVP in which the male entity told me to 'go.' Patience hears noises in the kitchen, walking noises. Once she came home to find a sweater neatly folded. Hair dye was spilled on the toilet seat and it featured a face, after it dried. Next door, a man was shot and was found dead in his bathtub. Patience has heard scratching on her wall.

INTERVIEW WITH DEBORAH HART

Deborah Hart, Property Manager of Black Butte Hotel, tells me the history of the Black Butte Hotel: "I moved here to Weed in 2007. I was staying with a friend and looking for a job. The job I found was being the Property Manager of Black Butte Hotel. Some of the prominent figures that stayed here, when it was a hotel, were Buck Owens, the country singer, and John Wayne. This place was a brothel back in 1917. Georgia Clark was the owner and she had prostitutes working on the second floor. There were gunfights. Chinese workers from the railroad came through the saloon. Prostitutes would hang out from the second floor balcony to entice men. Some of the activity that I noticed: a) I was lying in my bed. I saw my beaded curtains open up by themselves, and they split right in half and opened as if someone was walking through them. b) There was a prostitute that was strangled in the closet in the room that I live in. I live in room #6. I would sometimes feel someone pulling my feet while I lay in bed. If I lay on my side, I feel like someone is pushing me on my side, like they are trying to roll me. c) Donald Lee, a tenant, has told me that he has heard voices, banging on the walls, lights going off and on, when there was no one around. d) I have many tenants that hear phantom footsteps down the hallway; some tenants have been touched. Some tenants have felt negative energy in my closet and then later I learn that a prostitute had been strangled in my closet. e) I have heard my name called by a man with a high voice or a woman with a deep voice. The basement in the saloon was used as a work shop.

This was a place that was used as a secret drinking spot. There are stairs that are built that go nowhere. There are underground tunnels beneath this hotel, which prominent men from Weed would go into so they can rendezvous with some of the prostitutes. We have an attic that has a door that mysteriously opens. In the stairwell, tenants feel very strange; some tenants feel like they are being pushed down the stairwell. Since we are near Mount Shasta, I have seen UFOs that look like a butterfly without a head, or a Manta ray, with lights on the wings and transparent.

I have seen a glowing ball that was on top of Mount Shasta. The glowing ball grew bigger and bigger and then blinked out. On this night, I have been observing the skies, looking for UFO activity, I haven't seen anything yet.

SPECIAL NOTE: Thank you Debbie for providing us with Room #7. Getting Our Breakfast On! Black Bear Diner - Mount Shasta, CA

INVESTIGATION AND RESULTS: We captured an EVP in the cubby hole, which sounded like a baby crying. We captured an EVP of a man saying four unintelligible words and we captured the EVP in which Levi Morgan says 'no' that he was not pushed down the stairs. We are capturing designer orbs. Some of the investigators have seen shadows moving about in their peripheral vision. Two EVPs captured by EVP Queen Shari Aresta in Room 6 - a female voice moaning and an EVP of a woman saying 'help me.' Could that be the prostitute that was strangled in the closet?

SEANCE: We conducted a séance in the saloon; we saw moving lights in the poker room. We heard tapping and banging on the wall. We heard female and male voices coming from the poker room. The table where we held the séance, the table moved twice. Two of the investigators were touched on their shoulders and legs. The Property Manager went into the poker room and something told her in her ear to "get the f - - - out!" She ran out terrified. I went into the basement by myself and obtained an EVP of a man mumbling something.

THE REVEAL: This place is validated as 'haunted' due to the EVPs we obtained and the disembodied voices we heard with our ears. I have no doubt that ghosts of the past - residual and intelligent - haunt this incredible establishment.

< Black Butte Saloon

Paul Dale Roberts, HPI Esoteric Detective aka The Demon

Warrior Haunted and Paranormal Investigations Internationalhttp://www.knighttalkradio.blogspot.com/ for HPI Stories!Managed by Staci Butler, HPI Twitter Account Managerhttp://alldestiny.com/index.php/paul-dale-roberts/ Email: pauld5606@comcast.net Paranormal Cellular Hotline: For Investigation or Advice: 916 203 7503

The Secrets Of Mount Shasta And A Dweller On Two Planets

An early woodcut of Mount Shasta-garden of the gods.

Early settlers loved the beauty and majesty of Mount Shasta and settled nearby despite the sometimes harsh weather.

Some Thoughts On Modernizing And Editing "A Dweller On Two Planets"

By Sean Casteel

Modernizing and editing the classic New Age book *"A Dweller On Two Planets"* was a lengthy and painstaking exercise. The primary text channeled through Frederick S. Oliver is 327 pages and contains more than 150,000 words. It is a marvel of good writing that such a lengthy piece of work never fails to hold one's interest throughout.

Nevertheless, the book needed some updating. The modern reader would not have had an easy time maneuvering through the repeated usage of words like "thee" and "thou" and other archaic words and phrases. Oliver would often use words that have long ago passed into history as either too formal or too dated, with the original meanings lost in some limbo of language. There were a few typos of the more normal kind, but as with most books from this bygone age, it was very well edited and nearly without error of any kind. So in that sense, the work was easy.

What impresses me most about *"A Dweller On Two Planets"* is how reverently Christian it all is. Oliver clearly takes us on an occult journey and pulls no esoteric punches, but he also bears witness to the divinity of Jesus Christ frequently and with an overt and honest faith. He advises the reader that to tread the righteous path of truth to heaven, we must combine both occultism and Christianity and not see the two as mutually exclusive. This seems to me to be as refined as New Age thinking can get, in spite of the fact that the book was first published over 100 years ago.

The Secrets Of Mount Shasta And A Dweller On Two Planets

Much has been made of the fact that Oliver seems to predict television and cell phones that transmit the user's photographic image, and there is no denying that he is a true prophet in that sense. But I believe the real significance lies in this pairing of Biblical truth with occult truth, which leads us to the sure and certain coming of a world paradise under Christ.

On the way to that inspiring hope, we are provided with fascinating glimpses into other dimensions and various levels of the afterlife. The book revolves around a karmic morality story in which the main character's sins and virtues are balanced over two of his lifetimes. Perhaps in his redemption we can also find our own.

Black Butte as seen from Weed, California

A Dweller on Two Planets

Phylos (Frederick S. Oliver)

NOTE BY THE AUTHOR

Friends, thirteen years have become past time since the words of this book were dictated; publication has been delayed purposely, so that statements then made might gain strength through the fulfillment of many of the predictions to be found within these covers; predictions which at that time were wholly unverified, and were, moreover, regarded by science as chimerical. Prophecy would be impossible in a Godless universe; and were it not that vibration is the law of laws, no mind could come into unison with the Creator or any of His ministers; each living being is minister to the creature immediately inferior. Today we witness the faith of those who have believed in my words swallowed up in knowledge: many of the predictions have been realized; all will be eventually. So it is that today, in the middle of the final year of the century, I add THE MIGHTY CAP-STONE:

The Division of the Way Has Come; the Midnight Hour of the Cycle Which, More Than Any Other, Formed Life's Great Divide, Has Struck. When I first dictated for this book there was only, as it were, a few seconds left to the closing of the Sixth Day. But now for some seconds the initiation of that saying has been fulfilled of Him who sits upon the throne: "Behold! I make all things new." The Hour has struck. And now, "the one overcoming shall inherit all things and I will be his God, and he shall be my son." This is for those who set their hands to the Plow and their feet to Furrow, and *looked not back, while yet the Sixth Cycle was*. "But as for the cowards (a halt between two opinions) and the unbelievers (in anything above earthly, finite things) and the abominable, and takers of life, and passion and lust-servers, sorcerers, idolaters and swervers from truth, their portion is the (Great Karma of the World) second death." While the foolish ones were gone to buy oil, the bride-groom came, and they who were prepared entered in with him to the feast, and the door was shut. When the foolish returned the door was not opened unto then. Beloved, remember these words which were spoken by the apostles of the Christ; that they said that in the Last Time before the end of the Age "there will be mockers walking after their own impious lusts (10). These indeed blaspheme what things they do not understand; but that which they know naturally, as do the irrational animals, in these things they are corrupt (19). These are they who sepa-rate at the Dividing of the Way, going in the finite direction, not having the Spirit (7), and are placed as an example, to endure the retributive justice of an age-ending fire."

I have made many references to America as being Atlantis come again; much has, in a general way, been said of the beginning, rise, growth and destruction of that ancient prototype; a hint has been given here and there, more by inference than by specific statement, that while America should be peer and even more than Atlantis, just because she is Atlantis returned on a higher plane, she must endure the woes as well as retrace her pre-carnate glories. The penalty visited upon Poseid was the crowning sentence of that Age. Century after century in the majestic march of Time has gone by since the sun looked down upon a wild waste of ocean waters where, but a few days before, there had been the regal Island-Continent. Another cycle has reached its end, and its last hour has chimed. All that which is imperfect in the now-closed Sixth Day is come, in a stately, measured but inexorable way to face judgment by the standard, Truth. Neither spot nor blemish can not hope to stand nor continue before it. Neither can anything be amended so as now to escape its karmic penalty, for the seal of its full time is set upon it. "The one acting unjustly, let him be unjust still; and the filthy one, let him be filthy still; and the righteous one, let him righteousness do still, and the holy one, let him be holy still. Lo, I come speedily, and the reward of me is with me, to give back unto each one as the work of him shall be found." The Great Karma unfailingly sets each evildoer back to the point he reached before the animal forces in riot obtained control over the human. This is the reason that those who lost supremacy over their lower selves in the Sixth Cycle won no place in the Seventh. In the closing years of the spent cycle, one deserted his helpless wife; surely, he really deserted his birthright in the New Age. Another sought, being weak-willed, to drown worries in wine; he virtually drowned his soul's advanced merits. A wife was faithless to her wedding vows; the Door of the New Time is fast against her. A thief stole, what? His own life's rewards. One man deprived another of physical life; he also erased his own name from TODAY'S roll-call. One swore to keep a vow, but broke it often; in this New Day, after the grave shall claim his physical being, he shall not again awaken, having lacked the will to live. A man was buried with high honors who, at merciless cost to his fellowmen, enriched his bank account; a gravestone near as costly as pure gold stands above his mortal carcass, aye, and under it is also the dead hopes of resurrection. She sold her body; purchased and purchaser form an unhallowed company in Yesterday's catacombs, from which they shall not emerge to see the light of Today until, in cycles far from now, "death and hell give up" their inhabitants. Such is a brief glimpse into a Closed Record. Turn the page. Another did deeds of love; love and doers thereof live through all the days, forever. One smiled when a smile was heroic and cheered faint souls; one visited the sick and prisoners; one clothed a naked stranger; and one gave half of her last crust, though only to a starving dog. Verily, all these shall receive their reward in the Day now dawning. The bad are not all bad, neither the good wholly good. She who lived a life of shame, yet kept a hope for better things burning in her inmost heart, and longed for death to release her, since man would not:

"Looked beyond the shadow of the late unhallowed years, to the far, far distant upland, where yon glimmering light appears."

Truly, she shall be chastened, and made new, in the glory of To-day; but the chastening is a weary ordeal, and slow. As the Great Karma handles her, so   it handles all others, for it is Christ's mercy, which heals every soul's hurt. During many, many centuries, prophecy has looked forward to the end of the Age as a time of awful woe, and has pictured dread scenes of terminal horror. Am I come to say that all these predictions shall fail? Is the book of the Apocalypse mere allegory? If only it were! But as the Poseid age was stricken, this one must also be which has just passed.

Shall America, the Glorious, together with the rest of the world, meet similar woe? Alas, worse, though not by water but by fire. Shall all be wiped out of existence, leaving a planet in ruins? Toward the purpose of full obedience and the coming into harmony with divine law shall the lash be applied; words may not portray the scenes. This is the Message of the End of the Age:

"The day of vengeance is in mine heart, and the year of my redeemed is come nigh," says the prophet Isaiah. "Behold, the day . . . that burneth as an oven," says the prophet Malachi.

The Hour has struck. And yet in all of this there is no mystery, no supernatural penalty, no capricious infliction by an offended personal God, and nothing of "man's necessity, God's opportunity." It is all of Man's own doing. He has wandered from the Way, and has, for the God-nature in him, which he should have revered and nourished, substituted worship of Self and of Mammon; has cast out Love, and placed violence, lust, greed and all the riotous animalism in him in command of his life. *Man is his own judge and executioner.* Man is the type and the universe is the print; Nature patterns after Man, not Man after Nature. He, a being, of free will, has caused all the coming woes of judgment to be inevitable; he must endure; as he hath sown, so must he reap. O Man, forgetter of Love, of Mercy, of Right; breeder of Hate, of Cruelty, and of the inhumanity that has and continues to make countless millions mourn, is it possible that you have been blind to the handwriting on the wall?

Alas, yes, you have! Rampant is the Spirit of selfishness, of greed, of merciless gain; its hand guides the trains and steamers, clicks the telegraph keys, operates the telephone and cables, makes a mockery of free speech, shackles the press so that it dares to utter only that which cannot offend its master; every human enterprise, all national policies and international mutual respect, all things, even the churches, are willing vassals to this fiend, SELF. What then? Ruin is on all sides, the human race and all lower creatures its victims. Masons at work on a high wall shout as a brick falls: "Stand from under!"

Aye, stand from under! A world is falling! Pile no higher the racial and individual misdeeds now awaiting atonement; weary enough the awful reckoning of the Great Karma without additions to its terrible length that even now stretches ahead, a seeming eternity. Frenzied millions of men and women, boys and girls, no longer free save in name, are menaced with starvation. Hungry, cold, half-clad, shelterless only too often, denied the chance to work, however willing they may be, corporation-owned machinery their competitor; monopoly and trust-ridden, sleeping or waking. This inhuman picture is the rule, not the exception. You know this full well. I state nothing new in this regard, and the awful facts are underdrawn instead of exaggerated.

All of this, although in a far, far less degree, has been so at the ending of every age, was so in Poseid and is therefore now repeated. But it can never be so again after this, for HERE THE WAY DIVIDES. Poseid survived; so also shall they of the Sixth Age. In the full time by fire the Reaper shall reap, and no place will be found for physical safety by the unchanged of heart. But the time of it shall be foreshortened, else no flesh could remain alive. Stand from under! The roar of armed hosts must succeed the thunderous mutterings of the times. No more is there any chance to prevent the coming retribution (albeit it may seem unduly deferred), for the causes have had their way. Too late is it to even modify the result of the misguidance of that Spirit whose hand sways the helm.

A short but sharp conflict, Sanguinary past belief, even now reddens on the horizon. The trained armies, millions of men active or in reserve, that are now engaged in conquest, fevered with war, will only for a little longer, comparatively, submit to having themselves and loved ones ground under the heel and strangled by the hand of that organized thing, Capital, which, itself merely the natural fruit of selfishness, nonetheless is a riotous animal principle, compelling the few to be masters of the many, denying the God-born declaration that all men are created free and equal, and warping it to seem a giant lie. Soon millions of trained soldiers will turn upon the visible representatives, the wealthy and worldly prosperous, who in reality are not more responsible than will be their assailants, of that Relentless Force behind all human enterprise. Later they will break up into lawless bands bent on satisfying Ishmaelitish tendencies, each self-server's hand armed against his fellow creatures. Then will the pent-up hate, the savagery and selfishness, begotten by ages of selfishness and ruled by unbridled animalism, break in a storm such as the world has never yet seen, no, not during all the ages I scan, ages forgotten for untold thousands of years. That loveless conflict will initiate that which, Nature completing, will leave living but one where now are many. Hard and fast after the human conflict will come pestilences unparalleled, sweeping the wide earth over, for in that day none will pause to bury the slain until the evil is wrought, nor then, for the dead of the plagues will be as thousands for every one by violence. And all this because the love that should grace and soften men's hearts, each for all and all for each, dried up and became a mockery in the close of the ended cycle, leaving but scattered oases, few and far between.

Nature follows Man. For this reason, the waters of Earth will dry out, rains be withheld, cyclones sweep, and an earthquake come such as was not since a man was on the earth; aye, I am mindful of Poseid! But all of this will occur only through natural causes, and in consonance with the selfishness, lust, greed, anger and general depravity of the Type. As these things blaze in the human breast, so shall the air, dry and vapor-less under brazen skies, develop solar heats more fierce than history ever knew. A parched earth, furnace-like, piling all flesh mountains high; pestilences stalking unchecked. O ye! You are blind to the Handwriting on the wall, which flickers still, though written for a spent cycle. Turn now and read, while yet the last midnight stroke reverberates. The disciples asked the Great Master, saying: "Teacher, when will these things be?" And He said: "When you see Jerusalem surrounded by encampments, then you may know that the desolation has come near. . . For days of vengeance these axes, to be fulfilled of all the judgments."

Friends, do you know the meaning of the name Jerusalem? That it means "Vision of Peace?" Truthfully, it does. One by one during the years all the signs of the end of the Age but one were fulfilled; but these were "only the beginning of sorrows," for still the Spirit of Liberty lived here and there in the breasts of lovers of their fellowmen. That Spirit wrapped itself in the glorious folds of the Stars and Stripes and proclaimed the imperishable declaration of human equality, granting to all that freedom which Americans for themselves demanded. But now the "Vision of Peace" is finally encompassed by armies, the last gap being filled with *blue-coated soldiers* forcing Mammon's commercial shackles upon alien peoples in tropical islands. Ah, the Starry Flag droops; mournfully low above the freedom-birthright sold for a mess of pottage. My People, O my People! As you have sown, so you must reap. The Vision of Spiritual Peace is wholly clouded by the dust of armed camps, and no gap is left un-obscured. "Then shall the end come." A Son hath continually called from on High:

"Stand from under! Get into the shelter of that Cross."

In all the time of atonement, must those who thought no wrong indeed suffer? Ah, thought no wrong. In every life, whether a theist's, an atheist's or merely one ignorant of any doctrine of belief, there comes a time when the inward Spirit beseeches the soul to go up higher. It pleads again and again and yet again so—as long as a faintest hope remains. Omission too, hath its penalty: "How shall we escape if we neglect so great salvation?" echoed throughout the past Age. Fire burns a babe's fingers as badly as it does an adult's. There were and are those who lived and live the Cross. These shall not suffer, not even if bodily death overtakes them; they have no Karma to atone for.

What is the Cross? What is Christ? I have said, long ago, but I will restate it: the Divine stream of Life, the Indefinable God, that is, the long arm of the Living Cross. Directed, purposeful Human Will is the short arm. This will power is our call upon His Name that is never denied. Jesus, the Man of Nazareth, gave us a pattern. He sacrificed self for us. He said: "Follow me." Also: "If any man will come after me, let him deny *himself*, and take up *his* cross and follow me." This self is the lower self; it is the animal. All animals are in man concreted. No hyena is so treacherous, no tiger so ferocious, no hog so brutish, no weasel so destructive; no animal creature of any sort is so perfect in its own peculiar nature as is the man who suffers any or all of these animal characteristics within him to run riot; and this is because his human soul is enslaved to the animal. Animal is only force undirected, whether it exists in a body or not. Directed, guided by will, it ceases to be animal. But in yielding to that guidance it must give up its free lawlessness, something never pleasant and often painful. It is sacrifice, always. Its symbol is the Cross. He sacrificed self for us on this same cross of the Causeless, Divine Stream which contains all things and flows when or where no man knows. I would not minimize Calvary; it is very, very real and the one great fact forever! "Follow me." On that same Cross, day by day, aye, moment by moment, employing our wills, as He directed, that we may grow unto His likeness, we also, following, must sacrifice self, sacrifice the animal in us, that is, in God's service we must never cease to direct those vagrant forces which in running riot turn Earth into a veritable hell and supplant Love with Self. It is written that "a little child shall lead them." Surely and in truth, the "little child" of the Spirit in the New Time shall be ruler over the menagerie within the man, and that man shall therefore be able, even as Quong, the Tchin, to rule any animal outside of himself. A vast power, this. And because of it, in the New Time, no longer shall any beast, whether in human form, or in lower animal body, or merely apparent as a raging tempest or a disease, be free to do evil.

When the Spirit in Man comes fully into its own, "He shall rule them as with a rod of iron," this riotous throng. Rule them to their own good; cut them off suddenly, even as Quong cut off the puma from furthering its own will. He shall destroy that previously unbridled animal, by the Cross converting it into a servitor to the Father. All things must become new TODAY, because conditions will change so soon that they who would hold fast to the old will find nothing either in Nature or elsewhere that will continue to yield to the old powers.

And now here, of all places, I would indeed not be vague in expression. The Seventh Cycle is that of the Spirit. TODAY existence will demand a spiritual eye, and ear, and that every sense is raised to the Heights. The very means of dealing with Nature will no longer be gross, but will become as in Hesperus, manageable only by those who, using the Cross in their every life-act, swerve never to either side of the way, never, either in the least or greatest of the deeds they do. Committing error, even that good may come, cannot bring anything but pain and penalty. None of the evildoers can be lost, finally, for God wastes nothing. He converts all things from lower into higher, inexorably, surely. Some must endure the retributive justice of the Great Karma. The majority must experience more or less of this fire of transfiguration; the wrath of God is Love's severity.

Then will come those times when "all things are made new." What do you think now? Shall not America, and the rest of the world, be more glorious than you have ever dreamed? Aye, truly. She won't have the great population that the census-takers imagine. There shall be few where there were many; tens replacing thousands. But there is not greatness or magnificence in numbers; remember the Saldans and Rai Ernon; which was greater, he or that ill-fated host? Yet never shall a soul be lost; God has a place for everyone.

It is written that after a thousand years Satan shall be loosed for a little season. That is well. For the Race possessing such amazing powers, though few, will be the people. But there will be some who have attained these powers through mere intellect; they will abuse their privileges, having not the Spirit, and these sinful ones will the Perfect in Evil attack, that karma shall overtake them. Having had much given to them, of them shall much be demanded, which is why their karmic atonement will be more intense than words can depict.

The wrath of God is love's severity. All shall be converted from lower into higher.

"A glory shines across the coming years, the glory of a race grown great and free. 'Twas seen by poets, sages, saints and seers, whose vision glimpsed the dawn that is to be. A shining shore is by the Future's sea, whereon each man shall stand among his peers, as equal; and to none shall bend the knee. Awake, my soul, shake off your doubts and fears; Behold the hosts of darkness fade and flee before the magic of the Morning's face; And hear the sweet and wondrous melody that floats to us from far-off golden days—it is the choral song of liberty. It is the anthem of the coming Race."

(SIGNATURE OF PHYLOS, IN ATLAN CHARACTERS.)

PHYLOS, THE THIBETAN. (Otherwise named, in fullness, Yol Gorro, author of this book.)

A DWELLER ON TWO PLANETS

OR

THE DIVIDING OF THE WAY

BY

PHYLOS THE THIBETAN

This is before the coming of a new Heaven and a new Earth, in which shall reign the Prince of Peace for ever and forever, as the Old shall be passed away, for lo! on earth there is nothing great but man; in man there is nothing great but mind.

"Never utter these words: 'I do not know this, therefore it is false,' One must study to know; know to understand; understand to judge."—Apothegm of Narada.

"There are more things in heaven and earth, Horatio, than are dreamt of in your philosophy"—Hamlet.

This book is dedicated to progressive thinkers everywhere, but especially to the "Invisible Helper" who has made possible its presentation to the world.

26: 17 :: 25.8 + 30 : 24

AMANUENSIS' PREFACE

By permission of the Author, whose letter addressed to me follows as his preface herein, and to meet the natural curiosity and satisfy, so far as any personal statement from me will, any honest inquiring mind, I humbly appear in order briefly to give the major facts concerning the writing of this—even to me—very remarkable book.

I am an only child of Dr. and Mrs. Oliver, who for many years have resided in the State of California.

I was born in Washington, D. C., in 1866, and brought to the State by my parents two years later. Prior to commencing the writing of this book, in 1884, my education had been comparatively limited, and extended to a very slight knowledge of the subjects herein treated.

My father, a well-known physician, died a few years ago, my mother surviving him. Both were daily witnesses of most of the circumstances and facts surrounding the writing of this book. But further than to state this, I do not think myself called upon to introduce my family into the work, nor, in fact, myself, except in so far as it is necessary for me to appear and do my personal part as the amanuensis.

I feel that I am mentally and spiritually just a figure beside the Author of the great, deep-searching, far-reaching and transcendent questions presented in the following pages; and I read and study them with as much interest and profit, I imagine, as will any reader. At the same time, I feel, with no sense of the natural pride of an Author of such a book, that it is a work of unselfish love, and will help to the betterment of an upward-struggling world, searching ever for more light, and feed the hungry for knowledge of the great mystery of life and of the ever-evolving soul, through Him who said—"I AM THE WAY; FOLLOW ME." In these days of doubt, materialism, and even rank atheism, it requires all the courage I possess to assert, in clear unequivocal terms, that the following book, "A DWELLER ON TWO PLANETS," is absolute revelation; that I do not believe myself its Author, but that one of those mysterious persons, if my readers choose to so consider him, an adept of the arcane and occult in the universe, better understood from reading this book, is the Author. Such is the fact. The book was revealed to me, a boy, and a boy, too, whose parents were mistakenly lenient to such a degree that he was allowed to do as he chose in most things. Not lacking in inclination to study, but very lacking in willpower, continuity and energy, I gained little in educational triumphs, and was pointedly criticized by my teacher as "lackadaisical, even lazy." So, when I was a little past seventeen years of age, "Phylos, the Esoterisist," took me actively in charge. Intending to make me his instrument to the world, that profound adept showed what seems to me a rare faith, for I was without any solid education, as generally so considered, and was minus any special religious background, and for my only advantages, had willingness, love of the remarkable, and an uncolored mind.

For a year my occult tutor educated me by means of "mental talks," and my mind was occupied to such a degree by the many new thoughts with which he inspired me that I paid no heed to my environment, worked automatically, if at all, studied and read not, and scarcely heard those who addressed my exterior senses. Then my father decided to stop my "approaching imbecility," as he called it; for I had avoided explanations, and had said nothing of the talks with my mystic teacher, whom even I had never seen but a few times. To parental pressure I yielded, and told my—to me—divine secret. To my relief it was not discounted. Instead, after telling the long story to both parents, they expressed a desire to hear the mysterious stranger also. This my tutor would not grant, but he permitted me to quote his words, talks and addresses, and at length I became so proficient that I could repeat what he said almost as fast as he spoke to me. A circle was formed at home, consisting at first of my parents, W. S. Mallory (now of Cleveland, Ohio), and myself, as hearers, and Phylos as teacher. Later, Mrs. S. M. Pritchard and Mrs. Julia P. Churchill were present. This was in Yreka, Siskiyou Co., Cal., early in the eighties, where the writing of this book was commenced in A. D. 1883-4, but was finished in Santa Barbara County, California, A. D. 1886, where it has ever since remained in the manuscript, at the command of the author.

It will have added interest to many who love, or have become interested in CALIFORNIA, to know that within full view of Shasta, one of her loftiest mountain peaks, this book was begun and almost finished under the inspiration of that spirit of nature which speaks ever to those who, listening, understand.

How the Author differs from us common mortals, and how, by his occult methods, he possesses the power to dictate—"reveal"—as he has done and still does, may be better known by studying his remarkable record, set forth in this book—his personal history.

In 1883-4, A. D., in sight of the inspiring peak of Mount Shasta, the Author began to have me write what he told me, and, curiously enough, he dictated the initial chapter of "Book Second" first of all. Other chapters, both preceding and succeeding, were given at intervals of a few weeks, or even months, sometimes only a sheet or two, at others as high as eighty letter-size sheets being covered in a few hours. I would be awakened at night by my mentor and write by lamplight, or sometimes with no light, but in darkness. In 1886 the main work, as I remember it, was done. Then he had me revise it, under his supervision, and this work was as erratic as the other. In fact, the whole thing was as if he had the manuscript already prepared when he first began dictation, and was indifferent as to what portions were written first, just so all were written. Had I been a medium in the sense usually understood by the believers in spiritualism, as I understand it, the writing would have been automatic, and I would not have been forced to dress his words so much in my own language, and in that case no revision would have been necessary. But I was always conscious of every surrounding, quite similar, in fact, to any stenographer—with this lack of equality to such an amanuensis—that I was not then a shorthand reporter. Realizing how useful in taking my preceptor's teachings the possession of this art on my part would be, I learned to write stenographically, although never an expert.

Twice was the work revised, twice he had me go over this erratically written manuscript, which, as I have said, was mainly written backward. So strangely was it given that I had almost no idea of what it was, or with what it dealt. On one occasion, when I had written over two hundred sheets, mostly backwards, i.e., the sentences rightly last coming first, so fast and mixed that I had no idea of its sense, he bade me burn it without even reading it. This I did, and to this day I have little idea of what those pages contained, or why he had me destroy them; nor will he tell me. The book was finished in A. D. 1886, though for the purpose of publication the manuscript has been thoroughly edited by a literary expert, that any error therein due to my own limitations and mistakes in transmission as a scribe should be eliminated.

In the year 1894 the manuscript, as finished in 1886, was typewritten in duplicate by Mrs. M. E. Moore of Louisville, Kentucky, and she has had possession of one of said copies ever since up to midsummer, 1899. The Moore copy has never been changed by even a letter since it was written, evidence of which has been judiciously preserved. Said manuscript was copyrighted by me in 1894, and owing to an addition to the title, again in this, the year 1899.

During all this time I have not been permitted, nor was I able, to have it published. In the interval, many of the things spoken of in the shape of scientific and mechanical rediscoveries dealt with in the book have been brought to pass. The high attainments of the Atlanteans, lost for thousands of years following as the result of the engulfment of their great continent, have been and are rapidly being brought to light and utility, bearing out the prediction of the Author.

Witness the discovery recently of the Roentgen or "X-ray," not even dreamed of in 1886, yet in the book you will find a long treatise concerning "Cathodicity" and the amazing powers of the "Night Side of Nature," of such practical use to and so well understood by the people of that wonderful age. Also note wireless telegraphy; it, too, is herein, scattered all through and referred to in this book, precluding the possibility of interpolation. Again, regarding there being but "One Energy" and but "One Substance," now beginning to find able champions and general scientific acceptance, in place of passing it by as a chimera for the elementary hypothesis so long held by chemists. This also is an integral part of this book; though it is not more than two years since an article appeared in Harper's Magazine seriously advancing this belief of fin-de-siecle science as a novelty. These are but major examples of what was set forth in "A DWELLER ON TWO PLANETS" in 1886, together with many more predictions of the immediate oncoming of what the Author terms rediscovery of the secrets buried with Atlantis; and it is promised that we, as Atlanteans returning, are going beyond her fallen greatness, and that by slow, synthetic steps, we are coming up to surpass even those wonderful attainments, as the ever-expanding and growing mind and soul of man climbs ever higher in the rounds of his evolution.

To all earnest, though perhaps skeptical inquirers, I may say that the evidence as to this book being finished in 1886, and before the latter-day discoveries became known, abundantly exists and can be clearly established, to clear away any cobwebs that might otherwise take hold in their minds and prevent them from accepting the book for what its Author claims—the truth.

Upon the ability of the careful reader to so accept this book as history and not fiction, much depends, in lighting up the Path for their souls. I am rather in expectation of another work, but whether I will have it, or some other scribe will get it, I do not know. If it comes as promised, it will be one for the inner eyes of those who profit by this work and seek yet more of the counsel which will place their feet firmly on the "Narrow Way of Attainment."

In writing, I am always conscious of the presence calling himself Phylos, whenever he chooses to come to me, and sometimes I see as well as hear and speak with him, though vision is rare. Clairvoyance and clairaudience would account for this. I hear—and speak or write—what is said as I am directed. Often, after being shown the mental picture, I am left largely to express it in my own language. At such times I am as fully conscious of my surroundings as at any other time, though I feel lifted as into a Master's presence, and gladly do for him the work of transcription. If the good counsel and loving care I have personally received from my wise friend had been faithfully and persistently remembered and followed, instead of so largely slighted or forgotten, often to almost fade from my memory during his absence, I should undoubtedly have been a better example than I feel that I am of the grand lessons he sets forth in this book.

I have never represented myself to any person, nor to the public, as possessing mediumistic or any other quality, nor have I ever used the same at any person's request, for love or money. Whatever my talents or qualities in these things may be, they have only been used as a sacred gift. With such influences as have surrounded me in this work, I can gratefully and truly say that I have never been tempted to do otherwise, if I could; and have ever received exceedingly more good than I feel that my services have returned.

Now the question arises, do I believe this Book? Unhesitatingly, Yes. There may be points that I can accept only on faith, like any other reader, feeling that a day will come when, if I shall be faithful, I will be instructed by the Spirit to which he testifies. There certainly will be criticisms from some as to the manner of the writing of this book, and as to the truth of my statements regarding it, as there has so often been by those who prefer to believe that all such claims are but author's fictions. I have come to personally know the truth of some of the things mentioned in this book, in the course of the fifteen years that I have had in this connection. I have had many experiences, which have been mentally confirmed at least, either of the direct statements of the Author, or tending to strengthen the absolute confidence which I feel in him who I reverence so deeply. I have often, even as "Christian" in "Pilgrim's Progress," fallen. But the Path is there. Does the sun cease to shine because fogs obscure it? Then is it not for us to follow the Path, forgetting persons, and looking to the spirit, as we read Phylos' Book?

F. S. OLIVER.

The Secrets Of Mount Shasta And A Dweller On Two Planets

LETTER FROM PHYLOS, AUTHOR OF THIS HISTORY.

January, 1886.

Today, my brother, the masses of humanity on this planet are awakened to the fact that their knowledge of life—the Great Mystery—is insufficient for the needs of the soul. Hence a school of advanced thought has arisen, whose members, ignorant of the mysterious truth, yet know their ignorance and ask for light. I make no pretenses when I say that I—Theochristian student and Occult Adept—am one of a class of men who do know, and can explain these mysteries. I, with other Christian Adepts, influence the inspirational writers and speakers through an ability to exert the control of our trained, and therefore more powerful, minds over theirs, which are enormously less so. Hence, when the people ask for bread, our media give it to them. Who are these, our media? They are all men or women, in churches or out, who bear witness of the Fatherhood of God, the Sonship of Man, and the Brotherhood of Jesus with all souls, irrespective of creeds or ecclesiastical forms. Because these, our writers and speakers, have wrought for human good, so shall, and so does, good come to themselves, bread from the waters. It is proper that the leaders of the mental van should receive generous remuneration. And they do. But at this point enters a different phase. Observing the cry for more light, more truth; observing also how great is the recompense, up springs the imitator, who has no light of inspiration, no conception of the real truth, not of the laws of the Eternal. What does he do? Watch! With a pen whose shaft is imitation, and whose point is not of the gold of fact, but of the perishable metal of selfish greed, this person writes. He dips his pen into the ink of more or less thrilling sensationalism, muddy with the dirt of immorality and nastiness, and he draws a pen picture illumined by the tallow-dip of lust and corruption. There is in his work no lofty aim to inspire his readers; he deals with the lowest aspects of life, and, ignorant of the inexorable penalty for sin, has no atonement to demand of his characters. While a little allured by brilliant word-painting, the reader goes to the end and is ever-conscious that the cry of his soul for the bread of infinity has been answered not even by a stone, but by a handful of mud! No good purpose is thus brought about; nothing taught of the real

51

laws or philosophies of life; it drags down, but never elevates. Whosoever shall utter thus, upon them shall come retribution, and they shall be judges upon themselves, and executioners also, out in the open sea of the soul, where their own spirit will have no mercy for the misdeeds of the soul. Other imitators there may be, who, fired with a genuine desire to do good, will mimic intuitional utterances, and, however poor the work, if the motivation has still been to do good, in the measure of that resolve shall the Most High judge that whatever is for good is not for evil. But let them beware who, for money or profit, are tempted to give stones or mud!

And now, my brother, I have another subject to speak upon. Readers of my book, "Two Planets," may consider awhile over those passages concerning the sin of the Princess Lolix and of Zailm, the legal nephew of the Emperor Gwauxln. They may say that the mention of this fact, though liable to occur as one of the varied experiences of life, is nevertheless out of place in a book whose aim is highly moral. But I ask those who know my work, is it? Is it inexcusable to speak of those grave but common crimes if the author can treat them as examples of broken law, and demonstrate the working of such law so clearly before this unthinking world that men and women will be afraid to break it, fearful of the penalty, which cannot in any way be evaded? I think it unjustifiable to keep silence under such circumstances. I have, so far from overdrawing the estimate of the penalty of crime, not given the entire atonement picture. I know whereof I speak, for this, my brother, is my own life history, and words have no power to depict the utter misery which the carrying out of the punishment has caused me! If but one soul shall be saved like misery, and similar or equal sin, or less or more error, then am I content. I have sought to explain the great mystery of life, illustrating it with part of my own life history, extracts which cover years reaching into many thousands; and the greatest of all Books has been my text. I add not thereto nor take away, but explain. Peace be with thee.

PHYLOS.

Addendum:—I feel myself vastly indebted to many bright writers and authors for numerous quotations I have used here, without making credit at the time; it is impossible to render this award to every individual by name, hence I must do so concretely, just as the world finds itself forced to express its aggregate gratitude, not by words of laudation, but by shaping its life in conformity to the noble Precepts in poetry and in prose, devised to humanity as the legacy of all the ages. As the world is helped, so has my work been; I hope I have returned help for help.

Sincerely, PHYLOS.

A MARVELOUS PREDICTION.

The preface is mine to say what may properly please me. It was so given me by the Author.

A subject not specifically treated by Phylos in his book, but not forbidden me by him, I feel it almost due the public to give here, most especially as it was told me by him while I was summering in Reno, Nevada, in the year 1886. I at that time embodied it in a short story, which I dated, but more to the point, read to a young lady friend, Miss S. This fact she can testify as being fact, for it was partly written under her eyes, was criticized by herself, sister and mother, and, finally, was written upon paper bought for the purpose from her father's drug and book store.

Phylos stated to me then that inside fifty years, considerably inside, he thought, mundane scientists would have discovered and applied electric forces to the astronomical telescope. Just how, he did not state, although he did give ample enough details so that one familiar with those subjects probably would have been able to seize upon and work out the idea successfully. He said that electric currents unimpressed with vibrations such as produce sound, heat and light, until resisted, would be superadded to the light vibrations constituting the image beheld through the telescope. This would be accomplished through the media of well-known so-called chemical elements, whose then unrecognized higher powers remained to be discovered.

The result was described to me as awe-inspiring and marvelous past earthly dreams. Thus, he stated, that upon sung and stellar bodies so distant that hundreds of them only (even in this A. D. 1899) seem as a faint speck through the most powerful modern telescopes, to this electro-stellar-scope, by proper amplification of the electro-luminous waves, would be made so plain to earthly vision that objects not visible to the unaided earthly sight would be easily perceptible on the most distant stellar body, however remote from the mundane beholder. Further, Phylos says that he did not embody this subject in his book because Atlantis did not know of it, despite her marvelous scientific attainments. Hence it will be no "rediscovery," but a distinct step in advance of anything that Earth has known—Solomon at last outreached, so far as his time-honored saying applies to our planet, at least.

Respectfully,

THE AMANUENSIS, FREDERICK S. OLIVER

Los Angeles, October 11, 1899.

Footnotes

21:1 Revelations, XXII, 18-19; also I. Tim. VI., 3-12.

MAP OF ATLANTIS From *A Dweller on Two Planets*

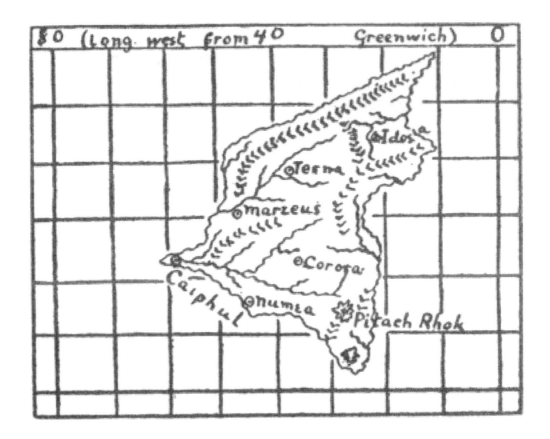

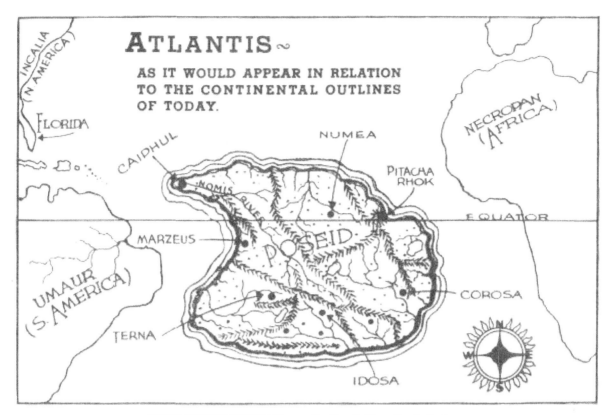

MAP OF ATLANTIS From *An Earth Dweller's Return*

ATLANTEAN WORLD MAP From *An Earth Dweller's Return*

BOOK THE FIRST. DIVIDING OF THE WAY

CHAPTER I. ATLANTIS, QUEEN OF THE WAVE.

"Why not?" I asked myself, pausing amidst the snow on the mountain, there so far above the sea that the Storm King was ever supreme, even while summer reigned below. "Am I not an Atlan, a Poseid, and is not that name synonymous with freedom, honor, and power? Is not this, my native land, the most glorious beneath the sun? Beneath Incal?" Again I queried: "Why not, aye, why not strive to become one amongst the foremost in my proud country?

"Poseid is the Queen of the Sea, yea, and of the world also, since all nations pay tribute of praise and commerce to us—all emulate us. To rule in Poseid, then, is not that virtually to rule over all the earth? Therefore will I strive to grasp the prize, and I will do it, too! And thou, O pale, cold moon, bear witness of my resolve"—I cried aloud, raising my hands to heaven—"And ye also, ye glittering diamonds of the sky."

If resolute effort could ensure success, I usually achieved whatever end I determined to attain. So there I made my vows at a great height above the ocean, and above the plain which stretched away westward two thousand miles to Caiphul, the Royal City. So high was it that all about and below me lay peaks and mountain ranges, vast in themselves, but dwarfed beside the apex whereon I stood.

All around me lay the eternal snows; but what cared I? So filled with the new resolve was my mind—the resolve to become a power in the land of my birth—that I heeded not the cold. Indeed, I scarce knew that the air about me was cold, was chill as that of the Arctic fields of the remote north.

Many obstacles would have to be overcome in the accomplishment of this plan—for truly, what was I at that moment? Only a mountaineer's son, poor, fatherless; but, the Fates be praised! not motherless! At the thought of her, my mother, miles away, down where the perennial forests waved, where snow seldom fell; while I stood on the storm-kissed summit, alone with the night and my thoughts—at the thought of my mother my eyes grew moist, for I was only a boy, and often a sad enough one, when the hardships which she endured arose to mind. Such reflections were but added incentives to my ambition to do and to be.

Once more my thoughts dwelt on the difficulties I must encounter in my struggle for success, fame and power.

Atlantis, or Poseid, was an empire whose subjects enjoyed the freedom allowed by the most limited monarchical rule. The general law of official succession presented to every male subject a chance for preferment to office. Even the emperor held an elective position, as also did his ministers, the Council of Ninety, or Princes of the Realm—offices analogous to those of the Secretarial Portfolios of the American Republic—its veritable successor. If death claimed the occupant of the throne, or any of the councilors, the elective franchise came into activity, but not otherwise, barring dismissal for malfeasance in office, a penalty which, if incurred by him, not even the emperor was exempt from suffering.

The possession of the elective power was vested in the two great social divisions, which embraced all classes of people, of either sex. The great underlying principle of the Poseid political fabric might be said to have been "an educational measuring-rod for every ballot-holder, but the sex of the holder, no one's business."

The two major social branches were known by the distinctive names of "Incala" and "Xioqua," or, respectively, the priesthood and scientists.

The Secrets Of Mount Shasta And A Dweller On Two Planets

Do my readers ask where that open opportunity for every subject could be in a system which excluded the artisans, trades people, and military, if they happened not to be of the enfranchised classes? Every person had the option of entering either the College of Sciences, or that of Incal, or both. Nor was race, color or sex considered, the only prerequisite being that the candidate for admission must be sixteen years of age, and the possessor of a good education obtained in the common schools, or at some of the lesser seats of collegiate learning, as the Xioquithlon in the capital city of some one of the Poseid States, as at Numea, Terna, Idosa, Corosa, or even at Marzeus' lower college, Marzeus being the principal art-manufacturing center of Atl. Seven years was the allotted term of study at the Great Xioquithlon, ten months in each year, divided into two sub-terms of five months each, devoted to active work, and one month allowed for recreation, half of it between each session.

Any student might compete in the annual examination exercises, held at the end of the year or just preceding the vernal equinox. That we recognized the natural law of mental limitation will be obvious from the fact that the course of study was purely optional, the aspirant being at liberty to select as many, or as few topics as were agreeable, with this necessary proviso: that only possessors of diplomas of the first class could be candidates for even the humblest official position. These certificates were evidence of a grade of acquirement which embraced a range of topical knowledge too great to be mentioned, otherwise than inferentially, as the reader proceeds. The second-grade diploma did not confer political prestige, except in the matter of carrying with it the voting privilege, although if a person neither cared to be an office holder, nor to vote, the right to instruction in any educational branch was nonetheless a gratuitous privilege. Those, however, who only aspired to a limited education, with the purpose of more successfully pursuing a given business, as tuition in mineralogy by an intending miner, agriculture by a farmer, or botany by an ambitious gardener, had no voice in the government.

While the number of those unambitious ones was not small, nonetheless the stimulus of obtaining political prestige was so great that not above one in a dozen of the adult population was without at least a secondary diploma, while fully one-third had first-grade certificates. It was owing to this that the electors found no scarcity of material for filling all elective positions under the government.

Some uncertainty is possibly left in the mind of the reader as to what constituted the difference between priestly and scientific suffragists. The only essential difference was that the curriculum at the Incalithlon, or College of Priests, embraced, in addition to every high-grade feature taught at the Xioquithlon, also the study of a wide range of occult phenomena, anthropological and sociological themes, to the end that graduates in the sciences might have the opportunity of fitting themselves to minister to any want, which men of less erudition and less comprehension of the great underlying laws of life might experience, in any phase or condition. The Incalithlon was in fact the very highest, most complete institution of learning which the world knew then, or—pardon what may seem to be, but is not, Atlan conceit—has known since; and for that matter, will know for centuries to come. As such an exalted educational institution, students within its halls must necessarily possess extra zeal and determined willpower in order to pursue and secure graduation certificates from its board of examiners. Few indeed had found life long enough to enable them to acquire such a diploma; possibly not one in five hundred of those who made honorable exit from the Xioquithlon, itself an institution not second to the modern Cornell University.

As I pondered, there amidst those mountain snows, I decided not to attempt too much, but a Xioqua I determined to be, if any possible chance existed; although I scarcely hoped for the possession of the eminence conferred by the title of Incala, I vowed that I would make an opportunity to compete for the other, if no occasion presented otherwise. To obtain the proud distinction would require, in addition to arduous study, the possession of ample money to furnish the expense of living, and the maintenance, at its highest, of an unfaltering energy of purpose. Where could I hope to obtain all this? The gods were believed to help the needy. If I, a lad of not yet seventeen summers, who had a mother looking to me for support and the necessities of life, with nothing that could aid me to attain my aspirations except native energy and will, might not be placed in that category, then who were the needy? I think there should be no more evidence of dependence necessary, and it was indeed proper for the gods to step in and help.

Filled with such reflections as these, I climbed yet higher towards tho top of the sky-piercing peak, near the apex of which I stood, for the dawn was not far distant, and I must be on the highest stone to greet Incal (the sun) when He conquered Navaz, else He—chief of all the manifest signs of the great and only true God, whose name He bore, whose shield He was—might not favorably regard my prayer. No, He must see that the supplicating youth spared no pains to do Him honor, because it was for this purpose only that I had climbed alone, amidst these solitudes, up that trackless steep of snow, beneath the starry dome of the skies.

"Is there," I asked myself, "a more glorious belief than this which my country-folk hold? Are not all Poseidi worshipers of the Great God— the one true Deity—who is typified by the blazing sun? There can be nothing more sacred and holy." So spoke the boy whose maturing mind had grasped the really inspiring exoteric religion, but who knew of none other deeper and more sublime, nor was he to learn of it in the days of Atla.

As the first glance of light from behind His shield stole through the dark abyss of night, I threw myself prone in the summit snows, where I must remain until the God of Light was entirely victorious over Navaz. Triumphant at last I then arose, and making a final profound obeisance, retraced my steps down that fearful, downwardly sloping ice and snow and barren rock, the latter black and cruelly sharp, thrusting its ridges through the icy coat, showing the ribs of the mountain which stood, one of the peerless peaks of the globe, thirteen thousand feet above the level of the sea.

For two days all my efforts had been to reach that frigid summit and cast myself, a living offering, on its lofty altar, thus to honor my God. I wondered if He had heard and noted me. If He had, did He care? Did He care enough to direct His vice-regent, God of the mountain, to aid me? To the latter, without knowing why, I looked, hoping in what may seem a blind, self-serving stupidity, for him to reveal a treasure of some sort, or—

What is that dull metallic glint in the rock whose heart my iron-shod mountaineer's staff had lain bare to the rays of the morning sun? Gold! O Incal! It is so! Yellow, precious gold!

"O Incal," I cried, repeating His name, "be thou praised for returning answer so quickly to Thy humble petitioner!"

Down in the snow I knelt, uncovering my head out of gratitude to the God of All Being, the Most High, whose shield, the sun, poured forth his glorious rays. Then I looked again on the treasure. Ah, what a store of wealth was there!

As the quartz rock splintered beneath my excited strokes, the precious metal held it together, so thickly did it vein its matrix. Sharp edges of the flinty stone cut my hands, so that the blood flowed from half a dozen places, and as I grasped the icy quartz which did the deed, my bleeding hands froze fast upon it, a union of blood and treasure! No matter! And I tore them loose, unheeding the pain, so much was I excited.

"O Incal," I exclaimed, "Thou are good to Thy child in so liberally bestowing the treasure which shall enable a realization of his resolution, before the heart has a chance to grow faint through long-deferred hope."

I loaded into my capacious pockets all that I could stagger under, selecting the richest and most valuable pieces of the gold quartz. How should I mark the spot, how could I find it again? To a born mountaineer this was no hard task and was soon accomplished. Then onward, downward, homeward, joyfully I swung, with light heart, if heavy load. Over these mountains, indeed not two miles from the base of my treasure peak, wound the emperor's highway to the great ocean, hundreds, of miles away on the other side of the Caiphalian plains. This causeway once reached, the most fatiguing part of the trip would be over, although but one-fifth of the entire route would yet have been traversed.

The Secrets Of Mount Shasta And A Dweller On Two Planets

To give some idea of the difficulties encountered in scaling or descending this giant mountain, I must remark that the final five-thousand feet of the ascent could be made by only one tortuous route. A narrow gorge, a mere volcanic fissure, afforded foothold of the most precarious character, all other parts of the peak being insurmountable cliffs. This meager support existed for the first one thousand feet. Above this point the cleft ceased. Near its upper end a small cave existed, rather higher than a man's stature, and capable of holding perhaps twenty people. In the farther end of this rocky room was a hole—a crack wider horizontally than in the perpendicular. Entering this crevice by crawling, serpent-fashion, the venturesome explorer would find that for several hundred paces he must descend a rather sharp incline, albeit the crevice in the first dozen steps so widened, or heightened, that a more or less upright posture could be assumed. From the end of its descending course it twisted and again increased in size so as to form a tunnel, ascending by tortuous windings, its walls affording sufficient support to make the climbing safe, although pursued upward at an angle of about forty degrees, while in some parts an even greater degree of perpendicularity marked the passage. In this way an upward climb of thirty odd hundreds of feet was accomplished, the winding and curving of the route greatly increasing the distance covered in a vertical rise. This, reader, was the sole method of reaching the summit of the highest mountain of Poseid, or Atlantis, as you call the island-continent.

Arduous as was its passage, there was more than enough room in this dry old chimney, or watercourse, whichever it was. Chimney it certainly had been, originally, though now water-worn to such an extent as to render the idea of its igneous formation, de novo, merely conjectural. At one part of its course this long hole widened into a vast cavern. This led away at right angles from the chimney, and down, down, until far in the bowels of the mountain—thousands of feet it seemed in the dread darkness—he who ventured so far found himself on the brink of a vast abyss, which had no visible side except that on which he stood; beyond this, further progress was impossible except for winged things, as bats, and bats were there none in that awful depth.

No sound came back from its frightful chasm, no brightness of torches had ever revealed its other shore—nothing was there but a sea of eternal inky blackness. Yet here were no terrors for me; rather a fascination. While others may have known of the place, I had never found a companion with enough temerity to brave the unknown, and stand by my side on the horrid brink, where I had stood, not once only but several times in days gone by. Three times I had been there, impelled by curiosity. On the third occasion I had leaned over the edge to seek a possible further descent, when the stone upon which I was—a huge basaltic block—loosened from its place, fell, and I barely escaped with my life. It fell, and for several minutes sounds of its descent came echoing back to where I stood; my torch went with it, and far down in the depths its sparks gleamed like fireflies as it struck projecting points of the rock before it finally disappeared. I was left in that deep darkness, weak from my great peril, to make my way up and out — if I could. If not, then to fail and die. But I succeeded. From then on, I had no curiosity to explore that unknown gulf. Through the chimney which led past the upper end of this abysmal cavern—between the upper end of the outer fissure in the cliff and the summit's side, five, or six hundred feet below the apex of the mountain—I had been many times; I had often been over the spot where a chance blow of my staff revealed the golden treasure, yet never found the precious store until I had asked Incal for it, urged by the pressing burden of my necessities. Is it strange that I felt absolute faith in the religious belief of my people?

It was into the dark chimney that I had to go when I left the snowy summit—out of the sunlight and fresh air, into dense blackness, and a slightly sulfurous atmosphere, but if I left the morning brightness, I also left the fearful cold of the external air, for inside the tunnel, if dark, it was warm.

At last, I came into the small room at the head of the thousand-foot crevice which would take me to the easier slopes of the lower and middle third of the mountain. In that room I paused. Should I return for another load of auriferous rock? Or should I go directly on my homeward way? At length I turned and retraced my steps. With the noon hour I stood once more beside my treasure spot. Then down again with my second load, till the weary toil ceased almost—for I was standing then at the entrance to the great cavern, four hundred feet from the little room at the head of the outer crevice—four hundred feet of pretty steep climbing. After a moment's pause I resumed the short but sharp ascent, and was soon in the little room, with only a dozen feet at most between myself and the free air. Sinuous, the long tunnel was, considered as a whole, yet it had some passages as straight, as if cut by tools along a line. The four hundred feet, more or less, which separated the room where I stayed my steps, from the entrance proper of the cavern, was such a straight stretch, and perhaps on that account as difficult to traverse as any part of the whole tunnel. Indeed it would have been impossible, except for its rough sides affording some slight foothold. Had the place been light, instead of filled with the blackness of darkness, I could have seen directly into the cavern from the apartment in which I was resting. The warm air induced me to sit or rather lie down at this point, even though I could not see, and so, as I rested there, I ate a handful of dates and sipped a little of the melted snow-water which my water-skin contained. Then I stretched myself out to sleep in the warm air.

For how long I slept I did not know, but the awakening—ah! the terror of it! Blasts of air so hot as to almost scorch, swept over and past me, laden with stifling fumes, and sending back a hoarse murmur as they rushed up the passage to the summit. Howling, groaning noises came up on the fervid breath from the abyss, mingled with the sound of tremendous explosions and deafening reports. The biggest cause for terror was a glow of red light reflected from the walk of the cavern, into which I found I could look with unobstructed freedom, and through whose depths shone flashes of red and green and blue, and every other color and tint, gases on fire. For a time, fright held me fast, so that without power to move I remained gazing into the awful hell of the blazing elements. I knew that the light and heat, both momentarily increasing, and the stifling vapors, the noise and the quivering of the mountain, all pointed but one and the same meaning—active volcanic eruption. At last, the spell which numbed my senses was broken by my catching sight of a spurt of molten lava which dashed up the intervening passage, projected a number of feet therein by an explosion within the cavern behind. Then I rose up and fled—fled across the floor of the little room and crawled with insane energy of haste through the horizontal entrance, which seemed never so low as that moment! I had forgotten that I carried gold in my pockets, and the fact only came back when I felt the retarding weight of the precious rock. But with the exertion to escape came a certain degree of calmness, and the restored presence of mind bade me not throw away the treasure. Reflection convinced me that the danger, although impending, was probably not immediate. So that I again crawled back into the little room and taking a sack which I had left there, filled it with all the ore I could carry. I undid a leather thong from my waist—a cord forty feet long—and looping one end to a point of rock, at the upper end of the crevice, I lowered the sack to the other extremity of the small cord, and then climbed down after it. Shaking the loop from the rock above, I repeated the performance again and again as I descended. In this way I reached the bottom of the crevice with the larger portion of my two loads of ore. From this point onwards my route lay along the crest of a rocky ridge, not very wide, but sufficiently so to form an easy path.

I had just started along this ridge when I looked back over the way I had come. At that instant, a shock of earthquake occurred that almost sufficed to throw me to the ground, and out of the little cave, where I had slept, shot a puff of smoke, followed by a red gleam—lava. Downwards it splashed, a fiery cascade, and a most glorious sight in the gathering darkness, for the sun was not yet set. The entire mountain was west of the ridge on which I stood, and it being near night, my position was in deep shadow.

Out along the ridge I fled, leaving my sack of gold and much that was in my pockets in the safest place that I could choose, high above the bottom of the gorge, along which the lava must flow. At a safe distance I paused for rest and scanned the fiery torrent leaping down the gorge, now some distance away, on my right, but in plain sight. "At least," thought I, "I have as much gold-rock—more metal than rock, it appears—left in my pockets yet, as I shall find myself well able to carry, now that the strength, born of excitement, is fled. So that even if I get not that I left behind, I have a great store of wealth. Therefore, Incal be praised!" How entirely inadequate to meet the expenses of seven years at college—and that college at the capital of the nation, where expenses were higher than elsewhere—were the twenty pounds, approximately, of gold-quartz, my inexperience could not tell me. That it was a greater treasure than I had ever possessed in my life, or even seen at one time, was an undeniable fact; therefore I was content.

A belief in an overruling Providence is necessary to most, indeed to all men, the sole difference being that men of widest knowledge require a Deity of power more nearly approaching infinity than do those of lesser experience; so those who realize the boundlessness of life, recognize a God of whom their conceptions are projected almost to omnipotence, compared to the conceptions which satisfy the ordinary human mind. Whether, then, the deity worshipped be a stone or a wooden idol, some inanimate form, or a Supreme Spirit of androgynous nature, it matters little. Those Beings—who order the course of events, executing the karmic law of the Eternal God, see the faith in mortal hearts, and suffer not that that law shall ever take its course in sternness, un-tempered by mercy. If trust in the idol, or the animate "god," or in the Supreme Spirit of God, should be allowed to perish because of the withering forces of sorrow and despair, then would human goodness tremble for safety and for continuation of its being. Such a catastrophe could not harmonize with God, hence, under the law, can never be allowed.

So with my belief in Incal, a belief shared by my country-people. Incal was a purely spiritual conception, and aside from the Eternal Cause, which no mind of any age of the world can sanely doubt, was existent only in the minds of his worshippers. And the faith was a noble one, one that tended to high morality, nourishing faith, hope and charity. What then though the personal Incal, symbolized by the shield of the blazing sun, was inexistent except in the brains of men? Our Poseid concept stood for us in the place of the Spirit of Life, Parent of all. That was enough to insure observance of the principles which it was supposed pleased Him best.

Surely the angels of the Most High Uncreated God, ministering then, as now, to the children of the Father, looked on the belief as it lay enshrined in my heart, and in the hearts of my fellowmen and women, and said, as they ministered: "Be it unto thee according to thy faith." The angels, beholding the hope that was in me to excel among men, had chastened me with fear as I fled from the burning mountain, but there came no disaster.

Onward I ran, as speedily as the nature of the path would permit. I had life and gold; so I praised Incal as I went. And the Spirit of Life was merciful, for I was not to know how insufficient for my needs was my treasure until the sting of disappointment was removed because of having found a more abundant provision. For several miles my course lay along the knife-edged back of the ridge. In many places awful gulfs yawned beside the path, so near that I had need of my hands to aid my feet. Sometimes these cliffs extended along both sides of the trail, forming it into a narrow parapet. I was grateful for small mercies and thanked Incal that the god of the mountain bestirred himself not in the form of earth-throes while I was in those perilous situations. At a distance of three miles from the starting place, my path led me along the brink of a frightful precipice, while above reared the wall of a second cliff. Only the light of the burning mountain now illumined my steps.

Here it was that, as I climbed cautiously downward towards the basaltic brink, a heavy shock threw me upon my knees and almost sent me into the gulf. An instant later a dull boom filled the air with an insistent intensity of sound, and I looked back in fear. A huge spout of fiery smoke was rushing skywards, mingled with stones large enough to be seen at the distance I was from the spot. Below the brink where I clung, an awful grinding and crashing was going on; the earth trembled fearfully, and repeated shocks caused me to grasp the rock, in desperate fear of being thrown over the edge. Off there in front, the gorge which lay at my feet once skirted other ridges and spurs of the peak. Once, for a while, these ridges and spurs had been; now they were not! I gazed upon a scene of awful and confusing turmoil, lit by the volcanic glare just sufficiently to be perceptible. The solid hills and rocks seemed tossing and unstable as the waters of the ocean and they rose and fell in a horrid swell, grinding and crashing in genuine pandemonium. Over all, volcanic ashes sifted in a thick, ceaseless shower, while dust and volcanic vapors filled the air and hung like a funeral pall over a seemingly perishing world.

Finally the mad uproar and sickening motion ceased; only the steady glow from the still-flowing lava and an occasional throe of earthquake telling the Plutonic tale. But I remained lying on the ledge, faint and ill. Gradually the lava stopped running, and the light went out; the shocks came only at long intervals, and a peace as of death filled all the region, while the silent gray ashes sifted down, covering the stricken land. Darkness reigned. I think I must, for a time, have been unconscious, for when I stirred I was aware of a sharp pain in my head; putting up my hand I felt a warm, wet oozing from a place which smarted at the touch. I felt about and found a jagged stone which had fallen from the cliff above and struck me. Further motion proved the wound was not serious, and I sat up. Already the dawn was coming and, faint with pain, hunger and cold, I again lay down to await broad day.

What a different scene rising Incal shone upon, in place of that of the previous morn! When I looked at the proud peak, the red light of the sun showed that one full half of it had been torn apart and swallowed up in some mysterious cavern. Aye, truly,

"Mountains rear to heaven their head in their bald and blackened cliffs, And bow their tall heads to the plain."

Nearer by, where other ridges had been, and where the awful reeling of the cliffs had occurred, right at my feet, indeed, no more was any rocky spire, nor peak, nor cliff there forever! Instead was a great lake of steaming water, whose farther shores were veiled by the softly settling ashes and clouds of steam condensed by the cold air into a fine misty rain, the weeping of the stricken globe over its recent agony! Hushed, was all the noise; quieted, the trembling; ceased, the boiling streaming of the lava.

That part of the ridge where I had lain had escaped, for the most part, the general rending. But even it had suffered, so that the path ahead of me, which I had been accustomed to travel in my trips to the peak, was gone, a huge block of probably thousands of tons weight having fallen into the pit below, making absolute erasure of the path, which had crossed that very place. I sought another and, in climbing about in the dull light, came to a part of the ridge which lay on the far side from the sun, which, as yet, was not more than two perilously narrow ledges, lakes of hot water below, impassable steeps overhead. Suddenly a dull red bar of light shone across my course! Looking for its source, I saw that the light streamed through a wide crack in the beetling cliff above. The bottom of this crack was not far below me and, instead of becoming narrowed out, had a floor as wide as any part of the fissure, as if all above that point had been forcibly fallen, or "faulted," to one side undoubtedly the real explanation. I lowered myself to the level of this floor and, finding the crevice sufficiently wide, stepped into it, ignoring the fact that at any moment fresh convulsions of the volcano might close the cleft and crush me as between the faces of a vise. I did think of this possibility but, Poseid-like, put aside fear by reflecting that I was trusting in Incal, who would do whatever was good for me.

The stricken cliff showed, here and there, veins of quartz with porphyritic sheaves, forming ledges running through the granite masses. Clear to the top, this narrow cleft extended, and though really some two or three feet wide, its height made it appear very narrow. As I paused, filled with delight at the idea that on both sides of me my eyes rested on virgin rock never exposed to the gaze of any man since earth began, I noticed that which set my pulses bounding with wild joy— right by my side, but a little in front, was a vein of yellow, ocherous-looking rock in which I saw many spots of whitish, harder rock, the appearance of which was due to quartz bodies torn apart by the same shock which formed the cleft. These spots were thickly dotted with nuggets of native gold and with silver-like mineral. The ductility of the precious metals was exhibited in curious effects, the gold and silver being drawn out from the smoothly fractured surface into wires, which in some cases were a number of inches long. Again the faintness of hunger left me, and the pain of my aching head-wound was temporarily forgotten, as I chanted a hymn of gratitude to my God. Gone was the towering peak; destroyed was the sole route of access to the lofty summit which man's foot might traverse; but here, after the war of the subterranean fires was over, here was a greater treasure, nearer home, easier to reach—the excitement of joy was too great a strain on my nerves, already so weak, and I fainted! But youth is elastic and the health of those who are without vices wonderfully buoyant. I soon recovered consciousness and was wise enough to make my way home without stopping to waste further strength, knowing that my mountaineering instinct would be an infallible guide to my subsequent return.

I felt, in taking counsel of my mother, that her belief that I could not work the mine alone was essentially true. But whom should I trust to aid me and take an honest share of the wealth so obtained as recompense?

Enough, is it not, that I found the necessary help? Certain professed friends entered into a copartnership with me and, for the privilege of retaining the remainder of the proceeds, allowed me one-third of the profits, agreeing to do this without requiring any labor from me; and, with some reluctance, also agreeing to my demand that no part of the ownership should be vested in anybody but myself. I caused them to sign a paper to that effect and to seal it with the most inviolable sign possible in Poseid, namely, to make their signatures with their own blood. We all three did thus. So much formality I insisted upon for the reason that the suspicion was irrepressible that these men proposed to claim that they themselves were the discoverers of the treasure, and that I had, per consequence, no right to any of it. Today I know that this was the case. I know that the proviso in the contract declaring that the whole mine which they, my partners, worked in the then current year was the inalienable property of Zailm Numinos was all that prevented the intended robbery.

This stipulation made no reference to the discoverer, as such, but did state in incontrovertible terms that in the possessor of that name was vested the title to the property. I would have had, in the event of a difference arising between us, no necessity to prove how I became owner of the mine; no claim that some person other than myself was the discoverer would avail the would-be defrauders, for whosoever was the first to find the lode, the fact remained that I was the owner, and possession in this event meant every advantage through the law. At least, so it seemed to my ignorance. My associates were not so ignorant. They knew that the contract was worthless because executed in violation of the law. The day came when I knew all. I knew in later times that the laws of Poseid made every mine a tithe-payer to the empire, and that a mine worked without acknowledgment of this legal lien was liable to confiscation. It was apparent, also, that if my partners had not allowed themselves to be swayed by greed into keeping secret the whole agreement, and also by working in the mine, thus rendering themselves participators in an infraction of the law, that they would have become the legally recognized owners, simply through furnishing information concerning my acts to the nearest governmental agent. But I did not know these things at the time and the other two thought it wise to keep silence, for the reason that they were not aware of anything except the fact that they were violating statutory enactments of no seeming importance. Thus was the secret kept until a later revelation.

The means having been forthcoming, the removal of my residence from the country to the city of the Rai was next in order. Our farewell to the old mountain home and our installment in the new one in Caiphul will be passed over in silence.

CHAPTER II. CAIPHUL

The Atlantean people lived under a government having the character of a limited monarchy. Its official system recognized an emperor (whose position was an elective one, and not in any sense hereditary) and his ministers, known by a name signifying "The Council of Ninety," and also known as "Princes of the Realm." All of these officers had a life-tenure in office, except in cases of malfeasance, which term was strictly defined and its provisions severely enforced; and from the operation of the law relating thereto, no exaltation of position was sufficient to secure exemption for offenders. No governmental positions were made elective, with the exception of one ecclesiastical office, and lesser positions in the public service were made appointive in all cases, the appointees being held to strict account by the appointing power, emperor or prince, who, for the use of this power was responsible to the people for the conduct of his placeholders.

However, it is not the scheme of this chapter to discuss Poseid politics, but to describe the ministerial and monarchical palaces with which the nation furnished its elected officers, one for each prince, but for the emperor, three. In the main, the description of one of these buildings, both within and without, typifies that of any or all of the others, just as in the United States of America and other modern lands a governmental edifice is easily known to be such, by its general architectural features. A description therefore of one palace will serve a double purpose, that of presenting an idea of the most notable residence in the great Atlantean empire, since I will describe the main palace of the emperor;

and, secondly, that of illustrating the prevailing style of governmental architecture in the period during which I resided in Poseid. Imagine, if it pleases you, an elevation approximating fifteen feet in height, ten times that figure in width, and that fifty times its height represents its length. External to the plane dimensions, on each of the four sides of the platform, which was of hewn blocks of porphyry, an easy flight of steps led from the lawns up to the top of the elevation. On the sides, these steps were divided into fifteen sections, while on the ends the divisions were only three, each being divided into lengths of fifty feet. Between the two sections nearest the corners each division consisted of a deep quadrangular recess, into and around which the stairs ran in uninterrupted continuity.

The next, or third section, was separated from those on either side by a sculptured serpent of huge size, fashioned from sandstone and as faithful to life as art could make it. The heads of these immobile reptiles rested on the green sward in front of the stairs, while the bodies lay in full relief upon the staircases and reaching the top of the platform, wound about the massive columns which supported the pediments of the verandas of the superstructural palace erected upon the platform described, columns which formed a most imposing peristyle between the broad verandas and the steps. The succeeding division was a quadrangle in the steps, and the next, another serpent, and so around the building. It is hoped that this description is sufficiently clearly-expressed to give an idea of the tremendous parallelogram, encompassed with steps, guarded by monstrous ornamental, as well as useful, serpent forms, religious emblems, signifying not alone wisdom but also the appearance of a fiery serpent in the skies of the ancient earth, initiating the event of the separation of Man from God.

Alternating with these forms were the recesses, relieving what would otherwise have been severely straight and wearisome lines. Surmounting this was the first story of the palace proper, its reptile-entwined peristyle holding aloft great veranda roofs, whereon were enormous vases holding earth to nourish all kinds of tropical plants, shrubs and many small varieties of trees, a luxuriant garden which perfumed the air, already cooled by numerous fountains playing in the midst. Above the first story, with its flower-filled porticos, arose another tier of apartments, surrounded by open galleries, the floors of which were formed by the roofs of those beneath. The third and highest tier of apartments had no verandas, although on all sides it had promenades, formed by the roof of the portico beneath. The same wild luxuriance of flowers and foliage rendered the stories of equal attractiveness. In all, song birds and birds of plumage were welcome guests, uncaged, but tame because they never received harm.

Attendants, with blowguns to project noiseless darts, quietly destroyed all predatory species, as also they did those which, having neither song powers, vivid coloring of plumage, nor the useful habits of insectivora to commend them, were therefore undesirable. Springing from the main roof of the palace arose graceful spires and towers, while the many jutting apartments, angles and groined arches, flying buttresses, cornices and multifarious architectural effects prevented any apparent heaviness in the design. Around the largest of the towers there extended from bottom to top a winding staircase, conducting to the rail-enclosed space on its summit, one hundred feet above the aluminum sheathing or roofing-plates of the palace. Agacoe palace was unique in the possession of this tower, differing thus from all other ministerial edifices.

It may be explained that the tower had been erected as a memorial of the departure of a fair princess from the loving care of her imperial husband into Navazzamin, the shadowy land of departed souls, some centuries before my day. Such was the Agacoe palace. Its uppermost floor was in use as a great governmental museum; the middle was devoted to offices of the chief government officials, while the first flat was magnificently arranged and furnished for occupancy as the emperor's private residence. As not uninteresting, it may be noted that the yawning mouths of the stone serpents recently described served as doorways (of the usual size) to certain apartments in the basement, a fact which gives an accurate idea of the enormous size of these lithic saurians. The monsters were made with an eye to artistic proportion; their bodies were of carved gray, red or yellow sandstone, their eyes of sard, carnelian, jasper or other colored silicious stone, while fangs for their yawning mouths were made from gleaming white quartz, set on each side of the entranceway.

So much sawed and hewn stone forces the modern mind to wonder if the Atlanteans obtained the finished product through the unremitting toil of slaves, in which case we must have been a barbarous people, whose political autonomy was ever menaced by the uplifting forces of the social volcano which slavery always creates, or else we possessed peculiarly efficient stone-cutting machinery. This latter is the correct assumption, for our machinery for that purpose, like an almost infinite variety of other implements for every sort of service, was our pride amongst the nations. Let me here make an assertion, not for argument but to be understood in the light of subsequent chapters, namely, that if we as Atlanteans had not possessed this wide range of mechanical inventions and the inventive talent which gave us these triumphs, then neither would you of this modern day have possession of a similar creative ability, nor of any of the results of such genius. It may be that you cannot understand the connection between the two ages and races while conning this statement; but as you draw nearer to the close of this history your mind will return to it and understand it completely.

Trusting that the effort has been successful to depict by words the appearance of Atlantean governmental edifices, let us next get an idea of the Caiphalian promontory, whereon was enthroned Caiphul, the Royal City, the greatest of that ancient day, within the limits of which resided a population of two million souls, un-encompassed by walled fortifications. Indeed, none of the cities of that age were surrounded by walls, and in this respect they differed from the cities and towns known to later historical ages. To call my records of this Poseidic age history is not outside of fact, since what I relate in these pages is history derived from the astral-light records. Nevertheless, it precedes the histories handed down in manuscript, papyrus rolls and rock-inscriptions by many centuries, seeing that Poseid was no longer known in the earth when history's first pages were chronicled by the earliest historian using papyrus; nay, nor even yet earlier, when the sculptors of the obelisks of Egypt and the rock-inscribers of the temples cut pictorial histories in enduring granite. No longer known was Poseid, for it is today approaching nine thousand years since the waters of the ocean engulfed our fair land and left no sign, not even so much as was left of those two cities hidden away beneath lava and ashes and for sixteen centuries of the Christian era thought never to have had existence. Excavators dug away the solidified lava from Pompeii, but from Caiphul no man can turn aside the floods of the Atlantic and reveal what no more exists, for were every day a century it were even so nearly three months of such lengthy days since the dread command of GOD went forth unto the waters:

"Cover the land, so that the all-beholding sun shall see it no more in all his course."

And it was so. In preceding pages the promontory of Caiphul was described as reaching out into the ocean from the Caiphalian plain and as visible from a great distance at night because of the glow of light from the capital. For three hundred miles westward from Numea the peninsula projected outwards from the plain, averaging almost to its extreme cape a breadth of fifty miles and rising much like the chalk-cliffs of England directly from the ocean to a height of nearly one hundred feet to reach a plain almost floor-like in its evenness. On the point of this great peninsula was Caiphul or "Atlan, Queen of the Wave." Beautiful, peaceful, with its wide spreading gardens of tropical loveliness,

"Where a leaf never fades in the still, blooming bowers, And the bee banquets on thro' a whole year of flowers."

Its broad avenues shaded by great trees, its artificial hills, the largest surmounted by governmental palaces, and pierced and terraced by the avenues which radiated from the city-center like spokes in a wheel. Fifty miles these ran in one direction, while at right angles from them, traversing the breadth of the peninsula, forty miles in length, were the shortest avenues. Thus lay, like a splendid dream, this, the proudest city of that ancient world.

At no point did Caiphul approach the ocean nearer than five miles. Though it had no walls, around the whole city extended a huge moat, three-quarters of a mile broad by an average of sixty feet in depth and supplied by the waters of the Atlantic. On the north side, a great canal entered the moat, a canal in which the outflowing waters of a large river, the Nomis, created an outgoing current of considerable swiftness. A current was thus naturally made to cause suction through the entire circle of the moat, of which the ocean supply entered at an ingress on the south side. In this manner efflux into the sea of all the drainage of the artificial circular island on which stood the city was allowed. Immense pumping engines forced fresh ocean water through large stone pipes and conduits all over the city, flushing the drains, furnishing motive power for all requisite purposes, for electric lighting and electric services of vast variety—but enough. Electric service? Electric power? Indeed we had deepest knowledge of this motor-force of the universe; we used it in countless ways which have yet to be rediscovered in this modern world of ours, and ways, too, which are every day coming more and more into recollection as men and women of that past age reincarnate in this.

It is not strange that you are incredulous, my friend, when I speak of these inventions which you have considered the special property of today; but I speak from a knowledge born of experience, seeing that I lived then, and live now; lived not only in Poseid twelve thousand years ago, but also in the United States of America, before, during and after the War of the Secession.

We drew our electrical energies partly from the waves beating the ocean shores, more largely from the rise and fall of the tides; from mountain torrents and from chemicals; but chiefly from what might aptly be termed the "Night-Side of Nature." High-grade explosives were known to us, but our employment of them was of much wider range than yours. If you could cause these substances gradually to yield up their vast imprisoned force without fear of an explosion, do you think that your machinery would long be propelled by clumsy, ponderous steam or electric engines? If a great steamship could dispense with its coal-bins and boilers and instead have dynamite in an absolutely safe compound form yielding, from what a man could carry in a handbag, force sufficient to drive the ship from England to America, or to send a train six thousand miles, how long would you continue to see steam enginery? Yet this was a power, and a least valued one at that, which we—possibly you; certainly I—knew in the Atlantean life. It will be again with you, because Our Race is coming again to earth.

But not alone this resource of power was ours; indeed, it was our forces of the Night-Side as an alcohol-vapor motor is to thy steam-engine. The Night-Side forces—what are they? At this place I will answer only by a counter-question, namely: The force of Nature, of gravitation, of the sun, of light, where does it come from? If you were to answer me, "It is of God," so then will I answer that, likewise, Man is the Heir of the Father, and whatsoever is His, is also the Son's. If Incal is impelled by God, the Son shall find how his Father does this thing, and shall presently do likewise again, even as Man so once in Poseid. But greater things than these which we did might you do; you are now, you were then; you are Poseid returned, and on a higher plane!

The original object for which the great moat encircling the capital was excavated, had, since long centuries, been fulfilled. That purpose was purely maritime, in the days when ships had been used as carriers, before the later general use of aerial vessels; and it had served this purpose in such stead as to win for Caiphul its proud title "Sovereign of the Seas," a name retained even when the original uses of its moat had become a matter of history. When the better means of transportation had replaced the old, then the ships, which for ten centuries had graced all the seas and waterways of the globe, were allowed to decay or were converted to other uses. Only a few sails now roved the waters, and those were merely pleasure craft belonging to novelty-loving people of leisure, who thus indulged their taste for sport.

This radical change was, however, no reason why the masonry quays of the one hundred and forty miles, more or less, of the moat should be allowed to go to destruction. This would have entailed the loss of valuable property through the encroachment of the unchecked waters, as well as the deterioration of the sanitary system of the city, besides which such a course would have destroyed the beauty of the moat and its environments. Therefore, in all of the seven centuries since we ceased to employ marine transportation, no sign of weakness had been allowed to threaten this great length of masonry.

The Secrets Of Mount Shasta And A Dweller On Two Planets

A marked feature of Caiphul was the wealth and rare beauty of its trees and tropical shrubbery, lining the avenues, covering the many palace-crowned hills, many of which had been constructed to rise two or even three hundred feet above the level of the plain. Trees and shrubs and plants, vines and flowers, annuals and perennials, filled the mimic canyons, gorges, defiles and levels which it had delighted the art-loving Poseidi to create. They covered the slopes, twined the miniature cliffs, the walls of buildings, and hid even the greater part of the steps which led wide-sweeping banks to the edges of the moat, overlaying everything like a glorious lush green garment.

Perhaps the reader is beginning to wonder where all the people lived. Truly the query is well-timed, and the answer will, I trust, prove interesting.

In the work of altering the configuration of the surface of the great promontory from that of a plain to the more beautiful variations of hills and their intervening depressions, the scheme pursued had been to make keyed-shells of rock, of enormous strength, in the form of terraces, and leaving arched passages wherever the avenues intersected such elevations, to fill in the interiors then remaining with a concrete of clay, rubble and cement carefully tamped. The exteriors were thereafter covered with rich soil on the levels and terraced for the support of vegetable life of all kinds. These elevations covered many square miles of the level once existent, leaving little that remained as plane surface except the avenues, and not all of these, inasmuch as quite a number of the thoroughfares ascended the rise between the hills or followed the ascending bed of some canyon until they reached the ridge at the head of the latter.

They then penetrated the divide and moved out upon the opposite side through an arched way, wherein tubes of crystal, absolutely exhausted of air, gave a continuous light derived from the "Night-Side" forces. The vertical faces and inclinations of the terraces, as well as the sides of the canyons, were made into rooms of varied and ample size. The entrances to these, and to the windows, were concealed under mimic hedges of rock, over which clambered vines and rock-loving

81

plants, thus removing from view the stiff ugliness of the metallic casings underneath. These apartments were arranged in artistic suites for the accommodation of families. The metal sheathing with which they were lined prevented moisture within, while their position under the surface insured an even degree of temperature at all seasons of the year. As these residences were designed and built by the government, the ownership was vested in the same power and the tenants acquired leasehold from the Minister of Public Buildings. The rental was merely nominal and only sufficient to keep the property in repair, furnish the expenses of the incandescent lighting and heating service, the water supply, and the salaries of the necessary officials to attend to these duties. All of this cost not above ten or fifteen per cent of an ordinarily skilled mechanic's wages. The mention of so much detail may be pardoned because, were it omitted, only a vague and unsatisfactory conception of life in this antediluvian age would be acquired by the reader.

The great charm of the residences lay in the fact of their retired situations, which prevented the dismal appearance of masses of angular houses, an effect of extreme ugliness seen in our modern days, but seldom, or never, in our Atlantean, cities. The result of this arrangement was that, to a beholder, looking from any high elevation, the city would have been conspicuous, to one accustomed to the modern atrocities of stone, brick or wood, chiefly for the absence of sky-piercing piles separated by narrow, dark, treeless and too often filthy tunnels, miscalled streets. Here a hill, and there another and yet another until the eye counted them by the score. There were one hundred and nineteen in all; here a lake, or there a cliff with a lake, or wooded park at its foot; gorges of mimic grandeur, little forests, so regularly irregular; cascades and tumbling torrents, fed from the inexhaustible supply of fresh water belonging to the city, their banks and shores covered with those plants, trees, and shrubs that love being close to abundant water.

Such, dear friends, would have been the scene presented to your eyes, if you could have gazed on Caiphul with me; maybe you did. And yet, Caiphul was not devoid of houses built much after the modern fashion, for the city franchise to build neat mansions here and there in situations and styles calculated to add to the beauty of the scene was a privilege of which anyone of means might avail himself, under official approval. Many did so. Museums of art, edifices for theatrical entertainment and other structures not designed for habitation were also in tasteful numbers.

I found, in going about the city, that the avenues, in certain instances, seemed to come to an abrupt termination in some grotto, whose interior was usually hung with stalactites pendent from the roof. Perhaps a slight turn occurred from the straight course, and thus prevented one from seeing through the grotto. In these places, shaded, high-tension, airless cylinder lamps cast a soft glow throughout the interior, making a moonlight effect very pleasing to one who came in from the brightness of the sunlight.

While, in the majority of cases, our people were accomplished equestrians, this mode of travel was not used except for physical culture and grace, electric transit being provided by the government. Indeed, the social reformers of these days of the Christian nineteenth century would have been in their ideal land had they been Caiphalians, and this because the government pursued the paternalistic principle so systematically as to have vested in itself the ownership of all the land, methods of public transit, and communications, in a word, all property, The system was a most beneficent one, which no Poseida wanted to see disused or supplemented by any other. Should a citizen desire a vailx (airship) for any use, he applied to the proper officials, who were on duty at numerous vailx-yards throughout the city. Or, to cultivate the land, he applied to the department of Soils and Tillage.

Perhaps it was desired to manufacture some product; the machinery was for lease at the nominal rate necessary to meet working expenses and the salary of the officers overseeing that portion of the public property. Let these samples suffice. Enough, that no political harmony exists in this modern time of the world like that which sprang from this paternalism on the part of our elected officials. Governmental paternalism is a thing regarded with jealousy and semi-alarm by modem republics. But it is today a different quality from what it was then. Ours was a paternalism closely watched and duly checked by the suffragists of the nation, and its life was essentially an advocacy of true socialistic principles.

I have not even now been so precise in details as to explain many of the most peculiar adjustments maintained between the political parent and its children, nor between labor and capital. But neither can I do so in these pages with any degree of propriety, because this is not a plea for readoption, in this age of the world, of methods pursued in that remote period. Yet, this much I can say, not inappropriately at this juncture, that Poseid had not in my day, the modern, yet also very ancient, annoyance of labor strikes, blocking capital and enterprise, starving the artisan, and causing more suffering on the part of the poor than such annoyances can ever bring to the doors of the rich. The secret of this immunity was not far to seek in a nation whose government was the voice of those people who possessed sufficient education to wield the power of franchise, and this, too, regardless of sex, because inborn in our national life was this principle: "An educational measuring-rod for every voter; the sex of the suffragist is immaterial." In such a nation, and under such a government, it would be strange indeed if industrial disharmonies could long disturb our social political structure. The broad principle of equity between employer and employee governed in Poseid; it mattered not what a person did for another person, but the whole equation hinged on this question: Was some service performed by one person for another? If so, the fact that the service was or was not accomplished by physical labor counted for nothing. It might be equally a service deserving compensation whether it was a physical or a purely intellectual service; nor was it held to be important whether the employer represented one or more individuals or the employee one or more people.

Our local enactments on the subject of industrial equity were complete and rather voluminous. While I care not to give in detail a reproduction of what may be termed labor law, a few excerpts are worthy of place. It will be well to preface these with a short history of their enactment, and thus show how, in that olden time, labor troubles quite similar, and fully as menacing to peace and order as any modern industrial upheaval, were finally and equitably settled.

On the "Maxin-Stone," to which legal code reference in full is made in the proper place, was found this vital seed of settlement of the fearful menace embroiling labor and capital, to wit:

"What time those who work for hire shall be oppressed, and shall rise in wrath to destroy their oppressor—lo! let their hand be stayed, that they shall obey Me. I say unto them: Harm not the person or the property of any man, not even though by that man they be oppressed. For are not all brothers and sisters? Are not all children of one Father, even the nameless Creator? But this I command: That they destroy oppression. Shall things, which are less than man, rule over and oppress their masters? Seek diligently my meaning."

The students of ethics interpreted this command to mean that the oppressed industrial classes should not harm the oppressing capitalists or their property. The rich classes were perhaps as much victims of circumstances as the poorer people; the remedy lay, not in blind anarchy, but in eradicating conditions. This was easy, if properly attempted. The oppressed were as a thousand to one of the oppressor. The majority of them held the elective franchise, and it was determined that, as the government was the people's servant, the proper method was to deal with the question at the polls, and not to employ violence against the rich. Therefore the call went forth amongst all the people to vote on the adoption of a code of industrial regulations and to vote its respectful submission to the Rai. Of the many articles and sections, I shall insert only those that are pertinent to modern times and troubles, so that if these selections are not articled and sectioned consecutively, the reason is obvious.

EXCERPTS FROM THE POSEID LABOR LAWS.

"No employer shall demand of any employee any service outside of legal hours of work without extra remuneration."

"Sec. 4. These hours shall not be less nor more than nine in number for physical labor in any period of twenty-four hours; nor less nor more than eight hours for sedentary employments chiefly requiring intellectual exertion."

This statute allowed the two parties to a labor contract to arrange to suit themselves when the working hours were to begin or end, with reference to the first hour of the day, namely, the modern noon hour. In regard to wage matters, the law was very clear. It held that as mankind was selfish by nature, that is, the lower nature, that he would operate on a basis of self-aggrandizement, the modern doctrine of "laissez-nous faire." Hence if he should not be motivated by the sense of duty to his fellowman to treat that man right, when right was not dictated by might, then the law must compel him to be fair. It is in this that the modern Anglo-Saxon world, which is Poseid (and Suern) reincarnating, shows one mark of the slow but sure upward progress begotten of time; proves that although man moves, as does all else, sensate and insensate, in a circle, yet that circle is like a screw-thread, ever progressing around and around, but each time moving on a higher plane. Poseid must be compelled by its advanced minds to do what is fair towards the weak. America and Europe are growing willing to do rightly, fairly, because it is the part of duty. Thus we behold modern employers often doing of free will what the ancient Poseid did because of law, namely, sharing profits with their employees.

The law then having gone to the lawmakers, the suffragists decreed that the government should establish a Department of Commissary, the duties of which should be to collect all statistics concerning the food products of commerce, also concerning all textile fabrics necessary for clothing and, in brief, all articles necessary for the proper social maintenance of individuals. On these statistical reports was to be founded an estimate of the cost of all such necessaries, amongst which books were reckoned as mental food, and the cost of these things for a year was calculated. Upon this calculation, day's wages were estimated by dividing the annual cost into the number of days. This rate was decided anew every ninety days, as the cost of the chief staples was found to fluctuate, hence the rate was not wholly stable, and the wages of any given three months' term might probably differ from those of any previous quarter.

Let me quote:

"Sec. VII, Art. V. Employers shall divide the gross profits of business operations upon the following plan: The wage, salary or payment for labor of each employee shall be paid in the sum directed by the quarterly estimate of living cost determined by the Department of Commissary. From the remainder, the amount of six parts in each hundred on the capital invested shall be set aside. This increment shall be and represent the employer's net profits. From the remaining income the running expenses shall be deducted, and of any sum thereafter remaining, one-half shall be invested to provide annuities for the sick or disabled, or assurance for the dependents of deceased employees. The remaining half shall be periodically distributed amongst the employees on the basis of their various compensations.

"Sec. VIII, Art. V. The whole of a body of employees is only equal to the Superintendent thereof. The Superintendent is equal to all the underlings. Hence, employers, when not themselves managers of the business, shall pay to managers a salary equal to the combined wages of the subordinates."

Truly, these labor laws and other matters have a modern sound. But civilization in all ages, among all nations, is accustomed to expressing itself in ways which, if modern language be used to describe them, will seem almost identical; so that in ancient Atlantis and in modem America the term "strike" may be properly used to designate a labor revolt; the same principle characterizes all other phases; for from age to age the world makes but slow progress, and is today not as far advanced in its present sub-cycle, nor as civilized, as it was in olden Poseid. This may seem a hard saying, but it will presently be understood.

Such, in the main, were the chief features of the industrial world in Poseid. The old-time strikes and riots out of which these laws were born disappeared and peace replaced it. The change was good and charitable, indeed, yet always the strong looked to see how they might evade the law, and though they did not succeed to a harmful extent, still the wish on their part entered the sum of karma. So when the modern world of the Christian epoch came to the eighteenth and nineteenth centuries, particularly the last named, then began the reincarnation of this Poseid era, and for a time the tendency to oppression again came uppermost. But overriding this tendency now faintly appears the willingness to do right for the sake of right, which, as applied to industrial matters, has of very, very recent years been manifested—a sign of the evening afterglow of the last day, now near striking its last hour, telling of a spent age. I particularly refer to the greater willingness of man to treat his fellow rightly, without being forced to do so by law. Truly, it is, as yet, only done because it is found to pay; but it would never have been found to pay if the reincarnated correctness had not induced experiments in profit-sharing to be made, in hopes of exterminating the strike iniquity and with the idea of harmonizing society to be active in doing as it would be done by.

Finally, strange and paradoxical as it may appear, this betterment is the direct child of the old-time rights extorted by might in Poseid, and today, reincarnated offspring of reincarnated oppression, as in Atlantis oppression sprang reincarnate from the grave of other ages gone before, previous to the wondrous memorial of Gizeh. But to more than mention this here would be to trench upon work given unto another by the Messiah; therefore only a hint can I give now, but more later. Suffice it then, that those were ages when man was struggling, with scarcely perceptible upward motion, from our fallen ancestry. Glory be to our Father that His children surely, if slowly, are by devious ways climbing His heights; many are their falls, but they shall rise again, not suffering the enemy to triumph.

It may be a seemingly inopportune intrusion, but I must here briefly describe the electro-odic transit system of Caiphul, and the other cities, towns and villages scattered throughout the empire and its colonies. The description is of the local transit-carriages only. On each side of every avenue was a broad tessellated pavement for pedestrians. A line of massive, bottomless stone vases in which ornamental shrubs thrived and foliage plants stood upon the curb, and on either side of these was a metal rail, placed at a height of about nine feet, and supported upon small cranes similar to those from which ship-boats are swung. At regular distances other rails crossed these main runners, rails capable of being raised or lowered to form a switch-junction, a simple lever effecting this process. These rails served as cross streets, there being in comparatively few instances any paved street underneath the rails on any but the great radiate avenues. On the maps of the City Department of Transit these main and cross rails looked like the web of a garden spider. For each transit-district there were multitudes of carriages, having an aut-odic mechanism, whereby they were made to speed at tremendous swiftness with their passengers. But collisions could not occur, as the conveying rods formed a double-track system.

CHAPTER III. FAITH IS KNOWLEDGE ALSO,
AND IT GIVETH TO REMOVING MOUNTAINS

There is a saying, whose origin is dim through lapse of time, to the effect that, "Knowledge is power." Within well-defined limits this is a verity. If behind the knowledge lies the necessary energy to realize its benefits, then only is it a true saying. In order to exercise command over nature and her forces, the would-be operator must have perfect comprehension of the natural laws involved. It is the degree of attainment in this knowledge which marks the less or greater ability of the performer, and those who have acquired the profoundest understanding of the Law (Lex Magnum) are masters whose powers seem so marvelous as to be magical. Uninitiated minds are absolutely alarmed by their incomprehensible manifestations. On every side of me when I came from my mountain home to my metropolitan abode, I found inexplicable wonders, but natural dignity saved me from appearing ignorant.

Little by little was I to acquire familiarity with my environment, and thereby gain a knowledge of the things which have been referred to since I first mentioned the exchange of country life for urban surroundings. But these attainments of pleasing authority over nature demanded a special course. That course of study had not yet been determined upon by me, prior to my introduction to the city, for it seemed that the part of wisdom was to concentrate my energies upon specialties and not to scatter force by attempting generalities. To this end I determined to live for a more or less extended period without seeking admission to the Xioquithlon, and resolved to devote the interim to observation. I had been an extensive reader of books, which I obtained from the public library in the district where my mountain home had been. From these I had gained no inconsiderable understanding of social polity. The fact that there were but ninety-one elective offices in the gift of the people, while there were almost three hundred millions of Poseidi in Atl and her colonies, and according to a late census which I had seen, thirty-seven, nearly thirty-eight, millions of electors held First Degree diplomas, thus entitling them to hold elective offices, disposed me to think it extremely improbable that such a high preferment would ever fall to my lot.

But if I could scarcely expect a ministerial office, I still felt that I might, if I fitted myself therefore by gaining a prime diploma, attain to a high political level and hold an appointive position, and some of these were almost equally as honorable as a councilorship. What special subjects should I concentrate upon? Geological research was very attractive to me, and by its numerous branches offered wide and alluring fields of opportunity. Then again, philology was almost as much so. My ability to acquire foreign languages was not inconsiderable, as I had found from studying a little volume descriptive of a land known as Suernis, a strange country, and of the language of which many examples were given. These I had without effort learned perfectly from once reading.

Several months of city residence at length found me determined to acquire all the geological knowledge that I could, for it was a study which I believed Incal had directed me to make, as well as to gain a knowledge of mines and of practical mineralogy. As coefficients, I purposed thoroughly to ground myself in synthetic and analytical literature, not just of my native Poseid, but also that of the Suerni and Necropanic languages. Thus have I named the three greatest nations of pre-Noachian (pre-Nepthian) times. One of these nations was effaced from the earth, but the other two have, after terrible vicissitudes, survived till today. Of them I will speak later.

The reasons which induced me to choose the curriculum which I have mentioned were that, as a geologist and coordinate scientist I hoped to make new discoveries of value and to place them in book form before the world, at least before the Poseid peoples, who esteemed themselves most of the world, an end scarcely to be attained otherwise than by this course of study. The influence which I hoped to gain through such publications might lead to my becoming Superintendent-General of Mines, a political place not second to any other appointive office. There certainly would be other studies required of me if I entered the race for a prime diploma, but the ones cited were the most agreeable and would constitute my main ambition. As an aside, I should say that those studies first selected, and afterwards mastered, led my nature to assume a bent which resulted, not many years ago, in my becoming a mine-owner in the State of California, and a successful one, too. It so much more firmly fixed my linguistic leanings that, while a citizen of the United States of America, I was a master not only of my native tongue, but also of thirteen other modern languages, such as French, German and Spanish, Chinese, several dialectal varieties of Hindustanie, and Sanskrit, as a sort of mental relaxation.

Please do not regard this confession as due to boastfulness. It is not. I only make it in order to show you, my friend, that your own powers are not matters of heritage only, but recollected acquirements from some one, or it may be of all of your past lives. Also, to give you a hint of profit, to wit: that studies today undertaken, no matter how near to the evening of your days, will surely bear fruit, not only in your present earth life, but in the experiences of subsequent incarnations also. We see with all we have seen, we do with all we have done, and we think with all we have thought. **Verbum sat sapienti**.

In the next chapter I will be devoting some pages to a consideration of physical science, as understood by the Poseidi. More specifically, I will refer to the prime principles upon which it was based, inasmuch as failing to do this would necessitate the taking of many statements **ex cathedra** which otherwise might be clearly understood at the moment.

CHAPTER IV. "AXTE INCAL, AXTUCE MUN"

In their consideration of natural laws, the philosophers of Poseid had come to the conclusive hypothesis and working theory that the material universe was not a complex entity but in its primal essence extremely simple. The glorious truth, "Incal malixetho," was clear to them, that is, that "Incal (God) is immanent in Nature." To this they appended, "Axte Incal, axtuce mun," "To know God is to know all worlds whatever." After centuries of experimentations, recording of phenomena, deductions, analyzing and synthesizing, these students had arrived at the final proposition that the universe—not here dwelling on their wondrous astronomical knowledge—was, with all its varied phenomena, created and continuously kept in operation by two primal force-principles. Briefly stated, these basic facts were that matter and dynamic energy (which were Incal made externally manifest) could readily account for all things else. This conception held that only One Substance existed and but One Energy, the one being Incal externalized and the other His Life in action in His Body. ₁

This One Substance assumed many forms under the action of variant degrees of dynamic force. Because it was the basic principle of all natural and a psychic, but not of spiritual, phenomena, allow here a postulate with which not a few of my friends will find themselves at least partially familiar, perhaps wholly so. Commencing with dynamic energy as first sensibly manifest in the example furnished by simple vibration, the Poseid position may be outlined as follows: A very low rate of vibration may be felt; an increase of rate heard. For example, first we feel the pulsing of a harp-string, and then if the rate of vibration be increased we hear its sound. But substances of other sorts, able to endure greater vibratory impulses, manifest under more intense action, following sound, first heat, then light. Now again, light varies in color. The first color produced is red, and thence, by a constantly increasing vibrating energy, orange, yellow, green, blue, indigo, violet, each spectrum-band being due to an exact and definite increase in the number of the vibrations. Succeeding the violet, further increase gives pure white, more gives a gray, then more extinguishes light, replacing it with electricity, and so on through an ever-increasing voltage until the realm of vital or psychic force is attained. This may truly be regarded as going inward from those manifestations of nature, of Incal or God, or the Creator, which are external; as going toward the internal from externality.

A very brief study will show you that the laws of the physical world continue inward to their spiritual source; that they are, truly, but prolongations the one of the other. But, before entering into the realm of vibration, whose doorkeeper is sound, we find that the One Substance vibrates in variant, but definite, dynamic degree, and that from there arise each and all of the diverse forms of matter. In short, the difference between any given substances, as gold and silver, iron and lead, sugar and sand, is not one of matter, but of dynamic degree solely. Do I tire you, my friend? Bear yet a little longer, I pray you, for it is an important matter. In this dynamic affection, the degree is no loose limitation, for if the vibratory rate be a shade different, lower or higher than in any special material which may be under notice, the variation will be different in appearance and in its chemical nature.

Thus to proper substantial entities definite if enormous vibrations per second may be imparted, and the resulting substance (for light is substantial) is, say, red light, [1] but if one-eighth greater it will be orange, and if more or less, then the resultant must inevitably be a reddish orange, or a yellowish, respectively. It thus appears that certain definite degrees exist as plainly as mileposts, and that these major degrees are absolute. In other words, the One Substance is not as readily kept between these greater definitions as upon them, a fact which explains the tendency of composites, or intermediate affections, to decompose into the definite or simple elements. Chemical compounds are not as stable as chemical primaries. The modern "wave theory," which states that sound, heat, light and correlatives are but forms of force, is only half correct. They are this, but they are more also. They are, in brief, expressions of the One Substance by specific degrees of the One Energy, and except that the rate of this expression is vastly greater in the case of electricity than in that of lead or gold, there is no difference between these widely diverse appearing things.

This is the energy the Rosicrucians named "Fire," that which gives entrance to that mysterious realm of nature penetrated only by the adept thaumaturgist, or magician. Call these students it whose will all nature bends obedient, by whatever name best pleases you, only bearing ever in mind that the real Magus never speaks of self or works, and is not known by his fellows to be what he is, except when an accident has revealed the secret. To this membership belonged He at whose command the winds and the waves were stayed on tempestuous Galilee. But He spoke not of Himself. Of that sublime brotherhood I will relate much before long. No better proof is needed that all the variant manifestations are but variants of the odic force, the Rosicrucian "Fire," than this: offer resistance to an electric current, thereby reducing or diverting it against an opposing force, and you have light.

Oppose to this light a combustible obstruction, and flame results. So might you go on to the discovery soon to be made by the world of science, that light, all light, of the sun, or from any source, can be made to yield sound. Upon this discovery hinge some of the most astounding inventions that your age has only dreamed of in its visions. But the primal discovery in this wonderful link, first of the sequence, will be the greatest of all, and so heralded. And this will be warranted, for the fact that it will be but a reincarnate unfolding will not diminish its importance to mankind, nor the credit of its rediscoverer. In brief, the truths of our Father's Kingdom are eternal; have ever been, will ever be existent, and only the discoverers themselves will be new to the fact. The fact not being a new one in itself, nor new even to the world, but only to this age of it. Poseid knew that light gives out sound when correctly resisted. It knew that magnetism gives rise to electricity in the same manner and for the same reason. Thus, the loadstone exhibits magnetism. Revolve it in the field of a dynamo and so cut the current and pile it upon itself, so to speak, and electricity develops. So, resist this and light appears; this, and heat comes; again resisted properly, and sound results, then the next energy appears as a pulsing motion. But these various processes may be "short-circuited" and all of the intermediate phenomena cut out.

Have I been wearisome in this discourse? If so, and I suspect that I have, the reward is at hand.

The Poseidi found that in the realm beyond magnetism were yet other forces, superior and more intense of pulsation, forces operated by the mind. And Mind is of our Father, and is the constantly creating source of all things whatsoever. Were the perpetual **vis a tergo** of divine creation to cease for one instant, in that instant the Universe would cease to exist. Now you will see the sublime beauty of the Atlan postulate not long since repeated: "Incal malixetho. Axte Incal, axtuce mun." For down from His heights, marking the descent by "force-falls" as a river marks its downward motion to its bed by cataracts, comes this supreme power. It comes far, oh! very far, down its course to the cascades of magnetism, electricity, light, heat, sound, motion—and far off where the bed of this Divine stream becomes nearly level, exhibits those little ripples of material differentiation which you call chemical elements, insisting on there being sixty-three, when there is but One.

From this knowledge came all the wondrous triumphs of that old age, and one by one they are emerging today after their long oblivion, till tomorrow when they shall awake in crowds, and press to rediscovery by threes and fours, and then by platoons and companies and legions, till all the treasures of Poseid shall be again on earth, in air, and sea. O, bright tomorrow of time, and fortunate all you who shall open your eyes upon it and its marvels. And yet, although so fortunate, you shall still find it well behooves you to temper all things by the spirit, and not to let the pace of physical discovery outstrip the advance of the soul. O, sad shall be found any day wherein man approaches the mysterious

96

treasury of his Father from the side of the blind physical eye. For if by this the whole world shall be gained, what shall it profit if it lose the soul?

Having thus acquired insight into a new realm, if it be new to thee, let me ask, and you answer me: How do you explain these two great phenomena, heat and light? They are not easy to explain. Cold and darkness are not merely the absence of heat and light.

Having given the basis thereof, now I will show a new philosophy:

I have said that the Atlans recognized Nature in its entirety to be Deity externalized. Their philosophy asserted that force moved, not in straight lines but in circles, that is, so as always to return into itself. If the dynamism operating the universe acts in circular progression, it follows that an infinity of increase in vibration possible to One Substance would be an untenable concept. There must be a point in the circle where extremes meet and run the round again, and this we find between cathodicity and magnetism. As vibration brought substance into the realm of light, it must carry it out. It does so. It conveys it into what the Poseidi termed "Navaz, the Night-Side of Nature," where duality becomes manifest, cold opposing heat, darkness light, and where positive polarity opposes negative, all things antipodal. Cold is as much a substantial entity as heat, and darkness as light. There is a prism of seven colors in each white ray of light. There is also a sevenfold prism of black entities in the blackest gloom—the night is as pregnant as the day.

The Poseid investigator thus became cognizant of wondrous forces of nature which he might bend to the uses of mankind. The secret was out, the discovery being that attraction of gravitation, the law of weight, had set over against it the "repulsion by levitation"; that the first belonged to the Light-Side of Nature, and the second to Navaz, the Night-Side; that vibration governed the darkness and the cold. Thus Poseid, like Job of old, knew the path to the house of darkness, and the treasures of the hail (cold). Through this wisdom Atlantis found it possible to adjust weight (positiveness) to lack of weight (negativeness) so evenly that no "tug of war" was manifest. This achievement meant much.

The Secrets Of Mount Shasta And A Dweller On Two Planets

It meant aerial navigation without wings or unwieldy gas-reservoirs, through taking advantage of repulsion by levitation opposed in over-matching strength to the attraction of gravitation. That vibration of the One Substance governed and composed all realms was a discovery which solved the problem of the conveyance of images of light, pictures of forms, as well as of sound and heat, just as the telephone you know so well conveys images of sound, only in Poseid, no wires or other sensible material connection was required in the use, at whatever distance, of either telephones or telephotes, nor even in caloriveyance, that is, heat-conduction.

To digress a little, it is to the employment of these and the higher forces of the nightside that seemingly magic feats of occult adepts, from the Man of Nazareth down to the least Yogi, are indebted for their possibility.

And now, let me close this chapter by saying that when modern science shall have seen its way to the acceptance of the Poseidonic knowledge herein outlined, physical nature will no longer posses any hidden recess, any mysterious inner parts, for the scientific investigator. Not earth, air, the depth of the seas nor those of interstellar space will hold secrets from that man who approaches from the Godward side, as did Poseid. I do not say that Atl knew the very all. It knew more than this day has yet uncovered, but not all. Yet, the search commenced then by them might be continued now by you, for America, my people, you were of Atlantis. Of either, I can sing, "My country, 'tis of thee."

Footnotes

61:1 NOTE—As in its outgoing impulse the Created draws away from the Creator, it looks back to its origin and notes its progression-marks, that is, its multiplied realizations of its increasing separation from its Source. The greater this separateness, the greater the field (Matter) wherein these points appear, because the divine element in the Created has noted more points, or in other things, more material objects as being between it and its source. Only when we look back at these things and we have sensed these thought-forms of God, do we perceive matter, for when we look forward to reunion with Him, matter disappears, giving place to Spirit.

62:1 NOTE—Red light is stated to occur at 395,000,000,000,000 vibrations of that "ether" which by Phylos is termed the last form of matter below where matter ceases and mind begins. And the highest visible light vibration is placed at 790,000,000,000,000. So says science. But Phylos says: "Vastly higher than the high purple range where light ceases ordinarily to be visible, the One Substance again vibrates visibly. As a synchronous harp-string that responds to the key of low C, for example, struck on another harp, will also respond to every C in the whole register, be it low or middle or high, so the One Substance responds at 831,000,000,000,000; at, again, the next octave of vibration, and again at the next, where it becomes visible as the fatal Unfed Light, called in Atla the "Maxin," and again, by the Tchin as the "Vis Mortuus."

CHAPTER V. LIFE IN CAIPHUL

The new life presented very many novelties to my mother and myself, coming into the midst of urban environments from the mountains, as we had so recently done.

After learning more about its conveniences, I very readily harmonized myself with the new requirements. My attire I altered to suit the city styles, while my bearing being reserved, I was enabled to appear at case, an appearance supported in continually increasing degree by the fact that I steadily gained in self command.

The indoor life of a student, when I had enrolled myself for attendance at the Xioquithlon, proved so weakening to one accustomed to unhampered freedom that I found myself obliged to follow some scheme which would afford me needed exercise.

After some thought, together with fortuitous information which I gained, I went to the District Superintendent of the Department of Soils and Tillage and requested that official to show me some piece of land which I might cultivate, not necessarily for profit, but for exercise, telling him that I was a student.

The Superintendent, with official indifference, laid before me a platted map of the lands adjacent to Caiphul.

In speaking of distances, I have consulted the probable convenience of my readers, and used feet, yards, miles, and so on, as nominal quantities. I refer to this now, remembering that our system of measurements was founded on a principle similar to the modern Gallic or metric system. But its unit was not the ten-millionth part of the terrestrial quadrant. Instead, it originated from the great Rai of the Maxin Laws. As previously remarked, this monarch had introduced all conceivable reforms, and among others was this of replacing with a uniform system of measurements the clumsier, though not wholly unscientific, method previously in use. The circumference of the earth at the equator, as determined by astronomers, had served as a basis, just as the modern metric system of a fraction of the quadrature of the earth's north and south polar division does today. But this standard was not regarded with unfailing confidence; it was feared some error had crept into the original calculation, and while if it had the rod of gold used as a register would have served all purposes, being unchangeable, still such is the human wish to be as perfect as possible, that, as I have said, the fear of an error annihilated confidence. Every man who chose to do so set up a private standard, based on any scheme which suited himself, a condition of things which led to deplorable fraud throughout the empire.

The Rai of the Maxin instituted a system so admirable that it was immediately accepted as absolute authority, more especially as no man doubted that it came from Incal.

The Rai had a vessel constructed of material which underwent the smallest known contraction or expansion under the influence of cold or heat. This vessel was interiorly a perfect hollow cube, of the exact size of the Maxin-Stone. A massive tube was also made of the same substance, some four inches in interior diameter. Into the cubic vessel was poured precisely enough distilled water, of a temperature of 398 degrees Fahrenheit, to fill it, and leave no bubble of air within the hollow. This water was then drawn off through a faucet into the tubular vessel, the same low temperature being carefully maintained. The exact height of the water was then graven on a rod of the same metal of which the vessels were made. The next step was to heat the water to 211.95° Fahrenheit, both this and the other process being performed at the sea level on a uniform summer day. Under the heat, the water expanded in an appreciable degree, and the almost boiling point was marked as in the other instance, and the difference on the rod between the two graven lines was made the unit of lineal measurement, from which all other measures were derived, that of weight being the weight of the hollow cube full of water at 398 Fahrenheit. I use the Fahrenheit thermo-metrical scale because to you our Poseid scale would be "pardon this digression," since it reveals another of the phases of life in that long-past age.

To return to the Superintendent's office. This person, having laid before me a map of un-rented areas—it will be remembered that there was no owner of land except the government—turned to other business, leaving me to study the plat at pleasure. Running my eye over the printed descriptions, I found that a tract of about five acres, on a part of which was an old orchard of various kinds of fruit trees, was to be had at a distance of some eight "vens" (nearly the same number of miles) from the city, but farther up the peninsula. Its former tenant had leased it for a period of fifty years, but by reason of his death the property was left vacant and was consequently again for disposition.

The fact that students were often hard pressed for means on which to live was taken into account by the government, which in all of its dealings with this class allowed better terms than were accorded to any other social division.

The property under consideration attracted me from its description, viz., "An area of approximately eight ven-nines (five acres) with a dwelling of four rooms, spring water piped over the house; one ven-nine devoted to garden flowers, and six to fruit trees fifteen years of age. Terms (with all conveniences) to students-one half of the fruit crop, and all perfume flowers grown, delivered to the Agent of Soils and Tillage Department. To other persons than students, four tekas per month (ten dollars and twenty-three cents). Not leased for less than one year."

I decided to lease the place, for I learned that "all conveniences" meant vailx transportation, telephotic (naim) service, and a caloriveyant instrument, which latter would save fuel, energy to be converted into heat for cooking and other purposes being transmitted by the "Navaza," a range of material forces called in these your modern days "earth-currents," but also including those of the higher ether, a range which you will eventually find and utilize as did Atlantis, for are you not Poseid returned? I have said it. You lived then; you live now. You used all these forces then; you will before long use them all again.

Having decided to take the property that was shown me, I so stated to the official, whereupon he furnished me with a blank contract, helping me to fill it out properly. As a glimpse into that long-ago, historically significant time, I give a copy of this leasehold:

"I, ... year., of age, of the .... sex, and by occupation a ...., do covenant with the Department of Soils to lease block .... in district .... described as follows: .... And I do agree to take .... this for .... years, the same being smiled upon by the Most High Incal."

I took the place for a term of eight years, expecting to be a resident of Caiphul during at least that period of time as a student of the Xioquithlon.

It seemed no small thing that I could have conveyance by vailx from my leasehold to the Xioquithlon, and thus enjoy a daily trip through the air. Vailx, like the modern cab, might be sent for by telephone and respond for service in a short time after the call.

It was customary with all newcomers in the city to make a visit to the Agacoe palace and gardens as early as might be convenient after their arrival. Two hours in each week the Rai (emperor) sat in the reception hall, and during these two hours visitors thronged the corridors and passed in double ranks before the throne. After this ceremony, all who chose were free to wander unrestricted through the gardens, visit the menagerie, where every known species of animal was kept, or to go through the grand museum or the royal library. With many it was a pleasurable custom frequently to spend the day at Agacoe, on which occasions lunches were brought and a quiet picnic held under the great trees beside fountain, lake or cataract.

I must now return to that time when my mother and myself were wholly unfamiliar with city usages, in order that the reader may accompany us through scenes of novelty. Let us begin with the visit to Agacoe. An acquaintance, at that moment gained, guided us to the palace, taking us with himself in a car into which he ushered us. At this time these cars were a novelty to me, and consequently their manipulation became a subject upon which to inform myself.

Our friend took a small coin from his purse and dropped it into an aperture in a glass-fronted box at one end of the car, The coin could not miss falling in such a way as to rest in the bottom of a glass cylinder, a very little greater in diameter than the money itself. Two metal points which projected into the lower end of the cylinder, but did not approach each other nearer than a quarter of an inch, were in the bottom of the tube. When the coin fell upon these a little bell rang, and our friend then raised a lever in the carriage, which lever had a lock-bar over it until the bell rang. This bar had, with the closing of the circuit by the coin, automatically slipped back, at the same time ringing a bell as above noted, thus releasing the lever.

When the latter was raised the car moved suddenly but easily out of the station. It swung from its overhead rail, only the peripheries of its large suspensory wheels being visible, for together with their axles they were mostly hidden by a long metal case which extended from one wheel to the other, and within which, a low, humming whirr could be heard, a sound produced by the mechanism of the motor apparatus. The plan of making the passenger do duty as engineer and conductor also was a good one, seeing that the processes required so little knowledge or trouble. As we left the car at the main entrance depot below Agacoe terrace, our friend replaced the lever, the bell rang again, the coin dropped from sight into a strong box underneath, and the vehicle was ready for other passengers.

At the grand entrance, a gate which was a marvel of architectural beauty, our friend bade us adieu, entered a car which hung from another track, and was soon disappearing at lightning speed to some yet more distant destination. Glancing at the directory, which hung above that particular line, I saw that it bore the legend in Poseid characters, "Aagak mnoiinc sus," that is "City Front and Grand Canal," to make a free translation. Wishing to inform myself concerning our friendly guide, I asked someone who had watched the arrival of our little party with interest who the gentleman was. The reply given was:

"A great preacher who foretells the destruction of this continent and bids all men to live so that they will not fear to meet One who, he says, is the Son of Incal and who shall come upon the earth in days yet very far off. He says that this Son of God shall be the Savior of mankind, but that many shall not know Him until He shall have been put to death. Twelve shall know Him, but one of them will deny Him in the hour of His last peril. Indeed, it is a subject of very exceeding interest, albeit one I do not very well understand; yet as Rai Gwauxln says, Be good to him! Show this preacher all favor, and say of him, 'He speaks the truth,' and therefore is he attentively received by every one."

Reader, even in that far past age of the world truth was dawning, and this, in the morning of the cycle, was a first ray of the bright sun of Christianity, the orb which even yet is not arisen in the fullness of its glory. I had that morning ridden in the same car with the first prophet who announced the coming of our Lord Jesus Christ, exhorting all of his hearers to live so that their souls might be turned as virgin soil to the rising Sun of Truth, and thereby be made ready to receive the Master when, after the death of their then possessed corporeal bodies, they had returned to earth from Devachan as reincarnated souls. Sowing the seed by the wayside! It fell on me when at a somewhat later period I heard the prophet speak in impassioned eloquence to the specially assembled Xioquithli (students). I know it fell on fallow soil, when I compare my life now with the lives past; yet, for long, the seed lay dormant, and while it did so the bitter experiences of sin and error arose and swept my life outward on a wave of scorching fire, which required another incarnation to heal the scars it left.

As we stood beneath the portal at the grand entrance to Agacoe, we, unsophisticated mountaineers could not know, when a uniformed guide accosted us, that the emperor, on his throne half a mile distant, was in that same moment perfectly aware of our personal appearance and also of the very words we used and our tones.

The Secrets Of Mount Shasta And A Dweller On Two Planets

To me the soldier said:

"And you, where are you from and what is your name?"

"I am called Zailm Numinos, and come from Querdno Aru."

"This visit—is it your first, or have you been here before?"

"Not before this; neither I, nor my parent here by my side."

"So! I will provide you with a conductor. You will find him at yonder gateway. One more question, if it's all right: What is your mission in Caiphul?"

"I am come to study xioq in the Inithlon; my mother is here to keep our house."

"All right. You may go."

This conversation occurred at the great portal giving entrance to the terrace above. The sentry sat behind a richly wrought gate of bronze metal and gold, very slight, but all sufficient to bar un-welcomed progress. At his back was a large mirror in the heavy arch of the portal. This reflector was suspended by two burnished copper rods in such a manner as to prevent it from touching the side of the niche at any point. Could I have looked behind it, I would have seen an arrangement of metallic cords much resembling those of a piano, together with much other machinery which at the time would have meant nothing to my untutored mind. How was I to suspect that this brightly polished metal sheet in which, as in a calm lake, the whole interior of the archway was reflected, was an ingenious automatic messenger?

That some one of the myriad wires behind it was vibrant to every possible inflection of the voice, or to any sound whatever, and that when I spoke every briefest sound I uttered was sped along the natural earth-currents which sprang from nature's Night-Side responsive to the control of man, and heard by the Rai on his throne. No more did I dream that, simultaneously with this telltale, our imaged reflection was like-wise conveyed to the same august presence. But such were the facts. A few steps brought us to an inner gate made of fenestrated iron plates which, upon the pressing of a button at the side, arose between standards to give beneath. At this point we found the guide whom the guard had provided. I deemed his silence an indication of gruffness, not knowing that he had received orders, before we came up to him, which directed him to conduct us to the royal presence and needed from us no repetition of our wishes. His quiet remark, "I understand," when I began to tell him what we desired, prevented more words on my part, for I felt a sense of injured pride at his reserve, so different from the freedom of my mountain associates; and there were so many of these haughty city people! I determined to give this man a lesson, and considered how I might best let him know that I thought his manner overbearingly out of place for one in his station. That he already possessed all necessary information concerning us I did not imagine, since, if the distance from his post to the other gate was not great, it was obviously too far for our low-spoken tones to have been heard. The unsuspected mirror had done its work here also, although we knew it not.

"Come," said this haughty fellow, "I will conduct you and your mother."

"Mother!" I thought. "How does the fellow know that one so fair and so young looking is my mother? She might be my sister, or even my wife, for all he knows." The supposed presumption of the man irritated me, for I was proud not only of my mother's youthful appearance, but also of my own fondly fancied mature looks; I had not infrequently been told that I looked seven or eight years older than I really was. Had the foolishness of such a pride in my personal appearance been fairly presented to me, instead of feeling an ill-defined resentment at a seeming presumption, I would have laughed at its absurdity, and put it aside as unworthy of one having such high-aimed ambition. As it was, it merely resulted in stiffness of demeanor as a retaliation for the imagined overbearance, and, mostly to my own detriment, caused somewhat of an obliviousness to sights and surroundings I had better have noted at the time. Though I did not laugh then, by reason of the obtuse view caused by my ignorance, I have laughed, since, as I looked back over the record of the past. So many thousands of years as have since elapsed may make it seem laughter at long range, but, "'Tis better late than never," fitly applies here!

The Secrets Of Mount Shasta And A Dweller On Two Planets

We seated ourselves as directed, in a car of lighter build than those used on the public avenues, and also of a different shape. It was not until we were fairly in motion that I realized how absolutely different was its construction and propulsive method. Well-used as I wished to appear to all these novel things, I gave a telltale start when the conductor touched a lever and the vehicle rose into the air like a soap-bubble, steadied itself, and then darted up the incline to the edge of the level ground surrounding the palace. Here we left the cigar-shaped vehicle and entered a car which ran upon rails.

When we were again in motion, we made a half circuit of the building, and then shot across the plateau directly into the dark, yawning mouth of one of the great stone serpents. Instead of ascending at the same angle as did the body of the reptile, our car glided along on a horizontal plane. As we entered, a sudden illumination lit up the gloom where an instant previous all had been darkness. From this pleasant surprise my attention was attracted to the brilliancy of the walls about us, which seemed to flame with red, blue, green, yellow and all other tinted flashes of fire, so that I can find no simile more fitting than comparison to the sunlit dews on the myriad webs of morning lawn-spiders. I forgot my own haughtiness, and asked concerning the cause of this dazzling effect, and was answered that the mansions had finished the walls with a mortar in which colored grains of glass had been incorporated.

In the midst of our admiration our horizontal progress ceased, and I saw that we were at the bottom of a sort of well, around the sides of which the track coiled in upward spirals until it seemed to cease just beneath a ceiling vaguely visible from the light cast upward by ourselves as we swiftly circled the incline. As we came directly beneath the ceiling a sweet toned bell rang twice, and immediately afterward the entire ceiling slid noiselessly aside, allowing our carriage to pass through. Behind us the well again closed automatically and we found ourselves in a splendid apartment, of which the size was not apparent, owing to the many swinging screens of a deeply reddish-purple silk, the royal color, as well as to the foliage plants, which made miniature sylvan vistas. The flowers and songbirds, the fountains and perfumed air, with the cool shade after its heat outside, for we had not been long enough in the elevator-well to become cool, all made what seemed here a paradise.

The ceiling of this great room was visible only here and there, being in most places hidden by petulant vines. Through all this harmony of vision, trembling in the air, over, under, around about were sounding entrancing musical cadences, to which, as to an inspiration, the birds replied in rivaling chorus. In and out, amongst this Eden-like scene of color, sound and scent, past choice statues and fairy, graceful fountains, our car glided with a noiseless speed which from its even motion aided the illusion that we remained still, and all the vision of delight shifted about us as about a center. And this was a marriage of art and of science; from their union sprang the fair dream, a triumph of human skill and knowledge!

In every direction cars were coming, going, or at rest, containing people dressed as for a gala day, the various distinguishing colors of their turbans denoting their social rank. Poseid, like other countries then and since, had its social castes, as the governmental, the literati and ecclesiastics, the artisans, a limited military, which served it as a police and sanitary corps, and so on through the usual familiar list. The apparel of all classes was fashioned in the same general style, until it came to the headdress—all of the people wore turbans—which article of raiment differed in color according to caste. Thus, the turban of the Sovereign was of pure reddish-purple colored silk; of the councilors, a wine red, and of lesser officials, a pale pink.

The turbans of the soldiery were deep orange for the ranks, and lemon chrome for the officers. Pure white marked the priesthood, and gray the scientific, the literary and artistic classes. Blue distinguished the artisans, mechanics and laborers, while, green denoted all who, for any reason, either immaturity or educational lack, did not enjoy the right of suffrage. Notwithstanding that these caste indices were strictly adhered to, they resulted in good, rather than otherwise, for caste conceits did not find place among those who wore any color but green, since dignity of labor was a feeling of such vigor that there was no envy of one class by another. As for those who unavoidably wore the green, those who did so because of not having come to their years of majority would grow out of the color, while those who lacked sufficient education to entitle them to another hue felt the stigma attaching to their grade to be a reason for extra efforts to attain a more honorable station in life.

While I had been studying the various topics presented for thought, our car was deftly made to avoid collision with that of a lady who came swiftly onwards, apparently heedless of her course, while she was putting in place a loose end of her gray turban, showing as she did so the flashing rays from a ruby, a gem that only royalty might wear. Our car wheeled into an increasingly long procession of carriages and presently carried us into a second apartment. But, the royal maiden of the gray turban and ruby—my thoughts were still with her! How radiant was her beauty! It was my first sight of the Princess Anzimee—but I must not anticipate!

The apartment into which we were now come was smaller than the one we had just left, but yet of no mean extent. Everything here was of brilliant, flashing carmine, except an elevation in the center of the room. This was of circular black marble steps, or small terraces, the top of which was twelve feet across, being surmounted by a dais of some dark wood, upholstered in black velvet.

It should here be remarked that black was a representative hue and included the symbolism of all colors, thus denoting, as used on the throne, that he who sat there belonged to every class; and this was the fact, since Rai Gwauxln was not only sovereign and chief of the army, one of the high priests, a literate, scientist, artist and musician, but was also well acquainted with the duties of artisans and machinists.

In front of the silver railing which surrounded the throne our carriage stopped out to one side of the moving line, obedient to a gesture of the emperor. The guide bade us alight and, opening a little gate directed us to ascend the steps of the dais to the feet of the Rai. My heart beat fast as I obeyed, and though pale with apprehension for no apparent reason, I had myself well enough under control to offer the support of my arm to my mother, and I think I never walked more proudly erect in my life. At the top of the steps, we kneeled and waited the command to rise again, nor had we long to wait.

As we arose Rai Gwauxln said quietly:

"Zailm, you are young to be a student so ambitious as I know you to be."

"If it pleases you for me to be so, I am happy," I answered.

"Have you learned what the primary schools have to teach to the young? For this must be before you can gain admission to the Inithlon."

"Yes, I have, Rai."

"If you would, Zailm, please confide to me what studies you chiefly prefer?"

"Zo Rai, I count it a high honor to speak. Of my own desire, I have not chosen any studies. Yet, I do not doubt that Incal Himself has ordered my preference, indicating geology above all else. He has also given me a natural disposition, which, if I consult, directs me to study languages and literature. I am not yet decided, but think well of these branches of xioq. But geology He directed through a wild experience."

"You do interest me, lad. Yet this is an hour of state duties, and I must not neglect my people who come before me to pay respects to their monarch. Take, therefore, this pass, and at the fourth hour come again to the portal at which you entered into Agacoe. I bid thee welcome."

I took the present and on my way down the steps of the marble terrace saw that it bore the inscription, "Rai's presence. Permit bearer."

We had with us a packet of dates and pastries and were therefore under no necessity of leaving the gardens for luncheon. Our guide took us again in charge, and after learning that we desired to remain within the grounds about the palace, threaded our conveyance through the mazes of the building once more, letting us out of the carriage beside one of the pillars of the peristyle. From the point where we alighted, and where we parted from the guide, I looked about to ascertain the direction of the grand entrance, and seeing that it was in the east, I escorted my mother to a seat under the side of a giant deodar, or, as they were called in after centuries, "Cedars of Lebanon." On a bough over head sat a mockingbird, or, as we call them, a "nossuri," signifying "songster of the moonlight," in reference to the habit of these lovely, gray-coated birds to fill all the still, moonlit air of night with their wondrous melody. Not that they do not sing by day; indeed, the bird was even then singing, but the naming these "nossuri," from "nosses" (the moon) and "surada" (I sing), was a distinctive Poseid ornithological term.

At the appointed hour we went to the place designated and, presenting the passport, were shown into a conveyance, and after again ascending the eminence the guide ushered us into a small apartment of most luxurious appointments. By a table almost hidden by books sat the Rai, listening to a well-modulated voice which was relating the latest news of the day, but the owner of which was not visible. The Rai turned as the usher announced us, dismissed the servitor, and bade us a good evening. Then he turned to a case shaped something like that pleasing instrument, the modern music box, and turned a key in it with a soft snap. Instantly the voice of the unseen speaker ceased in the middle of a word, and I knew as we complied with our sovereign's request to be seated that I had for the first time heard one of the vocal news-records of which I had so frequently read. During the ensuing hour I related the story of my life, its hopes, sorrows, triumphs and ambitions, in answer to the questions of the genial yet not seemingly old man to whom any living person might pay homage and suffer no loss of dignity, because his regal courtesy showed how very manly a king or how kingly a man might be.

I told how each new fact had only added to my appetite for even greater knowledge. Then I recounted the experiences of my trip to the summit of Rhok, a recital interrupted as I made mention of the name of the mountain. "Rhok!" exclaimed the imperial listener. "Do you mean to tell me that you ascended that awful height, in the night, alone? A mountain which all our maps say is inaccessible except to vailx?" "It is possible, Zo Rai, that the only route was known to but a few of us mountaineers; I have read that it was thought inaccessible; but—" I hesitated, then the Rai said, quickly:

112

The Secrets Of Mount Shasta And A Dweller On Two Planets

"Yes, speak! It was to take the measure of you that I have listened to your recital, for well do I know everything you have told me. I could have told it before you did, and can tell all the rest of what you will say; I wanted to hear you to assess you; your story I have known ever since I first saw you. I am a Son of the Solitude," he added. I was silent, for the thought shamed me—that he already knew all. Seeing this, he said: "Go on, my son. Tell me the rest; I wish to hear it from your lips, for I am interested in you for yourself."

Thereupon I resumed the interrupted narration, and described my rendition of homage to Incal, and the petition for His aid; His quick granting of my prayer; then of the eruption of the volcano and the peril in which it had placed me. At this the Rai remarked: "Then you were an eyewitness to that outburst of the earthly forces? I have been told that it caused great local changes, and that there is now a lake of extensive size where there wasn't one before, at the foot of Rhok; it is nine vens across."

I was still unsophisticated enough not only to be curious as to whether the Rai had seen the eruption, for I did not understand the significance of his being a Son of the Solitude, and as to his knowing about all my adventures, though I did not doubt that to be a fact, I took it to be due to a keen judgment of possibilities that this knowledge was his. But as an addition to my unsophistication I asked the Rai if he had seen these things.

"Guileless youth!" said the Monarch, smiling, "I do not often find so frank a person! You are indeed a son of the mountains! But you will not remain that way for long, I fear, in this your present environment! I will answer your question even as you ask it. Know, then, that no large convulsion of nature can occur that is not immediately automatically recorded, both as to its approximate extent, and its location, and a lighted exhibition of every portion of the affected locality shown forth afresh from instant to instant. All I had in this case to do to see this depiction was to go into the proper office, which is in this building, and there the whole scene was before me quite as vividly as it could have been for you, because I was able to see the outburst, and also to hear it, by means of the naim. Truly, what I saw lacked one element which doubtless made it a little more vivid to you than to me, that of bodily danger; but as for me this element was nil—you will someday know why—therefore the scene lacked for me no element that mere presence could have added."

I marveled greatly to learn of such instrumentalities concerning which Rai Gwauxln had informed me, and pondered with delight the prospect that I also might someday personally know and have access to them. The Rai resumed:

"You said that you found treasure of native gold in two separate places. Did you ever try to recover that which you obtained before the eruption occurred? No? It matters little. Zailm, it is said that ignorance of the law is not a valid excuse for its infraction."

The demeanor of the Rai had become one of great gravity, and I felt a foreboding not at all agreeable.

"Still, I am convinced that you knew nothing of the involved violation of the statutes when you failed to report the finding of the treasure. I shall not, therefore, punish you." But here the emperor paused, lost in thought, while I, not until then aware that I had done anything wrong in the view of the law, paled so visibly with apprehension that Gwauxln smiled a little, and said:

"But they who now work this mine, and they who receive the gold-dust and ore shall not so escape. With them it is a conscious crime, made worse in that they not only ignore the statute but also defraud you. From you, I will require only so much atonement as there may be in demanding their names of you."

This command I was forced to obey, even though I thought with regret of the wives and children of the culprits. They were innocent; must they suffer along with the real transgressors? The Rai seemed to know my thought; or if he did not, he at least spoke in accord, asking:

"Do these men have wives, families?"

"Yes, it is so!" I replied, so earnestly that once again the monarch smiled and, encouraged, I begged him to be lenient for the sake of the innocent.

"Do you know anything about our punitive system, Zailm?"

"Very little, Zo Rai; I have heard that no malefactor ever comes from the hand of justice without being better, but I imagine the treatment to be very severe."

"As to severity, no. And as to the other, if men are made better who have erred, so they will not be likely to again err, would not that redound to the advantage of the families of the criminals? Behold, I will have these men brought before the proper tribunal, and you will see the process of reformation. I think you will thereafter desire to learn anatomy and the science of reformatory punishment, as an addition to your other studies in Xio. Furthermore, I assure you that you will in no way suffer confiscation of that mine, but will possess it; and if you will give it to the national treasury, while you are a student, you will in no way suffer a lack of money. Afterward, when the years of study have been completed, if you are successful as a student, lo! Then I will make you superintendent of that mine. And if you prove yourself faithful over its few things, I will make you master over many things. I have spoken."

Rai Gwauxln touched a service-button, at which point an attendant entered, to the guidance of whom he entrusted me and my mother, bidding us: "Incal's peace be with you both."

So ended an audience which influenced the course of the years and bent life's great twig, making me feel a proud consciousness of being a repository of the trust of a revered friend, a consciousness which has ever proven most patent in this world of trials and temptations.

CHAPTER VI. NO GOOD THING CAN EVER PERISH

As antedating the reign of Rai Gwauxln, attention is called to a period of time embracing four thousand three hundred and forty years, inclusive of the main events of Poseid history. This interval, notwithstanding its long duration, had been singularly free from internecine wars, and, while not wholly unmarked by martial events, was certainly more peaceful than any subsequent world-epoch of equal length occurring within the one hundred and twenty centuries whose lapse furnishes the incidents of this history.

At the initial date of the period referred to, the Poseidi, a powerful, numerous race of mountaineers, semi-civilized at best, but of splendid physique, had swept down "like the wolf" and had, in many bloody contests, finally conquered the pastoral people of the plains, the Atlantides. The war was long and fierce, consuming years in its duration. The admirable valor of the hill-tribes found almost its equal in the desperate courage of their primitive foe; one body of combatants fought for life and, like the Sabines, for the preservation of their women against capture by mate-seeking tribes, while the other warred for conquest and, like the Romans, for wives. It was superior strategy which finally gave victory to the Poseid hosts.

As time went on, racial coalition obliterated all distinctions, so that the union resulted in producing earth's greatest nation. Inconsequential civil wars had several times made a change of political complexion, so that Poseid had seen itself governed by absolute autocrats, by oligarchic and by the theocratic rule, by masculine and by feminine rulers, and at last by a republican monarchial system, of which Rai Gwauxln was the head, when I lived as Zailm, in Atlantis.

Gwauxln was of a long line of honorable ancestors, and his house had several times furnished successful candidates whom the people had placed on the throne during the seven centuries that the present political system had ruled.

Such is the synopsis of the history of Poseid, which I gathered from a volume drawn from the Agacoe library. I might relate other scenes, other features, of that long historic period, and show how Poseid came to found great colonies in North and South America, and in those three great remnants of Lemuria, of which Australia is but the one-third left to the world by that cataclysm which sunk Atlantis; also of how Atlantis founded certain large colonies in eastern Europe at an age when there was no western Europe, and in parts of Asia and Africa. But I will not do so here, although by and by reference will be made to our Umauran possessions, when such reference is relevant to the subject matter of this history.

Fatigued with late reading in the absorbing history, I arose and went out into the quiet ravine in which our abode was situated, and my tired eyes rested upon a scene which in the glorious moonlight was one of fairylike beauty.

In the bed of the ravine, quite near, was a miniature lake, but nonetheless a lake in seeming, because it was in fact only a good-sized pond. Bits of shore, then steep banks, flower-hidden; the song of the nossuri, and the calls of various other birds and furry-folk of the nighttime, intermingled with the soft plash of falling water, the voice of the cascade which fed this lacustrine gem. Somewhere out of the night came the sound of flutes and harps and viols in harmony, rising in swelling cadence or lulling with dreamy languor, as the light breeze rose or fell. Over all shimmered the silvery rays of Nosses, round as a shield in her soft brilliancy, and oh! So beautiful! Presently, I turned from the lake and looked down the ravine along which a few people were yet moving, despite the lateness of the hour, the fourteenth since the beginning of the day at meridian. Here and there the gleaming white rays of householders' lamps were observable, shining from underneath some seeming ledge, revealing the presence of quaint windows or doorways. But not on these did I gaze over long. I could not, with the wonderful Maxt, the greatest tower of human construction in the world, rising in the perspective. In the very mouth of the canon it seemed to ascend, with nothing between itself and me to interfere with the view. Although apparently near, it was in truth over a mile away from my dwelling.

In this year A. D., 1886, chemists count the process costly which produces the metal, aluminum. In that day, forces arising from the Night-Side rendered inexpensive the production of any metal which might be found in nature, either native, or as an ore. As it might be done today if you could but know how, and that day is not far off when you will again uncover the knowledge. So, in that time, we transmuted clay, first raising its atomic speed so that it became white light of a pale illuminating power and then reducing it to the, so to speak, chemical "milepost" of aluminum, and this at a cost not nearly so great as in this modern day it takes to get iron from its ores. The mines of native metals, as gold, silver, copper, and so on, were valuable then, as now, requiring no processing save smelting. But a metal which might be obtained from any ledge of slate rock, or a bed of clay, was so inexpensive as to be the chief base metal in use. Of aluminum was the giant tower of the Maxt constructed. I could see its base from where I stood, an enormous cube of masonry, then the superstructure round shaft of solid metal of the tower proper, a dully white, tapering column, lit by lunar rays. From base upward, my gaze traveled until it rested on the top, its topmost point nearly three thousand feet in height. Entranced by this crowning triumph of the scene, I gazed at the heaven-piercing shaft; sentinel over the garden city, warding off the lightnings, when the lord of thunder was abroad; and all my thought was of its grandeur, and its majestic beauty.

"How often, oh, how often, In the days that have gone by-"

I have stood and gazed on some scene of loveliness, or of perfect beauty —handiwork of God, or possibly of man—God in man! And, as

The Secrets Of Mount Shasta And A Dweller On Two Planets

I have looked, my soul sang with praise, and my breath was the breath of inspiration. Always in such an experience, the soul, be it that of man or beast, takes an advance step. However much a soul may be steeped in sin or misery, synonymous terms, an inspiration breaks over it, and bears away a little of its sordidness, a little of its pain and fever.

So, therefore, the glories and marvels of Atlantis the Great were not in vain. You and I, reader, lived then, and before then. The glories of those long-dead centuries seen by us have lived enshrined in our souls, and made us much, aye, most, of what we are, influenced our acts, soothed us with their beauty. What, then, though the forms of the dim, mysterious past are rubbed away from all existence save in the record of the great book of life, the soul? Their influence lives, and forever. Shall we not, then, strive that our labors may ennoble, may live in soul and in spirit, and be looked back upon by ourselves and others, even as I, here, look back upon the record of my dead, but ever-living, past? It is a great joy thus to have attained the eminences of the spirit which enable me to scan the history of lives from which I passed through the portal of the grave; lives which now I am returned to gaze upon through the eyes of a different personality, a personality strung, greatest one of a chain, like pearls upon a thread, teaching me I AM I! Smoky, some of these pearls; black, others, or white or pink, aye, some are even red! Could tears add to their number, I would have more. Oh! So many more, for the white ones are so few, and the smoky, the black and the red, so many. But my pearl of great price is my last life. Of white is it, and by my Master was it cut cruciform. When He gave it me, He said, "It is done." Verily so! It marks the junction of the finite with infinity. So is it the period set to all time, for me, save I elect.

CHAPTER VII. CONTAIN THYSELF

It was in the time of the annual brief period of rest from study that I made my arrival to the capital city. In this vacation the Xioqua and the Incala participated, the majority seeking their homes first, for a season, but generally soon returning to the capital, in order to enjoy the special pleasures of the resting time. But some went over the ocean to Umaur, or to Incalia, that is, South or North America, respectively; others went only to the more distant provinces in Atlantis itself.

Thus far the reader has had to guess what sort of religion the worship of Incal was; it may even have been inferred that Poseidi were polytheists, from my reference to the various gods of this and that title, class or grade. Truly, I have said that we believed in Incal, and symbolized him as the Sun-God. But the sun itself was an emblem. To assert that we, despite our enlightenment, adored the orb of day, would be as absurd as to say that the Christians adore the cross of the crucifixion for itself; in both cases it is the attached significance that caused the sun, and causes the cross, to be held in any sort of regard.

The Atlantides were given to personification of the principles of nature and of the objects of the earth, seas and skies; but this was purely a result of the national love of poetry, and could be mainly traced to the favor which popular fancy had accorded to a chronological epic history of Poseid, wherein the chief men and women figured as heroes and heroines. The powers of nature, such as wind, rain, lightning, heat and cold, and all kindred phenomena were gods of various degree, while the germinal principal of life, the destroying one of death, and other of life's greater mysteries, were characterized as the greater gods; but each and all were but offspring of the Most High Incal. It was an epic related in metrical measure and rhyme, constituting a poem whose every line exhibited the master touch of genius. Its authorship was lost in the night of time. It was supposedly the work, however, of a Son of the Solitude. There was an addendum embracing later events and epochs, but it was a markedly inferior work, and was not valued as highly as the body of the poem.

As a fact, the worship of Incal never included anything other than the adoration of God as a spiritual entity, and the "gods" had no portion in the religious services held on the two Sundays of each week, that is, the eleventh and the first days, for with the Poseidi a week consisted of eleven days, just as a month comprised three weeks, and a year eleven months, with one or more "leap-year" days at its end, as the exigencies of the solar calendar might require, these days being a regularly recurring holiday season, as New Year's Day is now. That so many gods and goddesses seem to have been venerated was due to the national influence of the epic history spoken of, and it was but a habit of mind to speak of them at all.

In our monotheism we differed little from the religion dominating the Hebraic civilization; we recognized no divine trinity, nor any Christ-spirit, neither any savior except the endeavor to do the best we knew in the sight of Incal. We considered all mankind as the sons of God, not any one mysteriously conceived person as solely His son. Miracle was an impossible thing, for all things we deemed rationally referable to unchangeable law. But the Poseidi did believe that Incal had once lived in human form upon the earth, and had cast off the gross body of the world to assume that of unfettered spirit. He had in that time created mankind and, as the Poseidi were evolutionists, that word, "mankind," embraced all the lower animals too. In course of time beings of the genus homo were evolved, one man and one woman, and then Incal had placed woman spiritually highest and above man, a position which she had lost through an attempt to enjoy a fruit which grew on the Tree of Life in the Garden of Heaven. But in doing this she had, according to the legend, disobeyed Incal, who had said that His highest, most progressed children should not enjoy this fruit, for whosoever did should surely die, because no mortal being could have immortal life and also reproduce its kind. The legend read: "I have said unto my creatures, attain perfection and study it evermore, and such is endless life. But whosoever enjoys this tree cannot contain self."

The form of punishment meted out was the rationalistic, as the woman's attempt was to attain forbidden pleasures and she did not, uninstructed, know how. Her hand slipped from its grasp on the fruit and its side was torn out, so that its seed dropped on the earth and became flint-stones, while the fruit still adhered to the tree and became of the likeness of a great fiery serpent, whereof the breath scorched the hands of the culprit. Feeling the pain, she let go of her hold on the Tree of Life, falling prone upon the earth and never fully recovering from the injury. Thus man became the superior being through the development of his nature by the necessity he was under of preserving his mate and himself from the cold and kindred conditions which came along with the flint-stones. (The last Glacial or Ice-age). Having fallen back into these material conditions, reproduction of species was a necessity once more, and so the law of continence supposedly commanded by Incal was broken. Death thus entered again into the sum of human reckoning and, until the Word be observed, no man could know a deathless condition. CONTAIN THYSELF! On this depends all knowledge; no occult law is so great as this. Use all things of this world as abusing none. (I. Cor. vii., 31).

Such was the popular belief regarding the creation of human kind by Incal. The higher priests held to a religion which was virtually Essenianism, although for obvious reasons the populace was not aware of this fact. The date of this fabled occurrence was theologically supposed to have been preceded at least 9 thousand centuries, and some semi-authorities set it at even a more extended period than that.

Incal, the Father of Life, was not supposed to punish His children except that He made the laws of nature self-executive, His immanent will, and if any one transgressed these the guilt was inexorably punished by nature, it being impossible to set in motion a cause without a consequent effect; if the cause was good, so also was the consequence. And in this they were undeviatingly correct; no mediator can avert for us the results of our misdeeds. [1] The Poseid nation believed in a heaven of good effects for those who put good causes into operation, and there was a region filled with bad effects for the wicked; the two places were adjacent, and those who were neither wholly good, nor wholly bad, were supposed to live on a middle territory, so to speak. But, both of these post-vital conditions were included in the Shadow Land, as the word "Navazzamin" may be translated, literally, "A country of departed souls."

Though the religion of Incal was one based on cause and effect, nevertheless a slight inconsistency appeared in the more or less prevalent belief that He was supposed to reward the very good.

Today, my friend, you stand on the threshold of a new unfoldment. The religion of today is even yet tinctured by this concept of an omnipotent, but manlike, Creator, heritage of a dead antiquity. But you are living in the final years of an old Human Cycle, the Sixth. While I choose not at present to explain what this means, I will do so before I bid you God's peace. But I will say that humanity's new conception of the Eternal Cause will be more lofty, more sublime, purer, wider and more of an approach to boundlessness, than anything of which the long gone eons of time have ever dreamed. Christ is indeed risen and has come unto His own, who before long shall know Him as no exoteric man has ever known Him. And, knowing Him, they shall know the things of the Father and do them, because it is written, "I go unto my Father."

GLORIA IN EXCELSIS!

Faith shall soon be knowledge. Belief shall be twin with science, and the Word shall blaze as a sun of glorious new meaning, for true religion means "I bind together."

RESURGAM CHRISTOS

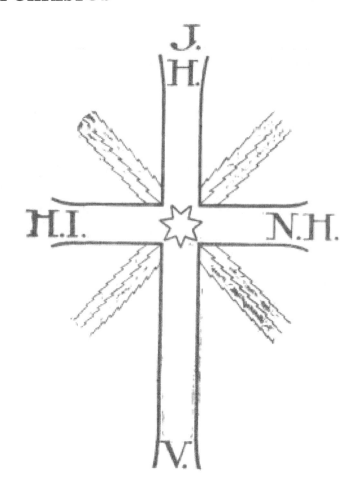

"Close Not the Ends of My Cross."

The Exoteric Church has closed the ends of His Cross. For that reason they are exoteric, and shall not ever be esoteric until they open the ends of that Four-Way Path. Open your eyes and your ears.

Footnotes

90:1 NOTE.—Do not confuse "undoing" with "atonement." Christ atoned; we must undo.

CHAPTER VIII. A GRAVE PROPHECY

It was about the first hour of the first day in the fifth month which had passed since I began attendance at the Xioquithlon, and as it was the week of Bazix, it was consequently the thirtieth week of the year, and near its close, there being but three weeks left in B. C. 11,160.

With the Poseidi, the day, as the reader has seen, commenced at meridian, making twelve o'clock till one the first hour. From this hour in the last day of each week until the end of the twenty-fourth hour in the following, or first day in the next week, all business was suspended, and the time devoted to religious worship, such observances being enforced by the most rigid of all laws, custom. Today, A. D. 1886, there are those who argue that if a man is engaged all the week at sedentary labor, on Sunday he is obtaining natural recreation by going zealously into athletic sports, or upon a fatiguing excursion.

But I submit that as the body is the externality of the soul, therefore, as the soul is, so will be the body also. Ergo: if the soul is of God, then to return to the Father as often as possible is to be recreated, or rested, or refreshed. Perhaps not indoors; no, rather amidst His works, but ever with un-artificial, natural thoughts of Him uppermost. Hence, I am to-day not less in favor of Sabbath observance, whether it be the seventh day or any other of the seven days of the week, as now constituted, or the eleventh and first, as in Atlantis.

Still, I shall not argue my preferences, and will only make a restatement of the well-known physiological law that a periodic day of rest is necessary to health, happiness and spirituality. In Atlantis, any person was free to employ the morning hours even of the eleventh day in any manner most agreeable, whether at work or playful relaxation. With the first hour, however, an enormous and very sweet-toned bell pealed forth with an intense, reverberant boom, two strokes, paused a moment, then rang four tones more.

Thereupon all occupations ceased, and religious worship commenced. On the following day the great bell struck again, and throughout the length and breadth of a great continent other bells pealed synchronously. It was even so in the populous colonies of Umaur and Incalia, the difference in time being calculated, and one man in the great temple of Incal in Caiphul attended to this sweetly solemn duty. Then the season of worship was over, and the rest of the Inclut (first day) was devoted to recreations of every sort. This is not to be construed that the worship was of a gloomy nature, or severe; not so, nor was it continued through the night, any further than that every light allowed during that interval was rendered carmine red by blending the atomic speed of the odic force, so that it was the element of light and that of strontium combined, this being done at the odic depots.

About the third hour after the Sun day had ceased, a peculiar event occurred in my Poseid existence. As I walked leisurely homeward, not yet having summoned a vailx, but proceeding under the dreamy calmness of the influence produced by the music of a choice concert given to the public in the Agacoe gardens, I met a stately old man, also on foot. I had often met him on former occasions and, by his wine-colored turban, knew him for a prince. Upon meeting him now, the current of my thought was altered, and I determined not to go home at once, but to remain in the city for a time, perhaps all night. Just as I came to this determination, the older man smiled, but without stopping went on his way. I then noticed that, much as he resembled the prince I had in mind, he was not that person, and it must have been an illusion, for the turban of this man was pure white, not tinted. And somehow I felt that he had wished to speak to me, but for some reason had not. If I should happen there later in the day, I might meet him again and learn what he had to say.

The Secrets Of Mount Shasta And A Dweller On Two Planets

Pondering these thoughts I went into a cafe in one of the grotto-tunnels, where an avenue pierced a hill, and after ordering a luncheon, waited for it to be served. During the dispatch of the refection, a xioqene, or student with whom I had become friendly, strolled in, bent on the same errand. The repast over, we proceeded to the moat, where we took a water-sailer held for hire by a poor man who made his living from the rental of these craft to those who liked this seldom-indulged pleasure; the common mode of conveyance was by vailx. The breeze being fresh, we sailed out into the ocean through the exit-flow of the Nomis River, the great river which made a complete circuit of the city, traversing the moat and then emptying into the ocean. On account of this extended trip I was unable to be again on the avenue until after nightfall. When I neared the spot where my meeting had occurred with the white-turbaned stranger, this time in a car, which I checked from running over-fast, I saw his commanding figure standing in full view in the bright light of the tropic moon. It was quite a part of my expectations thus to see him, and this time I inclined my head in courteous recognition. As I did so the stranger said:

"Stop! I would speak with you, lad, with you alone."

Almost mechanically I nearly stopped the car, in obedience to his gesture to descend, and setting its lever so that the vehicle would move at about the pace of a slow walk, I let it go, knowing that if no one took advantage of the paid carriage, it soon would reach some station, and there be stopped automatically. When I stood before the priest, as I judged him to be, he said:

"Your name, I understand, is Zailm Numinos?"

"Truly it is."

"I have seen you often, and am informed concerning you. You have a laudable will to excel and to attain high honors among men. You are still a boy, but in a fair way to succeed as a man, as success is commonly counted. A boy conscientious at present, regarded with favor by your sovereign. You will succeed, and will come into places of high honor and profit, and continue well thought of by all your fellowmen. Yet you will not live the full term allotted to man on earth. In your shorter period a knowledge of love shall come to you. You will experience the purest affection man is capable of feeling for woman. Yet, notwithstanding this, your love shall not be a love crowned in this life period. And you will love again; you shall weep because of it. You will work some good in the world but, alas, much evil also. And because of an over-shadowing destiny, unto you shall come much sorrow. By you unto another shall deep misery of anguish come, and unto the uttermost shall you pay therefore, nor come out from there until thou hast done so. Yet, behold not in this life shall much be required of you. When you think least to do sin, then shall your foot stumble, and you will commit a sin which shall be for you a pursuing fate, inexorable. Even now, in the days of your innocence, you are treading upon the steps of your destiny. Alas! That it is so. You move near to the realization of your death, and death is but the least portion which shall overtake you; but you awaken and flee out of the caverns of the burning mountain and reach safety. Yet at last you will pass into Navazzamin, the world of departed souls, and lo! I say to you that you will perish in a cavern. Me, even me, will you behold as the last living being upon whom thy Poseid eyes shall ever rest. But I shall not seem then as now, and you will not know me for the one who shall smite the evildoer who will then have enticed you to your doom. I have said. May peace be with you."

Much I marveled at first to hear these words, thinking that perhaps the speaker was one escaped from the Nossinithlon (literally the "Home for Moonstruck" or crazy persons), and this despite the introductory circumstances under which we had met. But as he continued speaking I knew that this was an erroneous judgment. Finally, amazed, I gazed on the ground, knowing not what to think and filled with an indefinable fearsomeness. As he ceased utterance, and bade me peace, I raised my eyes to look him in the face, to find to my bewilderment that not a soul was in sight, but that I stood alone in the great plaza surrounding a fountain whose jet seemed like molten silver in the moonlight. Dumbfounded, I looked about on every side. Had I been dreaming? Certainly not. Were the words of the mysterious stranger true, or false? Time will satisfy your curiosity, my reader, as it did mine.

CHAPTER IX. CURING CRIME

During the subsequent four years after my strange meeting with the tall and straight white-haired old man who had prophesied concerning me, events, one after another, shaped themselves in harmony with his forecast. In all that time we never met; indeed I met him but once more before my death.

Before going further I must recall and finally dismiss from the scene the partners in my gold mine and also the one who bought the gold, knowing the act to be unlawful.

Several months had elapsed since the interview with Rai Gwauxln in his private apartments, when a youth wearing an orange-hued turban and upon its front a gold-mounted garnet pin, denoting him to be a guard in the imperial service, entered the geology room in the Xioquithlon and going to the instructor-in-chief, spoke in a low tone. Rapping on his desk for attention from the ninety or more students in session in the minerals class, the chief asked if a Xioqene named Zailm Numinos was present.

I arose in my place in response to the question.

"Come forward." The other Xioqeni looked interestedly on, as I went up, not without some trepidation, for I well knew what service was represented by the messenger, and there seemed to be a sternness in the tones of the instructor not at all pleasant.

"This courier desires that you will go with him before the Rai, who has so commanded. He is at the Tribune, of the Criminal Court, and you are needed as a witness."

Remembering what the Rai had said, I was considerably reassured by the import of the words addressed to me, and no longer especially apprehensive, went as required. Arrived at the Court of the Tribunes, I saw my mining partners there in custody, along with the incriminated purchaser of the gold. The judge of the court sat on the judicial divan on its raised platform, and by his side sat, in simple dignity, Gwauxln, Rai of the greatest nation of the earth; but he was nevertheless studiously observant of the fact that the judge was, as such, entitled to the place of first rank while in the hall. Several spectators were in the seats provided for the public in the auditorium.

There could be but one verdict concerning the malefactors, "Guilty as charged." This opinion was reached very quickly, and by the culprits admitted to be a just one. Immediately, an officer took the prisoners into another part of the building, where there was a well-lighted apartment, fitted with various portable and stationary instruments. He was accompanied by all persons present.

A chair with a head-clasp rest, and with other rests, clasps and straps for the limbs and body of the occupant, stood in the center of the room. A guardsman seated and firmly strapped one of the prisoners in the chair. This preliminary attended to, a Xioqa approached bearing in his hands a small instrument of which, from its general appearance, I knew the nature to be magnetic. He placed the two poles of this in the hands of the condemned man, and after a brief manipulation a slight, purring sound was heard from the instrument. Immediately the prisoner's eyes closed and his every appearance indicated profound stupor; he was in fact magnetically anesthetized. Then the operator carefully felt all over the head of the unconscious man, and this examination concluded, ordered the attendant to shave the entire cranium. When this order had been obeyed, he made a blue mark upon the shaven surface in front and above the ears. Feeling further, he made the Poseid numeral (or 2) above and a very little back of each ear. These operations done, he gave his attention to the spectators, but, on being spoken to by Rai Gwauxln, he paused long enough from making his proposed address to the audience to call me to his side from where I stood outside the railing. Then he spoke:

"In the prisoner I find that the predominant, most positive faculties are those which I have marked one and two; these are, number one, a grasping desire to acquire property, and his disposition is to do all things secretly, as may be seen from the exceeding prominence of the organs of secretiveness. While the skull does not extend upwards very high, but at number two is very wide between the ears, I should infer that here we have a very acquisitive individual, lacking conscientiousness and spirituality, and therefore the moral nature, almost wholly. As he has also a very destructive temperament, we have withal a very dangerous character, one which I marvel has so managed not to have exposed himself to this office for correction before. Why any one should hesitate, even voluntarily, to undergo corrective treatment causes me much wonder. It is something, I suppose, explicable on the theory that one on the low moral plane of this poor fellow is unable to see the advantage of being on any higher plane, but is able to see the immediate advantages due to the pursuit of nefarious methods. He is, in short, a man who would not hesitate at the commission of murder, could he see any immediate gain in it, and be wholly oblivious of after consequences. Is this true, Zo Rai?"

"It is," replied the emperor.

"My diagnosis of the case," continued the Xioqa, "having been confirmed by so high an authority, I will now apply the cure." He summoned an attendant, who wheeled out another magnetic apparatus contained in a heavy metal case. Having placed this in a satisfactory condition of activity, the Xioqa next applied its positive pole to that place on the head of the patient marked by the figure one, and the other pole he placed at the back of the neck. He then took out his timepiece and laid it on the metal case of the instrument, near a dial the pointer of which he adjusted. All was then still, except the low-toned conversation in various parts of the room, during the ensuing half hour. At the end of this time the Xioqa arose from his seat and changed the positive pole to the other side of the head, where the duplicate figure was marked. Then again a half-hour's quiet, broken only by the exit of some of the spectators and the entrance of others. When the half hour had again elapsed, the operator changed the pole to the place marked "two." This time only half an hour was given to both sides of the head. I had been told by the emperor to remain. He had only stayed a few moments after the beginning of the operation which was not new to him. At the end of the work on the first man he was taken from under the influence of the magnetic anesthetizer by merely reversing the poles of the instrument at a second application. The Xioqa lectured upon the theme afforded by the operation while the first patient was being removed. To the considerable audience that had, by this time, assembled, he said:

"You have seen the treatment of those mental qualities which tended through their predominance to warp his moral nature, something but partially developed. The process has been partially to atrophy the vascular channels supplying that portion of the brain where are located the organs of greed and of destruction. But mark well this point, after all is said, the soul is superior to the physical brain, and it is in the soul, the nature of the man, in which these criminal tendencies inhere, the brain and other organs being the seat of psychic expression—the business office, so to speak. Hence, merely to have mechanically hypnotized this subject would not accomplish our purpose. Hypnotizing is an in-drawing, and the cerebral blood-vessels contract and become partially bloodless; indeed, they may become fatally empty; this art is a very dangerous one. But the opposite effect is produced in aphaism (Poseid equivalent for the modern word "mesmerism").

The brain is filled with blood, and the reversion of the instrument cessated the hypnotic and initiated the aphaic process. It is at this moment that the mind of the operator may assume control of the mind of the subject, and suggest to the erring soul a permanent cessation of the error. This man has been so treated, doubly treated, since not only has the blood supply been partially cut off which went to those organs where was the seat of his weakness, but with my will I have impressed his soul to cease its sin, and I have supplied it with a work to execute which will have a counter action. He may be slightly ill for a few days, but his tendencies to sin will be gone. It requires a superior mind, which has gone wrong in several directions, to make a successful evildoer, and where the lower nature, chiefly a perverted sex-nature, predominates, there will be found the criminal. Atlantis has no debauchees, for if a person shows such a disposition, the State takes the wayward one in hand and operates upon the proper organs. But I need not dilate upon these subjects any further."

The first man having been taken away to receive careful nursing, the next of my former partners was placed in the chair. Examination of the cerebral development revealed that he was more weak than wicked; a habitual liar, and of libertine tendencies; one whose skull was mostly behind and above the ears. I need not pause to describe his treatment; it was on the lines of the other; mesmeric suggestion was the chief cure.

As I went to my home that evening, I resolved to add the science of prophylactic penology to my chosen curriculum. I did so. By practice of the knowledge of men then acquired I interfered with the karma of not a few individuals but, as the result has proven, the interference was in no case injurious, so that I have not today to answer for any harm done. I have sometimes wished that I had submitted myself for treatment at the hands of the State, for it would at least have prevented the commission of errors which have wrought much misery, to me, and to others by me. That I did not, is as well, not only on the principle that in our Father's kingdom whatever is, is best, but also because no one can, in any way whatever, shirk the responsibilities inbound in character by the karma of all preceding incarnations. To have so submitted myself for correction would have been an evasion of the ordeal, a sort of cowardly attempt similar to the act of the self-murderer who seeks to avoid trouble on earth by suicide, and who in every case escapes nothing, not one jot nor tittle of the law of God.

Instead, he piles his miseries and penalties mountains higher and prolongs through inexorable karma, and other earthly incarnations, his anguish. Thus it is with those who die by self-destruction; but those who die by unavoidable causes, involuntarily, are not visited by such penalties. So the Poseid culprits who could in no way avoid the treatment were benefited, whereas for me voluntary submission would have sown dragon's teeth for my pathway. Penalties, observe, concern not those who know and, knowing, do God's will.

CHAPTER X. REALIZATION

The government was accustomed to keep systematic track of the more prominent Xioqeni to whom it gave free tuition but the supervision was never irksome, indeed, was scarcely felt to be maintained by those under this paternal surveillance. Those who, besides being bright and studious, were approaching the last years of the collegiate septerm were admitted to those sessions of the Council of Ninety not of an executive or secret character. There were some especial favorites who, being bound by strict vows, were not excluded from any meetings of the councilors. Not one of the many thousand students but esteemed even the lesser privilege most valuable, for beside the honor conferred the lessons in statecraft were of incalculable advantage.

In the latter half of my fourth year of attendance there came to me one Prince Menax, who desired to know whether I would accept the position of Secretary of Records, a position which gave opportunity to become familiar with every detail of Poseid government. He spoke:

"It is a very important trust indeed, but one which I am happy to offer you, because you are capable of filling it to the satisfaction of the council. It will bring you into close contact with the Rai and all the princes; also it will clothe you with some degree of authority. What do you say?"

"Prince Menax, I am aware that this is a very great honor. But may I ask why you have given such a great opportunity to one who supposes himself almost a stranger to you?"

"Because, Zailm Numinos, I have thought you worthy; now I give you every chance to prove it true. You are no stranger to me, if I be much of one to you; I feel a trust in you; will you not prove it well founded?"

"I will."

"Then hold up your right hand to the blazing Incal, and by that sublime symbol declare that in no case will you reveal anything that takes place in secret session; nothing of the doings in the Hall of Laws."

This vow I took and, in taking it, was bound by an oath inviolable in the eyes of all Poseidi. Thus I became one of the seven nonofficial, unenfranchised secretaries, who were entrusted with the writing of special reports and the care of many important state documents. Surely this was no small distinction to confer on one out of nine thousand Xioqeni and a man, as yet, unenfranchised in a nation of three hundred million people. If, in some way, I owed it to merit, yet I was not more worthy than a hundred other of my fellow-students. It was due just as much to personal popularity with the powers that were, a popularity, however, which would not have been mine had I not in all things shown the same solid determination which had governed my actions on the lone pitach of Rhok, the great mountain.

Prince Menax continued, saying:

"I would have you come to my palace this night, it being convenient, as I have some things to say to you. I would prove to you your error in believing yourself unknown to me, merely because you are one of a large concourse of Xioqeni, each in pursuit of knowledge. I do know you. From me, and not, as you have always imagined, from your Xioql (chief teacher) did the invitation issue to you to attend the sessions of the councils-in-ordinary. The Astiki (princes of the realm) are always much interested in deserving Xioqeni; that is the reason for many little duties falling to you for execution. But I will not say more at present, as I hinder your studies. Remember then, the appointed eighth hour."

Menax held the highest ministerial office of all the Astiki, being premier and, in short, the Rai's chief adviser. My opinion of myself rose in degree when I felt that I was held in such high favor; but it rendered me full of gratitude and not self-conceit; it was true self-esteem, not vanity.

Although this was not my first visit to the palace of this prince, I could by no means claim familiarity with the interior of his astikithlon.

Winding my best green silk turban about my head and sticking in it a pin set with gray quartz, through which ran veins of green copper, thus denoting my social rank, I stepped to the naim and called for a city vailx as you would call for a cab. The vessel soon came, and though small in size was ample for the conveyance of two, or even four, passengers. Bidding my mother good night, I was soon speeding on my way, and the conductor leaving me to my own company I sat listening to the furious patter of the torrents of rain which rendered the night inclement in the extreme. The palace of Menax was not far distant from the inner quay of the moat where that great canal nearest approached my suburban home, not indeed ten miles away, and therefore the aerial trip consumed only about the same number of minutes before the bottom of the vailx grated a little upon the broad marble floor of the vailx-court, announcing arrival at my destination.

A sentry came up to demand my business and, having learned it, a servitor was summoned to escort me into the presence of Menax.

A number of officers of the prince's suite were in the great apartment, painstakingly engaged in doing nothing in particular, an occupation in which they were aided by several ladies resident at the palace. Prince Menax himself was lying at length on a divan drawn up in front of a grate full of pieces of some refractory substance heated by the universal force.

As the attendant conducted me before the prince and prior to my presence being announced, I had enough time to notice a group of officers and ladies, gathered about a woman of such exceeding grace and beauty that even her evident sorrow and distress, together with the distance of the corner where she sat, could not wholly conceal it. Her attire, her features and complexion denoted that she was other than a daughter of Poseid, inasmuch as she had not their dark eyes, dark hair and clear, but distinctly reddish complexion. She who sorrowed, and was in distress, was the reverse of all this, as nearly as my hasty glance could discern, at the distance between us.

Menax said, in salutation:

"You are welcome. All is well. Be seated. The night is stormy, but I know you well; having promised, you have come."

He was silent for several moments, and gazed steadily into the glowing grate; then said: "Zailm, will you attend and take part in the competition in Xio in the nine days given to the annual examination of Xioqeni?"

"I have so intended, my Astika."

"You are privileged to waive examination until the last year of the sep-term."

"Really? That is so in all Xioqeni?"

"I approve most emphatically of your determination. I did the same thing myself, when I was a student. I hope that you will pass, that you may be joyful at your success, though it shall not shorten your years of study. But after the examination, then what? You will have a month wherein to do whatever you want. I wish that I had thirty-three days' respite from my duties!" Menax paused in meditation, and resumed:

"Zailm, do you have any preferred plan for how to spend that vacation?"

"None, my prince."

"None? That 's fine. Would it please you to do me a service, and go into a far country in fulfilling the kindness? Once the brief duty is completed, you may remain there for as long as you want, or go wherever your fancy may lead you."

I was not averse to doing as he desired, and as the duty took me to a land barely mentioned before, the account of my long-ago vacation trip may be prefaced by a description of Suernis, now called Hindustan, and Necropan or Egypt, the most civilized nations not under Poseid supremacy.

The Secrets Of Mount Shasta And A Dweller On Two Planets

When nations seek to make religion absolutely dominant in their affairs, the result is sure to be fraught with disaster. The theocratic policy of the Israelites was a case in point and, as the reader will before too long perceive, Suernis and Necropan were examples yet earlier in the history of the world. And the reason is, not that religion is a failure; the force of this record of my life must convey the truth that I think nothing is better than pure religion undefiled. No, the reason why a successful theocracy cannot permanently thrive is that the attention of the promoters must be given to things spiritual to render the spiritual successful, and the things of God's Kingdom can never be the things of earth. Not, at least, until man is fully developed in his sixth or psychic principle, has become purified, by the fire of the Spirit, from all taint of an animal nature. Suernis and Necropan were possessed of a civilization which I now perceive to have been peer with our own, though so different. But because it possessed scarcely a salient point in common with that of Poseid, therefore the people of the latter country regarded it with a sort of scorn 1 when discussing it amongst themselves. But they were very respectful in their demeanor towards these people, for reasons that shall presently appear.

The differences in the two equally ancient civilizations lay in the fact that, while Poseidi tended to the cultivation of the mechanical arts, to sciences having to do with material things, and were content to accept without question the religion of their ancestors, the Suerni and Necropani paid but little heed to anything not mainly occult and of religious significance—practical principles truly, occult laws having a bearing on materiality—but nonetheless were they careless of material objects except in so far as the proper maintenance of life was concerned. Their rule of life was summed in the principle of taking no heed of the life about them, but neglecting the present they strove after the future. The vital principle of Poseid was to extend her dominion over natural things. There were those who philosophized over the spirit of the times, Poseid theorists, and these drew a prognostic picture of Atlantean destiny. They pointed out the fact that our splendid physical triumphs, our arts, sciences and progress, absolutely depended on the utilization of occult power drawn from the Night-Side of nature. Then this fact was put side by side with the fact that the mysterious powers of the Suerni and Necropani owed their existence to this same occult realm, and the conclusion was that in time we also would grow careless of material progress and devote our energy to occult studies. Their forebodings were extremely gloomy in consequence; yet, while the people listened respectfully, the failure of these prophets to suggest a remedy rendered them in some degree objects of secret contempt. Any one who shall find fault with an existing state of affairs, and be confessedly unable to substitute a better, is sure to meet with public ridicule.

We, as Poseidi, knew that the mysterious nations across the waters were possessed of abilities which virtually dwarfed our attainments, such as our power to traverse the aerial or marine depths, our swift cars, our subsurface sea ships. No, they did not boast such conveniences, but they had no need of them to carry on the course of their lives and, therefore, as we supposed, no desire for such apparatus. Perhaps our scorn was more affected than real, for in our more sober thought we acknowledged, with no small admiration, their supremacy.

However, we could speak with, and see, and hear, and be seen by those with whom we wished to communicate, and this at any distance and without wires, but over the magnetic currents of the globe. Truly, we never knew the pangs of separation from our friends; we could attend to the demands of commerce, and transport our armies in war times with a dispatch which could pass around the world in a day; all this as long as our mechanical and electrical contrivances were at hand. But what availed all this splendid ability? Shut one of the most learned Xioqui in a dungeon, and all his knowledge would be as naught; he could not, deprived in such a way of implements or agencies, hope to see, to hear or to escape without external aid. His marvelous capabilities were dependent upon the creation of his intellect. Not so with Suern or with Necropan. How to hinder one of these people, no Poseida knew. Shut in a dungeon, he would arise and go forth like Saul of Tarsus; he could see to any distance, and this without a naim; hear equally without a naim; go through the midst of foes, and be seen by none of them. What, then, availed our attainments if opposed to those of Suernis and

The Secrets Of Mount Shasta And A Dweller On Two Planets

Necropan? Of what use our instruments of war even against such a people, a single man of whom, looking with eyes wherein glittered the terrible light of a will power exerted to hurl in retribution the unseen forces of the Night-Side, could cause our foemen to wither as green leaves before the hot breath of fire? Were missiles of value here? Of what use, when the person at whom they were aimed could stop them in their lightning path and make them fall as thistledown at his feet? What, even, was the value of explosives, more awful than nitroglycerin, dropped from vailx poised miles above in the blue vault of heaven? None whatever; for the enemy, with prescient gaze and perfect control of Night-Side forces we knew not of, could stop the falling destroyer, and instead of suffering harm could annihilate that high ship and its living load. A burned child fears the fire, and in times past we had sought to conquer these nations, and failed disastrously. Repulse was all they sought to effect, and successful over us in this, we had been left to go in peace.

As the years stretched into centuries, our ways likewise became those of defense only, never offensive any more, and owing to this change on the part of Poseid, friendly relations arose between the three nations.

Atlantis had learned at last so much of the secret as to wield magnetic forces for the destruction of its foes, and had dispensed with missiles, projectiles, and explosives as agents of defense. But the knowledge of the Suerni was still greater. Greater because our magnetic destroyers spread death only over restricted areas circumjacent to the operator; theirs operated at any desired point, however distant. Ours struck indiscriminately at all things in the fated district; at things inanimate, as well as animate; at men, whether foes or friends; at animals, at trees—all were doomed. Their agencies went out under control, and struck at the heart of the opposing force, not destroying life unnecessarily; nor even molesting any of the enemy except the generals and directors of their forces.

Of all these facts concerning the Suerni, I had long before learned. Prince Menax asked me that I oblige him by going on a mission to that people. I had never seen the land of Suern and, having a desire to do so, felt well pleased that it was to be gratified. After consenting to do as requested, I asked the prince concerning the proposed duty, saying "If Zo Astika will tell his son what is required, he will satisfy a growing curiosity.

"Even so will I do," answered the prince. "It is desired to send the Rai of Suern a present in acknowledgment of certain gifts sent by him to Rai Gwauxln. While there can be but small doubt that these gifts were sent to induce our acceptance of seven score women, prisoners of war, who seem to be much in the way of Rai Ernon of Suern, nevertheless we cannot regard it as necessary to throw us a sop, and while the women will be allowed to remain, or go wherever they will so that they go not where forbidden by Suern, we choose to regard the gift of gems and of gold as a gift, and make due return for it. So says the council in quorum assembled. It seems that these women are members of certain strong forces of foolish invaders whose country lies far to the west of Suern. These people very unwisely made war upon the terrible Suerni. They had never experienced, nor seen so exerted, the wrath with which Incal arms His children of Suern, a wrath which mows down its foes as the scythe of the reaper lays the grass. Now, Ernon has a fertile country, and these ignorant savages longed to possess it, so they sent the Rai of Suern a challenge of war. To this Ernon replied that he would not make fight; that those who sought him with spears and with bows, and came arrayed in armor, would find him, and therefore be sorrowful, inasmuch as Yeovah, as the Suerni are pleased to name Him whom we called Incal, would protect him and his people of Suern, and this without strife and bloodshed. Thereupon the barbarians returned derisive language, and declared that they would come upon his land and destroy his people with the sword. So they gathered a large army, even ten score thousand fighting men, and many camp followers, and these, led by a dauntless Astiki, swept east by South to devastate the realm of Suern. But wait; there is in this room one who can surely tell more than I, and tell it better.

"Mailzis!" addressing his body servant, "bring to me the beautiful stranger."

The Secrets Of Mount Shasta And A Dweller On Two Planets

Mailzis obeying, the foreign woman whom I had seen as I entered the apartment of the prince arose in an easy, graceful manner which commanded my admiration. Arranging her attire in a not at all hasty way—quite, in fact, the reverse of one obeying a superior—she approached Menax. Arising deferentially, the prince said, "Lady, are you willing to recount to me that which you have told to my sovereign? I know that your narration is vastly interesting."

During these remarks, the stranger had looked not at the prince, but at me. Her eyes had been riveted on my face, not boldly, but intently, though obviously quite unaware of the fixity of her gaze. Nonetheless there was such a magnetic power in it that I was compelled to look away, strangely abashed by the glance, but feeling that yet it followed me, although I saw it not. It occurred to me that the fact of the lady's reply being couched in the Poseid language was indicative of her possession of a good education.

"If, Astika," said she, "it is a pleasure to you that I do this that you ask, it is also one to me. It is also much of a pleasure to me to repeat it to the youth you favor. I would prefer, however, that the maid, your daughter, was not here," she added, sotto voce, with a glance of antagonism toward Anzimee, who sat near us, engaged in perusing a book, apparently, but, as I fancied, not in reality. This jealous undertone was not heard by Menax, though Anzimee heard it, and presently arose and left the apartment in consequence. This action I regretted, and the cause of it I resented, as the Saldu quickly saw, and because of it bit her lip with vexation.

"It cannot be comfortable to stand; will you seat yourself at my right hand, and thou, Zailm, change your seat, also, and be at my left?" said Menax, reseating himself on the divan.

When this arrangement had been made, we were ready to listen to the recital. At this moment the valet, Mailzis, respectfully approached and, being asked his wish, said: "It is the desire of your officers and of the ladies of the astikithlon to also be present at the narration."

"Their wish is granted; bring also the naim, and place it near us, that the editor of the Records may take account, too."

The Secrets Of Mount Shasta And A Dweller On Two Planets

Availing themselves of his permission, the petitioners were soon grouped about us, some on low seats, others, higher officers, more familiar with their prince, stretched themselves on side and elbow in front of Menax upon the rich velvet rugs on the marble floor.

Footnotes

106:1 It has always been this way; the seed sown in the Acre with the corners marked by posts of which the first has but one side, the second five sides, the third six sides, but the fourth again only five, has ever been scorned by man. That seed grows a tree with seventeen-branches. So was Suern. In another day it would be watered by Poseid; later it must be in Poseid. Yet again this would be after it was pruned by its Sower. Then it must grow till the day's end, and become great in the next day. But greatest at the end of that day. I have spoken a riddle that whoever solves it proves him of the Tree I have spoken, and filled with *deathlessness*. Hear, O Israel! Seek, O Manasseh, and Ephraim, seek! Land of the Starry Flag, open your eyes, and thou, too, O Motherland!

CHAPTER XI. THE RECITAL

"Mailzis," said the prince, "some spiced wine for us."

In the enjoyment of this truly refreshing, because unfermented beverage, we listened to the following thrilling narrative:

"You are, I think, acquainted with my native country, since you have had commercial intercourse with the Sald nation. All here have likewise heard of how our ruler sent a great army against the terrible Suerni. Ah! How little we knew of those people!" she exclaimed, clasping her small, patrician hands in an agony of terrified retrospection.

"Eight score thousand warriors had my father, the chief, under his command. One-half as many more were followers of the camp. Our cavalry was our pride, veterans tried and true, and ah! So lustful after blood! Such splendid armament had we, glittering spears and lances— oh! A wondrous array of valiant men!"

At this eulogy of such primitive weapons her listeners were unable to repress a shadowy smile. For a moment this seemed to disconcert the princess, but not for long, for she continued:

"In this splendid, powerful fashion, ah! How I love power! We came, taking loot as we proceeded towards the Suern city. When we arrived near it, after many days, we could not see it, as it was in a lowland. But we felt assured of an easy victory, since captives whom we took informed us that no walls or like defenses existed and that no army was gathered to meet us. Indeed, we nowhere found walled towns in all

145

Suern, nor met with resistance, hence had spilled no blood, but contented ourselves with torture of the captives, by way of amusement, before we set them free."

"Horrible!" muttered Menax under his breath. "Heartless barbarians!"

"What did you say, my lord?" asked the girl, quickly.

"Nothing, my lady, nothing! I only thought of the splendid march of the Saldan host."

Though seemingly somewhat doubtful of the accuracy of this statement, the Saldu nevertheless continued her recital.

"Arrived, as I have said, we stayed our march on the brink of a shallow, but wide mountain pass, wherein the Rai was so unwarlike and unwise as to have his capital, and sent a messenger to announce our errand and offer him favorable terms of war. In answer there came with our flag-bearer a solitary, unarmed old man. Elderly is a better word. He was tall, erect as a soldier, and had dignity of mien that made him splendid to look upon. Aye, he looked as power incarnate! I ought to hate him, but he is powerful and I cannot choose but love him! If he were younger I would woo him to be my mate."

At this unexpected remark we looked at the fair speaker in amazement, not unmingled with other emotions, while Prince Menax asked:

"Astiku, hear I aright? Woo a man? Is it customary among your people to give unto woman the lovemaking? I had thought myself versed in the customs of every nation, ancient and modern, yet knew not this fact. However, strange things are to be expected of—well, a race which has but numbers to entitle it to recognition at the hands of people like the Poseid."

"Why not be frank, Zo Astika? Why not say what you're thinking, that civilized nations like yours consider such a race as the Saldi beneath them so far that even their customs are well nigh unknown to you?"

Prince Menax flushed deeply in ashamed confusion, for he was unaccustomed to prevarication, and replied:

"Candor is best, I admit; but I desired to avoid wounding your feelings, Astika."

With a ringing laugh, full of amusement, the Astiki said:

"Zo Astika, allow me to tell you that in Sald, either sex is free to woo its chosen one. Why not? It is sensible, I think. I shall follow our custom in this respect, if chance ever presents. My chosen one must be pleasing to look upon, and must be courageous like unto the lion of the desert, yea! Even the deserts from which he came unto the continent of Suernota. Ah, me; yes, if chance offers," she reiterated, with a little sigh.

At length she resumed wearily, sadly:

"The Astika, my father, chief of our armies, said to this grand old man:

"'What does your ruler say?'

"'He says: "Bid this stranger depart lest my wrath awake, for lo, I shall smite him if he obey me not! Terrible is mine anger."

"'What ho! And his army; I have seen none,' said my father with the laugh of a veteran to whom despised resistance is offered.

"'Chief,' said the envoy, in a low, earnest tone, 'It is best that you depart. I am that Rai, and his army also. Leave this land now; soon you won't be able to. Go, I implore you!'

"'You are the Rai? Rash man! I tell you that when the sun has moved one other sign, your courage shall not save you, unless you will now return and collect your army. Otherwise I will then send your head to your people. There is but this option. After that length of time I will strike and sack your city. Nay, fear not now for your personal safety; I cannot hurt an unarmed foeman! Go in peace, and by the morning I will attack you and your army. I must have a worthy foe.'

"'In myself is a worthy foe. Have you never heard of the Suerni? Yes? And you have not believed! Oh, it is true! Go, I entreat you, while you can still do so in safety!'

"'Foolish man!' said the chief. 'This is your ultimatum? Then so be it! Stand aside! I go not away, but forward.' Then he called out to the captains of the legions and commanded:

"'Forward! March to conquer!'

"'Withhold that order one moment; I would ask a question,' said the Rai.

"Agreeably to this request our men, who had sprung to place at the word, were now halted with arms at rest. In the very front ranks of the Saldan army as it stood on the little eminence overlooking the Suern capital, and the great river flowing near, was the prime flower of our host. Veterans they were, tried and true, men of giant stature, two thousand strong, leaders of the men less seasoned. I shall never forget how grand looked that array, no, never. So strong; the very mane of our lion-power, every man able to carry an ox on his back. The sun was caught on their spears in a glorious blaze of light. Looking upon these men the Suerna said:

"'Astika, are not these thy best men?'

"'Aye.'

"'They are the ones of whom it has been told me that they tortured my people, merely for amusement? And they called them cowards, saying that men who would not resist, to them should they serve death, and they did murder a few of my subjects?'

"'I deny it not,' said my father

"'Do you think, Astika, that this was right? Are not men who glory in shedding blood worthy of death?'

"'Possibly; if so, what matter? Perhaps you would have me punish them for such action?' said my father, scornfully.

"'Even so, Astika. And thereafter depart from here?'

"'Aye, that will I! It is a good jest; yet I do not have humor for jesting!'

"'And you will not go, though I say to remain is death?'

"'Nay! Cease your drivel! I weary of it.'

"'Astika, I am sorrowful! But be it as you wish. You have been warned to leave. You have heard of the power of the Suern, and believed not. But now, feel it!'

"With these words the Rai swept his outwardly-pointing index-finger over the place where stood our pride—the splendid two thousand. His lips moved and I barely heard the low-spoken words:

"'Yeovah, strengthen my weakness. So dies stubborn guilt.'

"What then befell so filled all spectators with horror, so wrought upon their superstition, that for a full five minutes after, scarcely a sound was heard. Of all those veteran warriors not one was left alive. At the gesture of the Suernis their heads fell forward, their grasp was loosed on their spears, and they fell as drunken men to the earth. Not a sound, save that of their precipitation; not a struggle; death had come to them as it comes to those whose hearts stop pulsing. Ah! What frightful power you have, Suernis!"

"For the Angel of Death spread his wings on the blast, And breathed in the face of the foe as he passed."

Sennacherib was unknown then; the Salda princess knew not of the poem; but we do, my reader, you and I; that is enough.

While describing the action of the Rai of Suern, the princess had risen to her feet from her place by the side of Menax, simulating at the same time the fatal gesture of Ernon of Suern. So apt had been this mimicry that the group of listeners on our left had involuntarily cowered as her arm swept over their heads. The Saldu noticed them shrink, and her lip curled with scorn.

"Cowards!" she muttered. A Poseida overheard the words, and his cheek flushed, as he said:

"Nay, Astiku, not cowards! Consider our involuntary shrinking as a compliment to your descriptive powers."

She smiled, and said: "Perhaps so." Then, overcome by her apostrophe to the dread strength of Yeovah as invoked by Ernon, a strength which even proud Atlantis feared, she sank back in her seat weeping.

A little wine revived her, and the narration was resumed.

"After the horrible silence that fell on all who had witnessed the awful sight, the women, wives and daughters of the higher officers began shrieking in fright. Many of our men, as soon as they could realize that the stories they had heard and discredited were no idle tales, fell to the earth in an agony of pulling terror. Ah! Then, then could you have heard pleading prayers to all the gods, great and small, in whom our people place trust. Ha! Ha!" laughed the princess, bitterly, contemptuously, "appealing to gods of wood and metal for protection against such awful power! Faugh! Since I may not live in Suern, being banished, I would not live again in the land of my birth! I want no more of people who idolize lifeless objects and deify them. No, Astika," she said in answer to a question from Menax, "I never worshipped idols; most of our people do, but not all. I have not proved an apostate. But I do worship power. I ought to hate Ernon of Suern; but I do not. Indeed, I would, if permitted, live in his presence and idolize his wondrous strength, which works death to his enemies. Not so permitted, I would rather remain with your people, who are a goodly race, and, if not equal to the Suerni, are still better and more powerful than mine own, ah! Far more so.

"My father knew better than to imagine this some trick of a wily people, knew now, after this bitter lesson, that the reputation accorded them by travelers was no idle fabrication of wonder-mongers. But he did not cringe before the Rai, he was too proud-spirited for that. While we gazed, stupefied, on the awful scene of death, another and no less terrifying, but more ghastly thing happened. We that were alive, all our host except the two thousand stood between our dead and the river west of the city. Rai Ernon bowed his bead and prayed—what dire alarm that action caused our people! and I heard him say:

'Lord, do this thing for your servant, I beg thee!'

"Then, as I gazed on the victims, I saw them arise one by one, and gather up each his spear and shield and helmet. Thereafter, in little irregular squads, they marched towards us, towards me, O! My God!

And passed on to the river! As they passed I saw that their eyes were half-closed and glazed in death; the movement of their limbs was mechanical; they walked as if hung on wires, and their armor clanked and clanged in a horrid, mocking ring. As, one by one, the squads came to the river, they walked in, deeper and deeper, till the waters closed over their heads, and they were gone forever, gone to feed the crocodiles which already roared and snarled over their prey all down the stream of Gunja. No one to lead, none to carry; each going as if alive, and yet somehow dead, this ghastly procession to the river, a thousand paces distant, so completed the horrible sense of fear that desperate terror possessed the great army, and they fled, leaving behind all things, and soon only a few faithful soldiers were left in sight; these remained with their commander and his officers of staff, ready to share with him the death which they expected would be meted out to all who remained. The women also did not all flee. Then spoke Rai Ernon, saying:

"'Did I not tell you to depart, before I punished you? Will you go now? Behold your army in flight! Its rout shall not cease, for thousands shall never more see Saldee, because they will perish by the wayside, yet not a few shall reach their homes. But you shall never more go home; neither you nor your women. But they will not stay in my land nor their own, but in a strange country.'"

"That haughty, but now humbled soldier, my father, bent on one knee before the Rai, and said:

"'Mighty Rai, what would you do with innocent women? You said my warriors were guilty; I admit it, nor do I exclude myself. But these, my women, they have harmed no man. Your words lead me to believe that justice is your ruling principle; your acts do likewise, for when you might have struck us every one, you did no more than make example of a few guilty ones. I implore you, then, have mercy on my women; perhaps on my officers also.'

"'On thy officers, yes; they are faithful to you, though they expect but death as their reward. Bid them depart with what still bides of your army. They are unused to caring for the needs of the body, so they will surely all perish, except I save them. Having power, I will use it mercifully. None shall perish by the wayside; not one shall hunger, neither thirst, nor suffer any sickness, O Yeovah! All the way home, nor lose his way, though none shall have to eat any food all the way. And about them shall wild beasts rave, and though not one have a weapon, no animal shall harm him, for the spirit of Yeovah shall go with them and be their shelter and their safeguard. Yea, more also, shall He do, for he will enter into their souls, so that they that are warriors shall be henceforth His prophets, and shall uplift their people and make of their name one which shall go down unto all ages; a famous race of educated men shall they be, and astrologers, telling of God by his works of heaven. Yet shall a further day come some six thousand years hence when the men of Chaldea shall again try to prevail over my people, and again shall fail, even as now, but you shall long have been with your fathers asleep from a second life, and safe in the Name ₁ whereby I work, before this second attempt. Do you call innocent women who voluntarily came in all the insolence of supposed power and invincibility to murder my people? Innocent! They who came to see the plundering of my cities and to revel in the sufferings of my people! Innocent! Nay, not so! Therefore I shall keep with you these wives and these maidens. Behold! I have said you shall not go from here; neither will these women yet awhile, but you — you shall never go again from this land. I will put you in a prison which has neither bars nor gratings nor any wall; yet you cannot hope to leave it.'

"'Do you mean that we are all to die, Zo Rai?' asked my father in a low, sad voice.

"'Not so; Zo Astika, do you think I condemn murder, yet would myself do it needlessly? No. Having said that you cannot leave Suern, neither is it possible for you thereafter, though neither bolt nor bar hinders, nor any man watches or keeps you.'

"It was piteous to see the partings between those who were to go and those who must stay. But then, such are the fortunes of war, and the weak must obey the strong. I had rejoiced in our fancied strength, nor cared who fell by it. Power, aye, power! I think, after all, that I felt a grim satisfaction in beholding you, Power, my god, work so swift destruction!"

* * * * *

The princess said these last words musingly, apparently oblivious to her surroundings as she sat with clenched hands, admiration depicted on her beautiful face and her glorious blue eyes with their faraway look, but oh! So heartless, so cruel, after all. Queenly in figure, commanding in personality, beautiful, wonderfully beautiful, the world now, as then, would call the Princess Lolix; indeed she bore a most startling likeness to your own fair American women. But these are not like her, really. She, lioness-like, sided ever with the triumphant power. But the real American maiden, sympathetic, true as steel, graceful as a bird, sweet as a rose just blown—like Lolix in these three last traits, but ceasing to parallel her further, for she of today clings to her father, her brother, her lover, come sunshine, come storm, success or adversity—faithful unto death. Such have their reward.

There came a day when Lolix was altered to be all that the fair modern maidens are. But it was not till after years. There are some kinds of roses which, while in tender bud, seem all thorns; but what marvels of beauty are they when they have at length opened their hearts to the sun and the dew!

It appeared that Prince Menax had not previously heard Lolix speak at length, but had for some reason waited this experience until I might listen. Consequently it was a revelation to him to hear one so fair, and even so sweet, reveal so heartless a nature as she exhibited in her speech, which was quite as much retrospective meditation, on her part, as recital. After some moments, Menax said:

"Astiku, you have related that his Majesty of Suern did not by you and your companions as you anticipated, reasoning from the national custom of your people to devote female prisoners of war to lust and ministrations to man's base passions."

"Astika Menax, you will not think me disrespectful if I shall now call you friend? I will confess it to have been very much of a surprise that

Rai Ernon did not so do. I could not have complained, for such are the vicissitudes of war. Instead, however, he declared that neither he nor the Suerni had any use for us; which is why he sent us into a foreign land. Is that — our destiny here — such a hard fate?"

"No! Never so!" replied Menax, his lip curling with disgust at the bare imputation. "Here you shall be supported by the government until perhaps Poseid citizens shall choose wives from among you; ours is a people of strange tastes, sometimes!"

"Thou art sarcastic, Astika!"

Except that the prince slightly raised his eyebrows, he offered no reply to her remark; even this notice was so faint that if I had not been closely watching his face, I would not have perceived it. After a more or less extended silence, Menax said that they were hindered from evermore returning home to Salda, because—

"No longer my home!" quickly interrupted the lady.

"Then the land of thy birth!" said Menax with some harshness, as he again lapsed into silence.

Lolix then arose and, clasping her hands, vehemently exclaimed:

"I have no wish anymore to see my native land. From now on, I choose my lot in Poseid—to call it home!"

"As you wish," said Menax. "You are certainly a most strange woman. For love of power you forsake gods and home and native land. Are the others, your captive friends—nay, hold! Maybe not friends, seeing that they are fallen under misfortune! are these, as you are, these women, forgetful of their country?"

Bending her lovely head, the princess fixed the gaze of her glorious blue eyes upon the upturned face of her critic. Two drops, teardrops, fell from beneath the long sweeping lashes, her lips quivered, and she clasped her little hands together with the words:

"Ah! Astika, you are cruel," then turned away and walked sobbing to the seat where first I had seen her.

Thus was the unopened rosebud mistaken for a thistle blossom.

As for me, a strange mixture of feelings possessed me, a commingling of wonder and approval. I wondered what sort of a nature it was that could be so heartless and thirst so greatly after power as to leave every natural tie for the sake of following it, and yet was so essentially feminine as to be pained at the expression of a very natural condemnation of such conduct. I pitied her because she was so innocent and was so sincerely honest in and through all her soullessness, and had so much without deception narrated her later history, evidently expectant of disapproval, and felt so hurt at the contrary effect produced. Finally, approval divided my emotions, because the prince had given a really deserved scolding, and one which, though its edge was keen, could not fail to have a beneficial effect. My reflections were interrupted at this point by Menax, saying:

"Zailm, let us go into the Xanatithlon ₁ where all is quiet and beautiful among the flowers. We shall be alone there, you and I. I would dismiss these people of my palace, but prefer not to disturb the Saldee maiden over there."

Footnotes

118:1 Yeovah or Jehovah.—Ed.

121:1 Building for flowers.

CHAPTER XII. THE UNEXPECTED HAPPENS

A very few steps took us into the great conservatory, or Xanatithlon, where bloomed all manner and species of flowers. In the midst was a fountain whose three lofty jets sprang into the arch of the great dome and sparkled during the day in the sun-rays as they filtered through the thousands of panes of many-colored glass. Now, however, when the dull roar of the rain falling on all without mingled its tones with the dulcet plash of the fountain, that object of beauty was flashing in the rays of numerous electric images of the Day King.

Intermingled with the myriads of natural flowers were many hundreds wrought in glass so perfectly that only close examination by sense of touch might say which were produced by Flora and which by the artist. These illuminants were suited in kind to the natural flowers of the plant, tree or vine on which they hung; on the plants there were but few, on the trees, higher above the floor, the number increased, while on the vines that clambered over arches and pillars, or swung pendent between high points overhead were a great multitude, casting throughout this floral paradise a soft, steady glow which was most delightful.

In the midst of these pleasant environments we seated ourselves on what to the eye seemed a pile of moss-covered rocks with cozy depressions among them, very comfortable, since in reality they were easy springs on which grew moss originally furnished by silkworms.

"Sit here, closer to me, my son," said the benign old prince, drawing me down into a hollow beside the one he occupied himself.

156

"Zailm," he began, "I hardly know why I called you this night; why I didn't wait for a time. And yet I do know, too; I had a mission to confer upon someone suited to perform it. There are others more experienced, yet I choose to give it to you; you know what it is."

It was very evident to me that this was not what motivated the Astika in his choice, and that it was not for this that he had asked me into the conservatory. He had relapsed into silence, which he presently broke by asking:

"Have you ever heard that my wife gave me a son, and that both wife and son are taken by death? Aye, one son, and a daughter. Praise unto Incal, I have her yet! But my son, the pride of my life, is gone unto Navazzamin, the destiny of all mortality. My son, oh, my son!" he sobbed.

When his emotion had somewhat subsided, he resumed:

"Zailm, when I saw you, at your first meeting with our beloved Rai—four years ago, was it not?—I was astonished at your likeness to my dead boy, and I loved you then, Zailm! Many a time have I gone to the Xioquithlon to observe you at work in your studies. Always have the summonses you have received at divers times to attend at this astikithlon had for their prompting motive sight of you! Yes, sight of you, lad, sight of you!" he murmured softly, gently stroking my curls the while.

"Few days have passed that I have not at some time seen you, either personally or by naim; yes, I have gone at night and stood by your window, that I might gladden my heart with the sound of your voice as you sat reading to your mother. I have watched you and been proud of you, Zailm, for in every way you have seemed as my own; your triumphs in study have made joyful my days, as has also the skill with which you have performed governmental commissions, for you were as my son! Then come and live here, lad, for I want you near me, in this my old age. Together we will float down the stream of life, you and I! Perhaps I go out first across the great ocean of eternity; then I will await you in the dim land of dreams, where is no more parting, neither pain nor sorrow. Come, Zailm, come!"

The Secrets Of Mount Shasta And A Dweller On Two Planets

To this tender appeal I replied:

"Menax, I have often wondered, during the years of my living in Caiphul, what your favors to me meant. You have long been more kind to me than any other, yet have ever been reserved and distant, yea, more so than others who could not care overmuch what befell me. Now all is plain. I have looked on you with affection and loving reverence, and treasured your kindnesses, and acted according to your few words of advice. Yea, Menax, we will go together hand in hand to the shadowy land of departed souls, you for me or I for you, waiting the other's coming, whichever the Harvester of Souls shall first gather."

We arose and tenderly embraced each other. As we parted our clasp, I beheld the only child of the prince, enframed in clustering vines that twined caressingly around her lovely form. As I looked upon her I thought of that other girl, the Saldu to whose story I had so recently listened. Nearly the same age, neither of them more than a year my junior, but so widely different from each other as types of womanly beauty. It is difficult to describe a person in whom the deepest interest of the heart is centered, and the greater this feeling the more difficult will be the portraiture. At least, it is so in my case.

The reader is aware how the brown-haired, blue-eyed, queenly girl of far away Sald appeared, how delicate her fair complexion, how high-strung and sensitive her nature, yet in spite of that, how cruel! But how can I picture her whom I loved, her with whom the hope of a chance meeting, even at a distance, made a great part of the pleasure I felt in going to the palace of Menax. She whom I had loved and enshrined within my heart nearly as many years as I had resided in Caiphul—how can I describe her?

If the Princess Lolix was on the threshold of womanhood, so was this fair one, the Princess Anzimee. Slight, delicate, womanly, the daughter of a long line of patrician ancestry; my senior and superior in the ranks of study at the Xioquithlon, if my junior in years; I loved her, yet carefully concealed the fact. Each of my friends who reads this will know what I feel when I avow unwillingness to describe Anzimee, and bid each to place in this Poseid life-frame the picture of his own best-loved one.

"Each heart recalled a different name, but all sang 'Annie Laurie.'"

Prince Menax caught sight of his daughter at nearly the same moment as I did, and a look of mild surprise overspread his face at her presence, when he had supposed the Xanatithlon deserted. Seeing this expression, the Rainu came forward and, kissing her father, said:

"My father, have I intruded? I heard you and this—this youth enter, but I did not know that you desired privacy, so I kept my seat and continued my reading."

"Nay, my pet, you have no need of excuse. I am, indeed, rather glad that you are here. But what, may I ask, were you reading? It will not be well for you to study too hard, and this, I suspect, was, or is, your meaning when your word is 'reading.'"

With a sweet smile dancing over her face and lighting her gray eyes, she replied: "You would make an excellent reader of the hidden mind! I was indeed studying, but the end justifies the labor. Whosoever shall acquire a deep knowledge of the science of medicine shall be in a position to relieve even those in the agonies of mortal pain, and to cure those less gravely afflicted. Is it not a work for Incal then, as well as for His children, and is not such an act, done for the least of these, something done also for Him?"

Two girls—Lolix of Sald, and Anzimee of Poseid! A wide continent separated their two countries, but an even greater distance was between the daughters of the two lands. Lolix, with no sympathy for those in pain, no sorrow for those in mortal agony; Anzimee, at the very opposite of such traits of character.

For a full minute there was silence, while Menax looked at the noble-hearted, dainty speaker. Then, clasping my hands with his right and those of Anzimee with his left, he said:

"My child, to you I give a brother, one whom I deem worthy to be such; Zailm, to you I give a sister more precious than rubies; and to You, Incal, my God! All the song of praise which fills my breast for Your blessings to me." Here he dropped the hands that had touched, together for the first time, and lifted his own to heaven.

How the touch of that little hand thrilled me before it was withdrawn. Was I worthy of all this love? No sin had so far stained my fair fame, and I felt at that moment entirely deserving. If ever it blotted my record, sin was yet to come; but with disquiet I thought of the strange prophecy on that night of long ago; for an instant only this feeling possessed me and then it fled.

I was much given to the habit of analyzing men and motives; it was a second nature, so to speak, to consider every question in every possible aspect. So, even now, I was querying myself as to the meaning of this latest experience. I knew that for Menax, who had so winningly asked me to be his son, I entertained the most profound respect and affection. My life would not have appeared to me too great a price to pay, if for it I could have bestowed commensurate benefit on him; and I loved life, too; there was nothing morbid about my nature, unless exceeding love for my friends be a sign of morbidness. I dwelt a little upon what my adoption meant socially and politically. You don't need to be told what it must have been to my ambition thus to be placed in so high a niche as I would occupy from now on in Atlantean estimation as the legal son of a high councilor, who by marriage was the brother of the Rai. All this time, while considering the situation, I was reserving as a choice sensation the pleasure of examining what was the kind of love I felt for her who was my sister, by adoption only, it is true, but who, herself the pet of inner circles, and the adored of the people of Caiphul, would appear before the world as my sister the moment Rai Gwauxln should officially approve his brother's course.

Ought I to feel pleasure or vexation? I looked at her whom I had dreamed of as my wife in case Incal in His goodness should see fit to grant me exaltation to high places. Could I hope to realize the dream, after this unexpected turn of fortune? If I had come to my high place by a different manner, then I could have hoped for the hand of Anzimee. But now! My great fortune seemed like an apple of Sodom, bitterness to my mouth. For I was her brother, legally, if not by blood ties. There was a chance that things were not so dark as they seemed, since such adoptions among the lower classes were frequent, yet did not act as a bar to marriage. So, thus again, the sun came from behind the clouds.

The characteristic most marked in the appearance of the girl before me was the simplicity of her attire. That evening, her glory of brown tresses was caught in a loose, unbraided fall at the back of her shapely head by a plain golden clasp, A long, flowing robe clothed her slender, girlish form. No costume could be more artistically, tastefully simple than this colorless, diaphanous fabric, tinged just enough with blue to seem pearly white. Shoulder-tips of pure carmine indicated the wearer's royalty. Her dress was gathered at her throat by a pill made of a golden bar whereon flashed large rubies, grouped about a center of pearls and emeralds, the whole heightening the color of her checks so as to make her seem some lovely human rosebud. Rich as it was quiet, the attire added nothing to the girl's own sweetly dignified loveliness. The pearls, emblem of her rank as a Xioqenu; the emeralds, mark of her not yet having attained political voice; the rubies, gems of royalty, worn only by the Rai, or one of his near relatives. Gwauxln's own sister was Anzimee's mother and the wife of Menax.

Poseid derived her greatness from her educational superiority, a greatness which recognized no sex in its learned ballot-holders. But if Atlantis owed all things to knowledge, it was nonetheless true that Atlantis' people of ability would not have been what they were had it not been for their wives, the sisters and the daughters, and more than all, the mothers of our proud land. Our grand social fabric was founded on and built by the efforts of sons and daughters who, for centuries, had respected the lessons impressed on their minds by fond, true, patriotic mothers. Next to that paid to his Creator was the homage which a Poseida accorded to woman. We loved our Rai, and the Astiki; we respected them as much as ever rulers in this world have been respected; but we honored our women more, and Rai and prince, sovereign and subject, were proud to acknowledge the holy influence which made all our glorious land of freedom one great home. America, thou art beloved by me even as was Poseid. Foremost amongst nations, you are so because of woman—and Christ. You will keep in the leadership position because of them, and eclipse all the world besides when the happy karmic day shall have arrived which places woman not below, not above, but by the side of man on the rock of esoteric Christian education, the granite of knowledge and faith, which withstands the winds and storms of ignorance. Built on such foundation, the National house shall not fall; built on other, great shall be the fall of it. Here is wisdom: myriad serpents are in a man; in you; keep them. Now you are slaves. Be masters instead. But, alas! This Way is narrow; few *will* find it.

CHAPTER XIII. THE LANGUAGE OF THE SOUL

"Zailm, my son, you heard the narration of the Saldu, Lolix. As you know, it is from things rising out of the occurrences by her related that you go on a mission to Suern. It is not a hard task, merely to make return of acknowledgment for the gifts presented and disavowal of our intent to keep as prisoners the people whom Rai Ernon sent there. We will give them asylum, but Rai Ernon must not think that we permit their presence for any purpose except to do him a favor. Concerning other business, tomorrow it is Rai Gwauxln's pleasure that you attend at Agacoe. But will you not remain here this night?"

"My father, I happily would stay; but is it not duteous that I go to my mother tonight and set her at ease? She has an infirmity of nervousness that can not well withstand my absence at night."

"Thou art right, Zailm. Yet soon it must be arranged that your mother be housed in some pleasant part of this astikithlon, so that you shall be under thy father's roof at night." I then departed from the prince and from the sweet girl who had been with us during a part of the evening, and went forth into the night. The rain had ceased, and the clouds, rolling across the sky in sullen blackness, had but one gap in their gloomy mass. In this single hole shone a great white star, which at times flashed red. As I looked at it, down close to the horizon, seeming that moment risen from old ocean's phosphorescent waters, visible from Menax Heights, I thought of the past; for this star had flashed brightly upon me while I awaited the sunrise on Pitach Rhok. So many years it seemed since that morn! Today this star is called "Sirius," we named it "Corietos." As I looked upon it, it seemed an omen auspicious of success, past, present and to come. Raising my hands toward it, I murmured:

"Phyris, Phyrisooa Pertos!" which is: "Star, O star of my life."

It seems a little unusual that the language which is translated thus should have a similar sound and import as today used by the people of my home planet. At that old day I raised my hands aloft and exclaimed: "Star, O star of my life!" Today I turn awhile from precipitating this history in astral word-things, turn to my Alter Ego, and say: "Phyris, Phyrisa." This is her own dear name, and signifies "Star of my soul." Peculiar, is it not, that twelve thousand years should pass, and I, member of another race of human beings, in another mansion, find so little change in the language of the soul?

CHAPTER XIV. THE ADOPTION OF ZAILM

When, according to request, I arrived at the Agacoe palace on the next morning, I proceeded directly to the private office there occupied by Prince Menax, expecting to find my father alone. But in this I was disappointed, as Rai Gwauxln was there with him. The two were in conversation when I entered, and did not cease, evidently not regarding me as an intruder. At last I heard the Rai ask:

"Should we not now go to the Incalithlon?"

"If it pleases you. And you, Zailm, accompany us."

A palace car was summoned by the Rai, and came rolling along into our presence without any person to operate it; came in at the door of the office, which opened to allow its passage precisely as if some court page had opened it. It wheeled into the room and came to a stop in front of us. All this was done exactly as if under a guiding hand. But no visible hand was there. This was the first time I had ever seen any exhibition of occult power on the part of Gwauxln; indeed I never saw many examples of his power, notwithstanding his high adeptship. Like all true adepts he was exceedingly wary of such object lessons, disliking to show his knowledge before those not possessed of sufficient common sense to know that any acts of the sort were but examples of the control of nature through an understanding of higher laws than the ordinary mind perceives in its natural surroundings; but I was not one who saw anything miraculous in the occult; if I understood not the process, I did understand that it was but the operation of some unfamiliar law. Hence Gwauxln was not averse to allowing me to witness his power at times.

The car conveyed us to the vailx-landing outside, where we found a vailx of small size, into which Rai Gwauxln courteously assisted first Menax, then myself, and himself entered last. Here was a spectacle worthy of note, the ruler of a mighty nation without the display of a single attendant, not more deferential to rank than to those of inferior station. True, as a Xio-Incali, Gwauxln had command over mechanical service which was more regal by far than a retinue of menials could be.

Like father, like son. Gwauxln, who was as a father to his people, was copied by them in his demeanor. They, too, were simple in habits, courteous in manner, and, though in many cases wealthy and luxurious in their habits in life, were entirely non-grandiose, as their Rai set them example.

The great temple of Incal was distant several miles, but a few minutes sufficed to bring us to its huge structure. Outwardly the Incalithlon was shaped like the Egyptian pyramid of Cheops, not quite so high, but covering an area twice as great. No windows pierced its sides, and sunlight or that of day never entered its interior. Besides a number of small apartments, the building contained one vast hall where there was space for several thousand worshipers. The Poseid habit of copying nature was followed in this sanctuary with extraordinary faithfulness. Instead of straight walls, or alcoves, or the ordinary arrangement of interiors, the enormous auditorium was in faithful semblance of a cave of stalactites and stalagmites. In placing all this calcite, utility was consulted with regard to the stalagmites so that too much floor space should not be occupied by them. But the stalactites, hanging from the marble ceiling, had been placed as thickly as space allowed and sparkled like stars in the light from the incandescent lamps swung midway between them and the floor below. From the latter point of view these lamps were concealed by broad concave shades so that their glow was wholly invisible from beneath, but shining upwards was reflected from myriads of sparkling white needles, filling the temple with a steady and soft, but powerful, light that seemed to emanate from no special point, but from the air itself, a light well-adapted to religious meditation.

We left the vailx and entered the unimposing but ample portal, and proceeded across the hall to the Holy Seat, in the back of the sanctuary. Within it we found Mainin, the Incaliz, or high priest, a man of wondrous attainments of knowledge, second to none in fact. To him we all made courteous gestures of respect, and then Prince Menax said:

"Most holy Incaliz, you know, in your great wisdom, upon what errand your sons have come before you. Will you fulfill our prayer by granting us your blessing?"

The Incaliz arose and bade us to follow him into the triangle of the Maxin, or Divine Light, in front of the Holy Seat. Deferring the relation of our subsequent action, I will describe this especially sacred part of the temple. It was a raised, triangular platform of red granite, several inches higher than the floor of the auditorium, thirty-six feet between its points. In the very center of it was a large block of crystal quartz, upon the perfect cube of which rose the Maxin. This seemed aflame, in shape like a giant spearhead, and it cast a light of intense power over all things around, yet one could look at its steady, unwavering white glow without desiring shade for the eyes, even though these were not strong. Over three times the height of a tall man it stood, a mysterious manifestation of Incal, as all spectators believed. In reality it was an occult odic light, and had stood in that one spot for centuries. It had witnessed the grander development of Poseid and its capital city, and had seen the original temple of Incal (a small architectural structure, unworthy of a great people) torn down, and the present Incalithlon built around it. It made no heat, did not even warm the quartz pedestal; yet for any living being to touch it was fatal in the instant of the rash act. No oil, no fuel, no electric currents fed it; no man tended it. Its history was peculiar, and cannot fail to interest you, my friends.

Many hundred years previously there had been for four hundred and thirty-four days a ruler over the Poseidi who possessed wonderful knowledge. This wisdom was like that of Ernon of Suern. No one knew from where he came, and not a few were disposed to question his statement, while all were in doubt, as to whether his meaning was figurative or literal when he said:

"I am from Incal. Lo, I am a child of the Sun and am come to reform the religion and life of this people. Behold Incal is the Father and I am the Son, and He is in Me and I am in Him."

He was asked to prove this claim, whereupon he laid his hand upon a man born blind, and the man received his sight and saw with the doubters that his deliverer stooped to the pavement of the triangular platform, and with his finger drew a square five and a half feet either way. Then he stepped outside of the lines indicated, and at once the great block of quartz appeared, a perfect cube, in the place. Standing by its side he placed his finger upon the rock, and blew thereon with his breath, As he withdrew the finger the Maxin, or Fire of Incal, sprang up, and thus had cube and Unfed Fire remained during all the centuries since.

It is needless to say the proof was satisfactory, and thereafter the mysterious stranger revised the laws and provided then the code which had ever since governed the land. He had said that whosoever should add to or take from his laws, that person should not come into the Kingdom of Incal until "I am come on earth for the final judgment."

No one had ever desired to disobey, it would seem, or at least no change had ever been made. The laws which this Rai had given were written by him with his finger upon the Maxin-Stone, and no works of sculptor's chisel were better done. They were also written upon a book of parchment leaves, and this he placed under the Unfed Light itself, which thereafter sprang from the surface of the Book; this had remained ever since, unharmed, unscorched. The wonderful writer had placed it there in sight of all the people who could enter the new Temple built in place of the old one. As he did so, he said:

"Hearken unto me. This is my law. Behold it also written on the Maxin-Stone. No man shall remove it, lest he die. Yet after centuries have flown, behold! The Book shall disappear in sight of a multitude, and no man shall know its place. Then shall the Unfed Light go out, and no man will be able to rekindle it. And when these things have come to pass, lo!

The day is not far off when the land shall no more be. It shall perish because of its iniquity, and the waters of Atlantis shall roll above it! I have spoken."

Once, in the history of Poseid, a Rai had come to doubt whether a man would surely die if he tried to withdraw the Book of the Unfed Light. He conceived the idea that as the Maxin sprang from the top of the Book alone, and not from its sides, that removal might be possible. So therefore he forced a malefactor to attempt the deed, fearing after all to try it himself, although in the tyrannous policy which he followed, he cared not whether the man died or not. That was a day of growing darkness and wickedness, when men had somewhat forgotten the Great Rai, Son of Incal. The unhappy wretch was made to grasp the Book, and withdraw it if he could. He found it impossible to move it, but yet was not destroyed by the Maxin. Grown bolder, and urged by the Rai, he tried harder. He pulled, and then his grasp gave way, and one hand passed through the Maxin. The member was instantly destroyed, cut off, gone, while the monarch, standing many feet distant, fearful of approaching near, was stricken in that same instant by an out-leaping flash of the Maxin, and no one ever saw him again!

That one example was sufficient! The error of their ways suddenly became very apparent to the evildoers, and administration of the laws was again in accord with their spirit, as with their letter. The day of the "Dismal Prophecy" had been looked for as the decades passed into centuries, but its time was not yet come, and though many alarmists set days when it would surely come, it came not, and the Unfed Light continued. According to the law, bodies of all souls which had passed into Navazzamin were cremated. This even included some animals. Those dying at a distance from Caiphul were incinerated in some one of the multitude of Navamaxa (furnaces especially for dead bodies) which the government provided all through the provinces, and if the incinerated body was that of a human being the ashes were taken to Caiphul and cast into the Maxin, as a ceremonial act. Those of the departed from Caiphul were taken as they lay in death to the Incalithlon, and being raised to the top of the Cube, were let fall face forward into the Unfed Light. In either case, whether as incinerated ashes or unaltered forms, the result was the same; that is, while there was no flaming, no smoke, no tremor of the Maxin, nevertheless the instantaneous disappearance of the object occurred at the second of contact with the marvelous Unfed Fire. Hence it had been sung by poets as the "Gateway" to the country which each soul must discover for itself. To die, without in some manner passing into the Maxin, either in corpus personae or by the ashes from prior incineration, was thought to be the most frightful calamity by the greater number of the people.

It might appear that people of such scientific erudition would not be so seemingly childish in religious conceptions as this. But truly, it was not childishness. Instead, it was an insistence upon such entire destruction of the earthly casket of the soul as to render certain the freedom of the real person from all earthly restraint in entering into Navazzamin.

Not that many people understood the esoteric significance of the rite; no, they but understood so much of the real meaning as the Incali had given them through comparing the earth-leaving soul to the seed which, sprouting, leaves behind it every fragment of the shell.

To return to the Incalithlon and the ceremonial of my adoption by Prince Menax.

As we stood beside the Maxin-Stone, Gwauxln bade me kneel, and then, placing his hand upon my head, spoke, saying:

"In harmony with the laws of the land, made and provided in such cases, Astika Menax, a Councilor of the land of Poseid, wishes to adopt you, Zailm Numinos, for a son unto his name, in place of one departed from here into Navazzamin. Therefore, as your Sovereign and his, I, Gwauxln, Rai of Poseid, do declare it to be as prayed for by Astika Menax."

The Incaliz completed the ceremonies by placing his right hand upon my head and his left upon that of Menax as we knelt before him, and invoking the blessing of Incal upon us both. As he removed his hands, he addressed me thus:

"Be you upstanding in the sight of Incal, that no man may accuse you truthfully. Do this, and your days shall be long. But even as you shall fail, so then shall your time be shortened. May the peace of Incal be with you."

Not one of the three hearers of the Incaliz understood him to mean that my days would be short because I would fail in righteousness, but the words were taken only as a warning. Yet I knew afterwards, all too late, what prescience guided Mainin in his words. Knew in a flood of bitter memory, which recalled how disloyal I had been to the high resolve on Pitach Rhok to be successful, as a result of being true to my divine, God-considering selfhood. But all this came, as I thought, too late. Too late was it, when I lay in a dungeon awaiting death, from which no mortal could save me, and dreamed that my soul sat on a lifeless shore looking across a limitless ocean and crying, "Ah! Where is the hope of my years!" Bitter and fiery was the remorseful agony, but my name was still on the Book of Life; still there, and not erased as I feared. Karma is inexorable and severe, my brother, my sister; but our Savior has said: "Follow Me." "He that has an ear to hear, let him hear." "Be doers of the word, and not hearers only."

As we turned away, an Incala, who had been present, began playing on the great organ of the temple; then the silences of the vast auditorium responded as no human voice could make them do.

"On the winds the bells' deep tones are swelling—"

The echoes rang again and again as the thundering voices of the great organ pealed forth, thrilling the soul with its mighty harmony. Rays of many-hued lights, some brilliant, some soft-tinted as those of a spectroscopic image of the moon, played from point to point in exhausted air-tubes, and as the colors changed, so did the notes of music, for every ray of light, whatsoever its source, is a pulsing choral note, if developed rightly. Thus the stars sing.

The Rai did not go with Menax and myself when the conclusion of our business was reached, but remained with the Incaliz Mainin. With him Gwauxln was more familiar, his friendship more deeply intimate than with any other human being. And the reason was that both he and Mainin were Sons of the Solitude and had been youths together in the days before public favor had marked the one for Rai, the other for

Incaliz, these both being elective positions, the office of High Priest being the only ecclesiastical office which could be filled by popular vote. And this exception was because it was considered true justice to allow the people to consult their own desires in this matter of choosing one whom all believed to be the most eminently good and perfect example of moral life, to be over them in this highest spiritual office.

But in the days of their youth neither had seemed to expect the preferment which the years had in store, and after the long course required of Xio Incali at the Xioquithlon, both had bidden the world of men adieu and had gone forth into the solitudes of the vast mountains, where only the Sons of Incal had abode, of all mankind. These men were the Theochristic or Occult Adepts of that olden age, the Yog-Vidya of their time. They were indeed guardedly careful of their wisdom, then as now; but to Gwauxln and Mainin they imparted it generously. They had no families then, nor do these students of God, of Nature, deviate now from the same celibate principles. None who hope to achieve their deep knowledge will mate. ₁

After years had flown, so many that men had almost forgotten them, Gwauxln and Mainin did what few had ever been known to do—returned to the haunts of ordinary humanity. My father, Menax, had been but a babe when Gwauxln went away, and the latter's sister was not then born. Yet when Gwauxln came back, the silvery threads of age already gleamed in the hair of the Prince Menax, while as for the Rai that was to be, he looked a little more mature, but otherwise unchanged from the youthful semblance of the days of yore. In the interim, his sister had come to the world, grown to womanhood, wedded Menax, and after bringing into life their son, Soris, and their daughter, Anzimee, had gone into the undiscovered country through the Maxin gateway. Mainin, too, was of a similarly youthful appearance.

Both of these "Sons of the Solitude" came back, giving as their reason for return that their presence was needed, and both were eventually chosen by the people to fill the respective positions which we have seen them occupying, positions rendered vacant by the death of the incumbents. It is only now, after twelve thousand years have slipped into eternity through the back door of time,   that I have come to know how much Mainin had to do with those events, and how wholly in the dark concerning his real character was Gwauxln and every other Son of the Solitude. Not to anticipate, is it strange that Rai-Gwauxln felt more pleasurable intimacy possible in his intercourse with Mainin than with any other person connected with his daily life? Or that he felt his finally exposed treachery more keenly than any one else could? I think not.

Footnotes

137:1 I, Cor. vii., 3, 4, 5, 7, 8, 9, 29, 31, 32.

CHAPTER XV. A MATERNAL DESERTION

On leaving my farm home that morning, I had told my mother all that had transpired, and said that she should have an escort to the palace, where, after my recent change of fortune, I expected her to go and live, in accordance with the instructions of Menax.

What an anomalous position was this. Here was I, son by adoption of one of the Imperial Princes, and by virtue of being recognized brother of his daughter, Anzimee, I was a nephew of my sister's uncle, Rai Gwauxln. Yet my mother was not related to any of these royalties, and had seen none of them, except the Rai, often enough to enable her to be sure of recognition should she meet them again. But I rejoiced when I thought of the opportunities she would presently have of more intimate acquaintanceship.

Having sent the promised escort for her, what was my surprise on returning to the palace at learning from my father that, instead of coming, she had sent a message in writing. I hastily broke the seal and read, in her fine Poseidic chirography, the simple command:

"Zailm, come to me. PREZZA NUMINOS."

I went. Somehow an icy feeling of apprehension was in my heart, a presentiment of something harrowing. When I arrived at the house, my mother, looking, as I thought, rather pale, said:

"My son, I cannot go to the palace. I have no desire to do so. I am overjoyed at your success in life; live then, in your high place. I may

174

not go with you. You are easy in the midst of noble society, but I could never be so. Perhaps you will say that for me you will give it up and remain with me. Do not do so. Lest you feel thus, it is best that you should endure the pain of knowing now rather than later. Listen: I have cared for you during the years of infancy and boyhood, and seen you arrive at man's estate. You need not this burden now. I will go back to the home of the mountains.''

"Mother, talk not so!'' I interrupted.

"Hear me through, Zailm! I will go back to the mountains with my husband, he whom thou know not, a good man, a lover before I married your father, and whom, having wedded this morning, the notice of it has doubtless by this time been published abroad. An Incala, who came past very opportunely, performed the simple ceremony. My other husband, your father, I loved not, but did detest, for it was a marriage arranged by my parents against my will, but alas! With my consent, fool that I was to give it! You are the fruit of that union, and to me came unwanted. For your father was disliked, abhorred, but dying, left you heritor, not of my dislike, that were too unjust, but, must I say it? an object of indifference. I have not been a lacking mother, for, as a matter of pride, I concealed my feelings. In a way I even love you; I love my friends; it is nothing deeper. I have now to bid you goodbye, having said which it is necessary to—''

I heard no more, for I had fallen unconscious upon the floor. Was this the mother I had idolized? For whom I had striven so hard in the earlier years and later, in Caiphul, before a new object to work for arose and led me from there with greater determination in the form of a double ideal, love of mother and love of Anzimee. O Incal! My God! O my God!

At last I came out of the horrid dream into which, without regaining consciousness after my swoon, I had passed, a heated nightmare of brain fever.

"Mother!''

As I uttered the loved word, Astika Menax, who sat by my bedside, turned away, his eyes brimming with tears.

"Nay, Zailm, be not troubled! You have been ill near unto death with brain fever these two weeks. I will tell you everything, tomorrow, perhaps. You came very close to going to await me in the Shadowy Land; but not long would you have had to wait, my light, for it would have been but a little while before I rejoined you, lad!"

Tho story is not long. My mother, being told that good care should aid her in nursing me, said that she would not remain at all, as she doubted not that the skilled care of Menax's private physician could do as well, or better, for me than she. Therefore she had gone with her husband to their mountain home. From the hour in which Menax told me this, at the cost of much pain to himself, the subject was dropped, and never again referred to by anyone.

Once, when I went near to the place of my birth, and sent a messenger to ask if I was welcome, he came back to my vailx and said that a man met him at the door. To him the message was given, and he said: "Say to your master that my wife bids him come." I went, but could see that she would rather I had not come. She gave me her hand, but did not offer to kiss me, as a mother is wont to do. Her manner—but spare me details of this last meeting and last time I ever saw my Poseid mother. She acted wisely in not going to the palace, constituted as she was; it is a painful subject; let it be dropped.

As soon as my health permitted me to go on my mission to Suernis, which was not until the new year had begun at the Xioquithlon, from attendance at which the Xiorain forbade me until the next year, Prince Menax took me to his private office.

"The Xiorain has ordered wisely," said Menax. "Oh! These younger minds, they are full of promise for the future! No scheme was ever better than this in which the students govern themselves, and on all questions concerning educational matters, even to the distribution and use of the educational funds provided by the government and the selection of tutors, their word is law."

On the table in Menax's office stood a lovely vase of malleable glass, into which, while fused, powder of gold, silver and other colored metals were mixed, together with certain chemicals which rendered the whole of various degrees of translucency, from nearly opaque to perfect transparency, the various ranges affecting the metals as well as the glass, and appearing in different parts of the same object. The beauty was not second to the value of the costly product. Menax pointed to the tall vase, and I read upon it this inscription, formed with rubies:

"To Ernon, Rai of Suern, I, Gwauxln, Rai of Poseid, return this in token of your appreciation of the Poseidi."

If any reader desires to see a facsimile of the original legend in Poseid chirography, the desire is here granted:

Turning from the vase, I asked:

"When shall I go upon this mission, my father?"

"As early as health and convenience permit, Zailm."

"Then be it the day after tomorrow."

"It is well. Take any company you may choose. There are none who cannot get leave of absence from the Xiorain, I think, should you wish fellow students for companions; at least they can probably obtain a vacation of a month, and you will scarcely care to stay longer than thirty-three days. Take also this signet ring, whereby I delegate you my deputy, being confident of your discretion in its use; its powers are those of Minister of Foreign Business. And take escort of courtiers, also."

To this I replied that I would not take a retinue, such as a staff of officers, since from the story of Astiku Lolix, I judged Rai Ernon to be one who would look with scorn upon such a useless appendage. This pleased Menax greatly, and he proudly said:

"Zailm, your language pleases me! I see you are wisely politic, and that you do consider well the probable quirks of those with whom you have dealings."

The Secrets Of Mount Shasta And A Dweller On Two Planets

During my illness Anzimee had shown much solicitude, and as I learned from the regular nurses, all the while I was outside the realm of consciousness, she had permitted no one else to care for me except when she was utterly fatigued, and not long then. As I convalesced, her presence was not bestowed upon me except at intervals. I took advantage of one of these visits to let her know that I was aware of her kindness during my delirium. She flushed, then said:

"You know that I am studying the science of therapy; what better chance to experiment could an eager student have than what you furnished me?"

"Yea, verily," I answered, but felt that there was a deeper reason than the experimental inclination, and that the indulgence in the latter was extremely, lovingly cautious!

To Anzimee I outlined a plan for getting the greatest possible amount of pleasure from my trip, after the state business at Ganje, the capital city of Suernis, should have been attended to. It was three years since I had been away from Caiphul to any greater distance than going to Marzeus involved. I showed her the route I intended to take; together we scanned the map, and I pointed out that from Caiphul on the extreme western cape of Poseid, my course would be east by north across the continent, the intervening ocean beyond it and between that point and further land. Then still on east across the country of Necropan, which country, now called Egypt, Abyssinia, etc., then embraced the entire continent of Africa, one government similar to that of Suern, and was inhabited by a people of similar powers, but not nearly so far advanced.

Africa was then not more than half its present size, while Suernis, which also embraced all of Asia, was much different from what it is to-day, but was a name more distinctive of the peninsula of Hindustan. Leaving Necropan, the route would be across the sea to India, or, as we knew the names, across the "Waters of Light" (in reference to their phosphorescence) to Suernis. From Ganje, capital of Suernis, our course was still eastward across the Pacific Ocean, as it is now named, to our colonies in America, called "Incalia" by us, because in that far, exactly opposite land, the Sun, Incal, was fabled as making his bed by that epic previously mentioned as the basis of Atlantean folklore.

From Southern Incalia, (modern Sonora) I intended to go northwards and skim hastily over the desolate ice-fields of the arctic regions. What is now Idaho and Montana, Dakota, Minnesota, and the Dominion of Canada were then covered with vast glaciers, the rear-guard of the glacial epoch, which was slowly retreating, very slowly, even in so late a day, geologically speaking, as the days of Atlantis, reluctant to end its frigid reign. The trip could thus be made to afford novel and pleasing contrasts-tropical, semitropical, temperate and frigid.

"Would our father object to my going also, Zailm?" asked Anzimee, wistfully. "I have not been away from Caiphul in five years.

"Indeed, no, little girl. He bade me invite whosoever should please me, and I know of no person who pleases me more than you. I have already asked a goodly company of our common friends."

So Anzimee went also. When everything was arranged, our party consisted of nearly a score of young people congenial to each other, a couple of officers of the staff of Menax, with the necessary servants and conveniences for a month's absence. Our vailx was of the middle traffic-size, these vessels being made in four standard lengths: number one, about twenty-five feet; number two, eighty feet; number three, something like one hundred and fifty-five feet, while the largest was yet two hundred feet longer than the third size. These long spindles were in fact round, hollow needles of aluminum, formed of an outer and an inner shell between which were many thousands of double T braces, an arrangement productive of intense rigidity and strength. All the partitions made other braces of additional resistant force. From amidships the vessels tapered toward either end to sharp points. Most vailxi were provided with an arrangement allowing, when desired, an open promenade deck at one end. Windows of crystal, of enormous resistant strength, were in rows like portholes along the sides, a few on top, and others set in the floor, thus affording a view in all directions. I might mention that the vailx which I had selected for our vacation trip was fifteen feet and seven inches in its greatest diameter.

At the appointed time (the first hour of the third day, as agreed with

Menax) my invited guests assembled at the palace, from the roof of which we were to take our departure. How careful I was of my lovely sister, and how proud of her beauty.

The princess Lolix, whom we had ever treated as a guest at Menaxithlon, came up to the platform where the ship lay, curious to see our preparations for departure. It seemed ever new to her to behold an aerial vessel leave terra firma. Not that anything of her wonder was expressed; she made it a point of pride to appear surprised at nothing, however novel or marvelous it might really be to her experience. Indeed, hers was a calm, even temperament, not easily aroused. I had not, in the five or six weeks since hearing her story, again seen her exhibit so much of any sort of emotion as she had that evening when I had observed that my attentions to Anzimee disturbed the Saldu, and I knew that the effect must be deep because of her inability to keep its appearance wholly secret. Considering that we were bound for Suernis, Lolix was not invited to go, as she otherwise might have been. But I did not forget to bid her a cordial and respectful farewell.

The current keys were set, and, just as the vailx trembled slightly before leaving the roof, Menax sprang upon the deck, thereby considerably astonishing me, for I had no idea that he intended accompanying us. In reality he did not, but to all questions he preserved a smiling silence.

Long as was our silver-white spindle, we had soon risen so high as to make us seem a mere speck to people on the earth beneath. Then for half an hour we flew at moderate speed through the high abyss, when a young lady called attention to an approaching vailx, following in our wake. Prince Menax, seated in a deck chair by my side, looked over the rail at the surface, more than two miles beneath, then he drew his heavy fur cape more closely about his shoulders, looked back over the hundred miles, more or less, of our course already covered in the half hour, and remarked that the other vailx was rapidly gaining on us.

"Shall I give orders to the vailx-man to increase speed, that we may enjoy a race?" I asked of the company, which, clad in arctic clothing, was occupying the passing time in sightseeing round about us on the open deck.

"Nay, not so, my son," said Menax.

I said no more, for it at that moment dawned upon me that the pursuer followed us by the prince's order.

Menax now arose, bade the company goodbye and a pleasant trip, and then, Anzimee having arisen also, he put his arm about her and came back to me. As I stood up he passed his free arm around me and thus we stood for some moments. Then releasing us, he ordered the two deck men to throw grapples across to the other vessel, which at that moment grated alongside. The next instant he stepped on board the other vailx and signed to loose grapples. Thus we parted, high above the green earth, two miles beneath, he to return, we to go onwards.

CHAPTER XVI. THE VOYAGE TO SUERN

Before us lay a pleasure trip during which we would travel many thousands of miles. We proceeded slowly when we came above the base of the huge bulk of Pitach Rhok, the mighty mountain, and ascended somewhat, so that we should be on a level with its high point. When at the place, nothing would suit the company except a stop on the summit, and together we all placed foot in the snows on the pitach, which thing was done chiefly to please Anzimee, who said that the place was very interesting on account of what had there happened to me.

Then, again, we were under way, descending from the higher altitudes in order to better view the thickly inhabited, though mountainous, country beneath us, between Pitach Rhok and east Poseid.

At the approach of sunset a dull roar arose to the ear, and soon the long white shore of old ocean flashed beneath a moment, and in a little time was far behind, with the waters, lead color in the twilight, beneath, behind, before and on both sides, no land in sight, and over one thousand miles east the country of Necropan. Without going at a full rate of speed, we could not expect to be above that land in less than two or three hours. But as it would be dark before reaching it, we slackened speed to a hundred and fifty miles per hour, closed the deck and went into the salon, where incandescent lamps lit up the darkening night-glooms.

A trip by vailx could never prove so monotonous as a journey in even the fastest of ocean steamships so often is today. The variety of scenery, the wide views possible, for altitude was dependent wholly on pleasure, the external cold being unheeded by people who sat in a parlor warmed by means from Navaz and furnished with air of the proper density by the same Night-Side forces—all this tended to prevent ennui. Then too, the rapid transit changed the aspect of things beneath so fast that the spectator, looking backwards, gazed upon a dissolving view. As an aside, the currents derived from the Night-Side of Nature permitted the attainment of the same speed as that of the daily rotation of the earth, *e. g.*: supposing we were at an altitude of ten miles, and the time the instant of the sun's meridian; at that meridian moment we could remain indefinitely, bows on, while the earth revolved beneath, at approximately seventeen miles every minute. Or, the reverse direction keys could be set, and our vailx would speed away from where it was meridian on the surface beneath, at the same almost frightful rate, frightful to one unused to it, as my reader is now, but one day will not be, if, as I hope, he or she will live to see vailxi rediscovered. Nor need the life be a very long one before then.

While we had such preventives of boredom, we lacked not commoner means of enjoyment. We had our naima, in the mirrors and vibrators of which our friends, however distant, could appear in image of form and of voice, life-sized and with undiminished vocal volume. The salons of the great passenger vailxa had libraries, musical instruments, and potted plants, amongst the flowers of which birds similar to the modern domestic canary darted about.

At about the tenth hour it was reported that Necropan was beneath, and at this surprising information, because at the speed I had ordered, we should have been at least six hours longer in coming to that country, I enquired of the vailxman his reason for increasing speed without orders. No good reason being given, I severely reprimanded the conductor, and ordered that a descent be made to terra firma, in order that we might travel by day over the Wasted Land, as our word Sattamund may be translated, which is the Sahara desert of today. This great wade some of our party had never seen, and to allow them the privilege we settled down to spend the night on an elevated ridge, high enough to be above malarious influences, for we were near where modern Liberia lies.

"The proud bird—The Condor of the Andes, That can sail thro' heaven's unfathomable depths, Or brave the fury of the northern hurricane, And bathe his plumage in the Thunder's home, Furls his broad wings at nightfall, and sinks down, To rest upon his mountain crag."

Though we called it Sattamund, or the Wasted Land, yet it was not such an arid region then as it is now. Water, if not as abundant as it was in Poseid, was abundant enough to give a wealth of tropical trees of the hardier sorts, sufficient at least to hide the nakedness of the slopes and hills of that old seabed. There were even a few saline lakes there, broad and blue, and it was around these that the population was centered. But the same dread catastrophe that overtook fair Poseid laid its terrible hand upon Necropan, and its beauty of lush greenery went out from the land, because the geological changes withdrew all the water from the surface, and hid it so that only artesian augers could find it. The same mighty upheaval tore the rocks through and through in Southwest Incalia, and today there is in that arid region scenery most fantastic, weird past the power of my pen to describe, where flows the Rio Gila, the Colorado, and Colorado Chiquita. But I will reserve the description, and when it is given it shall be in other words than mine, so that you and I, my friend, shall together have the pleasure of enjoying a fine word-painting.

In Poseid and Suern, and wherever civilization extended its scepter, it was the universal law, and mankind's pleasure, to obey the heavenly mandate which the general accordance with the solar life spirit taught us required the planting, instead of careless rejection, of seeds of goodly flower or fruit, for shade, for beauty, for utility, wherever it happened that a favorable spot offered, either in the habitats of man or in the virgin wilderness. Indeed, in such trips as our party was then taking, it was a matter of religious significance to take great quantities of seeds and to scatter them from the vailx-decks at nightfall, both as an offering to Incal, as His sublime symbol set in the west, and also that the dews of night might ensure germination, and this ceremony was also held to be an acknowledgment of the Goddess of Increase, Zania.

Thus the wilds came to bloom as the rose; and today the world is the inheritor of that sowing of seed; the indigenous cereals, the wheat, for the origin of which many ingenious but insufficient theories have been put forth, and the varieties of palms that make the tropics famed for the grace of their cocoas and dates, and every genera of the Chamaerops. And these things are because man, woman and child found pleasure in that olden time in "planting seed by the wayside." Go you and do like-wise, that the waste places may become full of beauty and be a joy forever. All hail to Arbor Days, which fulfill the injunction of Christ; they will surely make a return, and some a hundredfold. A small pocket now and then will hold many a seed for planting, and though you do not heed its sort, so that it be goodly, yet the Father has said, "It shall bring forth after its kind."

THE STORM

The morning dawned clear and cloudless and was altogether so delightful that we attempted scarcely any forward progress, moving slowly in order that the deck might be uncovered and the company allowed to sit out in the fresh air and warm sunshine.

Down below, a couple of thousand feet at most, we saw, through good glasses, various forms of human, animal, bird and plant life; and sounds came up to us in drowsy, musical monotone, as our vailx hovered above. Towards evening the winds began to blow, rendering it unpleasant to remain so near the ground. The repulse-keys were set, and presently we were so high in the air that all about our now closed ship were cirrus clouds, clouds of hail held aloft by the up-rushing of the winds, severe enough to have been dangerous had our vessel been propelled by wings or fans or gas reservoirs. But as we derived from Nature's Night-Side or, in Poseid phrase, from Navaz, our forces for propulsion as well for repulsion, or levitation, therefore our long, white, aerial spindles feared no storm, however severe.

As the windows, being frosted over, obscured our view, and as the night promised furious weather, we had the help of books, music and conversation with one another, and, through the naim, with our friends at home in faraway Poseid. No authority had Murus (Boreas) over the currents from Navaz. The evening had not far advanced when it was suggested that the storm would most likely be heavier, and the wind wilder nearer the earth, and so the repulse-keys were set to a fixed degree, making nearer approach to the ground than was desirable impossible as an accidental occurrence. We might, if it were generally agreeable, take advantage of our privilege and enjoy the sensation of being in the midst of the storm, ourselves safe and under full speed,

"And brave the fury of the Northern hurricane."

The partial novelty might make us sleep better, when, the evening passed, we should have gone to our staterooms. I, therefore, approved the plan, and gave orders to the conductor to descend to a height of about twenty-five hundred feet. Down we dropped. Our lights were made low in order to produce a partial gloom, the better to enjoy the full fierceness of the tempest, and we sat near the windows where we could hear, if not see. To the eye, nothing would have appeared outside except entire blackness; to the ear, the loud beating of the rain upon the metal shutters was plainly, delightfully apparent. Against the sharp points of prow and stem the wind howled and shrieked like an army of demons. At times when the vailx was struck, broadside by some counterblast, it would careen and tremble, but it kept on its way, determined as a thing of life. The experience was enjoyable, if not entirely novel, for it spoke to us of the power of man over matter, and taught us of the things of God, Incal to us, Master of all things and of ourselves, who by Him had this authority over the elements. When the sensation had become monotonous the lights were increased to proper brightness; again we turned to books and games and music, as we once more sought the upper regions of the atmosphere, which were quieter compared with those of the half-mile plane.

Anzimee and a girl companion sat apart from the rest of the company in a retreat formed of flowering vines draped across one corner of the main salon. In a short time she came from her nook to where I sat, wrapped in meditative obliviousness. Touching my shoulder as she came close, she said:

"Zailm, you sing; it would please me if you would take your lute and come to where Thirtil and myself have chosen seats, and sing to us."

She bent over my shoulder, blushing slightly, looking so altogether lovely that I simply sat and gazed in silent appreciation of her beauty.

The Secrets Of Mount Shasta And A Dweller On Two Planets

"Come, Zailm, will you?"

I arose promptly enough when I saw a shade of disappointment cross her face, as she interpreted my silence to mean unwillingness, and I said:

"Lo, Anzimee, I am but too pleased to comply, but how could I move?"

Without suspicion, she asked:

"Move? And why not?"

"Have you ever seen a bright hummingbird," I replied, "which, poised at a flower beside you, you kept still, almost afraid to breathe, lest it be alarmed to flight? Even so I could not move, lest—"

"There, there now! If I were not used to reading one's earnestness or other emotions in the eyes, I would say you are a sad flatterer. But, come."

"What shall I sing, little friend?" I asked of Thirtil, a demure, sweet little maiden, an art student, half-serious, half-frivolous in temperament.

"Oh, you ask me? Well, something, something," with a mischievous glance at Anzimee, "from your heart!" she laughingly replied. Anzimee blushed, but made no other sign, merely dropping her long lashes as I looked at her, while I said, "Truly! Then from my heart, this." (a popular favorite, by the way):

"Before the heart can know its own, Before the doubts of life are over, Love in our hearts must have grown, To the heights of heaven's shore. Truly, love is sought in vain, In other place than in the heart; True love always hath its pain, When from purity we part. May we cease from every strife, While in lovely verse enshrining Incal's blessing in our life; With His peace it ever entwining. So is melody divine, When the music of the soul; It is betrothing yours and mine, While the centuries unroll. Yet our hearts are young and gay, Seeking ever fairest bowers Where shall bloom from day to day, All the beauty of the flowers. There is one of all the rest, That alone for me is blooming; Deep the tendrils in my breast, Find forever their entombing. Shall I pluck it while in bloom, Ready for the gardener's gleaning? Could I take forever home What, unto me, is no dreaming? Yea, beloved, we shall rejoice In His bless-ing evermore; Listening to the gentle voice, That as One—we do adore."

Thus it was within the vailx, song and pleasure; outside was the storm, risen up after us. Into the teeth of the furious gale plunged our long spindle, giving no outward sign, even had any one been there to see, of the light and warmth, laughter and song, of the human freight and songbirds within its staunch shell, amidst the flowers, a drifting bit of the tropics, safe from wintry blasts. No sign, except for only the gleam of the crimson fore and aft lights.

While the others retired for the night to their various staterooms, I remained in the vacated salon until the announcement was made to me that we were above Suernis. No landing could be made, however, in the face of a gale blowing eighty miles an hour; such an attempt would have resulted in being dashed to pieces the instant we reached the ground.

In order that we might be wholly out of the range of the influence of the storm, I gave directions to rise above the level of the disturbance, if such a region of calm existed within reach, and there set the keys so as to stop all propulsion. Receiving this order, the conductor increased the repulsion force by means of the levers of degree, and we rose steadily up, up, up—above the clouds, above the rush of the hurricane, into a clear, calm atmosphere, intensely cold, almost thirteen miles from the earth's surface. Could we have had a view unobstructed by storm clouds, we were just about high enough to afford us a horizon of three hundred and fifty miles. Soon after this order I went to my room to bed. With the morning the storm had not decreased in fury; and occasional flurries in the air above us proved that the storm-area on the surface must be of vast extent. The cold outside was too intense to consider, even for an instant, the opening of the deck; the sky was almost black in the depth of its blueness; the sun, shorn of much of its dazzling brightness, appeared strangely dim, and the stars were visible. The steady motion of the air-dispensers as their wheels and pistons worked to maintain the interior air at a normal pressure was painfully apparent in the awful stillness, while the fizz of the air escaping through the fine crevices around the windows and edges of the deck made such a noise that I ordered the setscrews tightened and the ventilator pipes opened. Had the frost not hindered vision through the windows and, with the clouds, prevented a view of the earth's surface, a sight most peculiar would have been presented. The view toward the extended horizon would have made the apparent union of earth and sky seem almost on a level with us; but directly beneath, the fundamental separation from the solid globe would have seemed, not like a ball but like a huge bowl, ornamented with landscape scenes in its interior. As, however, we could not see, our songs, our reading, and our conversation went on, while the very faint beams of Incal, coming through the frosted glass, were supplemented by the same knowledge which gave us heat and air and position, to defy the cold and the rarefaction and gravitation—knowledge of Navaz.

At home in Poseid there was no storm, but Menax, at the naim, told us that the weather office anticipated one, the same one which we at that moment were waiting to see end. We waited until the sun set in the west and came in sight in the east twice.

Several times the Saldu appeared at the end of the salon, seeming in the mirror of the naim as real and present as if, in truth, a third of the globe did not separate us. Once, only, she spoke, and then in a whisper to me, as I stood near the naim:

"When, my lord, will you return home? A month? It is long, it is long!"

A report of even the smallest events of our trip was furnished to the news office, and was printed upon the discs of the public vocaligraphs, to use a word of modern sound, and long before any landing was effected by us on the soil of Suernis our fellow countrymen were acquainted with the story of our enforced suspension between heaven and earth while waiting for the storm to end. Speaking of the vocaligraph leads me to remark that the social superstructure of Poseid was maintained upon the broad basis of equitable laws laid down by the great Rai of the Maxin-time through the influence of free speech as made and molded by church and school, and expressed through the millions of vocaligraphs, the three rendering secure the integral homes which, gathered together, formed the nation.

At last the storm king withdrew his forces and the time had come for our descent. Down we swept from the vault of heaven, into Ganje, capital city of Suern. Have you ever been in the ancient and long-deserted city of Petra of Seir? That very peculiar city at the foot of Mount Hor, a city hollowed from the living rock? Quite likely not, for the followers of Mahomet make it hard to visit the place. But if you have read about it, then you have some idea of Ganje, in old Suerna, built in the cliffs of the river banks.

Such details regarding the manner of our reception are too trivial to fill this record. Suffice it that it was suited to the friendly international relations of Suern and Poseid, and to my station and rank as a high deputy. Rai Ernon was far less interested in the vase, and in the other gifts of gold and gems, than in the captive Saldani whom the tokens commemorated, particularly in the Saldu, Lolix the Rainu. I was startled at the monarch's close knowledge of the whole affair in all its details, and of my sickness and other incidents which were not matters of public note; but I betrayed no such feeling, since it was but momentary and passed as soon as recollection of Ernon's wonderful occult powers came to me.

Speaking of the Saldui, but especially of Lolix, he said:

"I did not send the Chaldeans to Gwauxln as objects of lust, neither as a retributive punishment, that by exile from their native Chaldea they might atone to Suern for their fathers, sons, brothers, or husbands who worked harm to Suernis. No, doubtless they were not more to blame than is a tiger which has a similarly destructive nature, but by the laws of Yeovah we find that ignorance of the law never exempts a wrongdoer from penalty. Law says in regard to sin: 'Thou shalt not.' And the penalty lies alongside, inexorably, and is dealt out unsparingly for disobedience. Law, therefore, appears not to be retributive, but educational. Having felt the punishment, no one, either man or animal, is apt to try the error twice out of curiosity. Nature makes no penalty easy, saying: 'When you have learned, then the punishment shall be more severe.' If a babe fell over a cliff, its death would be the result, though its innocence knew nothing of sin, just as surely as a knowing man might meet the same fate deliberately. Now the Chaldean women needed to learn that conquest, bloodshed and pillage is a sin. The Chaldean nation needed a lesson also. It received it, in the death of its prize soldiery. But such examples need finish; a diamond in the rough is surely a diamond, but how much does the expert cutter of stones increase its beauty and value! Not to release those women to them was to that nation what the faceting is to a gem. Do you not think that I am right?"

"Even so, Rai," I responded.

For several days we remained in the capital, and during this time were escorted over it by no less a person than Rai Ernon himself.

It was a strange people, the Suerni. The elder people seemed never to smile, not because they were engaged in occult study, but because they were filled with wrath.

On every countenance seemed to rest a perpetual expression of anger. Why, I pondered, should this thing be? Is it a result of the magical abilities they possess? By what seems to us of Poseid mere authori-

192

zation of will these people appear to transcend human powers and set at nothing the immutable laws of nature, though it cannot be said that Incal has not limited them as surely as He has limited our chemists and physicists. The Suerni never lift their hands in manual labor, they sit at the breakfast or the supper table without having previously put upon it anything to eat, or elsewhere prepared a repast; they bow their heads in apparent prayer, and then, lifting up their eyes, begin to eat of what has mysteriously come before them—of wholesome viands, of nuts, of all manner of fruits, and of tender, succulent vegetables! But meat they eat not, nor much that is not the finished product of its source, containing in itself the germ for future life. Has Incal exempted them from His authority as Creator of the world, which all men suffer, "In the sweat of your face shall you eat bread?" It is less burdensome, certainly, on those who walk His paths, or even those who partly do so, and whose rule of life is continence. Such are more powerful, have occult powers that no eater of meats can ever hope to attain, but surely they are not wholly exempt; it must be somewhat difficult to perform such magic feats as these. No one ever got something for nothing. These people gaze upon the foes who come to menace them in their homes—and they are not!

"It passed o'er the battle plain, where sword and spear and shield flashed in the light of midday—and the strength of crowded together hosts is shivered, and the grass, green from the soil of carnage, waves above the crushed and moldering skeleton."

What Poseida could do these things? Rai Gwauxln, Incaliz Mainin, but no more, at least none known to the public even by repute. But no man of all Atlantis had ever witnessed much display of such power on the part of either, and with the masses it was mere repute. I was favored beyond most Atlanteans in this respect.

I noticed in our visits in and about the capital a thing which cast a shadow over me, that his people did not love Ernon, however much they respected him and feared his power. That the Rai was aware of my knowledge of this dislike was obvious from his conversation.

"Ours is a peculiar people, prince," he said to me. "During many years, centuries even, it has had to reign over it rulers who come from the Sons of the Solitude. Each and every one has strived to train his subjects so as to fit some future generation for initiation, as an entire people, into the mysteries of the Night-Side of Nature, deeper than your people of Poseid have ever dreamed of going. To this end moral codes have been insisted upon as a coefficient of tuition in operative magic. But the effort has never produced the end sought; only here and there has an individual arisen and progressed; soon every one of these has fled away from the less energetic people and gone to the solitudes, to become one of the 'Sons' of whom you may have heard; generically we term these students 'sons'; specifically we would have to refer to them as 'sons' or 'daughters,' for sex is no bar to occult study."

It had long been a matter of interest to me to learn all I could of this band of Nature students, Incalenes, as they were sometimes called, from Incal, God, and "ene," to study. Thousands of years later, in the time of Jesus of Nazareth, these were called "Essenes." But Atlantis, which possessed such a wealth of literature, had, with a single exception, no books on the subject. In that exception, a little volume printed in ancient Poseidonic, the details were very meager; yet its perusal had been of great interest to me. As I now listened to Rai Ernon, my interest was reawakened, and I thought I might one day become a candidate for admission to the order, if—but that "if" was of a large size. If the study renders the student so wrathful in soul as I see the Suerni are, then I will have nothing to do with it. The seed was planted, however, and grew a little when I learned that the angry gloom was not due to occult study, except in the sense that the lower nature was rebellious against the purity of the study and cast up the mud of anger, rendering muddy and opaque the clear waters of the soul. It grew still more when the Rai remarked later on that "the girl Anzimee would one day be an Incalenu." But the growth was not great in that olden time; it was reserved for a life to come, when decades upon decades of centuries had flown, till now!

The Rai continued: "You of Poseid dip a little into the Night-Side, and behold! Out of it you gather forces which open the penetralia of the sea, and of the air, and subject the earth. It is well. But you require physical apparatus; without it you are nothing powerful. Those versed in occult wisdom need no apparatus. That is the difference between Poseid and Suernis. The human mind is a link between the soul and the physical. Every higher force controls all those lower. The mind operates through odic force, which is higher than any speed of physical nature; hence controls all nature, and does not need apparatus.

"Now I, and my brother 'Sons' before me, have strived to teach the Suerni the laws which govern the operation of this force. Through this knowledge Yeovah leads His children in strength. Hand in hand with this knowledge are physical acts, powers that come early in the study. So far have they gone, but will no farther go.

"Morality aids serenity of soul; hence it is profitable to the Incalene, above all things, to be moral. But man is an animal in his corporeal self, and the passions thereof are pleasant. Love is of twofold nature: love of God and of the Spirit, pure and undefiled, and love of sex, which may likewise be pure, though if the dominion of the animal in man be over it, and not so that of the human, it shall cause the man to sin, for then it is lust. I have sought that the Suerni may know the law, that they may be the masters, not the creatures, of circumstance. But because they know a few things of magic, and in the greater feats were aided by the 'Sons' dwelling amongst them, lo, they are content. And behold! They rebel against punishment on account of the lustful nature they do indulge, and curse me mightily because I exact obedience to the law, and penalty for the infraction thereof; and they curse my brother 'Sons' who do aid me, therefore is their wrath which it has so troubled you to witness. My people do things strange in your sight, O Poseida, yet have no wisdom why it is so, and work their wonders heedless of Yeovah. Therefore they are a brood of sorcerers, and do not work white magic, which is beneficent, but black magic, which is sorcery. It shall create for them great sadness. I would, O Zailm of Poseid, have taught these my people faith, hope, knowledge and charity, which make for a pure religion undefiled. Have I not done well? Gwauxln, my brother, have I not done well?"

Rai Ernon was sitting in the salon of the vailx, and now addressed Gwauxln of Poseid, whom I saw in the naim as I looked around.

"In truth, you have even so, my brother," said Gwauxln.

For some moments the noble ruler was silent, and I could see teardrops falling occasionally from beneath his closed eyelids. Then he opened his eyes and began a most touching rhetorical address to, and in some sort against, his people.

"Oh, Suernis, Suernis! I have given up my life for you! I have strived to lead you into Espeid (Eden), to teach you of its beauties, and you would not! I have tried to make you the vanguard of all nations and your name synonymous with justice and mercy and love of God, and how have you repaid me? I would be as a father to you, and you cursed me in your heart! Sharper than knives is ingratitude! I would have led you to the heights of glory, but you would rather lie in a wallow of ignorance, like swine, content to do what are marvels to other people, but yourself completely ignorant of their value. You are an infidel, ingrate race, believing not in Yeovah, content to live by the little you know, too slothful to learn, more ungrateful to Yeovah than to your Rai! O, Suernis, Suernis, you have cast me off and made my heart to bleed! I go. From your midst the 'Sons' go also, a mournful band of disappointed men. And you shall become few where you are many, a derision before men and a prey to the Chaldeans; yea, you shall dwindle and shall wait until the centuries—even ninety centuries, are fled into eternity. And in that day you shall suffer until the time of him who shall be called Moses. And of them it shall be said, 'They are the seed of Abraham.' And behold, even as now the Spirit of God is abroad in the land, immanent in the Sons of the Solitude, and you mock It, so in a remote day shall His spirit become manifest and shall incarnate as the Christ, and so shall the perfect human glow with the Spirit, and become First of the Sons of God. Yet you shall not even then know Him, but shall crucify Him; and your punishment shall go down the ages until that Spirit comes again in the hearts of those who follow Him, and finds you scattered to the four winds! Thus you shall be punished! From now until then shall you earn your bread by the sweat of your face. You shall no more have the regal power of defense, in case you use it for offense. I will no more restrain you. My people, oh, my people! Ungrateful! I forgive you, for you cannot know how I love you! I go. Oh! Suernis, Suernis, Suernis!"

The Secrets Of Mount Shasta And A Dweller On Two Planets

At the last word the noble ruler's voice lowered to a murmur, and he buried his tearful face in his hands and sat bowed in silent grief, except for a sigh of sorrow which once or twice he uttered. Several Suerni had heard his words, and these now left the vailx very quietly and went to the city.

"Rai ni Incal."

I turned to the naim as these words were uttered, and noted that a great shade of sadness rested upon the face of our own Rai, Gwauxln, as he looked upon Ernon—like himself, an Adept Son.

"Rai ni Incal, mo navazzamindi su," which being translated, is, "To Incal the Rai; to the country of departed spirits he is gone!"

Startled I looked around at the Suern Rai, who still sat silent as before, in the same position. I spoke to him, yet he gave no sign. Then I bent and gazed through his fingers into his fine gray eyes. They were set, indeed, and the breath of life was fled. Yea, truly, he had gone, even when he said "I go."

"Come to me, Zailm," commanded Gwauxln.

I went to the naim and stood waiting.

"Are your friends all within the vailx?"

"Yes, Zo Rai."

"Take then your guards and seek the palace of Rai Ernon. Call upon his ministers to come before you and tell them that their Rai is deceased. Tell them that you will take his body in charge and carry it to Poseid. Amongst the ministers are two elderly men and sedate; these are Sons. They are of that body of disappointed men who go forth from Suernis according to the words of Ernon. These two will know that you speak the truth when you say that Ernon of Suern has left his Raina in my hands to govern as I shall decide is most wise. But the others will not know and the Sons will leave to you the telling of the facts. Great shall be the anger of them that are not Sons, so that they shall try to destroy you by their terrible power, disliking to be told that they are deposed from authority. Nevertheless, do this and fear not; be of good cheer, for how shall a serpent bite if it hath lost its fangs?" When, according to these orders, I had the court before me, I spoke as directed by the Rai. It was received with a courteous smile by the two who by their demeanor I recognized as the Sons of the Solitude. But by the others great anger was shown.

"What! And you, Poseida, offer us such indignity? Our Rai is dead? We are pleased! But we, not you, will attend to the funeral rites. As to the government of Suern, we laugh with scorn! Be gone! We are our own masters. Leave us our ruler, and you, dog, leave this country!"

For reply I repeated with emphasis the assertion of my authority. I confess to having felt an inward fear when the brow of one of these never-smiling men clouded with intense anger, as he pointed his finger at me, and said:

"Then die!"

I did not outwardly shrink, though half expecting to perish on the spot. Neither did I feel any death tremor, though the menace, ever before fatal, was not withdrawn. Gradually the minister's fury gave place to surprise, and he dropped his arm, gazing at me in amazement. I ordered my guards to manacle and take him to the vailx. Then I said:

"Suern, your power is gone. Thus said Ernon. He has said that henceforth you shall earn your bread by the sweat of your face. Over this country Poseid shall rule. I, special envoy of Gwauxln VII, Rai of Poseid, do depose all you that are here from rulership, except those two who offered not scorn but courtesy. While they remain, which will not be long, I will make them governors over Suern. I have spoken."

Indeed, I had spoken, and that, to so great an extent, without authorization. I was in an agony of doubt lest Rai Gwauxln should rebuke me. But I would not reveal my real weakness to these ingrates. Instead, I took a roll of parchment and wrote from memory the form of commission of governors of provinces in Atlantis, appointing one of the Incaleni to the office. This I sealed with my name as envoy extraordinary, following that of Gwauxln as Rai, using red ink, for which I sent a messenger to Anzimee at the vailx. My reason for appointing one of the Sons as Governor was that only one would serve. The other chose to ask passage to Caiphul in my vailx. Then, giving the Governor his commission, a document which he received with the remark, "You are a man, indeed, no longer a boy"—words which, though so kindly meant, fell on heedless ears at the time, for as I made my return to the vailx I felt actually heartsick at what I feared had been the highest point of indiscretion on my part. I called for Rai Gwauxln, and when he responded I told him what I had done. He looked grave, and said merely the words:

"Come home."

Imagine now my distress. Not reprimanded, nor commended, but without any explanatory clue whatever, I was ordered home. Then it was that I sought Anzimee, and having found her in her stateroom I told her the whole story. Our Rai was known to be one who could be severe in his punishments, although these took the form of disgrace meted out, as public dismissal from office for being unworthy of trust. Anzimee was very pale, but said hopeful words:

"Zailm, I see only that you did right well. And yet, why was our uncle so gravely reticent? Let me give you a potion; lie here on this couch, and take what I give you."

She poured a few drops of some bitter drug, put in a little water, and handed the cup to me to drink from. Ten minutes later I was asleep.

Then she left the room and, as I afterwards learned, called her royal uncle to the instrument, where she laid the case before him. He was troubled at the effect of his words upon me, an effect not intended, as he told her, and one which would never have occurred if he had not at that time been engaged in solving the very complicated political problem presented by the new aspect of affairs through the decease of Rai Ernon. What further he said was: "Be not worried, because Zailm is called home for no purpose of punishment, since I am well satisfied and called him for quite another reason."

I slept for hours, and when I at last awakened, Anzimee, sitting beside me, told me all that Gwauxln had said. As it was then nearly nighttime, I decided to go to my own room and prepare for the evening meal. On the way I met the Son who was going to Caiphul with us. To this person it seemed a great novelty to travel as he was then doing, although his remarks on the subject were few.

It was, as I reflected upon it, something of a novelty to be piercing the air at the rate of seventeen miles each minute, a mile above the earth. I tried to fancy how it would seem to one like my passenger to be doing this thing; but after five years of familiarity with it as a means of travel, I had poor success in attaining a sense of his feelings concerning the experience.

As we traveled westward the sun seemed to remain as it was when we left Ganje, for its speed, or that of the earth, rather, was the same as our own. We had been on the way for five hours and had covered considerably over half of the distance home, the whole journey being something like seven thousand miles. The remaining two thousand miles would occupy some three hours for transit, a length of time which seemed to my impatient desire so long, that I paced the floor of the salon in extreme restlessness. I have seen, since the days of Poseid, a time when a vastly slower progress would have seemed swift, but then the past had a veil obscuring it so that comparison was impossible.

"Man never is, but always to be blest."

CHAPTER XVII. RAI NI INCAL—ASHES TO ASHES

On a casket in front of the Holy Seat, by the eastern face of the Maxin-Stone in the Incalithlon, lay all that was of the earth of Ernon of Suernis. In the triangle were gathered a few witnesses asked by Rai Gwauxln to be present, and over all shone the mysterious light which required no fuel, nor for its tall taper any human keeper. High above hung the white stalactite ceiling, casting down from its many points the radiance of the lights which no one could see from below.

"Close his eyes, his work is done."

Beside the restful form stood Mainin, the Incaliz, his hand on the shoulder of the dead Rai. After the mighty organ had sounded a mournful requiem, Mainin made the funeral speech, saying:

"Once more has a most noble soul known earth. How has it treated him who gave his life to the service of its children? Truly, Suerna, you have done a deed which shall clothe you in sackcloth and ashes for aye! Ernon, my brother, Son of the Solitude, we bid you adieu in great sorrow of soul; sorrow not for you, for you are at rest; but for us left behind. It shall be many years before we know you again incarnate. As for this, your poor clay, over it we will say final words, for it has done its work and is committed to Navazzamin. Ernon, brother, peace be with you forevermore."

Again the mighty organ played in solemn sadness, and while attendants raised the casket upon the cube of the Maxin, the Incaliz raised his hands to heaven and said:

"Unto Incal this soul, unto earth this clay."

The body, bound with light bands to the casket, was raised with it to an erect posture, trembled a moment in that position, and fell forward into the Maxin. There was no flame, no smoke, not even ash left behind the instantaneous disappearance of body and bed.

The funeral was over. As we who dwelled in Caiphul turned to depart, we saw that which no man then living had ever before beheld in the Incalithlon. Back of us, in the auditorium, stood groups of grey-habited men, wearing cowls like monks of Rome. There seemed great numbers of them, collected in groups of seven or eight amongst the maze of stalagmite pillars which supported the roof. As we gazed, these men faded slowly from sight, until over four score of Caiphalians seemed indeed small in number in the vast hall where so recently had been hundreds of Incaleni, Sons of the Solitude in astral form, gathered at the funeral of their brother. Yea, truly, had the Sons come to witness the impressive ceremony where all that was mortal of their dead fellow was restored to the keeping of the elements of nature.

"But no man knows that sepulcher, And no man saw it either, For the angels of God upturned the sod and laid the dead man there."

CHAPTER XVIII. LE GRAND VOYAGE

Rai Gwauxln directed me to attend some duties at Agacoe before resuming my vacation trip, although it was all arranged before the funeral of Ernon that my action in Suern was to his satisfaction.

When I obeyed the Rai, which was almost immediately, for we were all ready to resume our journey, Gwauxln, in the presence of his ministers of state affairs, tendered me the position of ruling power over the land of Suern. I was very surprised, yet felt that I might accept and in conducting the affairs of that country render good service. But the fact that I was still an undergraduate at the Xioquithlon made me hesitate. At last I spoke, saying:

"Zo Rai, I am aware that you have done your servant a great honor. Nevertheless, my liege, feeling that I have not thus far acquired the full knowledge I desire, being still only a Xioqene, I ask your permission to refuse the office."

Gwauxln smiled, and said:

"Even so. But the governor you appointed shall execute your duties for the three years intervening—the four years, I would say, since I prefer that you should not study at all this year—and thereafter you shall legally assume active duties. I have a purpose in this besides mere form; I believe that that man who has an object, a direct goal, in view, is more likely to win success than one without. It is a good stimulus. I do therefore appoint you Suzerain over Suernis, and dismiss you to your journey of pleasant recreation with your friends as soon as you sign your name to this document. That is well written, though your hand shakes a little because of your nervousness. Be calm." This last he said as, trembling slightly, I wrote the desired signature.

Once more we were on our travels.

Anzimee, the elf, persisted in calling me "My Lord Zailm" when she had learned the story of my imminent suzerain duties.

Our course was again eastward, although now farther south, for we did not propose to visit Suernis this time, but intended to proceed instead to our American colonies, as in the original route we had planned to do after leaving Suernis.

We crossed equatorial Necropan (Africa), then the Indian Ocean and the present East Indies, but then colonies of Suern called Uz, then onward above the wide Pacific, still eastward.

"Umaur! The coast of Umaur!" was the cry that called our little company to the windows to look at a dark, serrate line that bounded the eastern horizon. It was the distant range of the Andes, appearing almost on a level with our vailx, which, two miles high above the ocean, shot towards the hazy, black line. Below was the broad mirror of the blue Pacific, apparently without waves because it was so far beneath us.

Umaur, land of the Incas in a far later day. Umaur, where in eight centuries more they must find a refuge who should be so fortunately fated as to escape from Poseid, before, "Queen of the World" no more, she sank beneath the waves of the Atlantic. Eight centuries, whose lapse would see the proud Atlantean become so corrupt that his soul no more reflected the wisdom of the Night-Side because, the calmness of morality being fled, the key to nature's Penetralia would have been lost, and with it his dominion over the air and the depths of the sea. Alas, poor Atlantis!

But Umaur lay ahead of us, and ignorant of the misdeeds-to-be of our national posterity, we in our vailx stood gazing on the coast we were so rapidly approaching, and commented upon its majestic mountain ranges as seen through the telescopes. [1] Here we beheld a land where, after thousands of years, the conquering Castilians would come, led by Pizarro, and find a race under the rule of Incas, a name preserved through the many centuries from the day when their remotest ancestors fled from sunken Poseid, calling themselves "Children of the Sun."

AERIAL-SUBMARINE VESSEL, ENTERING THE WATER

Umaur was the region of the quarries of Poseid and of many of its rich mines of mineral wealth. Here, too, were vast plantations, and east of the mountains were regularly planted groves of the rubber tree, the genuine Siphonia Elastica of botany. Here also flourished the Cinchonas, as well as many other trees now indigenous to South America, colonized plants from Poseid. Until planted abroad by Atlanteans, these vegetable treasures never grew outside of Poseid, and today the wild forests of peculiar South American trees and shrubs are the direct descendents of our regularly cultivated farm and plantation products in Umaur. In that olden time the Amazon River ran within dykes across the continent, and the trackless wooded areas of Brazil were then drained areas of tilled soil, such as the adjacent territory of the Mississippi is today. Some day this river, "Father of Waters," in the north, will sweep un-resisted, un-dyked, across the lowland, which, even now, its surface is above in altitude. It will do this, because these things are certain to be in the mutations of the coming centuries. It will do this, also, because history repeats itself; think not that you shall inherit and reincarnate the glories of Atlantis and escape its shadows. All things move in cycles, but the circle is that of the screw-thread, ever around and around on a higher plane each time. But that time when these things shall come to pass, and no man be able to say nay, is still far away on the horizon of a future time, as far ahead as is the grand recession of the Amazon on the horizon of the past.

From the great orchards and plantations and homes of Umaur, in the north of that continent, to the desert wilds of its southern parts, where one day trouble was to overwhelm me, and from there north along the eastern coasts, we took our way, leaving the doings of the millions of our colonists, the Umauri, to the imagination of the reader.

Eventually we came to the Isthmus of Panama, then over four hundred miles in breadth; to Mexico (South Incalia) and to the immense plains of the Mississippi. These latter formed the great cattle lands from which Poseid drew most of its supplies of flesh-foods, and where, when the modem world discovered it, enormous herds of wild progeny of our ancient stock roamed at will. Buffalo, elk, bear, deer and mountain sheep, all offspring of the remotest ages. I regret to see them so wantonly slaughtered as they are; surely so old a stock might be spared.

To these broad valleys were to come, in later centuries, invading hordes in boats, and over the far northern isthmus where now are only vestiges of its former existence, the Aleutian Islands. They came from Asia, then, as now, to a large extent the home of semi-barbarians, except where the sway of Suernis had extended a civilizing influence by sending out the tribes which, in a later day, were to occupy so large a niche in history under the name of the Semitic ram. But the barbarians who went into Incalia, occupying the North American plains and lake regions—a future age should come which would find these hordes gone from the earth forever; and, later still, curious people digging from archaeological remains would say: "Here lived the mound builders."

Still farther north than this, in the present "lake region," were large copper mines, from which we obtained much of our copper, and some silver and other metals. This was a cold region, far colder than it is today, for it lay in the edge of the retreating forces of the glacial epoch, an epoch not over until much more recently than geologists have previously thought and even still think.

To the west lay what in early American days were called the "great plains." But in the days of Poseid they had a far different appearance from that which they bear today. Not then arid, nor very sparsely inhabited, though vastly colder in winter, owing to the nearness of the vast glaciers of the north. The Nevada lakes were not then merely dried-up beds of borax and soda, nor the "Great Salt Lake" of Utah a bitter, brackish body of water of its present comparatively small size. All lakes were large bodies of fresh water and the "Great Salt Lake" was an inland sea of fresh floods, bearing icebergs from the glaciers on its northern shores. Arizona, that treasure-house of the geologist, had its now marvelous desert covered with the waters of "Miti," as we called the great inland sea of that region. Extremely lush vegetation was on all the slopes of all the hundreds of square miles not covered with lovely bodies of water. On the shores of Miti was a considerable population, and one city of no small size, colonists all, from Atlantis.

Reader, do you remember a promise given in previous pages, in which I looked forward to a treat in scenic depiction, saying it was from another pen than mine? I redeem it now, for already the geologist is after me for having declared Arizona the scene of a lake or inland sea so vast as Miti, and so recently as twelve thousand years ago. I am reminded that he has decided from evidence afforded by erosion and weathering of the rocks in that amazing region, that while the Arizona desert was undoubtedly a lake or a seabed since the Paleozoic time when it was the site of a shallow ocean, nevertheless that lake was certainly "of an age older than the Pliocene, being probably in the Cretaceous epoch." My friend, no. Those gorges and stupendous canyons are not merely the gradual product of time and water and weather. Per contra, they are of sudden formation, the rending and cracking apart of the strata in a similar, but on a far more vast scale, than the volcanic outburst at Pitach Rhok, described in the first chapter of this history. The Arizona wonders and the gorge of the "Grand Canyon of the Colorado" were the result of an awful dance of the solid crust of the globe. Even now the lava beds of the rectangle between the parallels 32 deg. and 34 deg. north latitude and 107 deg. to 110 deg. longitude west from Greenwich, in the Mt. Taylor and Mt. San Francisco region, have few parallels on earth as regards size. All over this hideous work of destruction, when the sea Miti had fled away into Ixla (Gulf of California) the rains and torrents of eleven thousand winter seasons, and the desiccating, powdering influences of as many torrid summers, have smoothed and chiseled and wrought the ruptured, ragged surfaces into yet more fantastic shapes, and claimed the whole work as its own, denying the hand of Pluto as the major worker. And the geologist seems to have admitted the claim, and placed the lake time far back, in order to allow a sufficient term for the execution of the gigantic work. And it is not so, for I saw that lake only twelve thousand years ago. But now for the literary treat; it is taken from a very modern pen, but it is so faithfully descriptive of the appearance of the region today that I desire to enjoy its perusal with my readers. The words are those of Major J. W. Powell, U. S. Army:

"The canyon walls are buttressed on a grand scale, and deep alcoves are excavated; rocky crags crown the cliffs, and the river rolls below. * * * The sun shone in splendor on the bright red walls, shading into green and gray where the rocks were lichened over; the river filled the channel from wall to wall and the canyon opened like a beautiful gateway to glory. But at evening, when the sun was going down and the shadows were settling in the canon, the bright red gleams and roseate hues blended with tints of green and gray, slowly changed to brown above, and black shadows crept over below. Then it seemed the shadowy portal to a region of gloom. Lying down we looked straight aloft through the canyon cleft and saw that only a little of the blue heaven appeared overhead—a crescent of dark blue sky with but two or three constellations peering down upon us. I did not sleep for some time, as the excitement of the day had not worn off. Soon I saw a bright star that seemed to rest on the very verge of the cliffs overhead. Slowly it seemed to float from its resting place on the rocks, out over the canyon. At first it appeared like a jewel set in the brink of the cliff, but as it moved out I almost wondered that it did not fall. In fact, it did seem to descend in a gentle curve, as though the sky, in which the stars were set, was spread across the canyon, resting on either wall, and swayed down by its own weight. The star appeared to be really in the canyon, so high were the battlemented walls. The morning sun was shining in splendor on their painted faces. The projecting angles were as if on fire, and the retreating angles buried in shade; the rocks, red and brown, blazed from their setting of deep gloom below, but above all was a bright red fire. The light above, made more brilliant by the bright-tinted rocks, and the shadows below, made more gloomy by the somber shades of sunlessness, increased the apparent depth of the awful canyons, and it seemed a long, long way up to the world of sunshine—and was a mile!"

Even the wide waters of the Miti, set about with towering peaks in the olden days, beautiful as a dream, were not more grand and glorious than these awful gorges come to take their place.

From the city of Tolta, on the shores of Miti, our vailx arose and sped away north, across the lake Ui (Great Salt) to its northwestern shore, hundreds of miles distant. On this far shore arose three lofty peaks, covered with snow, the Pitachi Ui, from which the lake at their feet took its name. On the tallest of these had stood, perhaps for five centuries, a building made of heavy slabs of granite. It had originally been erected for the double purpose of worship of Incal and astronomical calculations, but was used in my day as a monastery. There was no path up the peak, and the sole means of access was by vailx.

In the neighborhood of twenty years ago, more or less, counting from this Anno Domini 1886, an intrepid American explorer discovered the famous Yellowstone region, and while on the same expedition went as far west as the Three Tetons, in Idaho. [1] These mountain triplets were the Pitachi Ui, of Atlantis. Professor Hayden, having arrived at the base of these lofty peaks, succeeded, after untiring toil, in reaching the top of the greater peak, and made the first ascent known to modern times. On its top he found a roofless structure of granite slabs, within which, he said, "the granite debris was of a depth indicating that for eleven thousand years it had been undisturbed." His inference was that this period had elapsed since the construction of the granite walls. Well, the professor was right, as I happen to know. He was examining a structure made by Poseid hands one hundred and twenty-seven and a half centuries ago, and it was because Professor Hayden was once a Poseida and held a position under the Atlantis Government, as an attache of the government body of scientists stationed at Pitachi Ui, that he was karmically attracted to return to the scene of his labors long ago. Perhaps knowledge of this fact would have increased the interest he felt in the Three Tetons.

Our vailx alighted upon the ledge without the temple of Ui just as nightfall came on. It was very cold there, so far north, and at such an altitude. But the priests within the heavy, well-built edifice never suffered cold, for Atlantis, drawing upon Navaz, had Night-Side forces at its call. The primary cause of our visit was our desire to pay devotion to Incal as He arose next morning. All night the brilliant beams of light from our ruby-colored lanterns flashed the tidings, to such Poseidi as might look our way, that a royal vailx was in the region. Next morning after sunrise our vessel lifted and departed for the east, that we might visit our copper mines in the present Lake Superior region. We were conducted in electric trams through the labyrinths of galleries and tunnels. When we were about to leave, the government overseer of the mines presented each of our company with various articles of tempered copper. To me he gave an instrument, similar to the modern pocket-knife, which I retained to the day of my death, and always valued highly on account of its extra fine temper, which kept a keen edge, good enough to shave with, and rarely required to be sharpened. The Poseidi were adepts in this now lost art of copper tempering. In return I gave the overseer a nugget of native gold. He asked me where it came from, and when I told him, remarked:

"Any specimen from the famous mine at Pitach Rhok will be highly prized by an old miner like your servant, more especially as it is presented by the discoverer of the mine himself."

Thus had the mine, found by me when an obscure lad, returned riches to the pick and shovel which had rendered it famed throughout the civilized world.

After taking counsel among ourselves, we decided not to make the farther northern trip, for every one of us had seen the Arctic ice fields at least once, while some of us had been there several times. Instead, we decided to remain in Incalia for a week longer, and spend the eleven days thereof in visiting, more at our leisure, the great territory where, although of course we did not know it, the Anglo-Saxon was one day to found the glorious American Union. History is said to repeat itself; I believe it does. Certainly races follow in the track of preceding races, and as the most important and populous part of all the North American colonies of Poseid had its habitat west of the great chain now known as the Rocky Mountains, so also the grandeur of America will be upheld by the western and southwestern States of the American Union.

Man likes pleasant places to live in; he likes those lands where Mother Nature is amiable and laughs with abundant harvests upon slight provocation; man likes to live in a fruit-land, and where shall he find anything more to his mind than this same southwest and west of the Incalia of yore? Along the ocean shore and back to the Sierra Nevada Mountains is the region where, under Poseid dominion, lay a province not second in beauty to the lake region along the shores of Miti. And its bar retained its fair charm, while that of the other has given place to drifting sands and cactus and the mesquite, and is the home of the Moloch lizards, rattlesnakes and prairie dogs. It is no more the

"Union of lakes and union of lands" that it was in that olden time.

When we finally left Incalia, that we might return home to Caiphul, the last of our colonial lands visible was the coast of Maine, for we journeyed eastward, then south.

For change we decided to forsake the realms of the air for those of the deep where the shark is king. Like all vailx of the class to which it belonged, ours was constructed for both aerial and submarine service, the plates of the sliding deck and the other movable parts of the hull being capable of very close approximation by means of setscrews and rubber washers.

To settle straight down into the ocean would be too much like a landing on terra firma. But being at a height of two miles, more or less, the conductor was directed to gradually reduce the repulsion current, thus diminishing our buoyancy so as to bring us into the water ten miles distant from where the slant commenced. He was further ordered to do this while maintaining a speed which would, though very slow for a vailx, be really swift, that is, he was to cover ten miles in as many minutes.

When we struck the water at this rate of progress the shock which the entering needle experienced was sufficiently great to cause its inmates to stagger, and little exclamations were made by the ladies.

As soon as we entered the water the repulsion was made nil, and its opposite, a degree of attraction greater than that of water to the terrestrial center of gravity, was set up, whereby we were enabled to sink to a considerable depth, despite the air contained in the vessel. The lights outside the windows were started, our speed modified to suit the element, and then we all gathered in the salon by the windows, darkness within and the waters lit without, enabling us to see curious tribes of Neptune which crowded about the strange illumination in their midst.

While thus engaged and while listening to the delighted words of an enthusiastic ichthyologist, I heard a familiar voice in the darkness. I knew it for that of my father Menax, and accordingly went to the naim. He could not see me because I stood in darkness, but I could see him in the great mirror, for at home he was in the light and his image was so transmitted, so that I saw not only himself, but his immediate surroundings, just as a person outside a lighted window at night beholds everybody and thing in the interior, himself unseen.

"My son," said the prince, "you should not have allowed your love of novelty to cause you to act so unwisely as you did in entering the ocean at even the slow rate of a ven (mile) per minute. I fear that you have a vein of reckless daring in your nature which will some day bring you misfortune. Incal punishes the reckless by allowing His broken laws to exact their own penalty. Be cautious, Zailm, be cautious!"

After the submarine experiences had become tedious, the opposite course of a rapid but graduated augmentation of repulsion was imparted to our vailx—a procedure not dangerous, as the other had really been—and soon our long spindle shot out of the water like some great bubble, then rose to where the raz, or repulse indicator, was set for its government, only a few hundred feet above the surface of the ocean. There, putting aside the closed deck, we sat in the bright sunshine and enjoyed the pleasant ocean breeze, which blew in the same southern direction in which we were going. Desiring to reach home by the next day, when the afternoon grew cool we closed the deck, arose high in the heavens so as to lessen atmospheric resistance and made the quickest speed we could towards the south. This, I should remark, was not nearly so great as either an eastern or western course would have allowed. Thus, traveling either due east or due west, we could proceed at the rate of a degree of longitude every four minutes. But north or south we cut the earth's currents, and just in proportion as a vailx-course deviated from east to west, in that proportion was its speed lessened, until going due north or south we could only travel at the comparatively slow rate of some hundred miles each hour.

We saw that if we traveled home by the straight course, we would not reach Caiphul under two days, and, having set our desires on reaching it by the next morning, the prospective delay was so tedious that we decided to run in on an angle. That is, we would head our vailx southeast for the Necropan coast, then from there southwest for Caiphul, and though the extra distance would be several thousand miles, the increased speed attained would allow us to reach our destination in time to take our breakfast at home.

Beautiful Caiphul, There's no place like thee; Queen of Atlantis And Queen of the Sea.

168:1 NOTE—When your science shall, like Poseid, approach Nature from its Godward side; when, instead of ascending to that key-force of all Nature, the Odic force, from a synthesizing of environing phenomena, you shall look from Odicity down all the river of Energy, then you will have all that Poseid had (being yourself Poseid returned), even its vailx, its naim, and its telescopes. The telescopes of Atlantis were not such crude instruments as yours are. Not the most remote star which sends a beam of faintest light across the depths of space, but that star could be brought so near to us in seeming, that had so minute an organism as a leaf been lying on the "ground" of the star, it was visible to our eyes. Do you refuse to believe? Deny this proposition: that light is not alone a reflection or refraction of force from a substance, but is a prolongation of every substantial form, for as much as only One Substance exists, though many are the dynamic variations thereof, these are mistaken by you for different substances. There is but ONE SUBSTANCE: Light from Arcturus, let us say, is the prolonged substance of that star. Machine-made electricity is, per contra, unimpressed, formless force. One can be made to reinforce the other—the Formless to acquire the image of the Formed. Do you now see principle of our telescopes? Thy mind jumps far to the leading edge, and I hear you ask, "Is Mars inhabited? Is Jupiter? Is Saturn, Venus?" Ah! My friend, I will not answer yes or no, for when the Poseid view of Nature reappears on earth, you will KNOW. Seek and you shall find; but seek correctly. Walk the cruciform Way.

173:1 The Three Tetons we situated in northwestern Wyoming, but Wyoming as a territory was not in existence at the time referred to, having been formed in 1868 from parts of Idaho, Dakota and Utah. A small part of Yellowstone Park is in Idaho.—Kings Handbook of United States.

CHAPTER XIX. A WELL-MET PROBLEM

Work awaited me upon my return to Caiphul, work to which I might attend without harm to my delicate health, in fact rather tending to its improvement, furnishing a proper degree of mental stimulus, without involving any of the severe tension of study.

On the day of my arrival home, Menax said to me in a way which set me to thinking:

"I understand that the people of Suern have lost the power which they have had up to now of providing themselves with food by seeming magic. It must be a terrible problem to them how to meet the cravings of hunger."

Whether Menax designed these words for the purpose of arousing me to a sense of my duties in the premises or not, I had at the time no idea. But I pondered the situation very earnestly. It occurred to me that these people had few if any cultivated fields like our own; that they probably had no adequate knowledge of the arts of husbandry, tillage and like requirements, and, finally, that they were not possessed of muscles trained to effort. In fact they must be, in all matters of this sort, a kind of overgrown children. The more I dwelt on the problem, the more startling the situation seemed. I saw that they would, for at least a year, require having provision made for them. They would also have to be taught the methods of agriculture, horticulture, and care of cattle, sheep and other useful domestic animals. Later, it would be necessary to teach them such other arts as mining, spinning and metal working.

In fact, here was an entire nation of eighty-five millions of people coming to school to me for tuition in the arts of life. As the full force of the position came to my realization, it staggered me. Ah, poor me! I fell upon my knees on the greensward of the gardens and prayed to Incal. As I arose I turned and found Gwauxln regarding me with a most peculiar glance. His face was as grave as possible, but his splendid eyes were full of laughter.

"Do you feel equal to the task?" he queried.

"Zo Rai," I replied bravely, "your son is hard pressed. Equal? Yea; if Incal will give me guidance."

"Well," said, Zailm, you shall call upon the resources of Poseid to aid you, and they shall be at your service."

Not to be tiresomely long-winded, the schools were established, the food and raiment stations were placed in given districts, and the people of Suern, the great peninsula of modern Hindustan, with parts of Arabia, were taught the means of comfortable self-preservation and dependence upon their knowledge. Not all of this was done, that is to say, supervised by me, but the initiation of it, and during three and a half years the practical work of it was conducted by me and my vice-suzerains. Perhaps I was not grateful to Incal; perhaps I never thought a second time, in these days of prosperity, of the prayer of the moneyless and unknown youth upon Pitach Rhok. But perhaps I did, too. I rather think that I was never for one moment forgetful of that morning and its vows. Yet, it is a strange fact that human nature may swerve aside from what it knows to be the undeviating line of right; may be keenly conscious of every infraction and still be able to feel that it has been true to its vows. Moral lapses are the most frequent, those sins which are not strictly direct infractions of communal equities but rather of the Magdalen type. Strange, also, is it that mankind is seldom lenient to the victims, though generally quite sparing of censure for the real criminal. There can be no true justice in a decision on any subject in the world until, in crimes of this sort, equal penalty is meted regardless of sex. Does my proposition seem too sweeping? Consider then this: human justice is a system; if it be faulty in only one particular it is faulty in all things, since justice means perfection, and something that has a blemish is not perfection.

In the history of the Judaic race the later records of the deserving portion of the people of Suernis may be found. Truly, my people, we have seen glory together and long suffering. We have stood together since before the age that is, and that which passes, was! My seed of strong effort was sown in fallow soil, and it returned more than a hundred fold. The end is not yet; the harvest is not garnered, neither have the Chosen People come yet into their reward for the Great Tribulation since Ernon of Suern ceased to strive for them. The way was long, but they shall come at last from out of the desert they entered so long ago, and Yeovah will give His children rest! As Rai Ernon had said, the Saldee general never returned to his native land. He wandered about the city, little noticed by the people, and made his chief abiding place at the vailx of a certain Poseid deputy representative stationed with others at Ganje.

One day, having become quite friendly with the latter, the Salda asked that his friend give him the pleasure of an ascent into the air; he had never experienced a ride on a vailx and wanted to very much. At the time the deputy was busy, and promised to do as requested on the morrow. Accordingly, after dinner next day, which meal was served on the open promenade deck of the vailx, the ascension was made. The general had taken too much strong wine and was rather unsteady in his motions. One of the party was a Suerna who had been one of Rai Ernon's counselors. The general stalked to the taffrail of the vailx to look down into the nether air. Standing near was the Suerna. Neither liked the other, and the Salda, also excited by wine, became quarrelsome. The Suerna, the same, by the way, who had been so amazed by the failure of his occult powers when he made his attempt to kill me, gave the general a sly push, and he fell against the rail. Being heavy, his weight bent it so as to cause a still further loss of balance and he fell over the side, catching the rail with both hands in a very agile manner. Here, unable to raise himself, he hung, calling for help in an agony of terror. The Poseid captain was not a bad man, but he was somewhat stupid, as a result of a fall on his head, and while able to give satisfaction as a deputy, he was not able to rise higher than some such subordinate position. He had, previous to his injury, been a talented man, and was even yet an inventor of some small note. This was a talent that did him small service now, however, because so many others outranked him in the same direction. He had finally come to be a lunatic on the subject, and was ever seeking to utilize force or to economize power. While the captain was standing in stupid indecision, the Suerna stepped in and pushed him aside, himself grasping the terrified Salda by the arm. The next instant the ex-counselor and the Salda general were swinging, whirling towards the earth, over a mile below. Then the Poseida looked over at them as they fell and, his mind all occupied with his favorite mania for invention, exclaimed:

"What a waste of force! If only they could fall on some mechanism adjusted to raise a weight!" How it happened, the deputy never knew, he confidently asserted, and for lack of witnesses, together with his obvious stupidity, the court excused him.

When I learned of the event it was through the governor, whom I had appointed, who reported having relieved the captain from command of his vailx and deputy representative office, and the placing of another Poseida in his place. The Salda was the father of Lolix, and I thought it well to break the news as gently as possible to her. I was astounded, after having done so, to hear her calmly say:

"Pardon me, but how does this concern me?"

"Why, your father—" I began, when she interrupted me with:

"My father! I am glad. Shall I, who love courage, feel anything but displeasure at his cowardice in the face of death, because of which he was moved to cry out in terror like a child? Faugh! I call no coward father!"

I turned away entirely horrified, silent for lack of words to express my feelings. Perceiving my action, Lolix came to me, and resting her small, white hand on my arm, looked up into my face, so that my gaze was directly into her glorious blue eyes.

"My Lord Zailm, you seem offended! Is it so? Have I said anything to cause you offense?"

"Gracious gods!" I exclaimed. Then remembering a former estimate of mine, that the Saldu was only a child in certain respects, I said:

"Offended me? Not so, Astiku."

Then she slipped her hand through the bend of my arm and walked beside me. This little experience was the beginning of a longer one which, while very sweet for a length of time, still culminated in anguish there in Atlantis and, phoenix-like, arose from the ashes of the dead centuries, only a few short years ago. Truly, "the evil that men do lives after them."

Because it was so very obvious that her heartlessness was only that of un-development, I was not disgusted with Lolix. I spoke disapprovingly to her, indeed, but instead of turning away in unreasoning wrath at its existence, I sought to induce a perception of the enormity of such an offense as cruelty of heart.

According to the custom of her people, Lolix wooed me to wed her. Of course I could not consent to it, pleasant though it was to have this beautiful girl doing her best to win my regard. I could not, while I loved Anzimee. Of this love for my sweet, womanly little sister, I never told Lolix, disliking possible contingencies. But I did worse—I told her an untruth, for I said that the Poseid law forbade marriage with those of alien birth.

"Never an exception?" queried Lolix.

"Never one. Death is the penalty."

This was another falsehood, for in Poseid the death penalty was never inflicted, it being forbidden by the law of the Maxin book.

"Well, then, it matters nothing. You are young and strong, and of good courage and handsome. Because of that, I love thee. If the law forbid, it is all the same. None but ourselves need know."

The last barrier was fallen. Conscience slumbered. Thoughts of Anzimee were put aside as one would shun an accusing angel. Did I think of Pitach Rhok and my days of sinlessness? Or of the mysterious stranger whom I had heard in awe in the first of my life at Caiphul? Yea, I thought of these things. I thought of Incal, and I said:

"Incal, my God, if I am about to do wrong in thy sight, in disregarding the laws of society and marriage, strike me dead before I sin."

But Incal struck me. Not then, but afterwards through the ages. He struck not then; conscience slept the sounder, but passion awoke.

CHAPTER XX. DUPLICITY

The year during which I was not permitted to study passed quickly and uneventfully, except that complications deepened on account of Lolix. My affection for Menax became almost reciprocally as great as his love for me, which was limitless. But I did not tell him that which, heavier and yet heavier, weighed upon me as time lapsed, the secret affair with Lolix. To have done so would have been best, yet I dared not, for it would have lost me all that I most prized. At least I so feared then.

As time went on I began to query my position. Did I love this beautiful girl? Not as I loved Anzimee. "O, Incal, my God, my God!" I moaned in anguish of soul. Conscience still slept, but stirred restlessly. The fact that Anzimee was my adopted sister did not prevent her becoming my wife, for the law of relationship by blood was not violated. But my own acts barred the way.

My scheme to house Lolix in a palace on the far side of Caiphul from Menaxithlon was successfully carried out without exciting the suspicion of any one, not even arousing the jealousy of Lolix. Duplicity, duplicity!

Then I wooed Anzimee unrestrained by the presence of her who would have been a dangerous factor had she even suspected that the daughter of Menax was not my sister by the ties of blood. But my days began to be filled with fear, for I had sown dragon's teeth; the final revelation of such affairs as have evil for a guide is invariably sorrow and bitterness. Suppose Lolix did not tire of me, and I had neither the heart nor the will to do anything to cause her to do so, nature-laws were ever liable to cause a revelation of the facts which would be fatal to my hopes; and though I often cried in agony of soul that I was an unhappy wretch, conscience still slept. But mine was not a character to be deterred from my resolves by danger. If I was engaged in a game of skill with the Evil One for opponent, I would play to the best of my ability. So I determined to be rid of Lolix, a decision that was too late, for the fruit of our sin was come and a home secretly provided, for I would do no murder. These plans were carried out, all fortunately, as I thought, without any man being the wiser. But how to be rid of the really lovable woman, Lolix? Only a year remained before I would enter examination for my diploma at the Xioquithlon. If successful, I meant to ask Anzimee, whom I knew loved me in return, to be to me all that the honored name of wife conveyed.

At evening, or of an afternoon, nothing pleased Anzimee better than to walk alone, or with Menax or myself through the palace gardens, under the spreading palms and garlands of flowering vines which canopied all the walks, forming long, cool tunnels of green, bejeweled with Flora's most radiant hues. From the breaks in these verdant walls we could see the simulated lakes, hills, cliffs and streams, and beyond these could look out over palace-capped, vine-draped Caiphul and its half thousand hills, large and small. Walking amidst such scenes by the side of her who was so dear, is it strange that my soul was at such times eased of something of its burden of sin and woe?

So long did I defer action in the case of Lolix that I came to fear to take any course except to let events follow their own course. Yes, I lost confidence in my ability to solve the dangerous problem, fearful lest I should make a bad matter worse. Thus the days slipped by and the examination ordeal was close at hand. Neglect Lolix I did not, could not, nor had I desire to do so. Very often I was with her; indeed, with a strange blindness to the wrong involved, I divided my leisure between Lolix and Anzimee. I sometimes feared that Mainin, Gwauxln, or perhaps both, knew of my secret. They did, too, for their occult vision was too keen to allow them not to know the facts. But neither made any sign, not Mainin, for he cared not how much secret evil went on, as we shall see before long. Nor Gwauxln, not because he, like Mainin, did not care, but because he was merciful and knew that karma had more dreadful punishment in store than any man could possibly inflict, and his mercy refused to add to my penalty. So the cancer remained hidden from public gaze, and I did not know that the noble ruler was a sad spectator of my misdeeds. I do not wonder at his sad demeanor when with me as manifested in the last year of my studies.

Anzimee had postponed the time of her examination in Xio until the year in which I was to graduate, and so the festivities which always followed the examination as a mark of rejoicing over the success of those who received diplomas included her in the honorable list, for she had passed with high credits.

A dinner was given by the Rai to the successful contestants, and this feast inaugurated an extended season of high social dinners, balls, parties, concerts and theatrical performances, all in the same honor. Anzimee, arrayed in a robe of grayish silk, with her heavy coils of dark hair fastened apparently by a lovely rose, and upon her shoulder a pin of sapphires and rubies, was presented by Gwauxln at the state dinner to the new Xioqi as the "Ystranavu," or "Star of the Evening." This was a social distinction akin to the modern "Queen of the Ball."

Knowing that Rai Gwauxln would lead his niece to the table and be her escort, I took Lolix, as I had a right to do, for I was a graduate and the possessor of a diploma, and all such might choose a companion, who might or might not be a graduate. Lolix, for my sake, had studied hard during the last three years, and was now in her second year at the Xioquithlon, to which she went from the lower schools. I was growing proud of the girl, and felt most tenderly towards her; indeed, I would have been a most despicable person had I not, after her sacrifice for me. Several times I found Gwauxln looking intently at me—I sat not far from him—and once, as he passed me after the feast, he murmured sadly:

"Oh, Zailm, Zailm."

As may be imagined, this address did not increase my peace of mind.

The Secrets Of Mount Shasta And A Dweller On Two Planets

But that night passed without any further disquiet, as so many others had done.

As I walked with Lolix in the great hall of Agacoe, I remarked the many glances of admiration bestowed upon her beauty by the many gentlemen we met, nobles of high degree. She had indeed grown to have a loveliness of face and figure, and best of all, of character, which was no longer heartless, but very gentle since her sad experience of secret motherhood and consequent disbarment from its innocent joys, since the child might not be known as hers. She had had offers of honorable marriage and refused them, knowing even as she did so that the fact of their proffer was a proof of my having spoken falsely when I told her that the laws of Poseid forbade our marriage. But her love for me, if it suffered, was faithful and knew no lessening. And she kept the secret well and the more closely for my sake, wretch that I was! As I looked upon her, I felt that she was very dear to me. But Anzimee was more so, and therefore the hideous tragedy went on. I knew that from love of me Lolix had first repressed heartless remarks, then taken an interest in relieving suffering for its own sake, and so had become transformed from a beautiful thorn tree to a glorious rose of womanly loveliness, with few thorns indeed. Had I really any conscience deserving the name, that I did not come out before the world and take Lolix as my wife after all this boundless love for me? No, not in Poseid. Conscience had not slept; it had never been existent; it was yet to be born, and grow in a later time. Thus did the nemesis of judgment still withhold her stroke.

CHAPTER XXI. THE MISTAKE OF A LIFE

Comparison is good mental exercise. It is due to the reader and to myself, as well as to Anzimee and Lolix, to indulge a present mood prompting me to make an analytical comparison of these two women.

What was it that fixed so unalterably my desire to wed Anzimee and not Lolix? Both were gentlewomen, the first by nature, the second by— yes, by nature also. I was, however, about to ascribe the sweet charity of Lolix to the perception on her part of the misery she would feel, placed in like situation with those who suffered in very fact. But the ability to so perceive could arise only from its existence in her nature. No, it was her nature finally developed. Both women were refined, intelligent, and both were beautiful, though of types as widely variant as a blush rose and a white lily. Anzimee was a born daughter of Atlantis; Lolix was one by adoption. A small difference, surely, since both were in full accord and equally sensitive to the good, the beautiful and the true, in the polished refinement of erudite Poseid.

Truly, the relations between Lolix and myself were wrong, but she was not on that account less dear to me, nor was my regard for her less tender and loving. Her companionship had become a part of my life. If I had a sorrow or was despondent, she intervened with her sympathy and cheered me. My anxieties were also hers; my joys her joys. In everything but name she was my wife. Then why did I not acknowledge the fact before mankind? Because karma ordered otherwise. I loved Anzimee also. Through this love, karma operated to annul its own tendencies to espouse Lolix. And the mode of this operation was exhibited in my recognition of Lolix as possessed of every requisite to make me happy except in her one lack, that of psychic perception of the relation of the finite to the infinite. Absurd? No. That my soul craved such an ability on her part, and found it not, but did find it in Anzimee, was evidence of the growth of the frail seedling of interest in the occult life of the Sons of the Solitude, which had been somewhat matured by the words of Rai Ernon of Suern years before. Do you say that if a little such interest worked such error in life that deep interest would make for the losing of the soul, and so you will have none of it? Not so. It was the not being true to the ideal at that time gained, true with all my soul, that did the mischief, just as in the myth of Lot's wife, she had never been turned to salt had she obeyed, not curiosity, but the higher injunction.

Lolix had no dimmest perception of this psychic link between the things of earth and the things of infinity. I had; I knew Anzimee had; so I ordered my life so as to include her and exclude Lolix, whereby I did both them, myself and my conception of God (which is but a redundant expression, for no one finite can injure Infinity) a fearful injustice. But karma lay in wait for the evil of my life, demanded payment—and got it, every jot; no words can paint the suffering of the atonement. I scarcely propose to try and shall rest content if a realization of some part of it shall deter others from sin through the certitude that there is no one who can be a substitute for the atonement for evil done, and there is no escape from its penalty.

The Law of the ONE reads: "Except a man overcome, he shall not inherit of My life; I will not be his God, neither shall he be My son." There can be but one way to such overcoming, the ever-recurrent plunging into material incarnation, until the errors of the personal will are atoned and surrendered to the Divine Will. There can be no undoing by another, [1] and soon I will show why. Another cannot do your breathing for you. Reincarnation, the ever-recurrent imprisoning of the soul in fleshly bodies, is but atonement, is but penalty. If in His Name you become free, if in that Way you have overcome, and in place of being slaves to are masters over desire, you have undone sin. Then there is no more incarnation for you in the prison of this death, miscalled life. There is no other Way; the Great Master pointed none.

In atonement for my dark past I must by necessity return into the world, your world of sin, sorrow, sickness and pain, and disappointed longings for the peace that passes understanding. Is not my twelve thousand and more years of further wanderings in the far land of this world, far from my Father's house, and feeding on the husks called joy, suffering the fevers, pains and disappointment of hopes, enough of a punishment? Yet for a little while longer I must and, impelled by love, willingly do serve Him. Some souls shall have even more than I, if they turn not. Which *will* you? Will is the sole Way to esoteric, or occult Christian knowledge. Whosoever wills, shall have Eternal Life. But the *will* to overcome must replace our will of desire, as the fresh air replaces the exhalations of our lung. As the atmosphere is around about us, and, inhaled, becomes our breath, so the Will of the Spirit is around us and, entering into the heart that has determined to strangle the serpent into submission, suffers us not to know defeat. But I, and Lolix, refused this Breath, and unwilling, turned away. Oh! The horror, the pain, of those lost ages, lost with her! But regained by us both, in—*overcoming*. I am sorry to admit that such moral flaws could ever have warped my character, even twelve thousand years ago! *Will is the only Way to Christ.*

Is it not an appalling thought, to realize that, having decided to put Lolix away and to install Anzimee in her place by honorably wedding her before mankind, I was able to calculate upon my knowledge of Lolix and to depend upon her acquiescence in keeping my secret because of her unselfish love for me? Monstrous! I knew that Lolix did nothing by halves. Having given herself to me, she would not expose my evil, even though I rejected her for another; society had no reproach for a woman betrayed.

In pursuing my plan, I proposed to obtain the spoken affirmation of the love that had long been confessed by the outward behavior of Anzimee. Then I would tell Lolix all, reserving nothing, and throw myself on her mercy. Even after these many, many centuries, when—Laus Deo!—reparation is at last complete, I look at the record of this part of my life when I was Zailm, and wonder that the very confession does not scorch holes in the paper upon which it is written. Moral turpitude is a fearful thing, for, though conscious of its being sinful, I was but dimly aware of the hideous blackness of my action. Can you make a distinction, reader, between your horror at the one action sufficiently to take interest in the recital of my profession of love made to Anzimee, after I had hidden from my own sight the evil of my life? It may be almost futile to try; yet it is possible to forget anything out of sight, at least to such a degree.

"That one may smile, and smile, and be a villain."

More especially is it easy to smile when the evil is in such a far, far past tense, is atoned, and the villain is one no longer. You will pardon me if I hint the Way of atonement. Of all my thousands of years of my many lives, to which in this history I can but briefly allude, I draw for you one lesson that the weary pilgrimage has taught me, and in my soul I pray for you to heed it. For I am longing for my release, when I may go out into the blessed realms that my eyes have seen, my ears heard, and myself been amidst, with Him who opens and no man shuts, and shuts and no man opens. So know this, and these things; so long as any that read my words turn aside, and will not to know and do His Way, so long do you keep me out of my part in the Great Peace, until His spirit shall cease to strive with you, or hinder you. I am working and sacrificing that you may know that Way; and walk it. Yet some of you will, even at the end, be one of those that, denying Him, are by Him denied. Out of all the glorious systems of worlds, only Earth denies, for acknowledging Him by words and crying, "Lord, Lord," they still hate one another in their serpent-dominated hearts. Think not that I use any figure of speech when I say "serpent"; microscopists know better. "He that sows to the flesh shall of the flesh reap corruption; but he that sows to the Spirit shall of the Spirit have Life everlasting." They that are *alive* have crucified the flesh with its affections. Some will close the eye and the ear to my message I have from Him. By that shall the seed of Eternal Life be closed out of their souls, and they shall die. [1] But so many who in all things turn unto the Way shall for no reason be cast out. He said it who is true. Keep thy lamps trimmed and be wise, not foolish virgins.

Footnotes

188:1 NOTE. See foot note on page 236

190:1 NOTE—in this connection read the last age of this book, which closes the history given of a Life redeemed upon His Cross.—Ed.

CHAPTER XXII. ZAILM PROPOSES

My mind was filled with the question which I made paramount, how to phrase my proposal of marriage to Anzimee. Such occupation of thought is common to all lovers, of every race and nation, where matchmaking is not conducted by the parents.

Having set my time for the momentous inquiry, I sought Anzimee. The information that she had gone to Roxoi palace, one of the three set apart for the Rai but seldom used by him, was rather perturbing. Lolix resided at Roxoi, and had done so ever since the time when I secured her transference from Menaxithlon. But I was not daunted in my purpose of seeing Anzimee; so, while journeying across the city, forty miles to Roxoi, I pondered the new situation. I knew that the two girls were friends, and this fact seemed likely to complicate matters. Arrived at Roxoi, I found Anzimee in the gardens, seated near a cascade that tumbled over a fairylike cliff into a mammoth dewdrop of a lake. She was alone. As I came near she inquired, in a surprised tone:

"Where is Lolix?"

"Where?" I repeated. "I don't know. I was told that she was with you."

"And that was true. But she took my vailx and went away, saying that she would go and get you, so that the three of us might have a little outing together."

I thought rapidly. To Menaxithlon was forty miles across the city due south. The vailx must therefore take nearly or quite as many minutes going in that direction, and the same returning. Eighty minutes. That would be long enough.

Seating myself beside Anzimee, I took her hand in mine. I had often done the same before, and even clasped her about with my arm, but in a distinctly brotherly way. Now the simple touch of the fingers was electric in effect, and she could at once detect the intensity of excitement which possessed me. The fine language I had intended to use was lost, and instead of trying to regain it I said merely:

"Anzimee, would words deepen your certainty of my love for you? I can not command them; but I ask you, little girl, to be my wife!"

And for reply she answered in phrase as brief:

"Zailm, let it be so!"

What followed the reader may imagine; your own fancy will please you best, for surely the picture is not hard to draw.

When Lolix returned, I had departed, but not hastily, for she had been delayed in coming back, so that three hours had elapsed since her departure.

I knew that few things were more certain than that Anzimee would confide her joy to Lolix. But I had no misgivings, for I felt every confidence that Lolix would not betray our secret, however terrible the blow might be for her to bear. As I anticipated, Anzimee told the story of my declaration of love, and of her acceptance of me. When the whole story was told, Anzimee said that her friend looked at her a moment, then fell fainting to the floor. When she had been revived, she seemed so calm that even Anzimee did not question her statement that the swoon was due to nervousness. This was at the evening. Anzimee, filled with happy feelings, saw her friend in bed, dismissed the attendants, soothed her to sleep, and came home. These facts I did not learn until the next day. I thought it best to have a talk with Lolix at once, and so experience all the pain and have done with the anguish of it. Deluded mortal!

I went to Roxoi, and going into the Xanatithlon, awaited Lolix, to whom I had sent word that I desired to see her there. She came. Fully ten years seemed to have passed over her since I saw her last. Worn and pale, with great dark rings under her glorious blue eyes, into which the tears flooded as she caught my quick gaze. Poor girl! But what could I do? That was my thought. I was even a little conscience-smitten but very little, for the scales of sin were thick and very numbing to the soul.

She spoke first:

"Oh, my love, my love! Why have you done this? Do you think I shall live? I have known for a long time that no law existed to bar our union, and have waited for you to do what was right, confident that the day would soon come when you would ask me to share your proud name. But—O Incal! My God! My God!" she exclaimed, bursting into a flood of tears that were as quickly repressed. Then in a calmer voice, full of piteous heartache, she went on:

"Zailm, I love you too well, even now, to rebuke you! I am yours to do with as you will. I gave you my life long ago. I gave you my babe, and you placed it in a home where no man might suspect its parentage. Zailm, I have done more also—there was another that—that—O Incal, forgive me! I sent it in to Navazzamin, that it might not accuse you, Zailm! And now, I, whom you have called your 'blue-eyed darling,' I, who love you more than I do life, am put aside by you! O God! Why am I made to suffer like this? Why have I been stricken in this way?"

She broke into a storm of agonized weeping, and I did not try to stay the flood, knowing that sometimes tears are a blessed relief. Had she loved me like this? Fool! Not to have known it from her actions, which spoke louder than words possibly could. My heart struck me now indeed, and I prayed, prayed to God for forgiveness, and I prayed to her. Too late! Conscience came forth at last, born to strike, sprung like Minerva, full-armed for the combat.

When Lolix had recovered calmness, she said, in such heartbroken tones as had never fallen on my ears before:

"Zailm, I forgive you. Not even now will I betray you, since whom I once love I will love till death; afterwards, also, if love survive the grave.

232

If you have come to say the parting word, so be it! But leave me now, for I am almost crazed! Yet remember, my darling, that if your new life is not happy, though I pray Incal it may be, that there once beat a heart for you warmer, more loving, and perhaps truer, than I fancy you will find that of your new love. I shall not live long to be a shadow over your peace. Kiss me once as you would if I were your own wife in the sight of the world, as I am in that of Incal, and having died, you were about to give my body to the Unfed Light."

With these words she stopped, stood up and came before where I sat, and placed her arms around me, drawing me into an embrace. A moment thus, then her lips, chill as those of one who keeps company with Death, met mine in one long, sobbing kiss! She released her clasp, stood an instant, and was gone. So she left me. I sat for a long time in the midst of the flowers in the great conservatory at Roxoi.

"The blossoms blushed bright—but a worm was below, The moonlight shone fair—there was blight in the beam; Sweet whispered the breeze but it whispered of woe, And bitterness flowed in the soft-flowing strewn."

KARMA DISPOSES

That night the church's acknowledgment of my coming marriage with Anzimee would be announced by the Incaliz Mainin in the great temple, for in cases of high social rank it was customary like this to add extra formality to the publication. If, during the ceremony, a death was to occur within the Incalithlon, custom decreed that one entire year must elapse before consummation of the marriage rites. In any event one month must pass after the church's announcements, which were in consequence declared immediately following the engagement. For reasons of his own, Mainin the Incaliz desired that Anzimee should not wed any one; but as he had no authority over and but little acquaintance with her he kept silent respecting his wishes.

At the proper hour, Anzimee and myself stood before Mainin the Incaliz, within the Holy Seat. By our side was Rai Gwauxln and Menax, the five of us being the center of attention of the eyes of a great audience. In a clear, slow voice, the Incaliz began an invocation to Incal.

233

But in the midst of this service, a woman glided quickly across the triangle of the Place of Life, in the center of which was the Maxin. It was Lolix. She was as faultlessly attired as it was her pride always to be. Apart from the awful blaze in her eyes I saw nothing extraordinary in her appearance. But to have stepped into the Place of Life was an impermissible thing, and the act centered all eyes upon her. It meant an appeal to the authority of the Rai.

"What are you trying to do?" asked Gwauxln. "Zo Rai, in Salda, my native land, it was the custom to allow either sex to woo the other in marriage. I wooed this man, the Astika Zailm, not knowing that he loved my friend—how could I know? And now, I beg of you, deny the ceremony, as you have a right to do."

"Woman, I am sorry for you! But the customs of Salda are not those of Poseid. I do not grant your prayer."

I had felt a numbing terror that at last my crime was to be revealed. But the fear faded as the slender, graceful figure of Lolix turned and was swallowed up in the audience. Then the interrupted vows were renewed. When Mainin said to Anzimee:

"Do you declare it your wish to wed this man?" She replied: "I do."

"And you, do you declare it to be your wish to wed this woman?" To which I said: "Even so, Incal not preventing." As I made my answer the proceedings were the second time interrupted by Lolix, who again came into the Place of Life, but this time as hurriedly as if pursued. Opposite the Unfed Light she stopped, and said:

"Incal will prevent! See, I come to wed you now, Zailm, and here! The God of departed souls shall be our Incaliz, this dagger our wedding proclamation, church ceremony and all!

I should have prefaced the narration of the questions put to Anzimee and myself by explaining that after the invocation by Mainin, that person, Anzimee and myself, and the Rai with Menax, had left the Holy Seat and had gone into the Place of Life, so that Lolix now stood close beside me. As she spoke of the dagger her words were calm, but rapidly uttered—it was the calmness of insanity! Crazed by the course I had followed, Lolix stood there, her glorious blue eyes filled with the light of madness. With her last words still upon her lips, she struck at my breast with the sharp weapon. I warded the blow with my arm, which was pierced through by the forceful stroke. As she drew it out with a wrench, blood spurted over the granite floor. At sight of this she uttered a frightful shriek, saying:

"Mad! Mad! MAD!!!" and with one bound sprang to the center of the Place of Life, where she stood by the cube of the Maxin.

Anzimee swooned; Menax stood as if petrified, gazing at my flowing blood, while Gwauxln, pale but calm, spoke to a guardsman near:

"Arrest the maniac!"

The order of the Rai attracted the attention of Lolix, who said to the approaching soldier:

"No, no, don't arrest me. I was mad, but I am not. Whosoever shall touch me, him will I curse, and then die in the Maxin."

Being superstitious, the guardsman paused, for he dared not touch her, neither disobey the Rai. In his terror he turned to the latter and began to make excuse.

"Silence!" thundered Gwauxln. Then in gentle tones he said to Lolix: "Woman, come to me."

"Not so, Zo Rai! At this place beside the Maxin no one under the law may offer me violence. Here, then, I stay!"

Speaking thus, Lolix rearranged her slightly disordered turban, folded her arms, and then leaning back against the Maxin-cube, gazed calmly at the Rai. He made no motion, but looked first at her, then at me. Lolix, though still near to the Maxin, had assumed an erect position, no longer touching the cube.

Incaliz Mainin had stood quietly by during the excitement. He now said: "Aye, Astiku from Salda, there you shall stay, indeed, even longer than you think!"

He had spoken very calmly, even softly, gazing the whole time at the unhappy girl. When he turned towards the Rai, he saw a look of horror on his face, and hurriedly looked away again, finishing the reading of the marriage ceremony. I scarcely heard him, being engaged partly with my bleeding arm, and partly with Anzimee, who, but partially recovered, and still half fainting, leaned against me for support. When the ceremony was completed, Rai Gwauxln, placing a hand on each of our heads, said: "Not only a year must elapse before you may wed, but much longer! Zailm, I do forgive you your sins so far as it is mine to forgive, the human laws you have broken. As for your partner in wrong, never mind."

Then turning to Mainin, the Incaliz, he sternly said:

"Because of your accursed deed, you and I are forevermore strangers! Now I know you for what, alas, you are."

Having spoken in this, to his hearers, enigmatical and startling language, Gwauxln left the Incalithlon. Mainin also left. Menax, who had become curious regarding the unhappy cause of all this trouble, spoke to her as she stood by the Unfed Light. She neither answered nor moved. I approached near to her and said gently:

"Lolix?"

Still no answer nor movement. I touched her silken bodice, but received a shock which startled me like an unexpected blow! Her corsage was as rigid as stone. I touched her hand; it, too, was cold and stiff. Her face, even her wavy brown tresses, were alike rigid. Not only was she dead, but actual rock! Like one in a dream, too much stunned to be horrified, but still possessed of a strange curiosity, I rapped with my knuckles on the various thin edges presented by folds in her robe, and heard them sound with a metallic clink. I grasped a finger; it broke off, and then in a sudden wave of awful living horror I dropped it upon the stone floor; it broke into fragments like any fragile bit of rock. Still were the golden tresses, with which I had so often caressingly played, of the old lovely color. Her complexion, her blue eyes, even, were of the same natural hue they had been in life, but for all that her body was stone and her soul was forever fled! Her pretty foot, showing from beneath the hem of her robe, was not only as the rest, stone, but it was petrified fast to the stone pavement on which she stood. At last I realized all. This hideous deed was the work of Mainin in that instant he looked at Lolix in speaking to her. He had prostituted his occult wisdom, and for this Gwauxln had cursed him. Lolix's flesh and blood and clothes had all been transmuted into solid stone. This petrification was all that remained of poor, wronged, forsaken Lolix, a perfect statue which, if suffered by man to remain, might stand during the many centuries, till even stone at last crumbled to dust.

The awful meaning of it all came home to me at last. Was I primarily responsible for it? In that moment I knew that I was, knew that the murder was on my soul, as well as on that of Mainin, who had never found that opportunity, at least except by me.

Even in her temporary insanity Lolix had been true to me. Not one word had she spoken to involve me. If Gwauxln knew, and I was aware that he did, he gave me free pardon so far as human law was concerned. For the broken laws of Incal he could not extend pardon, that became karma, and there lay a weary width of desert sands of sin to scorch my feet in the passage I must make across them before I could tread the narrow way of attainment. The long atonement was before me. I gazed on the mute form of the girl I had so fondly loved, and loved yet, until Menax, who had become aware of the awful occurrence while I stood stupefied, but on whom the main effect was a desire to leave as soon as possible, pulled me by the sleeve:

"Come, Zailm; let us go home."

Giving one last remorseful look, I obeyed. Lovely Lolix. Her voice was still in death, and that through me! As remorse surged over my soul, I thought that I would now be glad to ask Anzimee to release me, confess all to her, and with her consent make Lolix my honored wife; but it was forever too late in that life thus to make reparation. No more could the tender glance of love flash on me from those starry eyes of blue! No more would my weary head nestle down on her shoulder, while with gentle caress she chased away my darker musings with a mild and gentle sympathy. Ah, ye gods! What had I lost? My life, that had seemed complete, and as a sphere like unto the full moon, was come, like that orb when it rises late at night, to seem torn and but half of itself, wrecked and ragged, careening through the nighttime of existence.

Anzimee knew nothing of the awful reality; she had been too much stunned by the sudden knowledge of her friend's insanity. She must not know if it woro possible to prevent her learning of it We went to our carriage and, solemn the one, stunned the other, and wildly remorseful the third, got in and went home to Menaxithlon. Home? I felt that the peace of home was no more mine! Life had become a desert over which stalked the skeletons of despair, regret and sorrow; overhead a moonless sky, underfoot in the night a howling waste of sand, blown hither and thither by careless winds. Lolix was gone, Anzimee would never be mine, as I felt in prophetic forecast of soul, and so, with bowed head, I sat in the midst of the desert of my days and let the phantoms dance about and mock me, unheeded.

CHAPTER XXIII. A WITNESS BEFORE THE CRIMINAL

States of mind, of feeling and of intuition are the only real things that exist. Jesus, although the Son of God, and John and Paul were all Sons of the Solitude; Hegel, Berkeley, Sterling, Evans; all real theosophists and all real Christians, are becoming Sons, and are in accord with those peerless nature-students of old when they say, "Spirit alone is real; all else is illusion."

If a man think himself ill, he will become so; if, per contra, he is cheerful under even the most adverse circumstances, he will not see that the world about is full of gloom; nor is it. It is only in himself, and he can change the world all into gall and bitterness for himself, although it is all a song for others.

For weary weeks I wandered about, stupidly, a leaden load of grief weighing on my soul, a feeling of dull despair which would have crazed a less well-balanced temperament. Had Lolix felt that way for even a little while? If so, and I knew she felt worse, if that were possible, God pity the bright, sweet and beautiful girl who had so suffered through me! I was tempted to suicide, tempted to sneak out of the back door of life, and I often felt of the edge of the razor-keen knife given me by the Incalian mining superintendent—how long before? Four years, really; four years? Four centuries, for anything I knew by my feelings. I stood by the Maxin in the long afternoons when I was alone in the temple. Or did I but dream that I did this? Aye, it was a dream of tortured sleep, for no one had admittance to the Incalithlon (except the Incala) on any other occasion than on days of worship or of special ceremonies, and then the edifice was always thronged. Anzimee crossed my desert at times, but though she spoke, and caressed me, and strove to arouse me, it was in vain; all her efforts fell like a ray of sunlight on the inky lusterless pools sometimes seen in deep forests. Left all alone with my remorse, for their unavailing efforts seemed to my friends more productive of harm than of good, and therefore they ceased them, I took my private vailx, and, to shut off all possible communication with the world, removed from it the naim. Then, no one knowing my intentions, I slipped away in the nighttime. I wandered then through the realms of the air, sometimes so high above the earth as to be in almost entire darkness, where the Nepthian Ring was visible and where even the air generators and heat furnishing apparatus were scarcely able to keep the air in the vailx dense and warm enough to support my miserable life.

Or, equally alone, equally in darkness, I made my vailx seek the depths of the sea where phosphorescent fish would have mistaken my craft for a larger brother, had I ever cared to light up. But my soul was dark, and of what use was it to illuminate the vailx when, with eyes to see, I saw not? So bitterly keen was my horrible anguish of soul that at last the body of clay lost its power to hold Me, and I arose above time and earth, and remained in that state for what seemed an endless period. No light appeared to be in the awful blackness, neither any warmth, but a darkness as of death, a coldness as of the grave. No person crossed my path; no sound was heard, save dull, muttering groans. But at length flashes of red flame leaped across my vision, then went out, leaving the gloom more wholly black than before. Horrid hisses, as of giant serpents, assailed my ears now; awful pain seemed to be dissolving my very soul. At last my nerves failed to respond to the racking agony, and sensation failed. Numbness seized upon me, and I exclaimed: "Is this death?" But only echo answered. The hisses had ceased; all was silent. Suddenly I felt a deep dread of the horrible solitude, so dark and cold and wet in which, somewhere, I could see a little light that seemed to render the intense darkness more smothering. I called aloud; reverberating echoes alone answered. I shouted and shrieked in wild terror. But in all the vast glooms around no sound save my own replying, reflected tones came again. The knowledge that my confines were limited came to me from the fact that my voice was sounded back to me after what seemed ages between utterance and return.

With this knowledge came the sense that I was free to go, and I arose from the place wherein I stood as if I was endowed with wings, and I fled faster than thought. Tall cliffs I found in the glooms, and in a short while peaks shone out in the glare from some flaming pit, but no creature was anywhere to be found; I was in a very universe of solitude. Alone, oh, alone! The awful, horrible despair that then seized upon me caused me to wail in more than mortal pain. My eyes were dry and my soul as if crushed. Despair so frightful held me for its own that I longed to perish. Vain wish. Then I remembered that I had an earthly body; to find even that would be some solace. On lightning lines I sped to it, to find it cold and lifeless save for a small glow of magnetic light in the plexus of the heart nerves and another in the medulla oblongata. But beside it I found, O, Incal! I found Lolix, weeping, praying to our God to restore—me. She did not seem aware that I had come, but sought me in the cold body of earth. Then I knew that I had been reminded of my corporeal self by that fond woman's soul pleadings. Such pleading, such anguish, I could no longer endure. I stood beside her, I touched her. Then she looked up and saw me. She looked long at me; then at my body. And then: "Zailm, is it you? My love, my love. Oh, take hold of me, before I fall!"

The Secrets Of Mount Shasta And A Dweller On Two Planets

She fell forward upon my breast, and in that time the body of me disappeared, and also all things, save the sandy waste where we then found ourselves together. . . . Then, before our horror-stricken gaze came a little babe, so tender in age it seemed just born. It was able to come to us, however, and it could utter wailing speech, which struck our ears like cries of mortal agony! It was dripping with blood, and its eyes were as those of a dead infant. With an awful shriek of anguish Lolix cried:

"O Incal, my God, my God! Have I not suffered enough but that my dead, my murdered babe should come to attack my soul? Zailm! Zailm! See! See! See our baby girl, murdered by me, for your sake!"

My heart seemed to stop beating in its fearful woe, and I stood paralyzed, gazing at the little one as it stretched its hands gory with the blood of untimely birth, and raised its glazed eyes—to me! Then I stooped and took it into my arms, holding it close, trying to warm its poor, cold little body, and I wept, aye, at last I wept great tears of real value, because shed for another. With a voice choked with anguish, I said: "Lolix, your sin is on my head, because done for me! Let Incal have mercy on me, if He will!"

Then a glorious radiance broke over the scene, and the Cross Bearer was beside us as we stood, clasping each other and our child. He whom I had seen by the moonlit fountain,

years before, stood by us again. On His breast shone a Cross of Fire, which leapt or fell again in waves of undulating, living Light. He spoke:

"Lo! You have called upon the Most High for mercy. Because unto that little child you have shown mercy, you shall receive it. You have come to Me, and I will give you rest. Yet, it shall not come to you until the day of the Great Peace enters into your overcoming heart. Therefore, in a far day, you shall reap a sorrowful harvest of woe, and repay all that you owe. When you come again, and also her with you, and are ready again to go into Navazzamin, you will find yourselves free of earth forever. Then, having received, you shall give. He that causes another to sin causes that other's and his own feet to slip and to turn from My way. He must atone his heart to Me first, then go again into the field of woe, yet not in a body of flesh but of spirit. And he must find his victims and struggle with them till he turns them back from where he led them. Thus he takes on his own back their burden he caused them to place there. Then he shall carry it for them until they, following his spirit-counsels to their souls, are come unto Me. And I will take that burden, that shadow, and it shall cease, for I am the Sun of Truth. Can a shade exist in sunlight? Can anyone pile shadows on the sun? Neither can anyone pile sins upon Me, and burden Me. That little one I will take unto Me; you have offended it, and it shall be as a millstone on your neck, casting you into the sea of earthly misery; yet you shall escape, for you have your name in the Book of Life. But now, rest! And My daughter, rest!"

I found myself in my body, unable to recall anything I had passed through. But I was weary and I slept. Nature came to the rescue of my tired soul, and for days I was in a fever, which passed into a coma, and from that I awoke, weak but well. Still, I was in a waking dream. And I dreamed that I was in the Incalithlon at Caiphul.

"O, the agony! O, sin's bitter cost!"

But at last I went back to Caiphul, after weary weeks in which I was lost to my people, aye, months, three of them. Back to my home. As I passed through the palace I met officers and ladies of the court, and attendants, to all of whom I had been a friend and who so regarded me.

They now gazed blankly at me, but spoke no word of greeting. Was my life known at last to a horrified world? No. This was not the reason of the strange demeanor of the people. I was unexpected, was supposed to be dead. During the hundred days of my absence, Menax, with Anzimee, had concluded that I was dead, had perhaps taken my own life. It would be happier for me had they thought correctly as to the first part of the matter.

Now I was back home, resolved to be open and frank in my relations with those whom I loved best on earth. I would confess my evil ways to them, and implore forgiveness. Once again—too late! Menax, long a sufferer from an affection of the heart, thinking me dead because I had not come to him nor to Anzimee, had not survived the shock which this belief caused him. I was told that for some weeks he was gone to Navazzamin. I dreaded to ask about Anzimee in case here, too, some terrible news awaited me.

In my misery I wandered about the city, and before long found myself by the great temple. A little door stood open and no one was near, so I entered by it, careless that admittance was denied all but Incali. I hoped to find in this sacred shade some relief. No one seemed to be within, and I wandered about until I stood in the triangle of the Place of Life. There, forgetful for the moment, I gazed reverently on the Unfed Light. Then I passed around to the other side of the quartz cube and— O God! There stood Lolix, still and cold! My very brain reeled. I went to her, and found her the same as when I looked last on her dear form, stone, only stone! How many years was it since then? A whole life may crowd into a day's length and centuries pass in a few weeks. O Lolix, Lolix, my accuser! In blank numbness of mind I laid my hand on her cold form, and shuddered at the chill, yet bent and looked into the eyes which saw me not, and kissed the dumb lips which made no response.

"Yet she would not speak, though he kissed in the old place the quiet cheek."

In her hand was a roll of red parchment; I ventured to remove it and look at its contents, if indeed it had any writing upon it. It had, and I read:

The Secrets Of Mount Shasta And A Dweller On Two Planets

"Because this statue is record of a despicable crime, I, Gwauxln, Rai of Poseid, do forbid its removal until I grant permission. Let it stand a silent witness before the criminal."

With a shudder I replaced the roll in the stony grasp, and almost fainted at the hollow rattle which it made as I did so. Was I that criminal? Not the one. But I felt as if I was. I would go to Agacoe and ask permission of the Rai to remove her of whom he knew I was fondest, but had lacked the courage or decision to say so to the world. Aye, circumstances made her more precious to Zailm than Anzimee was. I turned to leave that I might go to Agacoe. But I was startled when, on turning, I found myself facing Rai Gwauxln, gazing sorrowfully upon me. Startled only, for nothing surprised me any more nor ever gave me real terror. Before I had spoken he said: "Yes, you have my consent to remove her."

I felt no wonder at his anticipation of my request, although I noted the fact; indeed, it was deep gratitude which I experienced instead. I was muscular, and at once acted upon the permit. I took one long, last look into the deep blue eyes, and at the face, which seemed almost to smile as I bestowed a sobbing kiss upon the calm lips. Then I lifted her from the granite floor. The one foot that was exposed to view beneath the hem of her stony robe broke off at the ankle, just above the straps of her dainty sandal, as I lifted the slight but now heavy body. Then I raised her higher, and yet higher, to the top of the cube of the Maxin, and let her drop forward against the Quenchless Light.

"Kiss her and leave her; your love is clay." As she touched the Maxin-Light site she instantaneously disappeared, with no more disturbance of the tall taper than comes from the flight of darkness when the morning sun lights up the valleys. Calmly the Quenchless Light stood, unchanged as ever. As I turned away, I saw the little foot, whereon sparkled the sapphires and diamonds of the sandal strap-buckle, my gift! I succeeded in detaching the little remnant unbroken, but instead of putting it also in the Maxin-Light, I wrapped it in my mantle, glad that I had a token, even if it was only a stone foot.

I could not bring my courage to the point of asking my sovereign about Anzimee. No, I feared his possible and not unreasonable scorn. I would seek her and find out whether she was also dead, like Menax. If so, I resolved to take the first opportunity—the morrow might favor me, as it was the beginning of an Incalon or Sun day of general worship—and return to the temple, where I would bathe away my physical self in the unwavering flame of the Unfed Light.

Anzimee was not dead, however, but had not yet learned of my return. I found her, the sign of her great sorrow in her fine gray eyes, which, as we met, rested on me in a bewildered stare. Then, with one long sob, she fell into my outstretched arms in an unconscious condition. Poor little girl! I held her, I clasped her close to my heart, and while I kissed her pale lips, her black-ringed eyes, her sunken cheeks, my tears fell on her face like rain, the first tears my fevered physical eyes had shed through all my agony of soul. At last she awoke from her faintness only to experience a long sickness, in which her pure spirit came near bursting its earthly casket and, after several weary weeks, finally returned her to consciousness. When she was again moving about in her old quiet way, and although frail was able to endure the recital, I sat down in the Xanatithlon in the seat where Menax and I had sat so long before. Then I drew the slight form down upon my knees and, with my arm about her, told her all the sad story of Lolix and the miserable flight from Caiphul which I had made to escape the memory of it—alas! How unsuccessfully. No one can run away from self. Then, after the unrestrained confession, I asked her to forgive me. For some time she said nothing, but her arm stole around me, so that we clasped each other. At last she spoke:

"Zailm, I do forgive you—from the depths of my soul I do! You are only mortal. If you have sinned, do so no more. I do not wonder that you should have loved that sweet woman."

At this I drew forth the memento of Lolix, which I had carried with me, despite its weight, and without a word handed it to her.

"This is her foot? O Lolix! I loved you, also! Zailm, give me this. I would keep it in memory of my friend."

Then I spoke: "Anzimee, my wife, for you are to be mine, the world knows it, you have forgiven me. So has your uncle, our Rai. But it is still some months before we may wed till death. So I will go forth into Umaur, in the region where men are not, even in the south part, for in Aixa there are certainly mines, and in the sandy deserts there I will find gold. Not that I want gold, for I have millions, aye, three million teki, and much other wealth; but all that the earth will yield it is good for Poseid to have. I go, because I fear I cannot be in Caiphul and refrain from being always with you. In Umaur I can see you, and bear you, and love you, dear, for I shall not this time remove the naim, so that it will be much as if I were here. Therefore, kiss me, sweet one, a fond farewell, and I will be gone when the evening falls. Incal be with you, and His peace overshadow you!"

It was two thousand miles from Caiphul to that part of the Umaur coast nearest which I desired to go inland. But, thinking of Anzimee, the distance was passed unheeded until we lay above the region where now the geographies mark the great niter-bearing desert of Atacama. It was desert then as now. We found on prospecting its deepest sands, near to the base of the Andes, that these were rich enough in gold to justify myself and men in setting up the electric generator of water. This was an instrument containing several hundred square yards of metal plate surface arranged in banks like the gills of a fish, the whole encased in a tight metal box. An air current entering at one end of the case had to traverse every inch on both sides of the plate before it touched the farther end. As each plate was made and maintained very cool by Navaz forces, the result was rapid deposition of moisture from the atmosphere. In the example cited the generator was of the largest portable size, and the flow of water condensed by it was about a quart every minute, quite enough with which to do a considerable amount of mining in the economical way in which our mining machinery used water.

I had brought a horse from Poseid, and after mining arrangements were attended to, and the men placed at work, I had the animal made ready, and taking a case of mineral locators—light instruments operated by something similar to what would nowadays be called a pile la clanche—therefore not Night-Side electricity—instruments used for

247

The Secrets Of Mount Shasta And A Dweller On Two Planets

determining the location of mineral deposits on the principle of the electrometer—and with food enough for several days, I set out to prospect for valuable minerals. I also took a small, easily portable naim, so as to maintain communication with the rest of the world. I soon left this latter instrument in a cache, intending to get it when I came back, for I had not gone more than five miles before discovering that the instrument had been rendered useless by the loss of its vibrator. Where I had lost this essential I did not know, but I concluded not to go back after it. The loss, though no small annoyance, was a relief to my horse, for it reduced his burden by a number of pounds, no small matter, considering that I had a rifle, which I will not now describe, different though its principle from any modern weapon, in that its propulsive force was electricity, my mining tools, my packages of dates and nuts for food, my polar compass, pocket photographic apparatus, and a small generator, with, lastly, my bedding and my own weight.

That night I was far away, and the next evening found me over a hundred miles from the camp. As the sun sank low I found myself riding along the bottom of a deep arroyo. ₁ At a little distance I saw the mouth of what appeared to be a small cavern. This might do nicely to camp in overnight and provide shelter. My horse was well trained and would stay for hours within whistling distance of the place where I left him. So I dismounted and bidding him to remain near, went into the cavern. It seemed like a long tunnel, and without going further, I returned to my steed and took off his saddle. Then I laid under it the food I had brought for myself; for the animal there was abundance of grass growing about. The tools I also put under the saddle and, taking my electric rifle, was about to return to the investigation of the cave, when my horse pleaded for water, and as the ravine was a dry creek I proceeded to give him drink and take some myself. The creek bed was of smooth, cement-like rock, with numerous depressions shaped much like buckets. Beside one of these I set the generator, and soon the hole was full of water, cool and refreshing. I watered my grateful animal at this, and drank from the spout of the instrument myself. How good the fluid seemed! As I placed the generator, still running, back beside the hole, I little thought how I would need it soon, and be unable to get it.

The Secrets Of Mount Shasta And A Dweller On Two Planets

I found the bottom of the cavern to be of the same rocky character as the bed of the arroyo. I knew it was not mineral bearing, but my curiosity was aroused and I concluded to go to the end of the tunnel. In my pocket I had a small lighting battery and incandescent bulb, and when it grew dark in the cave by reason of my distance from the entrance, I used this to light up my pathway. For fully half a mile I found the cave to open on before me. At that point I stopped, overcome by surprise. In all that region I had not seen a sign of human presence, recent or ancient, until now. But before me, only partially exposed, stood a house, presenting its comer and part of two heavy walls of basalt. I dropped my light in my surprise, and it broke on the rocky floor, extinguishing the light. But it was not completely dark around me, for daylight filtered in from some source.

Long I stood there in that gloomy cavern, gazing upon the ruined house. From where had its builders come, and in what forgotten age? Where had they gone? Was this but a solitary building, or were there others hidden in the sands of the plain nearby, but not uncovered? Conjecture had here full play, for in all the annals of Poseid, covering decades of centuries with concisely written records, no mention was made of any people, civilized, or even savage, having had inhabitants in this "No Man's Land." The only reasonable conclusion was that I now gazed upon the relic of some people so ancient as to antedate even Poseid's forty centuries. At length I crossed the cave's short width in order to examine more closely this remnant of the dim past, a past forgotten even when Poseid was young. In the side of the building nearest to me was a doorway through the smooth, finely chiseled basalt blocks forming the wall. Partly ajar swung a door, apparently formed of a single slab of basalt about six inches thick by the proper proportions otherwise. Impelled by curiosity, I stepped into the room, which was easily done without disturbing the door from the position it had so long occupied. My reason greatly disliked the admission that even a stone structure should have withstood the effects of time for so long; but that was the only way to explain it, so I stopped guessing for the time being.

I found the three dimensions of the interior apparently equal, and about sixteen feet every way. There was just that single door to give entrance. Except for two parallel openings in the roof, formed by placing a stone of lesser width by a span on either side of the opening it would otherwise have filled, there was no break in the solid masonry. The floor, which was thinly covered, I found to be made of granite, the jointure of which was as perfect as that of the walls—not a sheet of paper could have been slipped between any two blocks. After exploring thus far, I leaned against the wall, near enough to the door to touch it without change of place, and letting my gaze rest on the barred grating in the ceiling, gave myself to reflection. How cold and gloomy it seemed in that lonely room, relic of a bygone age, forgotten by even so old a race as ours. The solid construction, the simple severity of its plan, all forcibly brought to mind the descriptions given of prisons in Poseid in ante-Maxin days. Was it the solitary example of building skill of its constructors in which I now stood, or was it one of a collection forming a buried city? How this particular building came to be clear of sand in its interior was easy to see. The rain waters had percolated through the shallow soil above, and had run through the crack which I have mentioned as giving light to the cavern. A part of the flow had gone outside, thus exposing two sides of the corner of the house; the rest of the water, running on the flat roof, had entered through the grating. Seeping this way through the sand in the room it had carried it out of the door standing open at the side.

Satisfied with my reflective study, I began to think of returning to the open air, and to my horse. As I turned to pass out, curiosity impelled me to swing the ponderous door on its hinges, if I had strength. Expecting that much effort would be required, I gave force to the action. Alas, for my superficial examination of the slab. I had observed no sign of a lock of any sort, and did not imagine any existed. Hardly any effort was needed to swing the deceitful door, and it went to with such quickness that I lost my balance and fell against the wall, striking my head so severely as to render me unconscious. When I recovered I found the door shut and securely locked. In my cursory notice of it I had not seen that instead of a simple slab it was made of the plates of stone, separated at the edges by a segment of a third plate, forming thus a hollow space between the outer surfaces. In that space there was concealed an arrangement of bolts and bars of stone, working on the gravity-drop principle and releasing the locking-bolts when the door shut tight to place. The ends of these, four in number, then shot into recesses in the wall, and the door was securely locked.

Being of a calm disposition, given to reliance on my scientific knowledge, the discovery that I was imprisoned did not discompose me in any great degree. Instead, I sought for some means of withdrawing the bolts. But none existed. I now thought in dismay that I had not a single tool with me with which to dig out of this gloomy prison. I then sat down to reflect on the situation. The longer I pondered, the more terrifying the aspect of things became. First, not a soul knew of my whereabouts. As I had no naim, my place could not be determined except by tracking me; this would prove impossible, because I had followed the beds of watercourses, long stretches of which were bare rock. I would not be missed for three days yet, as I had said that I expected to be gone for a period twice as long, and three days more than I had already been absent, before I proposed to return. No; there was no hope of escape, and now I realized how true were the words of Rai Ernon of Suern when he told me that a Poseida depended for his very life on his being surrounded by the creations of his knowledge in the realm of natural physics.

The food which I had brought with me was with my horse and outfit, as far beyond my reach as the stars. It might be that they would finally search for me and find my horse. But no, he would not be apt to remain three or four days alone in that awful wilderness; he would wander, perhaps go back to the vailx. But he would leave no trail to give a clue to my prison, for he would go as he came, over an unyielding, rocky stream bed. Hunger pangs again suggested that I had no food; I did not even have any water. Hope still remained, for was not Incal my protecting Father? How futile this, my hope! God, Incal, Brahm, call the Eternal Spirit what you will—truly he heeds the needs of His children, but those needs which seem to the child to be uppermost are not always so adjudged by the Eternal One. He operates through His children, whether human or angelic ones, making each one interdependent with all others, and thus men or angels may have for helpers each other, or perhaps only some animal brother. God takes note of a drowning mariner, but unless some brother is there to rescue, he may physically perish. He tempers the wind to the shorn lamb, but generally only through the fact that self-interest, or it may be some higher emotion, as pity, is aroused in the mind of a beholding man. Nay, it is only through the driving force of character, by our Heavenly Father implanted in the souls of His children, that He ever helps or saves. And this is mostly true: that the physical body must pray with muscular action if it would get an answer to its needs in physical form; the mind must pray through mental processes, and its answer will be in mental results, while the Spirit shall pray through its spiritual nature, and receive those values which are not perceptible to the natural mind. All this; but although the mind prays forever, and the body does no work, the results, unless a brother acts, shall not be for the body. And though the Spirit prays, yet if the mind pray not also, knowledge will not come to the brain. How shall the mind pray? By being in harmony with the Spirit. And how shall it have this harmony? By control through the will of the animal body, that it does not infringe the laws of that wholeness which is health.

When I sat in the cave house and prayed to Incal with my whole mind, yet, as I could not pray with my muscles, no release would come for the body, neither food nor drink. I might, on the mental plane, have influenced Rai Gwauxln to understand my predicament; this, to him, would have been clairvoyance; but this I could not do while the enemy who had aroused my curiosity to work my ruin intercepted all such clairvoyant messages; more especially I could not, being ignorant of the proper method. It would have been mere chance that Gwauxln would have been influenced by my mental tension of distress undirected by my knowledge. Meanwhile, unaware of how to use such powers, I dismissed thoughts of any possibility of escape in that direction. But I would pray to Incal. So I knelt on the cold, cruel floor, and prepared to invoke His aid. As I uttered His name I heard a musical laugh, albeit mocking, a sound which thrilled me with that dread terror which every man and woman has sometime felt, either in childhood days or in later life, that chill which shivers the senses when listening to some weird tale of horror, told by the fire's open grate, while the Storm King rocks the very foundations of the ground. Turning, and arising from my knees, I saw the Incaliz of the Great Temple in Caiphul.

"Why did you start at seeing me, as if you had looked on a demon?"

To this question I could give only one reply, that my sudden fright must have been from beholding him in that manner, since I was not accustomed to seeing men go about like ghosts, disembodied, yet not seeming to be so.

I felt a great joy at his coming, for I then believed that Incal had answered my yet unspoken plea for mercy by sending Mainin to my aid. And yet, why should I still be possessed by that unaccountable fear, the fear which overcame me upon first seeing him? I knew in the moment after its utterance that it did not arise from the cause attributed, his method of arrival to my prison, because I knew that as a Son of the Solitude he possessed the power to lay aside the gross body of earth as one would an overcoat and project himself to any desired place. I knew as I looked upon him that his physical body was in a trance sleep, thousands of miles away in Poseid. I had no such power to project myself, otherwise it would have been easy for me to let Rai Gwauxln know of my danger; at least, unknowing of Mainin's interference, I thought so. But as Incal had sent the Incaliz to me all was surely well.

The priest doubtless read my thoughts, for he said that he had become aware of my unpleasant predicament through Incal, and had come to assist me to escape. He must, however, leave me until he could get aid to me by dispatching a vailx from Caiphul. It would not take long, and meanwhile I must be of good cheer. And then he disappeared as he had come, and I was again alone, awaiting his promised return with a feverish anxiety not to be expressed in words. Hours passed, and he did not come, nor did anyone else. Hours grew into days, three days, and he did not come, neither did any relief. The pangs of hunger, terrible as they had become, were as nothing compared to my thirst. Once more the daylight ceased to filter through the grating overhead and the crevice leading to the upper ground. I had worn the ends of my fingers to rawness trying to release the bolts of the door; had sounded every inch to see if it did not contain a secret spring that would let loose some part of the prison wall. But fate had no such kindness in store for me. Seven times the light had gone out above me, marking seven nights since Mainin's visit.

Several times my torture of hunger and thirst had rendered me wildly delirious, with lucid intervals. In one of these lucid moments of comparative calm, as I lay moaning on the sandy floor, feebly calling on Incal for help, I heard the same low laugh that had heralded Mainin's first appearance. The sound fired me with temporary strength, and I sat up. I would have cursed the Incaliz for his long absence, which had meant so much suffering for me, had I not feared that in his anger he would leave me there to die. I no longer felt for him the reverence I had always felt, for I was certain now that he was not what men thought him. And I would have cursed him because of that, because of my inward sense that although his esoteric knowledge was great, and he was recognized as a Son, nonetheless he was black-hearted and an abomination in the sight of Incal, and that in him the Sons of the Solitude were deceived as the very elect. The reason I did not denounce him to his face was because of the fast-vanishing hope that he might still be induced to help me escape.

This time he came with changed manner. Now when he spoke, his first words were in mockery of my appeals to the great Father of Life.

"Ha! Much good may it do you to cry out to Incal or any helper. God! There is no God. ₁ Bah! How blind men are to pray to such empty ideals as their imaginings name 'God!' Men of Poseid say Incal is God; men of Suernis say Yeovah, and they of Necropan say Osiris. What madness and idiocy!"

Here I sat more erectly, and regarded him a moment before asking if he were not afraid so to blaspheme Incal and to deny his Maker.

"Do you think, Zailm, son of Menax, that I should do as I have if I thought any God existed? Is it news,—aye, it is news to you that I should desire to achieve the ruin of her called Anzimee—that I came from a former life on earth, aye! Many of them, filled with hatred of her who always up until now has caused me to be exposed to the laws of man? She cannot now, for in the Book of Fate I do not find it so written, so that either it is not there, or else I have lost my power to read fate, a thing I think not likely. But I will, through you, wring her heart to the depths, so that she shall cry out in anguish of soul! What has Anzimee done to me? Not as Anzimee, but as a powerful woman and seeress, before she was born in the earth as Anzimee. I follow her in vengeance. To wring her soul in agony I compassed the death of Menax, against whom personally I had no reason; I have almost done the same for you, although I have nothing against you. It was I that worked upon your curiosity so that you might find your death here. I had hoped to hinder your confession of your life-sin with Lolix unto Anzimee. Then, after you had met your death, and then been found by me, I would have gotten so much more misery for her out of the public exposure of your wickedness, for I had all the proofs well in hand. But that scheme is foiled; I care not overmuch; your death will cause her much torture. For that purpose also was Lolix led to do as she did, and you with her also, so long ago, for I lay My plans long ahead, being gifted with vast power of for piercing the future. For that same purpose shall the Rai be brought low, and finally she, who is the object of my most intense wrath, shall not know good from evil, so that her name shall be a scorn in the mouths of the people. Revenge is sweet, Zailm, sweet!"

My horror and my weakness together made it impossible for me to do anything but sit and stare in silent helplessness, even if any physical body been before me upon which to act.

"You are aghast at my evil? I am too old to fear failure, and am beyond the reach of the laws of men, at last. No man, nor all the men on earth, could deprive me of life or liberty. I have long known a secret which prolongs life many times the common length; it is a secret obtained from the deeper Night-Side of Nature. One day shall come when a Poseid shall know these secrets. It will be a sad day for it, I rejoice to think! I was old, old, when Gwauxln of Poseid thought me a boy with himself; so also thought the Sons of Solitude, for I was cunning in concealment. They still think so. I—yes, I will tell you, for you are even now as one who is dead. I have worked for three centuries in this present body. Did I not say that I am old? I have counteracted the good done by Ernon of Suern, so that he died of a despairing heart. I do this so that I may, if possible, wither all the hopes of humankind, turn them down from the infinite path, down to demonhood, death and destruction. Ernon worked to the exaltation of mankind; I to its depression; so we came in conflict, and I won. And why did he not know my hand? Because I have always worked in the dark, kept my own counsel, and obtained mastery over the evil hosts which are not human, never were, and never will be. And against Workers in the dark can no Son of Light prevail, for both work on the animal nature of man, which, having no light of guidance, takes the first offered support, thus favoring Workers in the Dark. But enough. I would not tell you so much were it not that you would not have much power thereby over me—ME, understand—were you alive instead of practically dead. Do you think now that I can have belief in a God? Bah! If God exists, I fear not; yet let Him punish!" [1]

And now a fearful, glorious and wonderful sight appeared. The night had come while Mainin thus confessed to me and gloried in his apical crimes, and called upon Incal to punish if He existed. In the total darkness of the prison, which, being physical gloom, could not veil the form of Mainin, there appeared that which struck terror to both our hearts, albeit terror of different sorts. A human form, which still was not of earth, surrounded by a blinding white light, stood before us. Was this Incal? Had He really accepted the rash challenge of the criminal priest? Upon His countenance rested a calm but awful expression, though not of anger or any human emotion. For an instant the wondrous eyes gazed upon me, then turned to Mainin. He then spoke, calmly, musically, and while I listened all my pain left me, though the words were of fearful import: "To feel the perfect calm over the agony steal."

The voice was like my conception of the tones of Incal, as He said:

"I shall not, O Mainin, list your crimes—you know them every one. You have been among the Sons, and they taught you all they knew, and about Me you learned more than they could teach, aye, centuries ago. I knew your way; I knew its evil, yet did not interfere, for you are your own master, even as all men are self-masters; few, alas, are faithful! But your height of wisdom, prostituted to selfishness, to sin, to crime, more completely than any other man has dared, is your destruction. Your name means 'Light,' and your brilliance has been great, but you have been as a light adrift on the seas, a lure to death of all them that follow you, and these have been numerous. You have blasphemed God, and jeered in your soul, saying, 'Punish!' But your day had not come. Therefore you were let go without rebuke. It made you bold, and you would go on, even now. But lo! Anzimee you shall not harm, for she is handmaiden of Christ, even my own daughter in service. You have well deserved the penalty, and because you have knowingly dared it, lo! Now shall it be dealt out to you. I would prefer that it was possible to avert it. But yours is one out of a myriad of cases, more heinous because you are wise, not ignorant. But because you are an ego, a ray from my Father, and now give out no more light, but darkness only, I will cut you off for a season, for you shall neither destroy more of my sheep, nor be let to leave unpunished the evil you have done. It would be better for you if you could cease to exist. But this may not be of an ego. I can only suspend you as a human entity and cast you into the outer darkness to serve as one of the powers of nature. Get behind me!" The High Priest had stood the picture of an awful terror, numbed beyond thought of escape, which indeed was not possible, for the Judge was Man, and more than Man finite—was MAN INFINITE, even CHRIST.

Now, however, as the Son of Light ceased to speak, Mainin uttered a howl of mingled terror and defiance. At this dread sound the Christ stretched forth His hand, and instantly Mainin was surrounded with a glowing flame which, on disappearing, revealed also the disappearance of the Demon Priest.

Thus had Mainin sinned, perverting his noble wisdom to evil and to sowing the seeds of sin, on and in the hearts of unsuspecting weaklings of humanity. He had sown and Suern was to reap, and through Suern, the world. But for this moving he himself was blasted from the Book of Life by a curse from the Son of Man.

Even those unfamiliar with only the material aspect of nature can find no difficulty in comprehending the destruction of the life of a man whose corporeal body was in far away Caiphul, when they consider that the earthly frame is no more an essential of the real man than the cocoon is a part of the butterfly, although in either case these things are essential to physical life.

Terrified by the awful sight of the blasting, I sank on my face on the floor. From this position I was told to arise by the Christ, who said:

"Such is the fate of the wholly selfish man. Fear not for your own safety, for I do not blast you; neither worship me, but my Father who sends me. I have reached the perfection of the Seventh Principle and am Man, also the Son of Man, yet more than any man, for I am in the Father and the Father is in me. But all men who *will* may follow me and be by me in the Kingdom, for are we not all children of One, our Father? I am He, *Christ*; that which I am, the Spirit of every man is. The penalty visited upon Mainin was not annihilation, which can not be; neither was it the death which is transition, but the death which lives no more as human life, but is out for a season into the outer darkness of devildom. Behold, I speak, and although you have ears, you do not hear, neither comprehend. But your hearing shall come to you, and you shall know, and shall lead my people. And lo! You shall lead them in a day that is to you still far away. But now you shall go no more to Atlantis, to live there, neither be seen by Anzimee any more, until she has gone from Earth twice and come again, and shall be called Phyris. Lo! I have said that these things should come to pass, and did prophesy to you in that city called Caiphul, and you heard me, yet heeded not. But now you will heed me, for I speak great words of GOD—and the world is His. Yet now no man knows me; but in a far day I will come again, yea! I will enter in and dwell as a perfect human soul, and make that Man first fruit of them that sleep the sleep which is change, so that by me he shall be exalted above Death. Then shall men rise up, and mock me, being unbelievers, and shall crucify me, yet shall I, who have become Jesus the *Christ*, not be harmed, but only my earthly house. And they shall be forgiven, for they will not know what they do. ₁ Peace I give to you. Sleep!"

Footnotes

208:1 NOTE.—A deep, narrow ravine.

215:1 Psalms lxiii, 1

217:1 NOTE.—"The fool hath said in his heart, 'There is no God.'"

220:1 St. Matthew, xii, 23.

CHAPTER XXIV. DEVACHAN

Obedient to this command I slept. When I awakened I was still in the prison, but all the suffering, all the tortures of hunger and thirst that I had endured were gone. Nothing seemed strange to me, not even when I arose and found that behind me, as a shell, remained the poor clay casket which had suffered so keenly under the pangs of starvation. All was as natural in seeming as are things in vivid dreams. I thought of Anzimee, and wondered if she, too, felt as happy as I did at that moment. I prayed that she might. Then I thought of the words of Him who called Himself the Son of Man, and wondered what manner of being He was. His talk had, for the most part, been without meaning to me; yet from it I understood that I was dead; that Anzimee would see me no more until after what dimly seemed an eternity, and not then as Anzimee, nor would I then be Zailm; yet I felt no regret over this long prospective separation. And in that time this Son of Man would have come again to the world, and left work for His brethren, the children of our FATHER, who in doing this work would be following after Him, and would become as Himself, in so far as to be disenthralled from time and from earth, and have all things, life and death. Yet, dimly understanding all this, I comprehended not its perfect fullness, for my natural mind was not able to grasp its spiritual meaning.

This, then, was Navazzamin, and I was what men call dead. It was much different from my concepts, as taught me by the priests of Incal, because it apparently differed not at all from earth-life, so far as I had as yet experienced. Perhaps it would if I were now to go and pass through the Maxin-Light. To do this would not be suicide, because I was already dead. No, it would purge away the earthiness which possibly prevented my finding the real Navazzamin which had been taught me. Would Anzimee and all others of my loved ones come here some day, and, should we meet and know each other here? Oh! It must be so, it must be so!

Filled with these reflections I stepped to the door, forgetting that its lock had previously prevented my exit. Only when it opened at my touch did I remember that it had defied every previous effort. Lightly I stepped away down the tunnel until I came to the daylight and to my saddle and tools, and yes, my horse, faithful animal! He was eating the grasses, and evidently made the overflowing waters at the generator his headquarters. Leave him? Not if I could avoid it! I was free at last! I looked around at the dry washes lying under the open sky, with their eroded monuments of clay, capped with wild pampas plumes. How gracefully these nodded in the light breeze, seeming to say, "Free now, free!" Then I went to my horse, to take him, forgetful that being dead I could not need such transportation. But he seemed not to see me, or to know my presence. This was a difficulty. I was used to conquering difficulties, but this was one where I was at a low what to do. I sat down and looked at the handsome animal. The longer I looked, the more perplexed I became. At last I got up in a sort of exasperation and talked very earnestly to the animal. No effect! Of course not! The more I talked, the more contented the horse became, as if he felt that I was near, and was satisfied. Finally I started away intending to leave him, since I could in no way influence him. This had great effect! The farther I got the more uneasy he became, as I was able to see, until at last he lifted up his head and neighed loudly. Once, twice, thrice, and then he started after me in a wild gallop! When he reached me he grew easy; but as I went rapidly onwards he followed. He was awake to a sense of my presence, though he could not see, feel or hear me. My mind was wholly occupied in getting this faithful servant to the camp. So, feeling no fatigue, nor hunger nor thirst, nor any sensation of the physical life, I walked clear into camp, all those miles, with that horse following contentedly after! When we reached the camp the vailx was there, but only two of the men, the others having gone in search of me, since I was now over-due in my arrival, thanks to Mainin. These men, like the horse, could not see me, but unlike him, neither could they sense my nearness. My utmost efforts were entirely unsuccessful, and although I stayed for two days, until the search was over and the men had returned to the vailx, to obtain further orders from Caiphul, I was unsuccessful still. One of the hunters was still out, and when he came back I spoke to him. He could not see me, but my presence affected him strangely. So I spoke again and again, till at last he sat down trembling by my desk in the salon of the vailx. A paper and a pen and ink were on this, and I said to the man: "Use that pen." To my partial surprise, he used it, but seemed in a deep sleep the while and mechanically wrote: "Use that pen." An idea occurred to me, and uttered words which had no connection of meaning, every one of which he wrote just as I spoke it. This was en-couraging, so I next said: "It is I, even Zailm, who say these things; I am dead. Go home to Caiphul." Of my body and its whereabouts I said nothing, feeling that it was properly entombed. But what I spoke in dic-tation was all written, not that the medium heard, but for the time I was the controlling intelligence of his body. The others took the message and hid it, and when the writer had come out of trance they asked him what he had written. But he denied having written anything. This seemed to satisfy them, the man was so obviously honest in his denial. So they went and gathered the equipage and animals into the vailx, and prepared to leave for Caiphul. Their action satisfied me, so that I thought no more of them, but began to wish I was at home. I reflected that I had left the disability of the flesh in the cave-house, so I ought to be able to go here or there, as had Mainin. I would try it. So I said to myself: "I would be at home, at Agacoe, where the Rai is, and he will be able to see me, and know all things of this matter."

With this utterance all things changed, and I found myself in the pal-ace of Agacoe. But neither Gwauxln nor Anzimee, who was there also, were seemingly able to see me, anymore than the man in the vailx had been. What was this thing called death, this barrier? Was death indeed the threshold between two conditions, communication to and fro be-ing impossible, as futile to attempt from my side as from the other? I had thought Gwauxln able to penetrate this barrier. But alas! I found myself no more able to obtain his recognition than that of the others. I knew he could see those who put off their fleshly shells in order to travel as Mainin had done, and resume them at will; why then not see me? Death perhaps meant more even than putting aside the body. I stood there a long time, wondering at this thing called death. As I stood by Gwauxln's side, having abandoned the attempt to impress him with a knowledge of my presence, a human shape came into the apartment. Shape? It seemed as real as any of the courtiers sitting by the arch of the doorway. None of these latter appeared aware of the new arrival; except the Rai, no one beside myself saw him, but continued their talk regarding the sudden death of the Incaliz Mainin, and disposal of his body in the Maxin-Light on the previous afternoon. I had been dumbfounded at the strange resemblance of the new arrival to myself, but I was immeasurably amazed to hear the Rai exclaim:

"What! Zailm dead! Dead?"

An attendant, hearing this exclamation, but seeing only the sovereign, hastily went to him enquiring his pleasure. As he approached he passed directly through the form which Gwauxln had addressed by my name! Neither the human shape nor the attendant seemed aware of the remarkable occurrence, but the Form, smiling, in reply said:

"Aye, Zo Rai; I am Zailm, but not dead, except in that I am free of earthly restraint."

Confused, almost stupefied by these happenings, I sank on a divan near me. Gwauxln could see what purported to be me was indeed a very image of me in looks, speech, memory of events, in fact really was the psychic counterpart of my life and self, but he could not see me. Mystery, aye mystery! How many had death to reveal to me? I had left in the Umaur prison a material image of myself; was it possible that there also existed an intermediate counterpart of both my material body and myself, which yet retained certain gross forms of life lost by me, making it visible while I was invisible? But as Gwauxln was a Son of the Solitude, why was he unable to perceive both my astral and myself? He was not unable, but would not allow me to know his ability. The reason, plain to me now, but not then, briefly is:—That a person in dying is separated into psychic elements which, not to be too detailed in the statement, are threefold, earthly, psychic and spiritual. Of these the highest is the I Am, the ego. The others are those above mentioned as spoken to by Gwauxln, and as left in the prison. Now, the ego seeks an exalted level; the "shell" stays in the earthly conditions until the body, finally dissolved, is "dust to dust." The exalted or egoic state is one of isolation. As spoken in Biblical records, ₁ a medium can go to it, but the ego, after a little while, cannot return to earth, nor know anything earthly save those extremely tense mental-spiritual states of one or many individuals who reach out for the things of God. And these things are not earthly. This is real mediumship. The genuine medium rises to the necessary height, but the ego cannot descend to earth, cannot deny the law of progress, except during a limited period after the transition called death, and then it is not retrogression. A medium is like an aneroid barometer, able to indicate the degree of ascension above the ocean of water, or of spirit. But he must be present on the level; the level cannot descend to him. Therefore it is that one in dying is a traveler to that border no one returns from. There is no return of the departed, except through physical rebirth and reincarnation. I leave it to you to find out that this is not transmigration of souls, for the latter postulates rebirth in lower animal form as a punishment for sin; such a thing cannot be. Retrogression is impossible, and the whole notion is just a corrupt falsity of conception, founded upon the misunderstood truth of reincarnation, whose successive rebirths are invariably progressive.

To return to the Rai and his determination not to see me. Gwauxln knew that I was not yet come into the proper state, and feared to interrupt my progress. Therefore he would not allow my "shell" to influence him, so far as I could determine. Having, however, by the contact of his supersensitive nature perceived the fact of my demise, he sought further, and though his actions denied to me that he saw me, he still put into operation forces to the result that I should presently be ready for him to come to me. But not until my mundane life was faded would he do so; not until I was gone forth into the "undiscovered country" of Navazzamin. Then he came, and the meeting was one of simple joy, of unaffected grace, between two souls equal before God, not in status of acquired wisdom, for in that Gwauxln was vastly above me, but in that equal brotherhood of the Spirit which I wish now reigned an oarth. It shall yet do so, for the Cross Bearer said, "You are all Children of one Father!" Behold, it is so!

When Gwauxln had come to me, the sphere of earth was in no way brought with him. To have carried earthly conditions with him would have been to remand me to earth, and have rendered me palpable injustice. No ego ever is permitted, by the very laws of its being, to go back to earth except a wrong thing is thereby suffered. The selfhood of an initiate may project itself into devachan, but the dweller in devachan (heaven) cannot go again to earth till it is born again there. Indeed! Why does the soul leave earth after the grave? It is because in devachan it assimilates the fruits of active earth-life. Right here is the explanation of the written Word of God: "Whatsoever your hand finds to do, do it with your might; for there is no work, no device, nor knowledge, nor wisdom, in the grave, where you will go." 1 True it is that in the grave nothing is done. In the following pages much will seem to indicate my "doings" between the grave and the cradle. But observe that the whole of earth had become a perfect blank to me. The soul cannot return save it re-embody in rebirth. To call it back is to cause revulsion of this process, and re-association with the astral-shell which the ego left behind at the death of the body. Such re-association revives the astral whereupon action and reaction take place between it and the ego, much to the detriment of the latter. All I "experienced" was only the fruits of what I had done; I could do no new thing, think no new thought, experience nothing not in itself the expression of something done before I came through the grave. And in this rearrangement and crystallizing of my past earth life, time cut no figure. The realness of it was only the reality of vivid dreaming; time had no part in that which was already done.

It lay in the power of the Rai to recognize me, but he would not, that I might not suffer harm. It similarly lies in the power of all forceful mediumistic natures (generally) belonging to the sect called "Spiritualists" to do likewise. These media can recall the departed, but at what dread cost to the departed ego, and reacting upon the medium to the latter! I say no process of Nature as ordered by our Heavenly Father may be lightly interrupted; every such act carries penalty proportionate to the understanding of the culprit; never light, and often of fearful weight. Had I remained to see, I would have seen Gwauxln, Son of the Solitude, go forth in his own astral shape, after retiring his corporeal to his secret chamber, that no harm might come to the body while he was away. And the shell-Zailm I would have seen go with him to the Incalithlon, and there I should have seen the Rai cause it to pass into the Unfed Light. But of all men on earth only the trained eyes of a Son could have seen what then happened. The "shell" would not have emerged from the Maxin ever again. What was this? Why destroy it? So that it might not go forth in the earth and impress sensitives such as the vailx-man whom I had impressed in Umaur, and whom my "shell" might otherwise continue to impress. Thus might have resulted much trouble, for this astral of mine was but faithfully repeating my final words before I parted company with it, when it said to Gwauxln, there in Agacoe, "I am not dead." It was even then like all other shells, its double composite nature only holding together during the limited period it could draw sustaining magnetism from my recently closed earthly correspondence.

In some cases such sustenance is sufficient for ages, in others, centuries, years, days, or even minutes, according to the earthward-turning, or the spirit-turning sympathies of the decedent. The astral is only vivified force, bearing the image in all respects of its ego, the I AM. Even prophecies made by "returned spirits," prophecies which come true after years, perhaps are but the impressed foresight of the ego at the moment of departure. For an instant it sees into vast future depths of time. And this glimpse is imprinted on its astral-shell. It is psychic form. If the phenomena set in motion by man are of that intensely vital created by Moses, Buddha, Zoroaster, then just as long as a believer of any one of these religious systems adheres, that long, but no longer the "shells" of these prophets will continue their derived existence. It is psychic force which is their controlling lever, formed force. It is this same force which holds the stars to their orbits, and the atoms to theirs.

The Secrets Of Mount Shasta And A Dweller On Two Planets

It is vital, and dual, being positive and negative. To separate the force or "fire element" of the ancients (ancients to you, not to me), was to cause the focus for such an Unfed Fire as the Maxin, and in later ages, in Israel the power in the Ark of the Covenant, alike with the Maxin, fatal to life. These focus points are portals into which the entire concourse of lesser forces of nature are absorbed upon contact. These foci are also the sole residence of the much sought "universal solvent" of the alchemists; needless to say that as some of these alchemists have been Sons of the Solitude, that therefore they have had the wonderful "solvent" to serve them.

It must be equally apparent why the secret has remained carefully concealed. These foci are the very auricles of the heart of the Universe, therefore any sort of formed force meets its Omega here. Consequently, when Gwauxln caused my astral to pass into the Maxin, he returned to the sum-undivided of cosmic force a quantity no longer of use to the formed world. On a very small scale indeed the medulla oblongata of the brain is such a focus, a maxin-point, where positive and negative meet. Were it not so, life would be impossible; destroy this maxin of the body, even by a needle thrust, and vitality instantly ceases. But enough. Gwauxln came to me, who could not go to him. Those not initiates do often thus rise in their sleep to their friends, but they fail at the point of not knowing how to do so voluntarily.

As one great point of my work is to explain these mysteries, I may spare yet a little space in rendering clear, past all mistake, how it is that those on earth can acquire the power of going to their friends beyond the Divide, but never these last come back to earth.

The barometer on a calm day registers at sea level a definite degree of air pressure, and at one mile above the sea, on the side of a mountain, let us say, the mercury in the tube has "fallen" to another definite but less degree. This is in both cases due to air pressure. If one now desires to know the pressure existing at a mile's height, will he go up to it, or will he bring that altitude down to himself? In storm weather the barometer "falls" also, the air is less dense, meteorological changes have taken place which in effect have brought the high aerial altitudes, *i.e.*, the conditions prevailing in high altitudes, down to the lower level. But thus has a storm been created; superior conditions have forced one. So it is that by the exercise of superior force a medium at a "spiritualistic séance" can bring back or down a soul which had gone on through the grave; but it will give rise to a psychic storm, and these are exceedingly costly occurrences. The Witch of Endor created such a storm when she forced Samuel down to earth again. Beware, O ye mediums! If you are, friend, a human "spirit barometer," you may rise to your friends, but never, if you value the soul's peace for yourself, or for them, seek to bring them down to your "circles."

Those who seek only the exciting part of this history will do well to omit perusal of the greater part of Book I, and leave it to the reader who seeks the reason and lemon of my life record, and how I am able to depict past scenes that took place more than twelve thousand years ago.

Through the crime of Mainin the Incaliz, I had been forced to seek my psychic plane, and because I was I, and am I, that plane is more or less one of isolation. That is to say, it was peopled with the children of my fancy, my experiences, my hopes, longings, aspirations, and my conceptions of persons, places and things. No two people see in the same way the same world. To Anzimee, with her knowledge, the world could not have seemed the same as to Lolix, who saw from another, and in some ways lower, standpoint, while to neither was it the same as to the wise minister, Menax; and with all three the view of life was different from that held by Gwauxln. So also the heaven, the devachan, of one person is filled with his concepts of life, while that of his neighbor on either side, so to speak, is peopled with other peculiar mental properties. Now the state after the grave, and his or her knowledge, aspirations and trusts of life is the condition of harvest, where no one acts, but where the rewards of action in the preceding life are paid; it is the land of Lethe, where is no pain, sorrow, sickness or agony, for these earthly conditions began on earth, and they unavoidably must be finished on earth. So karma decrees. Heaven is passive, not active, and the results of knowledge are there assimilated by the soul; that is, made so that the new birth is like the succeeding page of a business ledger—all of the old lives, with the last added in. I hope I have not been tiresomely wordy. I have not, if I have given a clear comprehension of what the relation really is between earth and heaven, and that the latter is to the former as the resting time of night is to the activity of the day. Let none suppose that the devachan of one who has committed earth-binding errors, and must by these bonds again reincarnate, is anything like the great Life with which are crowned those who are faithful unto the death of that serpent in the heart, animal lusts. The words can well portray mere devachan, but they are powerless to depict that Life. Finite can never compass Infinite. Then let the Infinite into your hearts.

Even so I pondered, in the presence of Gwauxln, Anzimee, and the others, who either would not or could not see me, my earthly powers were departing. The power which I had possessed a moment before of seeing persons, places and things of the world seemed fast escaping me, while glorious sights and sounds replaced them, sights and sounds akin to the day dream of the life just left, except that these were real to my senses, tangible and mutually reactive. Ah, well! If those left on Death's first shore could not see me nor know my presence, nor I see them nor their presence, why not unresistingly glide into enjoyment of the peace and the new sights and things which were come in place of the old? Yea! I would. Goodbye, old life; hail to the new.

As peacefully as a dream the sight of the palace and of familiar things faded from view, and I seemed to have come into a beautiful valley, hemmed in by azure hued mountains. Before me stood a building of unpretentious exterior. Irregular in its outlines, it seemed to have been built in sections, added as more rooms became necessary. What an altogether excellent idea that was, I thought. It was formed of slabs of rock, not quarried, but naturally scaled from the ledge. In places it was three stories high, in others only two, but mainly all the rooms were on the ground floor. What sort of people lived here? Certainly people whose architectural abandon was after my own heart. I felt, before seeing them, already friendly. Assuredly they lacked not the love of beauty, for covering the quaintly picturesque dwelling ran perennial vines, while all about lay tasteful gardens. Should I venture to intrude my presence? As I considered, a man opened a door near me and came forward. He had a very familiar appearance; where had I seen him? I had forgotten as completely as if I had never known the life which I had experienced as Zailm, the son of Menax. My senses were dominated by the feelings of boyhood, and the thoughts and ideas and simple knowledge of boyhood in the mountain home by Pitach Rhok. As the familiar looking stranger drew close he said:

"Do you know me, your father, Merin Numinos?"

While this settled the apprehension that dimly arose in my consciousness that I was alone, and therefore invisible to people, it only quenched the idea that had rapidly faded as I looked on the house of slab rock, the idea that I was dead. I no longer knew any such experience, and the knowledge of death had passed away so far as it applied to my own decease. I was filled with pleasure at the question of the man before me, and I now perceived that he was the father of my childhood's ideal, but not him whom my mother had always presented in disparaging light: she, you know, did not like him. But this thought did not present itself then; I only knew that I looked on him whom I recognized as my father. I was overjoyed at finding him, and I replied: "Truthfully, I know you well!" Then he asked: "Will you rest?"

"Being fatigued, I will do so, and no doubt be much benefited."

Then Merin Numinos led me into the great rambling house to what I must call a den, even though the name may seem inelegant. Den it was, certainly, but so charmingly, delightfully confused and disorderly; books and specimens of rocks, and all things which a boy loves were scattered about in that inextricable litter which fills the trim housekeeper with despair. My pleasure was unbounded, for I felt that I was a boy, only a boy, and had yet to reach maturity, the unknown possibilities of which seemed to fill my whole being with pleasant anticipation of the future; I was a lad of exuberant spirits let loose in his own realm, and in this room free from fear of the orderly mother who had elsewhere always restrained me. On a bed, roughly smoothed up in one corner of the shaded room, lay a pack of books from the district library, each marked, "Pitach Rhok District 5," in Poseid characters. These were in my way, and I laid them carefully, for books were always almost sacred objects in my eyes, on the floor, in order that I might rest on the bed. Then I laid me down to sleep upon the rude couch which had always seemed softer and easier to fond memory than any downy cushion in the Caiphalian life. Not that I knew this as I lay down. I only knew that I experienced a state of things just suited to my desires. I had no clear idea of any event of the old life in Poseid; no memory of death, nothing. All had gone like the events of some dream which we strive in vain to recall at breakfast next morning. And yet, when I came across things in the new state similar to those known and loved in the old, when I found things here such as I had been accustomed to dream of some day carrying to realization, then the new realities, which, after all, were not new, seemed wholly satisfactory, with the added charm of achievement, though I could not recall the old.

"The whole scene which greets mine eyes, In some strange mode I recognize, As one whose ev'ry mystic part, I feel prefigured in my heart."

Nature here, though presenting some novelties, was not different enough to excite special attention.

One day I arose and departed from the scenes of this reproduced boyhood's life. The curtain rose on things derived from the later life after leaving Pitach Rhok for Caiphul, and I found myself now in the midst of acquiring knowledge even to the great degree of a Xio-Incala, a degree greater than even any scientist of the modem world has achieved. But this phase of devachan soon passed, because, not having reached such a degree on earth, nor having even tried to do so, I had no real basis from which to draw devachanic scenes. Thus passed the time around me, sometimes with real egoii of deceased earthly persons who had worked with me intimately on earth, and so had with me to reap the results of the collaboration. At other times I was alone with my concepts, which, however, seemed as real as actual persons, for all seemed absolutely real. Lolix was here in her better aspects; but the sin of our day was held against our return to earth.

The Secrets Of Mount Shasta And A Dweller On Two Planets

It seemed perfectly natural to meet Anzimee one night as I wandered by the shore of a sea adjacent to an artificial wilderness, where all things were arranged in harmony with my ideal solitude to which, in Caiphul's busy whirl, I had one day dreamed of taking her when we should be wed. It was sweet when we met to hear her call me "husband," and the peace after action was all as delightful as I had imagined it would be.

But my pen is in advance of its proper place. To return to the den:

Without disrobing, for the air was warm, I lay down and slept. When I awoke I passed down the hallway into the garden. A change had come over. I was older; the landscape was different, and the houses were more like that which my more mature needs had painted as a necessity while I still lived near Pitach Rhok. No longer was a river in the foreground, but a broad sea with only the near shore visible. The change was correspondent with the later desires of my youth. These alterations, though startling as considered from an earthly, physical standpoint, were not startling nor even remarkable to me. What sort of life or condition was this which permitted such changes, yet did not present itself as anything extraordinary to me, the beholder? Even truth should not be told in excessively wordy phrases, and all that can be replied now is that it wag the life after death, to be slightly paradoxical. But this is not the Great Life with God.

Was time consumed in effecting these changes, or was this an Aladdin's lamp sort of land where a rubbing out of one and an installation of another set of appearances took place instantaneously? I did not even pause to consider, for no such conjecture occurred to me. To me things were real. Is earth real? Spirit, God, is real, and the earth and universe are the fiat, or externalized ideas of God. The things of earth are words of God's great Word, speaking to us. So, too, are the things of devachan or heaven. Both are real, oppositely so, but only real within us, not without us. I sought my father, Merin Numinos, and asked: "How long have I slept?" It was no more anything but a habit of thought to ask this, for I had no other motive. That, in the process of death, habits of mind do not suffer extinction together with life's memories of events, was proven by my action on hearing my father's reply:

272

"You have slept for several years."

"Years!" do you exclaim? It was no remarkable thing to me to hear this account of a Rip Van Winklian nap. No, but my habit of mind which took pride in neatness of personal attire caused me unwittingly to glance at my raiment to see if it were not the worse for such long wear. The allusion to several years attracted my attention, so that having found my attire presentable, though I still gazed at my clothes, it was in an absentminded way. I said:

"You say years; also another thing, 'you have slept ever since you came into this country.' Now, I ask you, have I ever been elsewhere?"

Receiving no reply, I looked up, only to meet a stare like that of a statue from my father. He evidently knew nothing of any previous state, nor, by the very form of my question, did I know more than he.

Death was another thing never referred to, because in the instant when promoted souls find it no more possible to impress their existence upon those left behind on earth, they recognize that they are in the midst of the change called death, of which they were perhaps apprehensive all their earthly days. As the exoteric religion then, aye, and now, also, taught but one death, the devachanee knew or conjectured no other. Hence, death to the disembodied soul was and is an unknown conception. Well, there is no such thing as death for a fact. Likewise pain and sorrow. Devachan the minor is like devachan the major (Nirvana), a state particularly referred to in Revelation xxi: 4. Now, my friend, I am not postulating an argument; I must refuse to argue, and though it smacks of medieval methods, still I must also refuse to reason with you. It is the purpose of this history to state what I know by experience; I state no theoretical ideas. If you will take any small matters left unexplained into the inner sanctuary of your soul and there meditate over them, then they will become clear to you, and be as the water which quenches all thirst, if so gained. Do you have ears to hear with? Then heed that counsel. I address only those who follow these pages for profit.

All the devachanee knows of is just one change, and that is so different from what he was religiously taught to fear, therefore many souls entering heaven conceive at the moment of death that no death exists, and that the teachings received on earth from priests were but ecclesiastical fictions. Nor are they so far wrong, for there is no other death than the mere change from objective to subjective states of being, save the second death, spoken of in my final page. To be paradoxical, death is different because not different, so far as they can perceive, from the swift view of the life just closed, a view all souls have, however brief it be. Hence it was that I was unaware of the fiction called death when I asked the father I found there if I had not always been there.

Religion taught in that old age as it now teaches, that with death came the cessation of all earthly sorrow. This is true for a time limited by the length of the soul's sojourn in devachan. These earth-born mists do not intrude there for the reason that being earth born they must of necessity have abiding places on earth and influence only those on earth.

"The evil that men do lives after them."

This is true; and in the form of crystallized disposition to do wrong, that evil lies in wait for their return to earth life; it is the wrongly so-called "Adamic" tendency to sin, and while the sinner is free of its power in devachan, the seed, like tares with the wheat, is ready to grow a harvest of sorrow along with the growing life of the new incarnated one; and until some good action shall atone for evil done, this evil will continue to grow. Fortunately, man has an eternity in which to make repayment, 1 and through following God's laws and being true to right, whatever its source, the tares are little by little uprooted. A good act is the erasure of a bad, and once performed is "often buried with the bones," thus completing the philosophy of Hamlet.

All about me were those I loved. As time seemed to lapse, I became conscious of the presence of one and another of my friends. Anzimee, Menax, Gwauxln, Ernon, Lolix without the shadow, all those and thousands more who have no name to the reader were there. They did not come; no, they were with me, each as I had conceived. These were my concepts, for they were subjective, not objective; they were my ideals, not real people; and they formed my world. It did not occur to me that they were not real. Did it ever occur to you, reader, that the world of your senses is the only world you have? That, if you had no sight, smell, hearing, taste or touch, that you would have no world even though your soul was imprisoned in a body thus dead, yet alive in a vegetative way? As the soul of each living man, woman or child, is different from every other soul, so also the world is different to every person—not the same precisely in any two cases. Now it is the record of the soul, made on imperishable mental substance, which constitutes much of the life after the grave; the record merges into a reality, and all seems equally real, just as real as when the combined senses first perceived it; in truth this afterlife is a reconstituted and inverted earth life, subjective now, instead of objective. My supposed friend may be a real enemy, yet if I die thinking of him or her as my friend, that concept is the one carried into the afterlife, and vice versa.

Thus, all about me were my friends. The things of my sense records, and the places, were the scenes where all these friends moved. But while I had my world about me in this way, a concept of me existed in the imaged world of every friend I had. Not that I was with them, but their concept of me was with them. Thus regarding the reality of all those concepts that were non-involute, simple and easily assimilated upon being remembered from the astral record, or, so to say, memory plates of the Soul, of every incident, small or great, simple or complex, impulse or even unconscious cerebrations. But now mark a feature of vast interest, inasmuch as it affirms what I have seemed to deny, any real association of the soul in devachan with other individual souls. Devachan would indeed be a dreary heaven if the friends of mundane life were never anything but "dream faces." Dreams they are, if the incidents created in our hopes on earth, and in devachan set forth as real to all seeming, were a simple fact. But if, on the other hand, it was so complex that to solve its equation required the joint efforts of two souls working in harmony, then also in devachan the results of this complex act affected both these souls, and during the assimilation of its results, that is, during the crystallization of such results into traits of character, both these souls would actually be together as ever they were on earth. If more than two people were involved on earth, so all these souls would congregate in devachan. When the process was complete, the separation came. So it happened that in one moment of as-similative experience all my concepts were only phantasms, merely the persons of one's nightly dreams; the next moment wore complex, as my associates were real egoii like myself. To me all this was un-known; all seemed real, and so, perhaps, was so. But it is pleasant to feel that one works with a loved son, father, daughter, mother, wife or other friend; that the consequences of the more serious events of our daily lives here will bring us again together in the heaven of our hopes; that the wife you take to your heart, and to whom on your confident loving plans for the well-being of your loved ones, to realize which both you and she must work nobly, earnestly, will come across the chasm which death spreads for your bodies, and be with you or you with her, there in Navazzamin. Pleasant, that your mother, father or other dear friend shall sometimes really be with you there; and that together you shall gather your various records, and enjoy in a seeming real that which was not on earth anything but a hope never materialized.

In meeting Anzimee, who still lived on earth, I met sometimes my conception of her, sometimes her own higher self. How was the latter possible? Because she so longed for me that it developed and enabled her to project her pure soul into my plane. This was not only pleasant and beneficial to her, giving her a hold upon things unseen, of which the apostle Paul speaks, but it was a holy joy to me to meet her that way; she could come to me, but I could not go back to her. There is no retrogression.

In communion with these ideals I had my reward, for nothing oc-curred contrary to my wish. But in experiencing this reward, I also un-consciously assimilated the value of the previous life on earth. Thus my connection with politics in Poseid had brought me in contact with men and manners, and from this contact were born schemes in which I was to have had a leading part. These schemes were now brought into the subjective state, and as such appeared to me to be in process. From these apparent actions my capacities were developed, and tests of the worth of my conceptions made. All of this resulted in making a con-crete deduction which became a part of my mental being; hence in a new incarnation I would come forth to mankind possessed of phrenological organs of increased power in the handling of political and social questions. Perhaps this power would not be actively employed, owing to other tendencies being stronger; nonetheless the power would be increased and ready for use upon demand. The same thing would prove true of all these souls really associated with me, both in previous-earth-and after-heaven, the results, values and summings-up of our contemporary devachan would give them new mental traits, or increase the force of their old ones, and reincarnation would reassociate us again on earth. And it has done so, or else I never would have written this history for your profit, dear reader. My education as a geologist at Xioquithlon was tested in this same subjective heaven, and from this came added ability as a geologist; in short, an intuitive knowledge of geology and desire for that study after reincarnation. Books would then serve to bring forth the geological bent I might manifest. I might go on with other instances of the summing-up and arranging process experienced by those who have both the grave and the cradle between them and earth. But this will suffice to hint to the reader that truths lie here and sweeten the "Thoughts of the last bitter hour . . . Of stern agony, and shroud and pall."

I hope, my friend, that this effort to render death less terrifying, by relating my own experiences of it, will be fraught with success, and that these words may so sustain you that you shall "Approach your grave like one who wraps the drapery of his couch about him, and lies down to pleasant dreams."

Zerah Colburn, the marvelous boy mathematician, did not acquire his knowledge in the schools of this modern age, but brought it, a legacy from the dead centuries, his past lives, his latent power was revealed. I will not argue with you, friend, that if you had had a past life on earth, you could "not have forgotten it, but would have brought memory of it with you." No, I argue not. I only leave it with your own intelligence to decide if I am not right, when you remember that habits of life grow from repeated actions of boyhood, the details and every recollection of which are gone. And knowing that this is so, decide, if you don't think it is absurd, that actions of a life experienced century times centuries past would be possibly recollected, more especially when all the intervals were spent on a different plane of life, a place where no single memory ever intruded, and could not by the laws of God. I know what I am saying.

At length there came a time when I cared no more for the appearance of action, nor for those concepts of persons, places, or things connected with seeming activity. Chiefly now I cared to remain in some quiet spot and listen to Anzimee, the real, not the concept, as she read to or talked with me. I slept much also. One morning I did not arise; I did not care to. I was not ill; no one ever knew illness in devachan. But I had lost all desire to see or hear more of anything. I did indeed feel languor, but not weariness. So I turned over again, facing the wall, and slept. It was the last occurrence in the last chapter of a life's long rest, which, though I knew it not, had covered twelve thousand years of the actions of men of earth. Death had never appeared in that home of the soul, for my concepts did not die, they only disappeared from the view of their creator. Even the real souls of men or women did not die. No. But when they came, one after another, to the retributive awakening at the cradle, if their lives in heaven were still associated with mine, if they had not gone elsewhere in devachan, as neighbors on earth separate and put the world between them, then they disappeared, just as my concepts disappeared when I had assimilated their value. They disappeared, because all the deeds of previous earth life had crystallized as traits of character, and they were ready for earth life again. Only myself could be conscious of my own change; I could not be conscious of theirs. I was ready for activity once more. I slept, and in this sleeping died out of that life of passivity into the waking of earth, a babe in a cradle. Born to see my Master in this life, and enter the Great Rest with him!

NOTE.—But one will come after me who shall tell you more of the Great Deep of Life than I. Await her words.—Author

End of Book First

225:1 II Samuel, xii, 28.

226:1 Eccl. ix, 10.

236:1 Do not confuse "repayment" with "atonement." Jesus makes atonement for us with God. We can only begin to repay, when, having obtained forgiveness through Jesus, we try to Live Him. Until we consecrate ourselves to Christ, we cannot have recognized that we are HIS because HE owns us. When we recognize this, then we recognize that HE owns us, and we own HIM. Then, but not until then, can we even begin to repay our karma. And if we "Go and sin no more," then HE will equalize our karma, and we will be released unto HIM, released or leased again! Karma closes for one who thus is atoned for, and his opportunity for reparation begins. For such a one, no more incarnation is necessary, for has he not the SON? And that is Eternal life. What do I mean by having the Son? And by being consecrated to Christ? In this, then, can only the church postulate? No, my friends. The Divine is eternal, infinite. The Human is finite. When the awakened man comes to know himself, he chooses which way he shall go. The choice is the crossing of the Divine by the Human; it is ownership by the Son which is within.

SEVEN SHASTA SCENES. INTERLUDE

I

If there are "sermons in stones and books in the running brooks," then is "Tchastel's" craggy pile a noble library in truth. In it the vastness, the grandeur and the solemnity of nature are expressed in mystic numbers carved in the eternal granite. On those stony, stratified pages Nature's students may read the doings of the gnomes, Mother Earth's treasurers. Here, too, in characters of lava, is written Pluto's kingly record. Aye! It is indeed Nature's own volume, bound between covers of snow and ice; and marking the treasures there is a silvery ribbon whose ends hang out of the vast tome, at the north one end, at the south the other, the name of the one "McCloud" river, and of the other the "Sacramento." Again, two lesser markers are in this sublime epic, viz.: "Pitt" and "Shasta" rivers. A volume of poems should bear a poetic title; so shall this. Can we bestow one more appropriate than the aboriginal appellation, "Ieka," a name retained and used by the earliest white men whose eyes gazed on that land, far northern California, land of romance, of gold and of adventure; retained through that intuitive recognition of eternal fitness which pioneer and trapper have ever, in all lands, exhibited toward existent nomenclature. For years the noble mountain bore, for white as for aborigine, the name it had fetched from out of the night of time, as its sister peak far to the north, Mt. Rainier, retained its primal christening of "Tacoma." But, alas, for human conceit! Alas, for man's vain discontent, unable to let well enough alone! To the one snowy mount came a Russian trapper, and thereafter "Ieka" was no more on the tongues of men, unless, indeed, it was still lovingly murmured by the dusky Modoc and his savage bride. To the other glittering peak went an egotistic Englishman. His lordship found "Tacoma" so beastly savage, "doncher know," and so over its Indian appellate he tacked his own patronymic. Time evens all things and "ever is justice done." The patriotic Americanism of the Northern Pacific Railroad topographers reinstated on the company maps musical "Tacoma," tossed to rubbish the imported name, and rebuked one egotist's vanity. That "Shasta Buttes" will ever know a parallel experience is problematical; if not, it is perhaps just as well, for American gratitude willingly concedes the privilege of nomination of this proud peak to its friend, and, in the '60s, champion of our national autonomy ————— Russia. So much for a kind of mental view, past and present, of this pride of the crags and peaks.

II

On the old wagon road which existed before iron rails linked Oregon's greatest city to the metropolis of the Golden West, there still stands, as for thirty years, not many miles from the State line, a station established for stage line uses, and "run" by "Daddy Dollarhyde." A lonely place, hidden amongst towering pines, which make regal clothing for the great "Siskiyou Ridge" of the Coast Range, extending in gloomy grandeur not miles, but hundreds of miles, Dollarhyde's appeals to the heart of the traveler as a Saharan oasis to the weary caravan. "It is a lodge in some vast wilderness," and in the days of this second "Shasta Scene" (A. D. 1884) was the only footprint of civilization for many a long mile.

Leaving Dollarhyde's, the road wound as directly as possible up a two-mile stretch of exceedingly steep mountain. Up this steep, long before anything even hinted that dawn would light those grand ridges, a youth, on foot and alone, was climbing. A tramp? Temporarily; down below, at Dollarhyde's, the rest of his party still slept. Up, up he toiled, stopping when the love of nature prompted him to "bold communion with her visible forms," and to listen to her "various languages"; pausing, the better to enjoy the exhilarating freedom, the beauty of the piney slopes, the whirr of the early grouse, and the chattering of squirrel and chipmunk. Once, enchanted by the exquisite charm of a crystal spring that leapt into and across the road, he stayed his step; and again, he stood gazing afar down into the gloom of a great canyon, which became lost to view "in the dawn's early light." The summit at last! But still no sun in the sky. All beneath was yet quietly resting beneath the sway of Morpheus. Ah! What is that? Away in the south is a huge, dim mass, dull gray below, but, where its peak holds aloft the sky, it is rosy, glowing pink. As the youth gazes, spellbound, Old Sol dispels the valley glooms, thrusts aside the night, and the new day is born. The rose tints are gone, but also the gray, and in their place appears a giant, pointed cone of purest white, albeit streaked at its base with black lines, each some awful gorge. It rises not like other mountain piles, from ranges rivaling its own height; no, all alone it stands forth from its high plateau, piercing heaven's blue, from base to summit, eleven thousand feet, from ocean's plane to apical peak thirty-five hundred more— Shasta, O, Mt. Shasta.

III

Of the youth, what? A year later we find him suffering a violent fever, the "gold-fever," which yet lingers in that region of once famed mines; lingers, though it be now A. D. 1890. Away up on a mountain's side with pick, pan and shovel he has camped where a little gold may always be found; where hope whispers he may find a "pile" some time, and fortune.

All through that region forest fires have raged many weeks; all the valleys lie hidden under a pile of smoke. But the miner on the mountain is above it all, and as he labors looks out over the undulating surface of the silvery, smoky ocean, down below. He sees a strange sight. No waves disturb this sea, which, nearly a mile deep, extends away beyond scope of vision. Two or three islands dot its expanse; these are all that is left to see of lofty mountain peaks whose bases are hidden. Perchance the words "smoke-ocean" seem figurative. Look heavenward from its bottom down in the valleys; the sun, appearing like a globe of blood, needs no colored glass to shield too sensitive eyes. Now go aloft to the miner on the mountain, looking down on, but seeing not, Yreka (town). With him again gaze at the "islands"; one only of them is not black in hue. It is the largest; sharp-summited, white, shrouded in eternal snows, Mt. Shasta rises, a noble island in the murky ocean about it, nine thousand feet.

IV

Night. Otherwise the same scene. Our miner sits in his tent door, meditating on the novel beauty of the scene before, below him. A north breeze has rolled the smoky sea silently away and left no sign. Beneath the tent outspreads a vast abyss, dark, silent, "the night's Plutonian shore." Our miner's fancy fills it with golden phantoms. Only the stars, "night's tall tapers," lighten the gloom. But far away east, over ranges of lesser mountains, dim shapes couched in the darkness, far away, miles real as well as seeming, a familiar shadowy shape of vast, uncertain size appears to shut from sight vision of some awful conflagration. Look! It grows, it brightens, till on the charmed eyes bursts a sudden, intense spark, then a full flame in Ieka's side—it is the moon at its roundest! And now Ieka's snows glow in its ray like molten silver, the dark abyss before, beneath the tent lightens, the phantoms flee, while over all, sublime, glorious, supreme, Shasta's silver image rises.

V

Traveling southward, miner no more, the youth bends his course. A year ago the golden phantoms died, the mine caved in, and "no man knows that sepulcher" in the wilds of Siskiyou. Winter wet had extinguished the flames and laid the smoky sea. But the succeeding summer saw all aglow again, matched by the lightnings of heaven. Our traveler is at the very base of Ieka Butte, and he and his steed crawl along the slopes and vales in the bed of the fire-born ocean of smoke as do crustaceans on the bottoms of aqueous seas. A flaw of wind decreases the denseness of the clouds, and above his head he sees an indistinct shape, lit feebly by the smoke-smothered moon, at its full now, as on that other night, a year ago. Beautiful through the murky air it is not; but when told that the point dimly seen overhead is the smoke-free, gleaming crest of Shasta, fifteen miles away as the crow flies, even though we gaze at it from its own base, we feel an indescribable sense of awe. And we liken the mount, with the flaming forests glowing at its feet and its own muffled form rising in obscured grandeur, to a silent sentinel by his watchfire, wrapped around with his cloak, and meditating on the trust he has kept, lo! these many ages, still keeps, and forever!

VI

Returned from the far south, and in camp. In camp at the timber line on Tchastel's side, awaiting the nightfall, and through the long afternoon gazing out over a wealth of scenery not in word power to paint. To the north "Goose Nest" mountain, its crater ever full of fleecy snow, rears itself aloft eleven thousand feet. Down yonder in that gemlike valley is the lovely town of Sissons; down, to our traveler, albeit on a plane seven thousand feet above the ocean. Night. But not in a tent door. No, on mule-back, he and a companion are toiling upwards. There is no moon, no wind, no sound, save a few strange noises arising from the nether regions. No moon, yet plenty of light, since the snow seems self-luminous, so that objects appear against it in sharp silhouette. How black the bleak rocks and ledges! And those glimmerings of light afar in the night, what are they? Lamps; lamps miles away, thousands of feet lower, yet in seeming not so far off. It is cold; oh, so frightfully cold, numbing the mind! And still as the grave. No sounds now arise to the ear; it is too high for anything but silence. So cold; and yet midday sun heat reflects from the snows as from a mirror, and then the temperature is fearful to feel, yet the snow melts not. Here is a hot, sulfur spring, one-thousand feet below the apex. Warm your chilled hands in the hot mud, wipe them quickly, lest they freeze, and climb on. Your eyes, could you see them, congested as they are in the rarefied atmosphere, the color of liver, would horrify you. Your breathing pains you; your heartbeats sound like the thuds of a pile-driver; your throat is afire from thirst. No matter; here is the top! Two o'clock a. m. in July, 188-. As yet no light, but faint dawn. But before long the soul is awestricken by a weird glow in the cut, which lights nothing. The beholders are filled with a strange disquiet; see the waxing light, and—in a fearful wonder, almost ter-ror—see the great sun, scarce heralded by the aerial rarity, spring from beneath the horizon. Yet all below is in "the darkest hour before the dawn." No ridges, no hills appear, no valleys, nothing but "night's deep darkness." We seem to have lost the world, and, for once, are free of time! The planet is swallowed up, leaving the mountain top's half acre the sole visible spot of all the Universe, save only the fearful splendor of Helios. Understand now, for you may, the sensations of Campbell's "last man." The world all gone, and self and comrade alone on a small spot in midair, whereon the almost rayless sun casts cold beams of strange, weird brightness. Look north. At a great distance in the night are four cones of light, Mt. Hood, Mt. Adams, Mt. Tacoma, and St. Helen's tall torch, all peers of our Ieka. As the Day King soars higher, lesser peaks appear, then long black ridges, ranges of vast extent, begin nearby, only to lose themselves in distant darkness.

Now the void of night vanishes, hills stand forth, silvery spots and streaks appear as the dawn lights lakes and rivers, and at last, with no fog obscuring it, in the distant west, seventy miles away, is seen a great gray plain, the Pacific's broad expanse. To the south, interrupted streaks of silver show where the Pitt and Sacramento rivers flow, while over two hundred miles away behold an indentation of California's central coast, marking the Golden Gate, and San Francisco's world-famed bay.

VII

Beside a roaring, dashing mountain torrent, falling in myriad cas-cades of foam white as drifted snow, interspersed with pools of quiet water, deep, trout-filled, blue, reflecting flowery banks and towering pine-crested ridges, "ribs of the planet," we pause. The day is hot, but the waters of this branch of McCloud river are cold—as the pristine snows of Shasta from which they flow to our feet and then away.

We recline on the brink of a deep blue crystal pool, idly casting pebbles into and shivering the image of a tall basalt cliff reflected from the mirror calm surface. What secrets could be around us? We do not know as we lie there, our bodies resting, our souls filled with peace, nor do we know until many years have passed out through the back door of time that that tall basalt cliff conceals a doorway. We do not suspect this, nor that a long tunnel stretches away, far into the interior of majestic Shasta. Wholly un-thought is it that there lie at the tunnel's far end vast apartments, the home of a mystic brotherhood, whose occult arts hollowed that tunnel and mysterious dwelling: "Sach" the name is. Do you find it hard to believe these things? Go there, or suffer yourself to be taken as I was, once! See, as I saw, not with the vision of flesh, the walls, polished as by jewelers, though excavated as by giants; floors carpeted with long, fleecy gray fabric that looked like fur, but was a mineral product; ledges intersected by the builders, and in their wonderful polish exhibiting veins of gold, of silver, of green copper ores, and marks of precious stones. Truly, a mystic temple, made far from the madding crowd, a refuge about which those who, "Seeing, see not," can truly say:

"And no man knows . . . and no man ever saw it."

Once I was there, friend, casting pebbles in the stream's deep pools; yet it was hidden then, for only a few are privileged. And departing, the spot was forgotten, and today, as unable as anyone who reads this, I cannot tell its place. Curiosity will never unlock that secret. Does it truly exist? Seek and you shall find; knock and it shall be opened unto you. Shasta is a true guardian and silently towers, giving no sign of that within his breast. But there is a key. The one who first conquers self, Shasta will not deny.

This is the last scene. You have viewed the proud peak both near and far; by day, by night; in the smoke, and in the clear mountain air; seen its interior, and from its apex gazed upon it and the globe stretched

away beneath your feet. It is a sight of God's handiwork, sublime, awful, never to be forgotten; and as your soul has satisfied itself with the
admiration of it, now in that measure be filled with His Peace.

BOOK SECOND

CHAPTER I

"I have called you friends, for all things that I have of the FATHER I have made known unto you."

With Chapter Twenty-four of Book First closed the last devachanic experience of a personal life history, a history enacted over one hundred and twenty centuries ago. It has its good and its bad phases. Under the social rules and customs of a people whom the modern world regarded as pure myth until after the cruise of the "Challenger" and the "Dolphin," there existed a personality whom those who have followed this history thus far know by the name of "Zailm," an Atlantean nickname no less pleasant-sounding than its significance is interesting, viz: "I live to love."

According to his narration, Zailm's youth was that of an obscure mountaineer. He was possessed of an overmastering ambition to make his name blaze among those of the noble of earth. He succeeded in his ambition, for his name, his wealth, his social and political position became of the highest of the aristocracy of a proud and, in myriad ways, marvelous people. If he failed in one particular, if his moral life became awry, his record in other respects was most commendable. For the one failure he paid dearly, and, if you credit his own apprehensions, the payment would not be complete for many a long, long year after you would have lain "down with the patriarchs of the infant world, with kings, the powerful of the earth, the wise, the good, fair forms, and hoary seers of ages past."

You have a view of Zailm, that boy so obscure, that man so celebrated throughout a land not paralleled today, nor ever matched since the old ocean rolled over it and the sun saw it no more in all his proud course.

From the perusal of that record I ask you to turn to the history of another personality, that of Walter Pierson, my own humble self. If the Poseida Zailm was proud to declare himself a Poseida, I am equally proud to say, "I am an American citizen!"

While I was still so young as to be unable to understand anything concerning my parents' death, except the agony of being left alone, I was orphaned by the fell stroke of an epidemic. I cried in my childishness, and begged to be allowed to see my papa and mamma, nor could I comprehend the statement, "They are dead and gone."

My orphaned boyhood was passed under circumstances of such sharp contrast to those years of my babyhood which knew parental kindness, that my inherent tendency to rove grew stronger, until at twelve years of age I became a cabin-boy on board ship, running away to accomplish my ambition. For many years thereafter I realized that actual hardship was an unforeseen part of the dream of travel and of sailor life; but its toil and trouble had to be endured.

My ability, willingness and honesty in service spoke in my favor so well that at eighteen years of age I found myself first mate on a splendid British merchantman. With this advantageous position, intervals in which to study such books as the captain, an educated man, had on shipboard, were mine, and I used the opportunity to excellent advantage, reciting my lessons to the captain, who took much interest in me. An invention for which many a seafarer has been grateful, and to which many a man whose life has been spent on the ocean wave has owed continuation of that life, paid me such a handsome sum, in royalties, that before I was of age I had no small fortune, which by wise investment soon gave me a sum to put in the bank with the assurance of a fair support for life. I did not continue long in marine service after my money began to accumulate, but left sea life to enjoy travel on terra firma. I had seen the chief ports of every land, and now was bent upon viewing the interior of my own country.

In the gold deposits of California, I added immense sums to my fortune during the years 1865-6, where I drifted after my discharge from the Army of the Cumberland, having served two years in that famous corps during the War of the Secession.

I gloried in the absence of two fingers, lost by a vicious fragment of shell at the battle of Missionary Ridge. I wonder if any reader remembers the morning of the 25th of November, 1863?

"All night the flash of rifles from the outposts had gleamed through the fog; and when day dawned it had not yet been determined whether the enemy had been forced from his almost unassailable position on the mountain. The morning was clear. All eyes in the Union bivouacs were strained towards the summit. Gradually the east purpled with strengthening light, and just as the sun rose, a squad of men walked out on the rock overhanging the precipice. Then, in full view of the watching tens of thousands, they unfurled 'Old Glory.' Amid thunderous cheers an army of veterans looked long through its tears at the Stars and Stripes, mute announcement of victory."

At the close of this saddest of wars, because the hands of fathers against sons and of brothers against brothers were raised, I presently found myself in the city of my birth, Washington, D. C.

Two months later I was in faraway California, in one of its most beautiful mountain countries, and formed one of a company of gold miners. So rich were the rewards of labor that we soon began to feel the work burdensome, and employed men to do it for us. Amongst these was a man from China. I say a man from China because he certainly appeared, from the very first, not to be one of the class sneeringly called "coolies," but a real man. "Coolies" were numerous in the town, some two or three miles from our mine, but Quong had nothing in common and did not associate with them; neither was he privately addicted to their habits of gluttony, gin-drinking or opium-smoking. His dress was that which always distinguishes the Tchin from other nationalities, but his features were not thus significant. Indeed, his high, prominent forehead, well-developed facial bones, bold eyebrows and delicate neck marked him as a man of high character, spiritual cast, splendid perceptive abilities and nervous temperament. His eyes—such eyes! Calm, clear, light gray, resting upon one with so kindly, unprejudiced and dispassionate a gaze, charitable, forgiving and strictly upright and conscientious himself, but always ready to overlook faults in others. Such was the appearance of a remarkable man. His speech was intelligible to everyone with whom he had dealings, yet it always seemed to me that his broken English, a commingled Chinese and Anglo-Saxon idiom, would have been wholly unintelligible gibberish in the mouth of any other Chinese. I am no Don Quixote, and do not propose to contend that it is not an evil of serious import to the white man of America, Australia and the people of the Spanish-American republics to be forced to compete with Chinese laborers or the commercial products of that nation. I think it a very real evil, and I sympathize with the Caucasian race. But in all frankness I would ask if the hordes of unskilled, uneducated, almost impossible-to-assimilate laboring poor of Europe are not an even greater menace? The immigration of either is fraught with fearful peril to the free institutions which I believe in, to the extent of having at the point of the bayonet risked my life for their preservation. But far be it from me to urge a spirit of strife; rather I counsel you to follow Him whose life meant "Peace on earth," and the true brotherhood of man. In deference to a correct sentiment, these pages will henceforth refer to my one Chinese employee as the "Tchin," or Quong (his given name), instead of "the Chinese."

After the change of policy which gave the hard work to hired men, my partners and I resided in town, although one or more of us were always at the mine in the capacity of overseers. We employed two gangs of workers that worked on alternate days, each thus giving but half of the time to labor, although the wages were not reduced in consequence. These easy arrangements made the men extra faithful, for they saw that our intention was not to get all the work out of them which they were able to accomplish, irrespective of their comfort or the fact that they were men not beasts of burden. That white men treated considerately like this will achieve more in the way of results than those who are made to work at their highest power every weekday hour has been my standard experience. Treat your fellowman as you would like to be treated were you in his place.

None of the men felt the least objection to Quong as a fellow-worker; most of them were ready to admit, indeed, that he did not seem like a heathen. They were right, for he was not one. His behavior towards everyone was respectful and manly, rather reticent, very quiet, but always so full of benevolent feeling that he won the affection of his fellow workers. They felt that he was a true man. On one occasion a new man was hired by the company, and he "didn't like pigtails." But in less than a week he fell ill, and, unasked, the despised "coolie" not only worked all day, but nursed the sick man through the brief but severe fever, sitting up all night, and only taking a few hours rest next day, his "off" day. No more was heard from the shamed objector to coolies, for he was completely won over, so far as Quong was concerned. Thus he, too, was proved a real Man, when the disease of bigotry was healed.

More than once the Tchin and I were companions on his leisure days. Sometimes we went to the town, but more often we turned our horses' heads away into the wilderness of the mountains. Without his guidance I would have surely been lost there, amid the vast gorges, with their shade of giant pines lying between the almost interminable ridges, those stem ribs of the planet. But Quong was never lost, never hesitated, though the night was upon us so dark on more than one occasion that I could not see my hand before my face, a fact I never quite comprehended at the time, though it is clear to me now. Once at such a time as this I felt the need of a light, so greatly, it was in a cavern which we had found, that he said: "Here, I give you light." I heard him break off a fragment of rock from the side of the wall of the cavern; next he put it into my hand, saying: "Have care now, it must not touch you; like lightning; would kill you." As may be imagined, I touched so little of the rock that Quong directed me to hold it tighter. Then a brilliant light sprung up from the tip of that rock, illuminating the entire cave like sunlight! Had this amazing thing occurred a few years later, I would have first called it an electric light. Then, reminding myself that no battery was there, nor any dynamo-electric machine, I would have done as I did do, sat down and gazed at the marvelous light, forgetful of where I was. As Quong would give no other explanation than he had already given, I was, necessarily, content; only I was not! But his ability to keep his course where not even the track of an animal was to be discerned was sufficiently astonishing, and I was often amazed at the man for not losing his way among ranges of sierra which stretched away to where the vast snowy peaks defined the horizon and kept the blue of the sky from blending almost imperceptibly with the blue of the mountains.

When we took such trips as these we were accustomed to leave the mine as early after supper as possible, that is, at half past five in the afternoon. If the other men were fatigued, Quong never seemed to share their weariness, although there was not a single fellow worker who did not admit that he accomplished more than any of them.

If the night was one of Luna's own, it was our habit to ride for several hours, frequently not halting before midnight, when we might be thirty or more miles from the mine.

On one of these occasions, when we and our horses were alone with nature and the night, we stopped in a remote solitude to wait for morning, to sleep or not, whichever we preferred. Quong sat down on a rock by the edge of a roaring crystal torrent and gazed in silent enjoyment upon the solitary grandeur of the somber pines and moonlit peaks. I left him there and wandered up the stream, till, on looking back, I saw that my friend was hidden from view by a sharp turn in the canyon. But heedless of this I wandered on, musing at the scene, "rock-ribbed; ancient as the sun."

It is not possible, for a person alive to the beauties of nature, to remain insensible very long to the more serious thoughts evolved by meditation pursued amidst the wilds, untroubled by man's sordid methods. Gradually my thoughts assumed a reflective cast, which, almost unperceived, became tinged with the dead black shadow of materialism. Many a time and often grim despair had seized upon me while pursuing to philosophical end the mysterious questions of the soul: "From where?" and "To what place?" Unreasoning faith had never held any place in my nature, and yet mine was a deeply religious disposition. "To reason is to be lost," thundered the church of those days, and it still maintains this attitude concerning reason as applied to faith. The queries which haunted others pursued me; but I lacked the Ingersollian desire to propound the question, which maddened me, to a world I did not doubt had enough misery already. But the despair which arose from the hidden questioning was no less intense just because it was hidden. Eagerly I read scientific works; studied anatomy, physiology, mechanics, the structure of cells and the essays of Darwin and Huxley, and I came to the same conclusions that have troubled the world so mercilessly in all ages. The gray matter of the brain, and the white cerebral substance, the medulla oblongata and vital magnetism, and the blood—these became so much phosphorized fat, haematin, and magnetic vibration; that same "unconscious cerebration" theory in fact, which even now disturbs certain philosophers. Thus joy and sorrow, and every other emotion, became a form of vibration, akin to sound waves, heat waves, light waves and undulation in general. I saw, in brief, my joy become a mere vibratory thrill of nerve tissue, similar, but more complex, to the throb of a violin string. My grief became a similar pulsation or wave. But neither were less intense; if my delight were mere pulsation of bundles of fibers proceeding from a cell or nucleus, principally composed of phosphorized fatty substance; if in passing, this delight but gave rise to a magnetic thrill, and a minute quantity of phosphoric acid, while any chance muscular exertion produced, ultimately, only relatively small amounts of carbonic acid and other excretory chemicals, nevertheless, it was extreme joy. And my grief over a deceased friend, if it produced exactly the same chemicals, having their formulas reducible to the symbols PO_4 and CO_2, etc., etc., was this emotion less agonizing, less painful? Nonetheless, when all questions were finished, when all were reduced to their ultimates, ever and forever I faced a blank wall, insurmountable, and everything ceased short of God. In my despair I cried: "There is no God, no immortality, and man differs from the oyster only in having a more complex organization. Only because I, believing thus, lack incentive to crime, am I prevented from lust, from murder; what clear evidence if I kill a man and no witness be there? When I, too, die, the clock of life is either worn out, or broken; both are irreparable, and there will be no resuscitation, nor punishment, for death levels all, equalizes all. Perhaps I myself am only a complex vibration of atoms, not dyads, but multi-atomic arrangements of matter acted upon by—what? Force, wave force, moving ether. We are but puppets, creatures of uncontrollable circumstances. 'Kismet,' says the Arab, and I must say so, too!"

Do hideous, natural causes of fright seek those moments to appall poor, despairing man when he is already a prey to shapes of awful oppressiveness to his very soul's life? I have thought no, and even the next moment thought so; soul in peril, and body also, for then in my path arose a terror, a huge grizzly bear, *Ursus horribilis*. "Surely horrible enough," I thought, as the animal raised himself in frightful posture. I had no weapon except a clasp knife, and the remembrance emphasized the reality of my peril. Wildly I looked about for a tree, to climb into the branches for safety. Nothing but giant pines were near; down the stream towards Quong were cottonwoods, but to go there was to put my friend, unaware of his peril, into extreme danger. Yet the bruin was rapidly forcing me to decide on the courses of flight, or remaining to be eaten, so I turned to run and—stood face to face with the Tchin! Calm and cool himself, he told me to have no fear.

Stock still I stood, amazed to see him walk slowly up to the grizzly which, from its fierce-eyed appearance, changed to a docile look, got down on all fours, and awaited the man's approach! Was Quong insane? I expected to see him torn in pieces; instead, he placed his hand on the head of the animal and said:

"Lie down!"

The order was obeyed at once, and then Quong sat down on the prostrate animal and fondled its great, stiff ears! Very gently, the bear licked the human hand, as gently indeed as if caressing its own cubs. What occult power was here? Was the Tchin a worker of miracles? Never before had any action indicated to me this ability of his. True, the example of producing the light in the cave was one, but it had not at that time occurred to me because I knew enough, and at the same time, not enough, to know that the production of electric light was a possibility, but not possible to any electrician or chemist in the way the Tchin performed it. It was not possible to ordinary science then, nor is it now any more so. But it would be possible to them if they would only use the proper occult method; it is one of the earliest learned and easiest feats performed by the novitiate. But I was not then a novitiate.

After a few moments Quong got up and, speaking to the conquered bear, said: "Go!" As obediently as before the shaggy beast lumbered heavily off up the canyon and was soon lost to view amongst the rocks and shadows of the night.

Once more the granite boulders shone silvery in the glorious summer moonlight; the dark pines swayed in the gentle breeze which, descending from its play with the whispering boughs, blew the spray of the rushing torrent over the grateful wild flowers nodding on the banks. And beside the rocks, the crags and peaks, the torrent and the pines, the moon shone down on two figures, two men. One stood wrapped in meditation; the other, not thinking at all, simply regarded the first with eyes where amazement still lingered. Neither moved, neither spoke. But one, at least, though he did not think, still felt. I felt how little difference existed between men, so that they were worthy men. I would have acknowledged the Tchin as my equal before the world; perhaps, indeed, as my superior. In the clearest nights some mists come over and obscure the face of things. So it is with the soul; in its clearest moments it knows Truth, only to forget in later moments how Truth seemed. Then, soon, the fogs clear away again. Sometimes, alas, it is after the obscured orb has set. So also the soul: death may get its darkness over it before the clouds of prejudice have melted, or it may not.

But there in the moonlight, the sky of my soul was also clear. But neither man moved, neither spoke.

CHAPTER II. A SOUL IN PERIL

Many days I pondered that scene in the mountains, marveling over the wonderful power possessed by Quong over wild animals. Did he know how he exerted this control, or was it simply a feature of his nature, sufficiently astonishing, truly, but still not understood by its owner? At Bombay, I had seen snake charmers exercise the same dominion over serpents, but it was an inherited ability, unexplained even by the operator. To questioners they would reply:

"So did my father, and my father's father, and his father. I know not, except he got it from Brahm."

But perhaps Quong knew the law which governed his phenomena; if he did, and knew one occult law, did he not know two, or more than two? I determined to ask him when the opportunity presented itself. While in Hindustan I heard that there were certain men there, not fakirs, but learned men who lived in the Himalayan solitudes, who worked magical feats of wonderful variety and power. Had Quong come from these; learned of them? Was he an occult adept, such as I had heard of? These were called, so I had been told, Ragi-Yogis, and to the curious person trying to learn more about them than the meager statement of their vast occult or theosophic wisdom, the native laity proved dumb as the Sphinx of Egypt.

I had an early chance presented to question my friend, who, well as I knew him, still proved more communicative than I had hoped.

It pleased me greatly to learn that not one in a hundred thousand Chinese had any occult wisdom whatever; pleased me, because I felt that if the degraded, groveling Mongol had such knowledge, then because it did not lift that unenlightened race it could not be of an elevating character. But all through the Orient, here and there, the magicians were to be found; the reasons for such secrecy, as they maintained, arose from the fact that before such knowledge as they were custodians of could be gained, the soul must be calm with that calmness which comes best from life amidst the wilds of nature. Now this may seem strange, but it is a calm which can hardly be maintained in the habitats of those addicted to meat eating, or of persons engrossed in the selfishness of common life. You may imagine that these students could seclude themselves from disturbance; men who wish to study do so seclude themselves, even in cities. Not so the occultist. For, from the social order and communal life of the world emanates an aura, or atmosphere, of its own disturbed muddiness, an aura fatal to the absolute peace required by the theosopher. I am impelled to remark at this point that what goes under the name of "theosophy" in the world today is an article so far removed from the genuine that the name has even already been laid aside by the silent nature student, who, now as ever, is a Son of the Solitude.

But to return to Quong and the question which I asked him. I attach his answer verbatim:

"Yes, in this land of the Starry Flag there are students known as the 'Lothinian Brotherhood.' Their lodges, called 'Saches,' are located throughout the western hemisphere; there is one Sach near here. No one not privileged could hope to learn where it is, or who its members are. Yet as I have led you, Mr. Pierson, to ask the question you have; as I have done this with consent of the brethren, to every one of whom you, who, however, know none of them, are yourself well known, to what do you ascribe my action?"

I could construe it in only one way; so I told the Tchin that doubtless they knew and favored my deep desire for occult fraternization, a desire ever baffled until that hour; I felt my Sonship; I did not know it.

"It is so; you are to be taken as a Brother Son by a class of men who seldom allow fraternity even to new affiliates, and never to any other persons whatsoever. But let this be clear to you forever; there is no order of mystic students anywhere, never was and never will be. The Lothins of America, the Yogis of Hindustan, do not gather together for study of occult lore. It is not possible so to study. He who attains, grows; he does not study as college students study. It is not in books. Each student of God is in himself the plane he dwells on, a radiating center of God-wisdom. The very vows asked of initiates are only tests to determine if in themselves they are that which they seek to affiliate with. The Theo-Christian indeed does live with others as to body, but because similars are mutually attractive only. The Kingdom of God is within you, or else (for you) nonexistent elsewhere. If you know this, then Christos will give it to you to know and become more, after which you also become, and thus grow, as the lilies of the field, which do not toil, nor spin, but are God thoughts externalized. 'I am the Way, the Truth and the Life,' said our Great One. You are, Walter Pierson, deservedly one of the Sach. And this right is because your life through the ages is known to them.

"My what? My life through the ages? Am I so old?" I asked, laughing at the supposed joke.

"You will learn in time, Mr. Pierson, in time," Quong said gravely, in meditative tones. "I am not speaking humorously."

The reason given for the interest taken in me made nothing clearer, so I fell to studying the question.

"No, you cannot guess why, sir," said Quong. "Look at me; you say I seem about thirty years of age. I am more. Multiply that figure by three and add its half, and you will be correct within one year. I have watched over you since your birth, using my psychic powers for the purpose, since until a year ago your present eyes have not beheld me. You are born with powers which you can develop so as to become wiser than I. If it pleases you, we will go to the Sach tonight. You are surprised that I, whom you have until now heard speak only in pidgin-English, as it is called, now use such fluent language. I have my reasons, believe me; maybe you find them obvious." In the afternoon I went to town, telling Quong that I would meet him there if access to the Sach was as convenient from there as from the mine.

On my way into town I met an acquaintance at whose very popular liquor saloon I had more than once taken refreshment, thinking it no harm, for I drank moderately. When we came near his place, on the main street, he insisted on my tying my horse and coming in to have a social glass with him. But the idea of acceptance jarred, and I felt that it disturbed the calm reflections which had filled my thoughts on parting with the Tchin. Quong never drank liquor, smoked, or was anything but moderate in his habits. But I entered, resolved not to take any form of spirituous liquor. The scene presented was familiar: men stupid, foolish, or excited from their indulgences, and public women mingling with the crowd in the place. Previously to the week just passed these sights were viewed by me with indifference. But now they seemed revolting in the extreme. One example of the satanic influence of liquor I saw with different emotions now from those of other days: a fair, beautiful girl, a moderate user of liquor, not reached to the depths as yet, but lacking restraint or inhibition, for all her education, culture and refinement; beginning life in the midst of the influences of school, church and home, in the far Eastern States, but fallen through a man's heartless treachery, and that cruel and equally heartless judgment of society—that pure sepulcher, outwardly stainless, but secretly worse than the victims it stones with its merciless opinions. All the worse is this hypocritical spirit because it lets the betrayer go free.

"Let him that is without sin cast the first stone." She was already passing her days in the midst of hell. And the original cause was liquor. Liquor? Yes, I knew her history. Her parents saw no harm in the moderate use of wine, and with the taste created in the girl's nature for the use, came that for "fast" society—and then ruin! Only eighteen years old, yet her feet had stepped on the embers of Hades. Was she lost, entirely lost? I hardly thought so. I believed her story, that all the glitter of erroneous ways, wine and fast society had been embraced in her eastern home because not discouraged by her parents. She said she had no care for those wild ways, but rather a disgust. I felt that she spoke the truth, for tears of genuine sorrow stood in the bright brown eyes, and I knew the possessor of such eyes had trod the path of sin, not through preference, but, as she said, "Through it seeming that at home no one cared what she did, until her disgrace, and then they had put her out and locked the doors of house and hearts against her." All this she told me while she sat in her own home, the finest in the little city, known as the "Retreat." She was occupying the day in painting, for her skill as an artist was only equaled by that which she had as a pianist. Her walls were covered with pictures of her own execution— such paintings! So sad and full of pathos. One was an ideal picture representing a fair maiden, with a feverish light in her eyes and a look of defiance on her face, sitting under a great tree on a lawn. Beside her was a young man, and before them was a serving woman with a tray on which were four glasses, two full of milk, two of red wine. With a smile of ridicule the young man placed his hand on the wine, and the girl, with flushed cheeks and defiant eyes, was reaching for the other glass of liquor, although it was evident that she preferred the milk. Behind her, unperceived by any of the three, stood a shadowy form, a man with a face of divine purity, who was gently weeping over the girl's error. Behind her companion was another shadowy form, black, and with a satanic countenance, his hand on the young man's shoulder and a smile of triumph on his evil features. Below the picture was the title: "The Defeat of Purity."

After I had studied long over the picture, I turned to its painter and said:

"That represents your life and its woe, does it not, Lizzie?"

She made no reply other than to break into a storm of tears. I waited for her anguish to stop, and as I sat, she dried her tears and replied:

"Yes, my woe. Oh, God! That I have fallen so low, and there is no hope! No hope! If I could, I would leave this sort of life and go away to begin anew where no one knew anything of me or my past. But I cannot, for I cannot get away; I have no means of support even if I could."

"Your art, Lizzie," I suggested, gently.

"Yes, my art, I know; but I fear not, for I have no means adequate to a beginning."

The Secrets Of Mount Shasta And A Dweller On Two Planets

It was from that girl's parlor I had gone forth when, in the evening of the same day, Quong and I went into the mountains, and the grizzly bear episode occurred. That was a week ago now, and today I stood in the saloon of Charles Prevost and saw Lizzie engaged in conversation with the barkeeper, over a glass of sherry.

Tho barkooper turned away to wait upon another customer, and at the same time I went up behind the girl and, bending my head close to her ear, said, almost in a whisper:

"Would you not prefer that sherry was milk instead?"

The hard look died out of the mournfully sweet face and a tear leaped to each eye and trembled there like a dewdrop, as she said, oh, so wearily: "Yes."

"Then come with me; let us go to your house."

We went, followed by the curious, misjudging eyes of the saloon idlers. Having arrived and having entered the parlor, I offered her a chair and took another myself. Then I said, as she looked at me wonderingly:

"Lizzie, let me rather say Elizabeth, for it is more stately, dignified, and so suits you better, you said you would rather it were milk; now, I know what you meant, that your soul yearned for the better life of which we were speaking last Monday. Well, I am rich; no one in the West dreams how rich. To me the loss or mere absence from my control of twenty thousand, or even more than twenty thousand dollars, would be unfelt; the income of a couple of months would replace it. Since we talked here last week I have thought of you many times; today I come prepared to—to, well, smother your pride, and accept this check on the First National Bank of Washington, D. C. Will you, Elizabeth, will you take it and go there? Flee from the misery of today and begin life there anew?" "But, but—how can I repay it, if I do; or how will you know that I do not waste it and abuse your confidence?"

"My girl, I do not want you to repay it ever, in any way, to me. Use it as I ask; as for me the Savior has said: 'He that gives even a cup of cold water shall in no way lose his reward'; and again He said: 'He that loses his life for my sake shall find it again.' If He promises life, Elizabeth, then what of money, which is so much less? I trust you. Will you take it from me as a 'cup of cold water' to save you from perishing?''

"Yes, if you give it in that way, I will, and as God shall help me I will be true to promise!''

How she kept her faith, dear reader, you will find by and by. But —— ——— City knew her no more, nor was a trace of her destination known to anyone there except myself. All that was known was that her finer pictures were boxed and consigned to a firm of picture dealers in New York City, via San Francisco and the Horn. This was a blind, for while the impression was sought to be conveyed that they were sold to the consignees, such was not the case, for nothing could have induced her to part with them except dire necessity. The less valued pictures were sold at an auction, along with her house and furniture, bringing quite a sum of money. Her own ticket, I was told a month or so later by a mutual acquaintance, a Catholic Sister of charity, may God bless those sisters! who went to San Francisco with her, was purchased for the city of Melbourne, Australia. The information surprised even me, and I thought her plans were deep laid, indeed. The Catholic Sisters gave me a small painting which Elizabeth had left for me. It was a picture of the Capitol at Washington, and under it the words in quotation marks, "Home, sweet home.'' The sister had never been in Washington and did not know what the subject of the picture was, nor had any other person seen it, so that not a soul but myself knew through the picture or in any way else where the fair, frail, but newly born to a high purpose, artist had gone.

Dismissing further special thought about her whom I believed to be saved, I began to reflect on my next actions. I felt, in thinking of my proposed visit to the Sach, as if I were about to leave the world; joining their order was, according to Quong, virtually, and perhaps in fact, leaving the world of ordinary humanity. As I walked along the streets after writing out the check for Lizzie, a windblown sheet of paper fell on my arm and remained until I picked it off. As I was about to let it flutter away, my own name on the paper caught my eye and aroused my curiosity. Then I read the entire note, and will repeat its words for your sake:

"Do not give the rest of your fortune away; so far you have given well, but do not rashly throw away the rest of it. Yet, as your mining days are practically over, as well as your life in this community, therefore sell your share in the mine. It is a good mine, and will bring a high figure; yet do not be discouraged if you do not find a taker for it now, but wait. Offer it now, for time is an essential.

M ————————."

Where did this message come from? I could not tell, and, strange to say, my usual abundance of natural cautiousness never suggested that the whole thing was an artfully planned scheme to defraud me. So far from such an idea occurring to me, I sought my partners and asked what they would give me for my third share of our joint property. The reply was not immediate. At last, one cautiously asked:

"Pierson, why do you sell? Do you fear the 'pay' is petering out?"

I replied that I did not, but had reasons of a private nature. Then, too, I wanted to go home. They did not know that I meant by the word "home," a figurative rendition; that home was not Washington, the city which they knew I had come from, and that instead, I meant affiliation with an occult brotherhood. They promised me an answer upon the next day. To this I agreed, but "next day" came not for more than a month; when it did, the interim had seen a "strike" at our mine, uncovering what was, in the belief of the company, millions of dollars. In the "pay dirt," lying on the "bedrock," a lode of gold quartz was found which, according to the assay, ran into the thousands of dollars per ton. Unconscious of this coming good fortune, I left my partners engaged in debate and went out upon the street. At the appointed place and hour of seven o'clock in the evening, now come, I met the Tchin. Our meeting place was beyond the town limits, and night had fallen when I arrived. He sat by a tall pine tree, and I did not see him until I had been there, supposing myself first arrived, some five minutes. It was the night of the full moon of that lunar period, and I sat musing on a rock by the roadside, thinking of the myth of Morpheus, who with leaden scepter wafts the many into the dim land of dreams, the only respite from woe that weary millions of sufferers ever find on earth. But Quong was not to usher me into peaceful slumber; he was not come as Morpheus, but he was to introduce me into a realm which, new to me, was old in the earth since the first flight of years began back in the eons of dead time, a realm that has existed from the time of the creation, the spiritual, far-away land of the soul, where the vagaries of dreamland are supplanted by verities stranger yet. I was about to enter on the path of Kabala, wherein travel those whose researches into the occult's innermost parts come from an antiquity of aged seers of times past. Would I prove worthy? Then the Tchin broke in upon my reverie with the bidding,

"Let us go."

Strange as it may seem, I was not at all startled at his sudden appearance. Soon we were among the rock-ribbed hills, and the pine forests waved above us, around us, and down the slopes beneath our feet. Deer roamed here, despite the comparative nearness to the habitations of men, and many a bright flower was faintly visible in the moonlight, peeping from its shy retreat, wood lilies, tiger lilies, violets. My thoughts dwelt musingly on these natural beauties and seemed to say, "How fitting that they who, in love of nature, hold communion with her visible forms should go, from listening to the tongues of the visible, to take note of the various languages with which she tells of things unseen." To the thrill of feeling which swept over me at the meditation, my very soul responded.

By the time we were fairly in among the forested mountains and the silences of nature, the night was well advanced. The moon's round shield now shone broadly upon us, or again peeped forth between swaying pines. Scarcely a cloud floated in the heavens, the air was warm and still, the entire scene seemed a most appropriate introduction to greater beauties which I felt were about to be presented.

Then, as I beheld Quong ahead with his blue Mongolian blouse, and in the act of uncoiling his pigtail to cool his head, the sight acted upon my deep-seated prejudice against the Chinese race and, like a ruffling breeze, swept over my placid soul and marred my enjoyment, my se-

305

renity. For a moment I forgot the superiority of manhood in Quong, and there arose within me a repugnance to investigating, in the company of a Chinese, things which impressed me as sacred. My vanity whispered that, because he was a Chinese, he was my inferior; yet for the world I would not have breathed a word of it to him. I almost felt inclined to return to town, nevertheless.

Quong's voice interrupted this disagreeable train of thought, and his words became a mirror to reflect my conceited egotism so faithfully that I was aghast, and wondered that my own sense of justice had allowed such vain ascendance of meanness. Swept away at last was every vestige of the notion that nationality was of the smallest consequence where real manhood was under consideration. Replacing the narrowness was the conviction that, while one race may have more numerous expressions of nobility than another, nonetheless the individuals of every race may leap the highest social barrier and stand equal at last, because it is the soul, not the casket, which springs aloft to God.

"What said the Tchin?" do you ask? This:

"Alas for human vanity! It produces more evil than any other emotion, makes men weak when they should be strong, cringe to prejudice when bravery is needed, and sows the seed of Injustice, from which grows the flower Intolerance and the ripe fruit Iniquity."

He then turned to me directly, saying:

"Brother, should the penalty earned by the depravity of the Chinese race be visited upon me, who have no part in their iniquity? Shall the good stone in the pile rejected by the masons of society be also cast aside? Perchance, it might become the head of the corner. Oppression by tyranny is rejection, for it denies a man's rights. Behold, then, what a pillar of strength is built of the rejected stones of the nations upon the rock of the American Declaration of Independence! Yet, let it not be built too high, and never of any but choice stone, whatever its source, lest it become of ill proportion and fall in ruin!"

"Indeed, indeed! I knew not that you could so easily understand my thoughts; nor did I know how illiberal I had grown through my vanity! Forgive me, my friend!"

"Ask not my pardon. I am not offended. But I saw clearly that you were doing yourself an injustice in allowing such play to prejudice. It was to set you right, not to humble you, that I spoke."

Somehow the beauty of the scene was enhanced in my sight. Like a gladdening rain laying the dust were the words of my friend, and my soul's atmosphere was cleared, so that all things appeared more lovely.

As we walked, a doe and her fawn stepped into the path before us. Their impulse, on seeing men, was to take flight. But Quong held out his hand and called them as if they were pets familiar with him. The animals stopped and returned along the path until within reach. He stroked them gently and as we passed on they followed behind. I was wondering if Quong, in his many solitary walks in the mountains, had not made a few pets, as, for example, these deer, and even the bear, when the idea was put aside by a new occurrence. As we came under an overhanging rock, a puma, or "California lion" (Felix concolor), leaped into our midst with the evident intention of having venison for supper. Indeed, had not the deer for which he sprang been too nimble, it would have been an instant victim; but it and its companion fearfully closed about Quong, and the latter, turning to the panther, said sternly, but in a calm, low tone:

"Peace!"

And there was peace, for the carnivore slunk down for an instant, like a whipped dog, then resumed a normal catlike attitude, and, purring, walked with soft, feline tread on one side, with the deer on the other side of the human mediator, and I, lost in amazement, brought up the rear. Truthfully, the fable of the lion and the lamb was realized in actuality.

"See, my brother, what it is to know the law and to live it; for I myself am a vegetarian, and the perfect peace such food allows renders my soul calm, so that I see the law as in a mirror. Behold proof of the truth in this occurrence!"

The Secrets Of Mount Shasta And A Dweller On Two Planets

As he ceased to speak we halted in front of a huge lodge of basaltic rocks, some hundreds of feet in height. The ledge was broken and twisted as if by some rending convulsion. All about the base lay huge fragments broken off the face of the wall. Against the cliff rested a giant block many tons in weight. Touching this with his hand, the Tchin said:

"Here is our Sach, our Temple, so to say; this rock guards the entrance to a remarkable place, to say the least, if viewed from an occidental standpoint."

I looked in vain for the doorway, or any crevice which might lead into a cavern. Meanwhile Quong laid his hand on the great cat with us and said:

"Go!"

And the lion, pausing not, went leaping along in bounds (for these animals have such a limber spinal column that they cannot run or trot like other animals not of the feline tribe), leaps by which it was soon lost to sight. Then Quong said:

"As it will not return here, these gentle deer would best remain; no other spot is so safe for them. Goodbye, my little friends!" Continuing, Quong said to me: "Have you found the doorway? It is not strange that you should fail, for it was constructed with the special purpose of baffling the curious."

Again he touched the enormous quadrangular block. Immediately it tipped on edge and leaned outward over us, causing me to spring away in terror lest it fall on me. "Be not afraid, my brother. See, it is under my control as if on hinges"; and he swung it back on its lower outer edge with wonderful ease, only keeping his own nearest hand firmly upon it. To my amazed query he replied that it worked to his will through magnetism. But I saw no magnet, and said so.

"Truth! In me is the magnet you do not see. Did it ever occur to you that the processes of all life are carried on by what for our present purpose may be called magnetism? Assimilation of food and drink, waste, excretion, all vital processes whatever? The magnet is in the cerebellum or back brain, and in the medullary substance of the corporae striatum, a veritable wound magnet. The force which causes the heart to act, the lungs to act, maintains bodily heat, and so on, is enormous; it amounts to many hundreds of thousands of foot pounds per day. He that knows occult law can make nature parallel this magnet, for the universe itself moves only because of the current, which flows from positive to negative, from one-half of matter into the other half, continuously. Here, now, is an occult secret: make a place of separation in this, the Fire of Life, and where the poles come in contact there shall force be in action. This block of stone, the door, is an armature in a natural field of force. Here on the ground is another."

Putting the door-stone back in place, Quong drew a circle on the ground about a foot across. Then in this circle a couple of lines in a simple cross, one north and south, the other east and west. As the four ends of the cross were contacted with the circle, a tall, steady flame sprang up, its spear-shaped cone trembling within itself, but being wholly uninfluenced by the wind, which had some time before commenced blowing in vigorous gusts. Then said the Tchin: "Behold the Vis Mortuus. Of all mankind only an occult student could bring it forth; only such a one could put it out, unless by accident. Touch it not; it would be fatal, on the principle that the greater contains all lesser forces, and it would instantly absorb the force of life, or of wind or wave, or projectile; it exists visibly here because it is on a miraculous symbol. You think that symbol might as well be of any other form? So think those who comprehend not. See that moth darting about the flame of the light; it will enter, but not be burnt; no, quicker—see! It touches, and disappears, and leaves no sign—yet the light is not hot, no, not even warm. I will put it out."

Suiting his action to the word, he drew a stick through beneath the dust on which the circle was described, and the light in that instant was gone. Then he made another circle, drew but one line across it, north and south, then stepped into the figure, one of his feet on each semicircle. Immediately his whole person was covered with a brilliant flame, so that he appeared on fire. I was exceedingly terrified.

"Do not fear for me! It is well with me. The other flame was negative odicity, and would have instantly been fatal to whatever motion touched it and have disintegrated its form; yea, a rock thrown into it would at once have disintegrated, or a cannon ball discharged from the muzzle of the piece would have fared the same. But this is a positive flaming of the Vis Naturae, and preserves life. I might stand here till the centuries mounted and be not weary, nor hungry, nor sick, eat not, nor drink, yet live; for this keeps all things untouched by time, as when they enter it. Do you now think there is no difference in symbolic figures? Indeed, yes. But my soul will not progress; so that although its use offers ease of living, I care not to employ its aid, except that when weary it gives me rest; ill, it restores health."

He broke the circle with his foot, and coming away, swung back the door-stone again and stepped within the tunnel disclosed behind it. ₁ I followed, the door was replaced, and I found that the passage led into the mountain. I was still thinking of the biblical legend of the rolling away of the stone from the mouth of the sepulcher of Jesus the Christ, and paralleling it with this act of the Tchin, aware now that neither were miracles, but manifestations of higher natural law, when we began to walk along the hall of the tunnel I following closely in the rear of my guide, whom I could hear but not see, for since the closing of the door-stone the blackness was appalling in its intensity. Mistrusting this blind guidance, I approached the wall, that I might feel my way, when suddenly all about me shone a marvelous white light. It was not coming from any point, but all the air was luminous, for I observed that nothing cast a shadow, either below, above or on any side. It was the same marvelous light I had seen once before in the cavern we had found together. After going about two hundred feet we came to a door made apparently of bronze covered with artistic cameo and carved figures of men and animals ranged about a double triangle inside of a circle. This door gave entrance to a large circular chamber not less than sixty feet across, with a domelike ceiling ten or a dozen feet high at its junction with the wall, but over twenty feet in the center. The same wonderful illumination was omnipresent in this great apartment as in the hall outside. But I asked no questions; I deemed observation the better way. Quong temporarily left me here, going into another room through a narrow doorway closed by a portiere. I devoted the time to looking about me, examining the surroundings. I found that the chamber, like its approach, was hollowed from the living rock, only that while the beginning of the hallway was in a basalt cliff, the room was in a different formation, being in mineral-bearing rock. The central part of the walls and ceiling cut across a wide vein of gold-bearing gray quartz of hard texture. This lode, fully twenty-five feet wide, had on one side a granite ledge, and on the other red porphyry of the variety chiefly found in the quarries of upper Egypt. Beyond the granite was another lode of metallic rock, and in this one side of the room was reached without cutting into other veins. The porphyry almost completed its side of the chamber, but not quite, as a second body of gold quartz was intersected, but not cut through. Now imagine the extreme beauty of such walls as these when polished like glass, thus enhancing the veinings of the clouded rock and brilliant beauty of silver and gold, both native and in their ores, and not a few other metals and minerals.

The makers of the wonderful room had "built like giants and finished like jewelers." But how had such an enormous task been accomplished, and when? A town of many hundreds of people lay but a few miles distant; but the inhabitants knew nothing of all this. It did not occur to me in explanation that its builders were of the Lothinian Brotherhood, and had formed their temple by the disintegrating force of the Vis Mortuus, into which I had seen Quong cast a stone and had witnessed its instantaneous disappearance. It was long afterwards before I, musing over memory's pages, thought of this solution to the puzzle of the existence of the Sach, or Sagum. But when I did, I knew it for the truth; knew that neither pick nor drill, nor any tool of human kind had been used, and that what I had thought the result of years of patient toil was but the work of a short time. Yet this was the fact, my friends!

On the floor was a carpet of oriental variety. The fabric was of long fibers woven together at one end, but loose like hair at the other; in color a quiet gray. A footfall upon it gave no sound whatever, any more than would a carpet of duck's down. Around the sides of the Sagum extended a wide divan, continuous except at the three entrances. Covering it and hanging down from its edges was the same silky fabric as lay upon the floor. The one article of movable furniture in sight was a singular looking stand made of brass, which stood in the middle of the apartment. Its top indicated that it was used as a brazier. I would have made sure of its real use, but refrained from asking, not desiring to appear curious.

"Weed, ask questions if you wish," said Quong, who had just returned. "Have no fear of seeming inquisitive. That is, as you suppose, a censer; its use will be made apparent." I was again astonished at my friend's occult powers, for his answer proved a clear case of mind reading. I now felt an unconquerable sense of fatigue and sleepiness, and without saying anything, or asking permit as I might more courteously have done, and would but for my being so sleepily stupid, sat down on the divan, and then reclined at full length; but this act seemed to arouse me so that I could not sleep. I tried very determinedly to do so before finally admitting to myself that it seemed impossible.

"So you can't sleep? I will aid you."

Again the Tchin had perceived my wish, for I had hoped as a last resort that he would offer to put me to sleep, having myself no doubt of his power to do so. He leaned over me, and touched a knob in the wall; a small door flew open, disclosing a number of shelves. From one of these Quong took a peculiar looking flute of reed pipe. Placing it to his lips he began playing an air which had a very familiar sound. Like some sweet, half-forgotten memory floating back from "Lang Syne," bringing an exquisite sense of pleasure and pathetic pain, so the wild, sweet notes brought to my mind a faint, indistinct recollection of some former delight. In trying to remember where—what—remember when—ah, me—sleep, had overtaken my senses.

It matters little how long I slumbered, whether minutes or hours; yet it must have been hours.

Footnotes

272:1 NOTE.—This was in one of the walls of one of the vast canyons which seam the sides of Mount Shasta, in Northern California.—Author.

CHAPTER III. TAKE THEREFORE NO THOUGHT
FOR THE MORROW

When I awoke, rich, delicate perfumes, and the low hum of voices greeted my still slumberous senses. On opening my eyes, I found that Quong was by my side, having either remained while I slept, or returned before I roused. In the center of the room, sitting on the floor, I saw about a dozen people, each clad in a long gray robe. Quong had one of these robes on his person, and to my astonishment, I found myself attired in like manner. A high caste Thibetan, two Hindoo pundits and an Egyptian were, excepting Quong, the only foreign brethren, the remaining persons being American and English. The Egyptian was to the Sakaza what the Grand Master is to a Masonic fraternity. Understand that he was not a teacher in the sense that a professor in a college is an instructor. He was in himself more of the Way, more of the Truth, more of the Life of God than any other present. And hence, as in himself the highest plane, he stood before the rest as a pinnacle each might study, and rise unto. This man alone was standing.

Perceiving that I had awakened, Quong said:

"Let us seat ourselves in the circle, brother, that the ceremonies of the evening may commence."

When seated we formed two in a circle of ten persons, arranged in a ring in the center of the chamber, our hands clasped on either side by our neighbors, and so around the circle. In its center stood the brazen censer, and beside it the Grand Master. Presently this person began to speak in the best of English, giving a clear, concise statement of the wisdom-religion of the Lothinians. He disclaimed the idea that anything which was performed under occult law could be a miracle, and declared that no miracle had ever yet taken place in the world, because a miracle would be a contravention of law, and what was a violation of law but evil? It being evil, Jesus the Christ would have been the last ever to have worked one. Not a man or woman, it was asserted, and it is true, comprehends how these laws operate, or understands anything of their nature, unless such man or woman is an occult student. The world of science is more ignorant of these mysterious forces of Nature than even the sect styled "Spiritualists," for these do comprehend a little, but so very, very little as to expose them to fearful dangers, handling as they do forces so terrible when abused that their field of operation might well give pause to the wisest ere they trod therein. Yet science soon shall know, following the Cross-Bearer. Beyond admitting me to free hearing of what was said and done, no notice other than salutatory courtesy was paid me; that is, I was not invested with any membership degrees; no degrees can be conferred, for each is in self the degree represented. But the Adept, as I clearly perceived, had spoken so personally direct that I knew he addressed me. This was when he said:

"There is within this sacred place of meeting one who hath studied deeply; studied as scientific modernism contemplates all life, and the study has always filled him with melancholy, yes, even despair. He has questioned of the stars, 'What are you?' and no reply has been given beyond that which astronomy offers: 'Worlds, suns, blazing orbs, mighty beyond power of mentality to conceive.' And of the grass, and it has said, 'I am of cells aggregated and vitalized by the spirit of nature.' The animal has replied, but in Darwinian terms: 'I am a form evolutionized, and come up from protoplasm.' He has seen Man to be at the apex of animal life, and so he says of himself: 'Lo! There is nothing but at one end the simple cell; at the other a complexity of cells aggregated. But to me the world and all its forms speak of action, and eternity; but of the immortality of man, of a soul or a spirit, or of God, no, no word! Death ends all!' O my brother! Does not this joy speak, and these griefs of yours, to you of anything but magnetic vibration? Are you blind to the message of God that the 'vibratory' joy or grief or 'unconscious cerebral action,' whereby you come to a given knowledge, is but the method of your life? And the animal, does it not say: 'Lo! I am a soul, and this animal body is fit tool for my soul powers, which, if they increase beyond the power of the tool to express, force me (the ego controlling) to cast it aside and seek a fitter tool in a body suited to my progress.' And does not man say to you: 'O brother in darkness, I am at the apex of animal life, truly; in my admirably adapted physical body is a fit tool to prosecute to the utmost any and all material processes. It brings me to the wall of all physical life, and behold! It enables me, the ego, to reach the top of this wall, and find that I am a spirit, not a vital stone. And because of my sight, I will leave behind the pursuit of materiality for that of spirituality, and go even unto my Father's house, where there are many mansions (conditions) of spirit, but where matter does not break in to corrupt nor steal the treasures.' Who has asked, let him hear me. I have spoken. May peace be with you."

I thought my friend Quong was speaking in a humorous vein when he said that the Adept, whose name was Mendocus, had not so much as opened his lips, or used his vocal organs at all. Not so, however; I was mistaken. Quong read my thought, and said:

"Nay, my brother, not in jest! Each of us has heard Mendocus, and to each it seemed that his national tongue was used; to me, my own; to you and five others, Anglo-Saxon; to the Hindoo pundits, their tongue. Because Mendocus spoke from his soul unto ours is the reason of this seeming paradox."

I thought at once of my Bible, which was a treasure to me above all other books, and of the passage wherein it is written:

"'Now when this was noised abroad, the multitude came together and were confounded, because that every man heard them speak in his own language."

In answer to the unspoken thought, Mendocus, the Adept, turned to me and said:

"Truly, they spoke to the souls of that multitude; it was no miracle, but law. The Bible is sound occult doctrine so far as the matter in it has escaped the revisers, and worse than revisers, the Roman Catholic interpolators and twisters of its truths. You do well to read it; I have read it through eighty-seven times."

Here another brother joined with the remark: "The hearers and the speakers were to each other as a perfectly attuned violin to its bow, every string ready to respond to the least master-touch."

To this Mendocus added:

"They heard the speakers as you heard me, not with ears, for no aerial connection is needed between souls in sympathy, but the consciousness of what was said existed as does the consciousness of one's own thoughts; you need not speak your thoughts that your ears may convey to your consciousness what thoughts you think. Neither are your ears of more use in comprehending me. Yet because the thoughts did not originate in your brain, but in mine, and so were external to your inner consciousness, therefore you supposed that you heard me with your ears, when it was your soul which understood, for I did not use my voice."

I now understood, in the light of the mind-reading power which these students had revealed, why no question had been put to me concerning my life, my thoughts or will in regard to affiliation with them; they knew these things, through this ability, without asking.

Mendocus, Master, now requested attention from all present, and then made an invocation to God and to all occult initiates in this world and elsewhere in the universe. At the conclusion of this petition, he slowly raised his right hand, then, after half a minute, he dropped it to his side and bowed his head. The wonderful light commenced to wane and, simultaneously with its disappearance, a blinding flash of light seemed to dart from the ceiling overhead, striking the censer by his side. Then came that inky blackness which follows the midnight flashing of the lightning of heaven; but it was not destined to last very long. Soon in the deep darkness there was a noticeable lightening which continued to increase until the whole interior of the Sagum was illumined by a lurid glow which rendered every object clearly visible. Like the other, it seemed not to emanate from any particular point, but it was as if the entire atmosphere was like red-hot iron, self luminous. The next instant I observed that the faces of the Lothins had assumed an exceedingly ghastly hue, bloodless in appearance as are the countenances of dead men. Their pallor was soon explained, however, when my eyes fell on the brazen censer standing in our midst. The gaze of every brother was fixed with unwavering intensity upon a small globe of blue fire which rested on the fire pan. I noticed also that the self-luminosity of the atmosphere was gone, and that the light from the blue globe cast shadows. Although in size it was not larger than a filbert, yet its intensity counteracted the luridness of the air. It was beautiful in the extreme, but not dazzling. On the contrary, it was cool and calm, resting the eyes. Evidently the light was the same as the positive flaming of the Vis Naturae with which I had seen the Tchin envelop himself. It trembled and quivered like a globule of molten, boiling metal.

Such absolute silence reigned, not even a sound of breathing being audible—that I turned a quick glance on my friends. Except for the glitter in their eyes as they gazed on the blue light, every one would have seemed only a perfect but non-vital semblance of a human being. Then my gaze reverted to the object which drawn their attention. It had been growing, and, now of a size of half a dozen inches, was gloriously beautiful. Although I had seen no human agency concerned in its creation, still I felt that it was produced by the occult knowledge of which I had witnessed so many other manifestations. Mind over matter. All of this was marvelous and novel to me, but I knew it was not a miracle, although magical. "What is magic?" do you ask? Magic is the comprehension of laws not ordinarily possible to grasp by means of physical experiment, because their phenomena in general lie higher than the physical realm, just a little lower than mental or psychic operations, and making use of some of the last to a major extent.

As I watched the blue globe, I gradually became in tune with the mental condition of the Lothins about me. Instead of wondering what were to be the perfected dimensions and what the object of this glowing ball, I contentedly watched it, with a sense of perfect knowledge of its ultimate size and use. But this intuition aroused in my mind no train of disturbing conjecture. I thought of nothing, absolutely nothing, taking no thought for the morrow, or the next moment. My intelligent friend, try this once; try to think of nothing; to have no thought, not even the one that you are not thinking. I doubt your success in the attainment of such a state of mind; but if you are, happily, successful, you will remember to the end of your allotted years on earth how great was the sense of rest, of peace, of perfect joy, felt, not thought of, in that moment. If you could attain and then retain such a mental state for half an hour, you would become clairvoyant and clairaudient during that time, and both see and hear across the leagues of earth; aye! And be conscious of the future, so that a prophecy then made by you would be found to come true in every detail, though in scope was over years mounting to centuries. You must perceive, then, what a beautiful condition the Lothins enjoy: the whole present, and each way, from the present almost to eternity, is theirs to know. These states of mind are long-lasting with them, and in the peaceful, inactive resting which is theirs at such times, they find themselves in contact with the architect of the world, and know His ways. Like Job are they then: hearing of Him by the hearing of the ear, their eyes also behold Him. ₁ Some few of God's works they can do, many more of them they can understand, laying the line on the foundations of the earth; entering the springs of the sea, knowing where light has its way, and the place of darkness and the bounds thereof; yes, in this still time of their souls God opens to them even the gates of death, through which they go and return. But though they know all this, and so, friend, you might, too, yet it is because the Creator shows them the paths to the place thereof; and He will show you if you enter the occult door through which Christ has gone unto the Father. Follow Him, and greater things than these you shall do.

Mendocus, Master, now perceived that the lurid glow of the atmosphere had been neutralized by the light of the blue sphere, which, full twelve inches through, rested motionless in completion, its glorious, radiant center of entrancing loveliness. He raised his hand slightly, as if giving an unspoken command. Upon this the sphere of light rose to a height of perhaps eight feet from the floor, where it hung without visible means of support. Again the hand waved in command, and the sphere moved horizontally over our heads to a point about fifteen feet from the center of the chamber. Here it was permitted to remain. Although every one present was intuitively aware of all that was about to occur, I will describe every incident for the benefit of my readers. Following the pure blue light came a sphere of intense indigo color upon the brazier, its process the same as that of its predecessor, and when complete it was assigned position thirteen feet from its neighbor, on the same eight-foot plane. Next came a sphere of violet, of equally intense brilliancy, differing only in color, not size. Then there followed a globe of pure red, then one of orange, another of pure yellow, and lastly one of glorious green. Every one was at the same height from the floor, and equidistant, approximately, from its neighbors. Any attempt at describing the extreme beauty of these iris-hued spheres would indeed be futile, as they hung, motionless, above our heads.

Once again the Master gave silent order, and the spheres began to move horizontally around their common center. Slowly at first, then gradually the speed increased until persistence of vision presented them to the sight as a great circle of light ninety feet in circumference; nevertheless the orbital revolution did not in any degree merge the colors into becoming white light. And now an additional feature of beauty was presented: as the seeming ring sped around, from each of its compound globes a shaft colored like its parent was simultaneously projected horizontally to the center, when, from the junction, a perpendicular column of light of purest white went forth, upward and downward, the one to the great quartz crystal in the ceiling overhead, the other to the carpet of gray below, for the censer had been removed from underneath. Thus was presented the spectacle of an enormous wheel, axle, spokes and rim, revolving at great speed, and all formed of imponderable light. Though it rested on the carpet, there was no scorching, for this was but Viviant Fire, positive, not the negative Vis Mortuus. Buddhism symbolizes the latter element as "Siva," the destroyer; it is the Fire of Death, the one wherein I had seen the moth perish and the stone disappear. There is an esoteric Buddhism as well as an exoteric, or religion of the masses, and the names of Siva and Vishnu, which to the exoterist are names of personal Gods, of the Destroyer and the Preserver respectively, are to the esoterist merely the terms distinguishing the obverse and reverse aspects of Nature, that is, growth and satiety, change and destruction.

Would power like this of the Lothins ever be mine? It seemed to me that if Mendocus, Master, had come to such wisdom, he, being but a man, could not do more than I—we were both souls. The wondrous temple in the heart of the mountain; the lighting of the darkness; the lifting of the great stone at the entrance; the Vis Viva and the Vis Mortuus; all this that I had seen and was to see, was only the work of men who had, in their calmness of soul and purity of heart and body, done these things because the Christ-Spirit, in the pure of heart, is perfect human and extends unto the Father. Could I not hope to attain the power of doing likewise? I asked myself, and knew that I could, for I was then in the peace of clairvoyance. But I did not see all that must intervene, nor all the events of the nearer future, nothing of them, in fact, but only the more distant perspective of my soul's destiny.

"Truly," said Mendocus, "but not now, not until a time of trial has passed. To you, as to all other occult neophytes, there will come moments of darkest doubt. And your very soul will weep in the agony of despair. No, you will not doubt the truth of hermetic wisdom at any time, but only your ability to acquire it. Study, then, the principles of truth, not its phenomena only. For its own sake it is more to be desired than its works, though usually less attractive to neophytes. Your doubts will result from an imperfect conception of your own self, a lack of perception of symmetry; giving undue proportion to certain facts, and upon finding these of less importance than your conception of them originally painted, your heart will fail you, for in themselves they are great, and if comparison declares them small, what power shall grasp the greater? Then will it be that you will fear you are only finite, and these things are infinite, and you will say to your soul: 'My weakness is to these things as twine used to capture leviathan.' But this is not so, for no creature is more than the Creator, and you are of the Father and joint Creator with Him. What shall prevail? Only Faith like that of the Spirit who over-lights Jesus and all them that triumph over time. Woe to you if you shall faint while striking out at the shifting clouds of doubt. Miserable indeed is the lot of such a one, for, excluded from the society of the Brothers because of his faint heart, he is still possessed of a knowledge of something purer, better, higher than the ordinary ambitions of humanity. After his glimpse into the greater possibilities of his being, he is scornful of resuming his former sense-relations with the world. He cannot descend to the world's level, nor raise his fellowman to his own height. So through the rest of his life on earth he is alone. My friend, there is no solitude so dreary as he has who is in the world, but not of it. Will you venture onwards, braving this peril? At this point there is still a chance of returning without incurring the danger which follows when further advanced. Do not set your hand to the plow if you cannot go to the end of the furrow; it is long and difficult to follow. The world has not so hard a task as this to impose in all its power. I offer you a choice."

Mendocus now watched me as I pondered the proposition. I felt that I could not in any event resume the old life; within me the fire was already alight, and the Sword of the Lord had cut off the old from the new, so that I felt it was between me and the past. No; "Onward, Christian Soldier," must be my song leading to victory. I was decided in my mind, though I had not as yet said so; but I had no need to utter aloud my decision, although, forgetting this fact, I was about to do so, when Mendocus said:

"You have, then, decided to go onward. I am sorrowful because of it. For though you shall emerge at last as gold burned in the fire, still the ordeal confronting you is fierce. But I will not allow that your feet go alone; for that would be unwise. I will so do for you that the step be not irretrievable, lest it perchance be as I fear. O, Brother! I fear that woe is yours!"

After this decision I was required to take vows of secrecy, whereby I was bound not to reveal any part of what I should learn in any manner which might give the hearer of my words practical use of what I told him. I might drop a hint which might be followed as a clue to the Voiceless Silence where the Flower of Life blooms; but, beyond a hint, my friend, I can tell you nothing. I have given many hints. Nor, were I to disregard my word, and divulge secrets of immediate working value, would you thank me. No, rather you would curse me. Why? Suppose we think about an instance: Suppose I were to reveal the secret of the Vis Mortuus, would you thank me? It is, remember, that force which may be projected in all its fatal strength to any distance and which is personified in the famous poem, "The Destruction of Sennacherib," in the line:

"The Angel of Death spread his wings on the blast."

Suppose I revealed that secret? How long would it be before the world would find that the unscrupulous among men were using it to work undetectable murder? And its uses are many besides, for it is the principle in nature which governs transmutation, disintegration, decay, destruction, death. All these, but never does it build anew; it is Siva, the Destroyer. Used correctly, it is a beneficial force, for without it there would be no progress in nature, because no change could occur—there could not even be retrogression, but utter stagnation.

Its sign is:

Much as that means to me, it can only be a hint to you. Study it if you will, and one day it shall be revealed to you. In reason you can no longer ask why occult matters are so imperatively secret, for it must be evident that this fair earth would be made by the unscrupulous into a very hell of misery and crime, were they not thus secret. For a time those who chose to subvert their knowledge would seem to thrive and prosper, even though the world about them suffered. But subversion of the law is violation, and the penalty at last visited is in tenfold degree upon those who went most astray in their blindness and sin. It would cause them to curse the giver of such wisdom. Nine-tenths of the people of this world are unable to govern themselves well; they cannot in saneness expect to be made sharers of such awful knowledge as Siva represents. Men and women are really not following the Christ until every part of their own nature is held in an iron grasp of merciless subjection to high principles. But study, my friends, study. Christianize the money power of this world, so that capital shall not work harm to men but good, and from good thus born the karma of the world will lead to the goodness of heart which gives calmness of soul; in that calmness your study will bear fruit, and then it will not be a mockery, in seeming, of your hopes for me to say "Study!" I rejoice in those earnest workers whose motto is: "Look up, not down; look out, not in; look forward, and not back, and lend a hand." Only this: the occult student gazes in, and not out! But these are not esoterists. Their name shall one day be great in the world, and though you who desire to study and know occult truths now may not see your hopes bear fruit in your present incarnation, yet in coming lives you will grasp these truths which elude you at present. Follow Him.

Before me, Mendocus, Master, had opened a view of life so radically different from the old, restless existence, that my heart grew warm, regardless of his prophecy that bitter woe was perhaps to be my portion before I could enter the haven of my desires. The fact was that my optimistic nature deceived me with a hope that somehow I could manage to avoid the threatened sorrow, and, having escaped its menace, could go happily onward. Alas, poor me! I knew nothing of karma, and in that day knew nothing of Zailm of Poseid. Otherwise, had I known, I would have trembled when the Master expressed his fears for my sake. I saw before me a great ocean of wisdom, flashing in the light of truth, its horizon defined only by the voyager's temporary inability to go farther, its depth measurable only by that of the Universe.

Free from the dogmatism of cramping creeds and of superstition, that ocean reaches out into the eternity which enshrouds the stars as well as the dust in mystery, that mystery which veils the Creator from the created, veils it from the joint Creator, man, too, just so long as his soul shall lean to creation instead of to the Creator, his Father. Veils it until the eons of time shall be swallowed up in eternity—beyond the stars, Earth, Venus, and Mars, when man shall cease to be man in becoming more than man, and Life the Less be gathered into Nirvana, sum of all the parts. I repeat it, sum of all the parts, for it is not in any way that horrible cessation of being which Sanskrit scholars have interpreted the word "Nirvana" to mean. They have misconceived the facts; it is not the end of life, except Life the Less, any more than the statement "God is nothing" (that is, not one thing, but the sum of all things) should be construed as a denial of the being of God, the Eternal Father of Life.

A change had come over the Master. Up to the present his attention had been that of one controlling a process. Now, with his back to the shaft of the wheel of light, he stood beside the censer, looking upward, his gaze like that of one beholding a sight pleasing, yet absorbing. At last he bowed his head and said:

"Welcome Mol Lang, friend and brother!"

I saw no one, but was aware that the person addressed could not be one of the Sach. Mendocus, Master, turned to the brazier by his elbow and struck it lightly with his outspread fingers, whereupon the fire pan became red hot. Then he thrust his hand into a pouch hanging from his waist and drew it out filled with a white powder, which he cast on the fire plate, producing a dense white smoke. I regarded this as a mere ceremonial offering of incense, and thought it savored of superstition, for I had now lost my intuitive perceptive power, and could only depend on conjecture. This idea was scarcely formed before it was abandoned, for the cloud of smoke rapidly took the human form, into which the solid appearance of genuine personality was introduced as the incense was consumed, until upon the glowing stand stood a man of commanding presence. Some men seem to be not of any distinctive nationality but very much citizens of the world, or, even more largely, representatives of the race, and one feels that they might be of this world or of any other capable of supporting human life. Such was the man before us. He was addressed by Mendocus as Mol Lang, of Pertoz, and though I knew no such country, I unquestioningly accepted this name.

His deep-set eyes, under massive brows, and a head of similar contour to that of the philosopher Socrates; his snowy hair and long, white beard, together with a soldierly erectness of person, made Mol Lang, the Pertozian, the very personification of occult wisdom, from my point of view; nor was I far wrong. His turban, which in fact was blue, mottled with brown, seemed, chameleon like, to assume different colors as the varicolored spokes of the wheel of light passed by, not through him, but he through them. He wore a long, gray robe, hanging down from the shoulders and belted at the waist. On his feet, of goodly, delicate shape, were sandals.

The Pertozian stooped and put his hand on the shoulder of the Master, making some remark, the import of which I did not catch, then stepped to the floor with a light bound, and with Mendocus went to the divan and sat down, engaging in an earnest conversation, which they held secret from the knowledge of the others. Do you ask where our clairaudient, mind-reading ability was, that this conversation should have been unknown to any of us? Unless one who knows that mind readers present are apt to exercise their ability desires to have them share his thoughts, they cannot. He preserves as an almost unconscious habit the mental desire of having his thoughts remain impenetrable, and to such a will no human power can break through the barrier it sets.

At length they returned to our circle, and Mendocus seated himself with us. The visitor then said:

"Though the men of Lothus have known others of my fellow Pertozians, few until this time have known me; none, indeed, but your Master. I have come to induct one of your fellows into the land of the departed, while another I take home with myself. To you, Lothins, I need not say that the body is like a coat, to be put off or on at pleasure by those who know how. I say this only for him known in the world as Walter Pierson, but to me is Phylos. And someday the world will hear of him as Phylos the Tibetan, yet he will not reside in Tibet in Asia, but shall be so called because he shall for a time live on the soul plane of the occult Adepts of Tibet. To you, then, Phylos, I say that when you shall be free of your mundane body, then if you would go to any sphere of heaven, to Neptune, or any planet or star, you only have to desire such transference of yourself, and it is accomplished. Will you go with me this night, which is now nearly morning?"

Where was this I was asked to go? I knew not clearly whether he meant the soul realm, or in fact just where he did mean to go. But my faith was strong, and I replied:

"Wherever you go, I go also, for I have faith in you that you will do me no harm."

The faith inspired in that hour by the gentle dignity and kindly love I saw beaming from those deep-set, calm gray eyes, has known in all these subsequent years no cause for regret; nor for the action which my faith then inspired me to make, this heart has only a feeling of supreme thankfulness that the Christ-Spirit at that moment put it into my soul to have that faith. I fancy I hear some reader, timid at the prospect of trying the unknown, which might for all I knew at the moment include my physical death, saying: "How was it that you felt so sure of Mol Lang; did you not fear he was a devil?" No, I did not, for I was under the protection of goodly men, into whose midst no demon could enter any more than night can reign beneath the noonday sun. At least one of my protectors (Mendocus) had arrived at an ending, so far as earth's present cyclic age can teach; the physical nature had no secrets from him; but the illimitable realms of the Father hold many "mansions" besides the universe of matter and the house of light, or the dwelling place of darkness. In this mansion of the material universe nothing remained for Mendocus to gain; he stayed but to give.

Death had no power over him; he was supra-mundane, and until he decided otherwise, he must live; only the word of God (the true Logos) he himself invoked could "loose the silver cord." Would you, protected by such a one, fear demoniacal influences? One other question of the multitude you may desire to ask, I will answer. You inquire how these highly favored ones of God can be certain of the truth of their intuitive perceptions, and I answer: the man who lives in his spiritual nature does not believe, but knows that his being is one with God the Father, the Great Parent. And his spirit speaks by the voice of intuition, informing him by a single flash of that which he would otherwise be long years in learning by external methods of investigation, if, indeed, externality could ever impart the knowledge. His spirit gives him from its own source, the Father, an effortless, instantaneous perception of facts, principles and things. I am reminded of the words of Mol Lang to me in this connection: "Phylos, some day you will comprehend this: Earth is a letter in a sevenfold alphabet; the stellar universe is but one book; its pages truly are myriad, its chapters legion, yet, besides this book, the library of the Creator is of endless number."

It occurred to me that we were the ones who should thank our visitor, and he not thank us at the conclusion of his remarks, for it seemed to me a lecture of wonderful power. A few minutes later he turned to me and said:

"Phylos, are you ready to go with me now?"

I replied affirmatively, as did Quong, whom the visitor called Semla, when the same question was put to him.

Gravely the Brethren arose and took the hands of the Tchin in their own, as one by one they said to him, as to one going into a far country not to return for years, and perhaps not forever, "Semla, may the peace of God be with you evermore; fare thee well." Then Mendocus, Master, said: "Semla, my peace I give to you."

I noted the difference in farewell speech, and at another time asked of Mol Lang and received the explanation that while the Brethren could not give peace, not yet themselves perfectly possessing it, Mendocus, Master, having it himself could give it, especially to one who, like Semla, was so near its attainment. To all these Semla said, quietly:

"Peace do I wish you."

To me no such farewells were given, for they said, "We shall see you here again." This was unpleasant to me, in the frame of mind I was in, but I concealed my feelings as well as I was able, and replied as kindly as they spoke. Then Mol Lang said, "Come."

He started forward to the door of the Sagum, and I would have followed without looking back, had it not seemed as if someone touched me. Imagining that some Brother wished to speak with me and had thus called my attention, I turned and saw something which will never fade from the tablets of memory! Lying on the long, soft silk of the carpet was a human form. Looking more closely I saw that this was my own physical form, my body, my materiality, in short. In the act of raising it from its position lying down were four of the brethren, two on each side. Others were doing a similar act for the corporeal shell of Semla. It was my consciousness that something was being done to my earthly body which I had mistaken for a touch. It had not occurred to me that I was without my mortal casket, so easy had been my disembodiment.

"Death is, after the agony of illness for those long sick, an easy and pleasant experience," said Mol Lang, in answer to my mental reflection. "If you were not to reenter your physical body again, this would be death for you," he added.

I was so greatly amazed at this last phenomenon that I stood still, saying nothing, as I watched the bodies being removed from the main apartment and laid on couches in a smaller room. Mol Lang then remarked:

"Essentially this is death. Behold then, bodily death is but a casting aside of the grosser forms of life, which have served their purpose. As you will return, this is not absolutely death for you. Semla will not return. His body is therefore dead.

When real death takes place, the gross body is cast off, and the sword of the Lord ⚔ cuts it off,

and Siva ⊕ takes possession of it and distributes it to the elements,

in order that Vishnu ⊘ may receive it for new uses from Brahm the Creator. Then the soul is free for a great length of time, compared to that spent on earth. Though the astral shell can come into spiritualistic circles and manifest through mediums, still the I AM does not come into any earthly condition until it returns for reincarnation; and then always on a higher, never on a lower, plane of progress, there still exists a penalty for sin, or, what is the same thing, incomplete severance of one's self from desires for earthly experiences. Will you prefer Earth to Life?

"We do not immediately go to my own home, but into that realm where those go who have died from earth into devachan, that is, heaven, or the 'Summerland' of the 'Spiritualists,' or the 'Land of the Obb River,' or, again, to 'that boundary from which no traveler returns.' Phylos, the sect known as 'Spiritualists' are in error when they speak of 'spirit communion' and regard it as they do, for no ego returns out of devachan unless it is forced, and this is harmful and vastly unjust to the ego. ₁ The astral soul and animal principle may thus return, but the I AM never. To the latter there is no past earth state; mind, I do not say for it, but to it. That is, it has no consciousness of anything earthly or of anything occurring on the earth. We can go to them, but they cannot come to us. Let us, then, go."

The mind works quickly, and before we had reached the bronze door, my consciousness had mastered the truth that death is not in itself agony; that it brings no startling changes, and does not invest the soul born into the hereafter with any wonderful power of foresight. In fact, there is only freedom given from the earthly body, and a few powers bestowed at that same time; nothing remarkable, considering that earth has no hold on the soul anymore. I speak of those who in mundane death seek escape from earth, having but little love for its conditions, though much love for its children. People like this have worked for their brethren and accumulated a good and high karma which takes them away from the imprisoning conditions of earth.

Mol Lang interrupted my reflections here, saying:

"One more thing; let us leave your second self, that part of you which perceives earthly things and preserves earthly memories. This is so that no disturbing comparisons may arise between that state into which you are going and the earth behind you, which you shall not see any more than they can who really die. But between you and earth I will preserve a vital link formed of your second natural principle, so that it shall not be death to you."

Then he said: "I believe I have no further use for this transient form."

Had an uninitiated observer then been present, the astonishing, not to say terrible, spectacle would have been presented to him or her of a man dissolving into smoke, for Mol Lang liberated the bonds of his smoke-form and it floated away in formless cloud.

Mol Lang laid his hand on my head, and as he took it away I no more remembered anything of the world. I dimly saw before me the bronze door of the Sagum; I knew that Mol Lang opened it, and that we three stepped forth, not into the long hall of the temple, but into an open expanse of green, sunlit meadow or prairie land. But it was no surprise, for I remembered nothing of any special features of earth life: I only knew that I was I, and that I was in a pleasant land; it was much like a vivid dream; no one in viewing a dream landscape is conscious of any other belonging to and seen only in waking hours; the faces in dreams are natural, not novel, not strange, and when seen are not compared with those known during wakefulness, for knowledge of the latter state is blotted out during sleep.

Mol Lang spoke:

"You have come through the gateway. Lo! Physical nature and laws do not reign here; they reign in the objective world, but not here, for this is the subjective world, in no sense physical or existent, nor perceptible to senses belonging to matter. Yet it is real, for Spirit is real, and subjective states, no less than objective ones, are born of the Spirit of the Father. This is another of the Mansions in His House. It is farther from the earth than the farthest star of the sky, because it is in no way of a material nature. Things of earth to the inhabitants of this world are only dreams, and vice versa. To either, the other seems unreal. This place we are in is the 'Far away home of-the soul.'"

I listened to Mol Lang and had ears to hear, so that I understood. Earth, of which he spoke, was vague, and knowledge of it was an almost forgotten dream. And the vagueness was because that principle of my worldly nature which was the seat of earthly sensing, and of memories of things perceived, was left with the body. This principle might visit a spiritualist medium and it would be called me. Yet it would not be me, but my shell, my link of connection between my spirit and my corporeal body. Friend, you will agree that an author is reflected in his autobiography; but that book is not the author. No more than is that which has its "actions, passions, beings, use and end" in the body the MAN. Yet that book may live and guide men to action. So may the astral shell of a man or woman who is dead. And the vitality of the medium may galvanize that shell so long as its influence governs any living earthly man or woman. Hence we see the phenomena of the "circles" of believers in spirit communion. There is no return of the ego (the I AM) to circles, neither communion from their plane down, though sometimes from your plane up to theirs. And yet you persist, my spiritist friends, in saying that I am in error. You say that what I call "shells" cannot be such because they tell of events after death. Yes; they do, I admit. And they do because they are but records of the ego which for a few brief moments at death is sometimes highly prophetic, and sees forward over every detail, frequently for coming centuries. Or again, the departing soul catches a glimpse of its own self-conceived devachan, and the record of this is imparted to the shell, which carries such views to the spiritist medium. Witness the often absurd description given of the character of the "spirit-world," and that through honest mediums, too. They give none of CHRIST, save where two or three are gathered in His name.

Mediumship is true; its ordinary explanation is false. The medium goes into a trance; then his or her vital force is transferred to the "control" which is but a shell, and not the true spirit or ego. Then the hearers enjoy a "communication." Like a reader of a book of record is that medium; events of the past are retold, and more or less accurate prophecies made; the shell lives for the present an energized life, just as Poe lives anew in the person of an elocutionist rendering "The Raven," from the rostrum. Just so long as the "Commentaries" influence mankind, just that long will the "spirit" of Caesar control mediums; and while the Book of Mormon retains its hold on the deluded masses of Utah, so long will the "Prophet Joseph Smith" influence sensitives. But I grow tiresomely wordy. Let us therefore turn to the world of effects, and see what it presented to our psychic perceptions. Will you come with us and see what we three saw as we went forth across the plain which confronted us at the door of the Sagum?

Footnotes

281:1 Job xiii.—5.

292:1 I Samuel xxviii, 14-15.

CHAPTER IV. PAYING LIFE'S REWARDS

"Phylos," said Mol Lang, "you shall now presently behold a man, all in a world of his own. He may not come to us, but we will go to him, and enter into perception of those things which he sees, and because we enter into his perception, therefore we shall be fellow spirits with him, not mere images of his conceptions. Then shall his environment seem as real to us as it does to him; nevertheless his world is (except for such visitors as ourselves, and those few, or perhaps many other souls who are on his identical plane) merely a world of him own conception; it exists not for him who is his neighbor, who will be, as we shall see, on a different psychic plane. Both persons will be existent in the Mansion of the Father, who thus gives His beloved rest.

"Let us enter into the state of that man; he is an inventor from the world of cause, and all about him shall we find evidences of his inventive dreams, which here seem to be real to him. On earth, he beheld in his imagination multitudes of his fellow beings using his adaptations of mechanical and natural forces. He had motor railways which were free to the public, none indisposed to pay were obliged to do so. And he had designs of coin, which the mint (owned by himself, as he had desired while on earth, so that he might correct abuses) minted free for use by the people. So also with all other things which he had hoped to see realized on earth. Yet he died without it, and coming to the world of effects, finds it all (to him only) a fact. We will walk across this plain to the grove yonder, a mile."

The Secrets Of Mount Shasta And A Dweller On Two Planets

For some time after this we walked in silence, each content to note the beauty of the scenery. Gurgling brooks meandered through flowery meadows, groves dotted the perspective, while far away on the horizon was a line of blue hills. When we came to the grove designated by Mol Lang I saw that we were at a station, where cars of strange appearance stood on a network of tracks. People were coming and going past this central point in all directions. The cars had immense spidery wheels, many yards across. A light flight of metal stairs led to the top of a tower; the tower was also an elevator, so that while some people walked up, others were hoisted to the top, where, several rods from the ground, they stepped into the body of the car; then an engineer on the car manipulated certain machinery, and the immense wheels began to revolve, swifter, swifter, and yet swifter, until the great, light vehicle could be seen moving at an amazing speed across the country, up and down hill or around curves with equal facility. "Let us take a ride," said Semla. So we walked up the spiral stairs, and there found a pleasant man in uniform, who asked if we would pay or not.

"Yes," said Mol Lang, "I will, but my friends will not." Thereupon he produced a coin of gold, and while the official was making the entry in his book, Mol Lang handed the coin to me to look at, and I saw that it bore a face of a man, and around the edge the superscription:

"MERTON FOWLER, THE PEOPLE'S FRIEND."

"What conceit!" thought I, whereupon Mol Lang smiled slightly, took the coin from me and paid it over. The official asked where we would go, and for answer Mol Lang said: "To the Falls." The official knew of no such place, but said that he would put us on a car, the engineer of which would know. He conducted us to a car on the other side of his platform, and having entered, we were soon speeding away like an arrow for swiftness. The stops which we made were numerous, all for the purpose, so the engineer explained, of complying with Merton Fowler's rule that all who rode on his cars must inspect his many inventions. The variety of these was bewildering to me, and so many of them seemed to be in operation solely for the purpose of demonstrating peculiar mechanical principles, that I will not consume space for description. At length, after traveling across half a world as it seemed, though not taking a tedious amount of time, we arrived at a splendid group of buildings. Then the engineer confessed that he knew nothing of the Falls, except that he had heard his master speak of them as existing. He would go to him. Accordingly the car ran up before a building which looked like an office, and there he put us in the charge of another person with directions to take us to Merton Fowler.

That gentleman we found in a palatial environment, where things were of great beauty, but where all seemed to be mechanical contrivances, and to exist for that great underlying principle of the designer, the systematization of his knowledge, and the putting of it to more or less utilitarian uses. It was a very paradise for a machinist, but I was not a machinist, and it fatigued me. The number of people was amazing. Mol Lang said that not all of these were mere ideals of that prolific mind, Fowler, but that on the contrary, many of them were real personifications, a few of whom were media like ourselves, but the majority "dead," that is, disembodied souls who were on the same plane of invention and realization as the real mind in control, Merton Fowler. He was the chief here, the others similar. I asked where the Falls were situated, and the inventor, Fowler, replied that a certain author of his acquaintance lived there, and had the pleasure of listening to a mammoth pipe organ made for him by the inventor, "By myself! All men whatever," said this egotist, "are beneficiaries of mine, and recognize me as the chiefest of humankind, and greatest of all living people!"

I turned away in contempt of such mammoth conceit and vanity, and as we left Mol Lang said:

"That man is arranging his concepts of a Christless life as gained on earth. When all is assimilated, he will reincarnate on earth, and from his early childhood self-conceit and self-admiration will be his ruling characteristics. In his last life on earth he sowed the seeds of the one to come. Here, he enjoys the growth of those seeds. Here, too, will the harvest mature, and when all gather, he will take it to earth again to replant. You might ask what good comes of perpetuating such vanity. I would reply: 'First, it is the law of God. Secondly, out of his future egotism will arise self-confidence.' His spirituality of temperament is large, his animal qualities well-balanced and strong, and the good of all his conceit will manifest itself next as a governor of those forces which will lead men forward. Before he died on earth he was a retiring man, timid, feeling himself never appreciated. When he next appears there will be a strong soul, and a leader of men to higher levels of life."

"Truly," I said, "all things under the hand of God work together for good!"

The Falls were in the devachanic realm of an author, who, while on earth, was a very pleasing writer, albeit extravagantly hopeful in his imaginative excursions and thought plays. This was, indeed, doubtless the reason of his popularity as an author. His mind dwelt on the sublime in nature, and on the good, the true, and the beautiful. Here in his heaven he lived his books, and found all about him the characters, the emotions, the delicate imagery and the sublime beauty which made his pages seem real to their readers, and over which tears of sympathy were shed by most perusers. To him also, these things, figments of his imagination when penned, were here become what his desire had always painted, realities, and he enjoyed the seeming actuality, nor knew it but as a dream of his life's nighttime. "Of what use, since it was only a dream?" I answer: these glorious creations of the imagination all make for that high spirituality, that keen sympathy of soul which shall soon bring about the universal Brotherhood of Mankind; it shall dawn with the dawning of the new century, creedless, boundless, asking nothing of any affiliate except high, unfaltering aspiration and action. And this author, who has been in his soul-home these many centuries, shall be one of its prophets, reincarnated.

We found the Falls in a vast gorge, deep as the Royal Gorge of the Arkansas river. It connected two great lakes of rare loveliness; the Scottish lakes or Lake Champlain are not more beautiful, though either were as great as Nyanza. Over a cliff half a mile high, and in the form of a double horseshoe, each more than a mile wide, were two magnificent falls of the river, separated in the center where the middle points of the two curves met, by an island. From this cliff rose three tall conical needles of rock, up, up, up into the air, over a thousand feet each one. Around each was a spiral stairway chiseled in the enduring granite of the stream, and from top to top of each swung a suspension bridge. From the one overhanging the falls run two suspension bridges swung on great cables, miles long, reaching as they did the shores on either side of the river by a diagonal course. I felt sure that the inventor, Merton Fowler, would have conceived no such bridge, because his mechanical training would have told him such lengthy bridge-cables would break from their own weight. But this author, who was no engineer, saw no such difficulty, and consequently his concept found no bar to execution in his imagination. As it was not objective, but subjective, it existed for him, and as we were temporarily on his plane, and perceiving through his senses, we also saw them and found them real; and to all on his plane they were real, subjectively real. But earthly eyes could not have seen them, for they see nothing except objective realities. And both states are real, but to those on the respective planes only. If the things of the spiritual are foolishness to the natural man, so are the things of the natural world to the devachanee. But I digress. The myriads of people, creations of the author's mind, used his bridge; they lived in a Utopia of his creation, and the whole was a very heaven. It all nurtured his spirituality, his reverence for God, his constructive sense even, as well as his sense of beauty. His soul has almost assimilated the whole of these "steps toward God" and it is almost ready to reincarnate as one of the deeply artistic, constructive, reverential souls of earth; one of the nobly beautiful, God-ward turning leaders of the race. Is he not a worker for the Father? "By their works you shall know them." And while and because he leads, he himself will draw nearer, with every passing hour, to God; nearer to Nirvana, that glorious resting time of all the lives, out of which the spirit of man shall wake to find itself more than Man, find itself one of these wonderful World-Spirits whose glittering forms fill the skies of night! Or servants of the Father in some other untellable way.

––––––––––

The fact must be sufficiently obvious that the life between the grave and the cradle, life in the world of effects, is a life of assimilation of results due to causes set in operation while on earth, the world of causality. It is the character-forming realm, where effects are so arranged as to present them as causes in the succeeding earth life; not in the shape of segregate influences, but as traits of character, giving rise to well-defined policies in life on the part of individuals. Like attracts like, and if parents have certain influences governing their lives at critical times, the soul in devachan, which is unavoidably seeking rebirth on earth, will seize the opportunity presented of finding its similars, similars at that time, though perhaps at that time only, like itself, but never so before, possibly never to be so again; suffice it if there be a concordant trinity at the time. There is no accident, no chance, in the Universe; all is immutable law, cause and effect. Zerah Colburn, whose early, advanced skills in mathematics while he was yet a little boy amazed the world, did not inherit his powers of calculation. Mozart did not inherit what neither of his parents possessed, though it is true that the maternal mind did provide attractive mental similarity by her own love for music, experienced by Mozart while still in the womb. A recurrence of traits absent for generations prior has been invoked to explain these cases of infantile genius when it has been well known that neither parent had the traits which seem to have been passed to the offspring. But that explanation will not wholly suffice. The question of heredity is a deep one; parents are moved by special influences, and children of that time are souls attracted from devachan to their mental similars. Such was the young Zerah Colburn; such the infant prodigy, Mozart. Zailm Numinos might have told you that Colburn was a noted Atlantean mathematician had he not neglected it in his history of Atlantis. And Mozart was Aleman the poet and lyrist of Spartan Greece.

Night seemed to be coming on; the air was pleasantly cool, and we found ourselves, after a long sail on a lovely body of water, standing on a shore whose sands and pebbles were of agate. Bamboo fringed the lake margin, and many graceful houses in quiet nooks dotted the varied landscape. The country bore some resemblance to the land of Japan, and indeed we found that we were in the concepts of an American who had resided for many years in Japan before his entrance to devachan.

The Secrets Of Mount Shasta And A Dweller On Two Planets

We went into a spacious veranda of a house of fine appearance, which in architectural style was a general combination of things, most comfortable. Contrary to Japanese customs, we found easy chairs instead of mats or rugs, and in these chairs we took seats, Mol Lang saying we would be welcome to do so. Before long a servant in Japanese costume appeared and placed a table before us, and upon it laid covers for five persons. Presently a handsome, elderly man, with a young girl, who, I judged, was his daughter, came out of the residence, and exchanged greetings with us, after the manner of true gentlefolk. This was, as Mol Lang afterward explained, the real ego about whose imagery all things in this place clustered. The lake, the tropical vegetation, the remodeled Japanese people whom we met, in short, all effects here, were arranged in accord with this man's ideals. In them he saw realized his dreams of a quiet, carefree, hospitable life, and because he saw them, we also saw them, for Mol Lang had insinuated our perceptions into this man's soul plane. With him we partook of a generous supper. Liquors were not on his table, nor could any have been found in all that soul land, for the man was a total abstainer. Of course, the people whom he believed he saw, and who, for him, resided in this, his country, used liquors no more than he, for they were either his imagination's concepts, or, if real individuals, were in sympathy with the master mind, else they would not have been there with him. But all this he knew not any more than one who in slumber dreams, knows at the time that the vivid dream personages and places exist solely for himself. Sometimes, truly, a night dreamer really goes away with another harmonious soul, the two being real souls on a psychic journey, it being no dream, but a fact.

This man, in all of his princely extravagance, his artistically beautiful buildings, the richness of clothing of the people whom he conceived, the statues, fountains, groves, all things, was but heartily drinking imagined joys, wholly unconscious all the time that they were subjective creations. They were all conceived for a single purpose, pursuit of which formed his chief joy, that of caring for the happiness of his daughter. She was his idol, his joy, the reason for being, he would have said. And she was a pretty girl, though not to my mind beautiful. She was engaging, witty, well educated, and accomplished. But I have seen many such, and thought of her as only one of hundreds I had known. We were invited to stay indefinitely in this home, and, upon Mol Lang's suggestion, accepted the offer. Days passed rapidly in this paradise, of which our host's home was the central attraction. He had great parks, and gave splendid entertainments to scores of happy people. His house was a palace in itself. The libraries, the art gallery, with thousands of fine paintings, all this, and more, made life so pleasant that several months had elapsed before our party of three bade him adieu. In it all we saw that the cheerful life was for the sake of the daughter, and held little pleasure for the father. The art gallery, too, was added to his home for her sake. The libraries were for both, and, as he said, he thought he took more pleasure in books than she did; to him books were sacred treasures. But it was in music that his soul found ecstatic rest. Such divine melodies and such exquisite technique and feeling as he exhibited in his rendition of fine music I had never even dreamed of, much excellent music as I had heard. It was as the fable of Orpheus come true. Hour after hour he played for me, while Semla was away with Mol Lang, and my soul responded in a thrill which swept it with sublime joy, until it seemed as if my being had become a person-less, throbbing, sobbing stress of harmony, that could flee on the winds and set the souls of men pulsing, beating in unison! I knew that the player was a companion to me in it all. We were two souls on the same plane, reaping identical experiences.

At last a day came when Mol Lang said: "My friends, let us go away from here, for other things claim our attention. A few hours here must suffice us. We will go where the daughter of this man really is."

My friend had, I thought, spoken of the months of our tarrying in this paradise in a figurative sense when he said "a few hours." But he had not; it was really only a few hours as the people on earth had counted the same interval through which we had so recently passed. Time is, after all, only a measure of so much done by or to him who experiences its lapse; myriads of people have lived a whole century during ten minutes of other people's time. Mol Lang's remark about our being ready to go where the daughter really was I could not comprehend at the time, nor did I know for years, all because my own astral had been left behind in the Sakaza on earth; I had no means of comparison of ideas. The place I was in was the only place existent for me; that is, it and the country of the author and that of the inventor, Fowler. These I knew of, and for them a memory shell had been formed by me as I went through them; not that I was conscious of such a process of creation; I was only aware of the memories which were retained for me, and which seemed part of myself. But Mol Lang explained only that the American really did not have his daughter with him, but only his ideal of her ever before him.

On our departure we went down to the lake and got into a boat, and as we traveled, somehow it seemed as if, without my knowing just how or when, we had left the boat and the lake, and were in a garden, walking amidst a profusion of flowers. It was without explanation, but did not particularly surprise me nor long occupy my attention. No one is ever astonished at anything in the psychic realm.

It was a city garden, and, situated on a hill, the residence of the owner commanded the view of a great city, extending in all directions. The house was evidently the home of a person of refinement, and while evidences of wealth were numerous, these seemed to be unessential additions for the sake of comfort, instead of a display of riches. No person could long be amidst the influences of that home, to which Mol Lang admitted us, without feeling that the owner believed herself to have a great and sacred mission in life.

"This is the daughter," said Mol Lang. "The girl whom we saw in the other home was the daughter, as the father imagined her to be when he died, leaving her at that age. See how different the woman is from his conception of her. I bring you here so that you may see what difference exists between the devachanic concepts of the soul and the objects conceived of. It illustrates the saying that 'heaven is what we make it.'" At that moment a lady entered the room, evidently on business; her manner was full of power. She seemed not to perceive us, and after a little I coughed slightly to attract her attention. Mol Lang smiled in amusement, as he said:

The Secrets Of Mount Shasta And A Dweller On Two Planets

"Phylos, you could cough for a long time, and she would not know of thy presence. Why? Because we are temporarily on the earth, and I have given you power to see earthly conditions, that is, while we are on the earth, for it might be all about us yet if we were in a different psychic condition, the earth would not be near, but vastly remote from us. This lady has not yet come to the change called death. She is one who labors to place woman on the proud basis of independence, proud, because rightfully hers. But woman will never attain to it until she does so by self-effort; nothing is won worth the having except by self-effort. When she so wins it, she will be by the side of man, not above him, for woman is not man's superior; neither below him, for she is not his inferior; but beside him, for man and woman are equal in all things. It will be a blessed day for humanity when this time comes. This lady and her sister workers are now guiding those dwellers of the earth who have not such clear understanding of the needs of the times; and they will succeed, more or less, during this century, but not brilliantly, since no great reform, nor anything greatly good, can succeed in any century, decade or year nominated by the number nine. Hence, human hopes will wax or wane, will seem to go forth to victory, but will meet only failure until the new century. Darkest of all the years will that be which is just before the dawn. This brave leader we see here will see Hope set in that last year like a star in the west, and she will die then, despairing, though hoping, with prophetic Mackay, that 'Ever the truth comes uppermost, and ever is justice done.'"

For a considerable time after this we were silent, for Mol Lang seldom spoke without definite cause, and it now served his purpose better to be silent. I spoke next:

"What good can it be, what good can be achieved through such bitter disappointment? Such heartache?" "That which comes always from all things. 'Man never is, but always to be blest,' is wholly true. And it is not from the hopes we are able to bring to realization in earth life that our devachan, our heaven, is made; but from those hopes, longings, aspirations and determinations which through life are our dearest desires because we have never been able to satisfy them. They have the most happy heaven whose high-soaring souls have always been forced

342

to be content with the mere view of Caanan from their mountain lookouts. Let no poor, disappointed soul on earth mourn because of life's unsatisfied longings, for we do not know today whether we are busy or idle. In times when we have thought ourselves lazy, we have afterward discovered that much was accomplished and much was begun in us. These beginnings are fruitful, indeed, for they bestow upon us our longed-for aspirations, 'over there' if we will, in His way."

During this discourse of Mol Lang I had glimpses of the whole, both of earth and of heaven. A thing which struck me with a feeling of peculiar anguish was that that gentle soul who thought he lived for his daughter, really had not that daughter with him, but only his self-created image of her. I had not thought of the fact that even on earth we do not have our friends, but only our concepts of them; that our supposed friend may really be our secret enemy, but if we know it not we remain happy in our ignorance. Mol Lang observed the feeling on my part and said, as he turned and placed an arm around me as we walked onwards:

"Phylos, beloved son, feel not so! When the day comes when this lady shall enter the devachanic life, then whenever and wherever she has ideals and concepts like those of her father, or he like hers, then the two of them will be really together, 'two souls with only a single thought.' It is the same on earth; only identity of thought makes nearness of souls. As the grand march of souls following after Christ draw nearer unto God, those planes where all souls are together in the thought and concept will be the planes mainly occupied by humanity, till at the glorious last, none shall be apart from any other, or from the Father."

The room and its earnest worker had faded from view. Instead of it we found that in front of us was a monastic structure, set on a lofty mountain peak which arose from a lake. Dim vistas of water, of wooded shores and silvery, shadowy isles were in perspective. Over the tower which rose from the monastery was a flashing crescent of purple light. I asked what place we were at now. The answer was:

"The Lunar Temple, a part of devachan, but having nothing to do with the moon. Here, where many occult students come after laying aside the earthly body, is a holy place of rest. Here are many theosophic adepts and neophytes; they saw then with eyes of spirit, hence had then, as now, much the same concepts of life; devachan to them is not, therefore, on the same plane as with other mortals, any more than their objective life was. Here Semla takes leave of us, to appear no more on earth until after fifty centuries of mundane time. He will then incarnate, not as a Tchin, but as a member of the American Nation of that far distant day, because his life has been mostly spent in that land this time. But now he enters into the rest he has earned; this is his devachan."

There, under the flashing purple light from the monastic tower, Semla took his leave, invoking upon us the peace of the Father.

Through ability conferred by Mol Lang, I had seen the nature of the life after death. For a few moments my soul was able to compare the newly gained knowledge with my old time ideals of nature. I thought, "If all this is but a dream, what is a dream? If this which seems real matter is not such—"

"Nay, my son," interjected Mol Lang, as I thought upon the nature of matter, "this is real matter. Why, what is matter, do you think? Matter is a One Substantiality, having not a single quality which any human sense can have knowledge of. But force also is one of the creations of the Father. And force has two polarities, the positive and the negative, absolute opposites. Now man on earth has certain senses; there are seven of these senses: sight, hearing, feeling, smelling, tasting, intuition, and one without a name. These last are not yet evolved, for the fullness of days is not come; the Fifth Day is; but the Sixth and the Seventh are not. With the last, man becomes greater than he has ever been. Only they that have ears that hear shall solve this saying. Five senses understand the positive dynamic affections of matter by Force, and behold, man senses the earth and some of the stellar bodies. But all these are of the positive, and so are in the Father's Mansion of Cause. These five senses are what the Apostle Paul called the 'Natural Mind.' But 'In my Father's house are many mansions.' And this, which is the briefer life after the grave, is His Mansion of effects, and it is the result of matter affected by negative force. Here the first five senses call all things pertaining to devachan 'mere dreams'; even wise Hamlet asks, 'What dreams may come?' But I say unto thee, both earth (cause) and devachan (effect) are material; both due in their every phenomena to force, but either state is perceived only by senses special to it. Man in one hath five special senses, and these know the earth, but call heaven a dream; and Man in the other has other seven special senses, and these know of devachan, but call earth a dream. Yet both states are really material, and similarly, both are unreal except to the Father. So Man is constantly dying from the one state and being born in the other, back and forth, and only that state where he is is real to him at any time. Myriad times does he repeat the process, incarnifying and discarnifying, and each time of rebirth on the earth finds him ever on a higher plane, until at last the concrete condition miscalled life is over, and the condition-less 'long devachan' (Nirvana) is attained. Then man and his Father are together and at one. Man came from God; unto Him must he go. But only a few have done this as yet, and of these Jesus Christ of Bethlehem is so far the only One who can truly say, 'I and my Father are one.'" Mol Lang had no desire that I should continuously retain the memories of the experiences just passed through; the separate facts were to become quite as unknown as if never observed. All was solely for the purpose of surrounding my soul with influences calculated to force me upward and onward, out of earth life, or desire for it, until at last I would come to realize that I had known something higher, and must return to the plane of the spiritual nature. Yes, the word is MUST.

After leaving Semla, with the new life open to him, Mol Lang and myself sought the lake, and after taking our seats on a bit of sandy shore, I asked questions as to the appearance of the scheme of creation to occult perceptions. It seemed to me that life must have a wider significance to him than to me.

"Phylos, it has. Grand as the vision of life seems to the ordinary man, made up, as it is, of his few years on earth supposedly followed by unending existence in heaven, to me it is infinitely more beautiful than even earth's loftiest vision can present it! Man's ideas are full of error; they involve the childishness of admitting that in the life on earth the multitudes who 'make in their dwellings a transient abode' are in the course of such a finite time, able to set in motion infinite causes which shall be carried out in psychic effects eternally. Only through the Great Master are any so able.

"I have so willed, my son, that the features of this visit to devachan shall be withdrawn from you, and you will remember them only as a vague, delightful dream, which shall have influence in leading you to the pinnacles of the Father and the summits of the soul. It is easy to erase these memories; I have but to disassociate the astral body formed here by your experiences, and you will thereafter know this state only when that astral shall control you as its medium. I will take you to my own home in Hesper, and there you will come to know my son, whose name is Sohma, and my daughter Phyris. Yet that knowledge also will I disassociate, after the time of it, and you will forget it all; yea, you will forget even me, and know only through the same mediumship, because your karma orders for you long years yet to come on earth, and atonement for evil works which have cried unto God for compensation, lo! A century of centuries, and longer. Christ has said: 'One jot or one tittle shall in no way pass from the law till all be fulfilled.' Unless you be released to Him.

"But you have asked a question. Hear the answer: I sow a seed, and it shall grow, and blossom and fruit, and though the sower is forgotten, the plant will not be. You will remember my words forever, not forget them for one hour, for such is my will, yet forget me completely.

"Besides the heavenly world, there are many more which are imperceptible to men. Yet matter and force compose them all. Many of them are worlds of Cause, but no merely human being is in them, nor can any earthly sense understand them or know of them. They are peopled, but by beings of whom some are good, and some are evil; in the sight of the Eternal Cause, relatively good or evil. That which exists under laws hostile to man is evil to man, though not in itself evil. But these 'mansions' are set apart from one another that they may not interfere. There is that which is astray, but in itself not evil, for in all the creation there is no evil eternal, for God is perfect.

The Secrets Of Mount Shasta And A Dweller On Two Planets

"The worlds of human life are seven in number; yet four of them are invisible, unknowable to earthly senses, and this is not because of remoteness, but the kind of force-affection of their ingredients of matter. Mankind occupies but one planet at a time, for like its present dwelling place (earth) the human race is but a letter in the Divine Library of Being. To be exact, the more advanced, occult souls do inhabit Venus, which I have called Hesper, and which was by the ancients of the Earth termed 'The Garden of the Hesperides.'

"Yes, Phylos, life does mean more to me than to you. I look at its stately march, and I see the battalion of being wherein I am but a corporal, progressing around its appointed seven spheres, of which only Mars, the Earth and Venus are matters which earthly perception can know; I see the human race progressively incarnating on each of its peculiar planets as it goes, every individual ego about eight hundred times, approximately, on each world each time the race comes to it, which is seven times also, making forty-nine world-carnate epochs. Each ego thus has incarnation and dis-incarnation periods to the number, more or less, of forty thousand. It is in these that, beginning as an irresponsible creation, far from human, as you would define the word 'human,' and ending as a Perfect Man entering into Nirvanic rest, that the scheme of the Eternal Uncreated Father is perfected. Yes, truly, man sins, but as his incarnations progress, he atones for every jot, every tittle. Karma is the penalty for evil doing, and it is the law of God; it knows no lessening of payment, accepts no vicarious price, but is faithful jailer over that prison which is life-action; whosoever is thrown into it shall not come out till every farthing is paid. Beware, then, of doing wrong, for you must bear the penalty, only you. Truly, life is long enough to make payment; it is better to have none to make! ₁

"We go now to a view of the truth that the spirit came from the Father, and returns to Him after it has fulfilled the law and the prophets; it lives in the worlds of cause a short span, but in those of effect a long span, for passivity is to activity as about eighty to one, and the lives are many, strung like beads on the one cord of the individual ego.

"Lastly, the ego coming from the Father has no sex; it is not man,

347

neither woman, but sexless. When it enters upon life it becomes double, so that in the earth there is a man, and there is a woman, and though the bodies and the animal souls and the human souls are different in the two, yet behold, their spirit is one and the same. Now sometimes the two, being of one spirit, are also husband and wife. Yet more often, they are not, for the age of harmony is not yet at hand. But it is of such singleness of spirit that the Bible says, 'What God has joined, let no man put asunder.' There is no man who could, if he would, so separate. But that saying is not of the carnal marriage, but of the spirit unit only. And the latter has no lust. But when the two shall, after the millions of years which lie between the non-esoteric Christian and Nirvana, come to know all the law of life, then the union will be as it was before the separation. You cannot really comprehend the truth now, but when you shall at last be done with earth life, you will then recall it and know. And knowing it, you will then tell the world of it. But not now. Now this is true: Mates in the Lord cannot know each other as such, until they both will to live after the rule of His Highway. And the latter has nothing carnal. 'Straight is the Gate and narrow is the Way that leads to Life, and there are few that find it.' Until they find it they do not find each other; neither are they released from incarnation in the flesh."

Mol Lang arose after this long discourse, in which he had briefly described the works of God. He said:

"I have answered you. Come, let us go from here, and you shall know my son, and my daughter, and my home."

He laid his hand upon my brow, and I seemed to sleep; when I was conscious again we were in an immense garden, and before us I saw a house which at once impressed me as being a real home. I say this because somehow occult study had seemed foreign to home life and influences. How entirely compatible the two are will appear nearer the end of this history.

I found on acquaintance with it that it bore out my first impressions perfectly, for it was the most genuine home that could well exist, and typified all human life in this world of Cause, Hesper. It was a home of human glorified beings, of occult students incarnate in exalted causal life.

Do you ask me how any portion of the human race came to be so far in the lead as the Hesperian contingent? The answer is that their seven-fold natures had been so far perfected by the trials to which the study of occult adeptism subjects its initiates, that they had become enlightened, responsible beings; they had drunk of the cup concerning which Jesus inquired of the children of Zebedee if they had the ability to drink it. And in consequence there had come to them the keys to that realm of spirit which no natural mind can understand. They had learned the sevenfold character of their natures, that man is a composite being, having seven principles, viz. the I AM, or ego; the body of the spirit, or spirit-body; the human soul; the animal soul; the astral reflection of the two lowest principles, by name, vital force and the earthly body thereby animated. Thus far, I regret to say, the mass of mankind is not developed much beyond its animal soul; a minority have the human soul shining forth; but only occult adepts have the Sixth or spirit-body developed, while none of whom the world knows except Jesus and Buddha are perfect in the Spirit of the Father.

I stood with Mol Lang, looking upon his home in Venus, the world to which Earth's children will come, leaving it deserted until another round shall return them, although on a higher plane, that of perfect love, "the greatest thing in the world." But now Hesper is the planet of this Christ-like love, its home in the course of nature and man's development. You will not all come, alas!

"Phylos," said Mol Lang, "my son is of nearly your own number of years; my daughter Phyris is the same age as yourself. Both will tell you of occult truths, as I have done, yet neither they, nor I, nor anything but the intuitions from your own God-given Spirit can teach you. If a soul has not in itself perception of God and His works, no man can teach it, for having ears to hear and eyes to see, he hears and sees, but does not comprehend. To me it is given of God to show you and tell you of those things which many prophets and righteous men have desired to see and to hear, but have not. Blessed are your eyes, for they see, and your ears, for they hear. Yet, nevertheless, you will return to earth and will forget, and restlessly long for a better state, but shall not find it again for many years. O Phylos, my son, if only you could even now know! But karma pursues you, seeking repayment. And karma shall have its dues, and you will then go free. Let us pray to God now, for I will speak no more of these things; I have spoken already. Hereafter Phyris shall tell you and show you in my place."

Then, in that Hesperian garden, we knelt together, and Mol Lang repeated that eloquent voice of the ages, so old, yet ever new, the prayer of our Savior. I think tears were in our eyes when we arose. Turning, I saw a lovely woman.

"Phyris, my child, he has come! Phylos, this is my daughter, of whom I told you."

It had so surprised me to hear a man who had so much of what untaught fancy calls Godlike power speak of his children, that Mol Lang had said to me in comment:

"Phylos, do you think that because I have wisdom which you have conceived that only God possesses, that I am not human? My son, I am more wholly and truly human because of being near to God. But the mass of people on earth are not fully developed even yet in the human principle; their lives, actions, passions, are centered in the Fourth or animal soul, and only the more exalted have reached the development of the human within them. When mankind shall come fully into its humanity, then Earth can no more be its planet; they must come here. Bear in mind always, that all you see in Hesper is only human, and so you will know more of what Man is, how glorious a being he is. Man is only partially human, and not filled with the Father, nor come into his Spirit body, and he must therefore marry and live in marriage, else the race would cease to reincarnate. Each ego must pay its debts. But many will die debtors to Him."

We three, father, daughter, and myself, went into one of the wide porticos of the brown Parthenon-like mansion, and sat down, being seated where we could see over the profusion of flowers in the great gardens. So beautiful was the scene, both near and far, that I was content thus to remain, unmoving. Here was no devachan, no scene of effects, but an active life in a world of cause.

This life differed from that upon earth in being broader, more perfect, more glorious than earthly conditions can produce in the present round. Ordinary life in Hesperus is all that the highest form of life can be on earth; and thus has all the wonderful development which exists in the midst of the secret occult brotherhoods of Earth. It is impossible to express adequately what perfection of physical life exists in Hesperus. But it is a perfection of the physical nature, amid ideal surroundings, all of which prepare the animal man to work for the human man, and he for the Spirit man, the I AM, or ego. Thus does the ego progress through matter. Is it not a sublime thought that reincarnation does not mean transmigration of souls? The first leads man ever up; the other, which is false, even in theory, merely a perverted notion of the first, might mean progress, but more often would mean retrogression, and in all this Universe there is no retrogression. Reincarnation is but a chance to expiate the errors of life, foremost of which is not overcoming and containing self. Will you not pay? Then you are doomed!

Footnotes

311:1 See note page 236.

CHAPTER V. HUMAN LIFE ON VENUS

"It is good to be at home again," said Mol Lang. "I love my home because here are my friends, and here is the congenial atmosphere of spirituality. I see about me the locations of my last objective incarnation, this present. For me there is no more birth, and no death of the body except through transition of the Logos. Here I passed the ordeal of the crisis and have become androgynous, for in me now are the feminine and the masculine; I am whole, not half, and I and my egoic mate are one individual We divided are one, and have come to the Spirit in the sense uttered by the Savior when He said, 'Be you therefore perfect, even as your Father is perfect.' And you, my son Phylos, will surely come into this same glory, for by your karma it is so fixed. Yes," said he, reverting to his first thought, "it is good to be at home."

The old man arose from his seat and paced with stately erectness up and down the veranda. "Old?" Yes, as earth counts age; for Pertoz he was just in early prime, not yet come to his two hundredth year by some forty-eight months. And age could never affect him anymore, for he had come to deathlessness; to bodily immortality. Of him, as of many, are the words of the beloved apostle, John. ₁ At that moment he was in his astral form, his physical body being in his sleeping-room, where he left it, in order to cross interplanetary space for me. Curious thought! An inhabitant of Venus able to visit earth at will! Yet it is not really difficult. It merely involves the leaving of the physical body and plane at one point, and entrance to the astral, or psychic plane. From this latter it is as easy to return to the state of cause at any point, be it Alcyone, chief of the "Pleiads, glittering in their eternal depths," or even further, beyond ken of the telescope, as it is to return to the place departed from. The whole difficulty is in leaving the physical plane at all, and for the advanced esoterist this is as nothing, because the normal state of his soul is always in the astral or psychic instead of the physical. The difficulty with a student is in the repugnance he feels to the thought of returning to an inferior state of being, like life on earth. But the Life of Love is: "I serve." So we return.

That we were in the astral, disembodied state was no hindrance to Phyris' perception of us, for like all Hesperians she had the sight of the soul as you have ordinary sight, a mere commonplace power. Her eyes, as indeed those of all souls on this high plane of being, have psychic clairvoyance as a normal possession, though not the less endowed with ordinary physical vision on this account. As in the long ago of Earth, her eyes were still the same clear, calm gray, the kind possessed by Jesus of Nazareth. They were windows for her pure soul, which seemed to be just behind them, gazing out. This slender, graceful girl was no devachanic ideal, although not gross enough to be visible to eyes used only to perception of objective, earthly states of matter; her sweet, grave demeanor, her light laugh at something said by Mol Lang, her perfection of physical life, all breathed the fact of her objective being, and bore evidence to the truth that her rule of life was obedience to the law. And yet I doubt if your eyes, my friends, could have seen her at all. No telescope will ever reveal human life on Venus; not that it is not there, but its forms are of the One Substance affected by a range of force rendering them imperceptible to earthly eyes. You will not think the air any less material, or electricity any less real, because your eyes cannot perceive them. Your eyes are very limited in their visual range; if the One Substance vibrates more or less rapidly than an exceedingly small length of time, producing correspondingly minute force wavelengths, your eyes cannot cognize such vibrations. It is the same with your ears and hearing. If your eyes and ears were not thus limited, you would see every sound and hear every sunbeam. Every rainbow would be vocal, while heat, which now you only feel, would furnish amazing wealth of sound and vision. So it is with the Hesperian people, their persons you could not see, their voices you could not hear, yet they would not be similarly limited in regard to your persons and voices. But so long as you imagine that because you have eyes you can see all that there is to be seen, and that your ears hear all that is worth hearing, so long will you depend on these organs, and gain that sort of false ideas of the Universe which must arise from entire ignorance of all except the tiny bit of creation you occupy. So long, too, will you depend on the telescope to reveal truths about other worlds; you will hunt for evidences of human life on the nearer planets, but you will never find any until you cease to expect that matter will reveal soul; it cannot do it, for the finite cannot reveal infinity. Turn it about; ask of the soul that it reveal itself and matter also, and all worlds will draw near to you, show their teeming vitality of life, and all nature will uncover such treasures as the hungry soul of science has never found before.

Phyris was able to look over all my past, over the other lives which I had yet to attain the power of recollecting. She knew every deed, thought and motive of it all. Had she oared to examine this history? No fear existed in my mind, for I did not know of such a past myself, and my ignorance preserved my peace of mind. I did not try to analyze the reason for my eager desire to win this maiden's good opinion. If I had, I should have complained bitterly to myself for being a presumptuous fool. As it was, I was happy in the knowledge of my purity of purpose.

Though dissociated from earth life, my soul development was but little more than before. Therefore, to me, Phyris seemed a sort of goddess; and to have estimated only as perfect human herself and her wondrous occult powers, would have been an impossibility with me. To have found that I was in love with her would have frightened me. I am glad that I was then prevented from having that thought. But deep in my soul it was true, nevertheless, and the leaven was working. Closer knowledge was not to have the effect of detracting from her exalted position; but it was to raise me to the understanding that these psychic powers were attributes of human nature, for in itself human nature is essentially godlike.

By the way, what is the mundane idea of God? You say that God is omnipotent, omnipresent, eternal. Very good. But the earthly idea of these things is very narrow. Conceptions can never rise higher than their source, therefore God is, although a noble ideal, not nearly so great to the world as He is to Hesperus. Do you say that I am inconsistent, denying my own high claims for Man, and that I am virtually negating the statement that conceptions can rise to the level of their source? I reply that the Father limits the height of the source. "What do I mean?" I mean that He speaks to only the partially developed human soul on the earth plane from the level of human principle in Himself, but from no higher plane. So the earthly conception of Him is that of a perfect Person, all-powerful, ubiquitous, eternal, but a person; whereas He is impersonal. But to the Hesperian, God speaks of Himself and His works from the level of Spirit, which is above soul; it is the level of the Over-Soul of Emerson. I hope you will study that statement, for nothing I have said means more, is more important than anything in this book.

I have said that the earthly conceptions of omnipotence, omnipresence and eternity are narrow. It is true. The first means only the most extravagant exercise or suspension of known laws, but scouts the existence of fearful, wonderful, unknown laws. Omnipresence means to the non-occult mind a variety of vague, impracticable ideas, only the few recognizing it as immanency and constant self insertion and creation. Finally, eternity; the mind readily agrees to unlimited, endless time, yet is aghast at a mere decillion, almost refusing to believe. Yet one is to the other as all to nothing.

At the time I first met Phyris my ideas of God were similarly limited, and when I saw her exercise powers which no terrestrial man ever dreamed that even God could possess, I was truly aghast. Love her? Not then. Respect her, adore her, as a Hindu does an image of his God, yes. But the seed was sown; its growth sure.

Mol Lang left me in the large parlor of his home, where we three had gone, and when only Phyris was here beside myself, I immediately was inhibited by a timid fear of my gentle hostess. Although she soon dispelled this feeling, I nevertheless felt relieved when a young man entered and she introduced me to—

The Secrets Of Mount Shasta And A Dweller On Two Planets

"My brother, Sohma."

As I looked upon the two, and remembered Mol Lang's appearance, I thought: "What splendid physiques these people have, how graceful and perfect every line; it is as if the body was molded upon the soul, and perfect in its every physical contact."

"Yes, you are right in your thoughts," said Sohma. He had replied to my thought, as Mol Lang and Phyris had: "You are right. We make our physical lives correspond to our rigid adherence to law, though that adherence is to us a second nature, not burdensome, nor even in its exercise consciously applied. Excesses, intemperance, indulgence of that nature so pleasant to the animal senses, these have no attraction, but instead are utterly repugnant. Vegetarians strictly, never taking life for any selfish purpose, is it wonderful that our material frames conform to our soul shapes?"

"Truly not," I replied, "but in my case how could conformity to law change the appearance of an unhandsome maturity? My body is already grown, completed in obedience to laws not wisely nor very closely kept. I see that you are possessed of occult wisdom, but I am not, and find it hard to remember what I have heard of it; as for making the knowledge practical, impossible!"

"Phylos, my brother, the occult adept is born, not made. His or her knowledge is from within, not from without. To you shall be given the key of the Spirit, and behold, the All-Knowing will enter into your soul, and though no man shall teach you, neither any book, still you shall become aware of all things, for all things are of our Father, and that is the Spirit. But before the Spirit can come in, the house must be swept, and, my brother Phylos, I would prefer that you are not destined to endure this ordeal. Yet the occult that knows all things is born of many lives, and in these has been evil. You are born this way also; it is karma."

Mol Lang had now returned clothed in his material body, and I alone was in the astral, yet not solitary in the sense of loneliness, for my friends were not separated from me as a result of our diverse physical conditions. True, I could not clothe myself in material form, for I was in Venus, and my body was in a distant planet. This condition was the reverse of disability, however, for in going from place to place I had only to desire to be in a more distant place, and I was there, though this power enabled me to have such freedom only in Hesper, and a sense of restriction consequently arose. Discontent was growing in my soul; I felt already a stranger on this high soul plane where my friends were born. Though I knew nothing of earth because my earthly self was in the Sach in the care of Mendocus, yet I had a most uncomfortable feeling of foreignness; a feeling that some other and previous condition, somewhere, was not strange, and I had a longing to be again in its familiar environment. Poor me!

Footnotes

316:1 NOTE.—Kindly see St. John xvii; 21-26.

320:1 St. John xvi; 13.

CHAPTER VI. AN INDIRECT ANSWER

An eminent author has said that "literary themes are necessarily limited; that authors cannot create as a fiction that which has no counterpart in fact." And this is absolutely true. Literature is restricted to ringing the changes on love, hatred, hope, despair, greed, indifference, envy, the gamut of our human emotions, in short. When these are presented in their threefold aspects, tragedy, comedy, or seriocomic, the scale is run, and the only further variations possible are the lights or shadows of faintness or intensity of emotion.

Perhaps the thought arises that in this history some new phase will appear, that Theo-Christianity has some new phases to present. Such an idea is doomed to disappointment. Indeed, the occult will be found to exclude even certain potent earthly factors of literature, all those of the lower animal nature, because these have no place in human life. Envy, greed, hatred, have no place in a nature which is close kin to that soul of love, Jesus. Indifference, sloth, despair, these can have no room in a soul which scans so absorbing a vista as that open to Mol Lang, yet so loving a soul that, like Jesus and Gautama, perfect willingness existed to turn from such sublime reward in order that they might lead their least brethren there also. You may say that such love as this is not animal when I say it is not human. Right. But it is spiritual; it is that love which only those who have begun to tread the Path know, knowing within the soul the advent of the Spirit. If any of you come to feel that You will not shrink, though karma demands that you also show that "greater love hath no man" than that he "give up his life for a friend," then brother, sister, you have known the birth of the Spirit within you. Blessed are you then.

No one can rightfully expect that by the relation of weird things I shall give him a half-hour's amusement; such is not my aim. This book is a work of love, done for a sacred purpose. The second coming of Christ is upon the world, not only as a time simultaneously arriving for all, but also unto each human soul as it becomes ready to receive Him in the heart, and do His work. 1 He is at hand now in the sense that if you will open your soul to receive His spirit, He is there to enter in. Truly, of the moment He comes to His own no man can tell the day or the hour; yet I say, tarry not for Him as a man or an external spirit, but as the Christ Spirit entering into your very being. And He shall not wait to come as a man, but come as the Spirit of Divine Love, just as soon as you are ready to make that your rule of life; and as the Christ and Father are One, so therefore shall you who hear and pay attention be glorified, and presently arise, depart from this world, and go unto the Life. Whoever has ears to hear, let him hear. Likewise He shall come as a person at the last. 2

I certainly have strange things to relate, but nothing weird, unreal or sensational. That which I say is from my Father, and can lead the earnest listener into the Path where the Christ led the way. What I say concerns a larger measure of life, Hesper, the planet of Divine Love. I hope to reveal some further idea than I have up to this point of the extent, kind and duration of occult life. Until now, I have given only rules; now I give the result of faithfulness to them. I hope to show what a glorious being man becomes through heeding occult law, the law of the Spirit I testify about. Upward through all the ages, with never any descent, Man pursues still the glorious march which shall eventually result in making him one with the Father—more than man finite, Man infinite! Angelic! But my pen is years ahead of my visit to Hesper. I must return to that time or else my words become merely words, erected like modem buildings, fourteen stories high.

My desire to investigate the occult truth did not diminish because of the rapid growth of my desire for a life more familiar. Yet ever and again

The Secrets Of Mount Shasta And A Dweller On Two Planets

I caught myself studying whether psychic truth might not be pursued where, ah! amidst—well, some set of conditions less rigorous to the animal instincts struggling within me, and setting me so far below my friends. You might as well hope to mix oil and water as to study the occult among unspiritual, earthly influence!

As a teacher, Sohma contented himself with telling me of principles, and not of marvels, in case that in pursuing wonders I should lose sight of causes; the fruit of a tree is always likely to be more attractive to the ignorant than is the tree itself. Here is a primary truth in regard to occult study: pay small heed to the marvels, or to magic, and all heed to laws, for the laws are the tree. The marvel worker is the least of the brethren, understanding not the laws of the others to any profitable extent. Know the law; know the marvels only incidentally; if you do not know the law, but only the marvel, then you are not following Him, nor shall you inherit His kingdom, though you could do more magic then the Tchin, Mendocus, or even Mol Lang. It was their possession of least value; may you also regard it that way.

During a stroll in the garden, I asked Sohma about his remark that though I should be given the key to occult wisdom, I should not be taught details. "Sohma, you say details are omitted, and effects also, and only general laws are to be taught me. Now, my nature seems incapable of learning much in that way. I seem to feel a different method is necessary, a method born of—of—" here I passed my hand across my brow in perplexity, for earth memories were not supporting me. "Well, I don't know exactly what; I seem to have some vague idea of a past life, somewhere, in which other methods of learning were in use. I do not know now, brother. I am lost." "No, not lost, Phylos; misplaced, ahead of your common place in life. But you make reference to the analytical philosophy, which reasons from effects back to a common cause. It is not a sure process, as witness the status of chemical science in that vaguely remembered life of yours. Chemistry is a proud science, though handicapped by clumsy analytical processes. It cannot tell what a grain of sand is."

Suddenly my chemical learning returned to me, in obedience to

The Secrets Of Mount Shasta And A Dweller On Two Planets

Sohma's will, although the surrounding circumstances of its acquirement were blocked. But with the return of the knowledge itself I became immediately argumentative, and I replied to Sohma:

"Pardon me, but chemistry can tell that. Sand is silica, silicic acid, and it is composed of the element silicon and the oxygen of the air, in the proportion of two of the latter to one of the former."

"Precisely. But you have not really told anything; you are as far from a finality as before. You say sand is composed of two primary elements?"

"Certainly."

"And being primary, cannot be reduced farther?"

"No, they cannot," I said, yet, remembering certain wonderful things I had already witnessed, I was beginning to be nervous.

"No! Are you sure?" he asked, persistently; and I, both from a feeling of stubbornness which his manner aroused and a determination to be true to my science at all hazards, replied:

"Assuredly!"

"Phylos, if it were not that your stubbornness was tempered with an admirable loyalty to principle, I should say that wisdom will die with you. But, my friend, your system of chemistry, with its sixty-odd 'primal elements' and its 'monads, dyads, triads' and so on; its simples, binaries, tertiaries and the like numerous compounds, is nothing but a fine working hypothesis, well adapted to producing the result it has produced, but because it is not the whole chemical truth, not capable of ever attaining that wholeness of results which marks the sublime constitution of nature. So far from leading to the truth these theories have just the opposite effect; they teach the many forms of matter, whereas its unity is the truth. As I said, though, the chemists of the earth have a good working hypothesis, one which will do until the better method of truth is found."

Sohma paused, at which point I asked what the better method was. He did not answer me in direct words, but instead he put before my mental vision a workshop, in which there were many kinds of instruments and machines in states either of completion or approaching completion, lying upon tables and benches. I saw here a clock, there watches, there again an old style typewriter; there were time locks and combination tools, besides many intricate mechanisms that even the sight of suggested no use for. At a little distance upon a table lay a confused mass of parts of machinery not put together. He said:

"Phylos, can you put these things together? In this pile are portions of clocks, typewriters, locks and so forth. You say you are not a machinist, and so cannot deal with these things. These things are not unfamiliar to me, who am a machinist. With all the parts before you, you could not construct a clock or other mechanism. But suppose you were to take carefully apart a clock now in running order, and study carefully all its relations, and do so by not one only, but by several of these instruments, then the whole would become familiar to you, and while merely taking one clock apart would not be likely to teach you, doing so by many would enable you to put them all together again as they were. That is the process of analysis, deduction and synthesis; it is the same, practically, in physics, or in mechanics or chemistry."

"But my friend," I said in dismay, "I cannot do these acts, not having the opportunity to experiment in this way."

"That is my point, Phylos. I will show you the better method I spoke of. Here before us is an invention of my own; practically I am its creator, and therefore I understand it. Here also is another identical machine, but it is in a separate state; its parts are a confused pile. Now you know nothing of constructive mechanics; I do, and I will point out to you the principal parts of the machine, which is in running order. Observe!"

Sohma went up to the machine, which stood, a marvel of mechanical beauty, its burnished brass and silver wheels, springs, cogs, chain belts, etc., showing through the quadrangular glass case. He spoke into the mouthpiece, explaining the machine to me as he did so. He said that he would remain near the mouthpiece, so that his words would be reported and printed and bound in book form. As he spoke he loosened a set screw. Then he said:

The Secrets Of Mount Shasta And A Dweller On Two Planets

"A microphone diaphragm sets strong currents of electricity in operation. These act only as my tones impact on that vocal diaphragm, whereby, as you see, carbon discs close other circuits, and operate levers carrying type upon their extremities. Observe that this vocal diaphragm is made of steel cords that possess sound, like those of a piano, and there are just as many of these as experience has demonstrated that there are vocal tones and octaves. Therefore, there is in one alphabet just that number of letters, and our written language consists in the proper sequential arrangement of these letters, either type, if printed, or symbolic handwriting, if written. Along with our spoken tones, then, if near such an instrument as this, we can 'utter' a printed volume. The congregate tones affect each its own chord; this in vibration compresses the carbon discs, sets going the instant electric current, the type lever does its work, the paper is carried a space forward and the next type strikes, and so on till the voice ceases utterance. The spacing between words, even, is automatically done, for, so long as one is talking connectedly there is a utilization made of the return of the carbon disc from its compressed active state, whereby a spring moves the paper carriage one space for every minor pause in the voice, and two for periods, but it is not sufficient for more than a double spacing motion. I am done speaking, nearly, and will move this lever up, thus releasing the stored force which arose from the motion of the parts, especially of the heavy balance wheel. No more printing will be done, but the reserve force will fold, cut and bind my speech, and when this is done, the last of the force stored, equal in all cases to the special work, is exhausted entirely by the ringing of a bell which signifies the end."

Though Sohma ceased to speak, the instrument still worked, and almost quicker than this sentence will be put in type, the bell rang and behold! Sohma's words in book form dropped into a little box at the end of the case. The instrument stood motionless in its case, and for the first time its compactness struck me; it was but eighteen inches high, by two feet in width and three in length, yet it had done all that marvelous work.

"Could you take this instrument apart and put it together properly again?" was the startling question, startling because I thought he intended me to do it! "No, my brother; but as its creator, knowing all its most obscure points, my comprehension of it and of other machinery, and of truths not mechanical as well, but scientific psychics, is a veritable spirit of knowledge, and observe: this spirit I will to enter into your mind, at least so far as concerns this mechanism. Behold it and know it."

Strange to relate, I, who previously knew almost nothing of such things, seemed in an instant to understand the whole of the delicate apparatus, as a watchmaker does a watch. Sohma, perceiving this, said:

"Such, Phylos, is that key to all wisdom that I spoke of. God, creator of all things whatever, shall one day enter into you. Then your spirit, which is a ray of His Spirit, shed into the darkness of life by Him, shall reunite with Him. And because He creates by constant Logos all things and states of Being, and is immanent in it all, knowing it all, so when He enters your soul, you shall know all things likewise, and, in less measure, truly, create also. You shall know that, in a chemical sense, only one element exists, operated upon by Force. Then all 'elements,' as you know them, shall be seen to be but different speeds of the molecular formation of the One Element by varying degrees of the One Force, and light, heat, sound and all solid, liquid and gaseous substances will be seen to be different not in material, but in speed only.

"That knowledge underlies all life, physics, chemistry, sounds, calories, chromatics, electrics and all and every possible aspect of nature. Such is the supreme law of God, and He is nature, though nature is not conversely God. Another law is that of compensation; may I tell you about it?"

I replied that I would be but too glad to listen, for his words revealed God in all things, whether high or low. So he continued:

"This law, then, not only governs all matter, but that which matter is the reflection of, Spirit, and the soul realm. I need say only a single brief instance in material nature, the screw plane. As the plane of a screw is greater or less in its inclination, so will its action be either rapid or powerful, but never both at once. If the thread be slight in pitch, the screw bar will progress through its nut very slowly, but, as exerted in a screw press, the crushing force will be enormous. Vice versa; if the pitch be steep, the screw bar will progress rapidly, as to wit, the screw nail, which may be driven into wood with a hammer, and revolve as it goes in.

"Now, in the soul realm, if a human being is content with the gradual, easy pitch of the Godward ascending plane of pure daily life, daily temptations to work in error, and too often fall, progress upward will be slow, but very sure. But, on the contrary, if eager to learn rapidly, it must meet in a few hours all the crushing force of temptations to err and to sin which the ordinary man meets distributed through many, many incarnations, covering ages, aye, eons of time. In the one case the Father gives sufficient daily bread of strength to men to enable them to progress very slowly, but with certitude. In the other, all the splendid reserve of resistant force of a very God is needed, for all the power of Lucifer, that high nature spirit who was incarnate in the planet which disrupted into the solar asteroid belt, upon the lapse, the failure of its Soul, all of his glorious power was not sufficient to carry him to victory, so he fell. Only the God-Christ in you can win this struggle. Truly, no mere human, so long as he remains Man, can have such a temptation; not yourself, not Mol Lang, my father, not even Gautama were subjected to such a severe test as was that sublime world soul, Lucifer, except relatively. I say relatively, for consider this: if a fly or an ant is subjected to all it can endure, then its pain at that point is as severe as that of a man at his breaking strain. But as Jesus and Gautama were tempted to the utmost and did not fail, therefore their victory was greater than Lucifer's failure, and when you shall come to a trial like his, you will doubtless succeed; though, again, you may fail. There is but *one* Guide; follow and win; *follow* not, and you will fail. ₁ It is a new idea to you to learn there is an animating ego, a world spirit, dwelling in each star, each planet, every stellar body, just as there is an individual soul in each human, animal or plant body. Yet this is true. It is also true that the spirits of men will progress; will face the supreme ordeal, and, if they pass victorious, will enter that long rest, heaven, devachan, call it what you will, Nirvana. But that is not the end, for life had a beginning—it also has an end. And the perfect human ego, emerging eventually from Nirvana, that long devachan of all the incarnations, emerges not as Man; it does not live, but It Is, and Its post-life existence is a state of Being which no human mind could understand, except inferentially it do so through the knowledge that that state is to Life as the senior to the junior. But before then is the *trial of transfiguration*; to it my father has come, I have not. If we fail, then that is the second death, ₂ but meet it we must, humanity must. But it is a long time until then, for it does not come until the striving soul be perfect, and be ready to leave the developing state of Human Life, to be judged according to (its) works for Him who made it. Do I tire you, Phylos?"

I replied that he did not, though it did seem that I grasped his meaning only to lose it again. Nonetheless I was eager to have him go on, imagining I understood, just as every Person you or I know is fond of thinking his or her comprehension of obscure subjects is perfect. Sohma smiled and said in reply that, when he was done, all that I would have gained would be the psychic bent favoring my progress, for I was destined to forget the very ideas I believed I was gaining. But he continued, observing that a favorable prejudice was a worthy thing, calling for his best effort for me.

"I wish you to observe this also: that if you think the judgment day, when according to its works your soul is charged and accused by your spirit, which is God in you, if you think that because that day may be in remote eons before it comes, and therefore you have ample time to lag, to err, I counsel you it is a fatal mistake. For if at the great trial any man fails it is because day by day, as the lives were run, he neglected his chances, either by omission or commission. Then shall such a man suffer the second death, be cast into the 'lake of fire,' in other words, their Spirit will depart from the soul and go to the Father, while the soul will be gathered into the sum of force, the 'Fire' element, that which is the sum of all lesser force forms, out of which life springs, heat and vibration. But this will not be until he who is in error has passed from his soul into his spirit. So the 'second death' ₁ is not of the sinner; it is the cutting off of all his, or her, spoiled work, and a chance to begin again, to build better; our Father does not damn His child, but only the imperfect work, the sinning soul. In our library you can see a book brought here to Hesper from the Earth, a book which speaks of the order of the Rosicrux, wherein this supreme Fire is written of. It is also that Fire once called in the Earth the Maxin. "Phylos, you will suffer the ordeal of the Crisis before other men; whether you shall succeed or fail no man knows except those who have passed up until now."

When Sohma ceased speaking, I looked around me, and found that while the clocks and typewriters, and locks and various instruments, were gone, the vocal printer was not gone; it was an actuality, the rest only concepts which Sohma had willed me to see. My mind was not trained sufficiently well to continue on a special line of thought so long, and while I imagined that I possessed a clear idea of all my companion had said, and was pleased by the notion, yet had I tried at that moment to recollect his meanings, I would have been embarrassed to find that I had nothing beyond vague ideas. Still, I did not try the experiment, but, content with the supposition of possession, my mind wandered to a new theme, and I asked Sohma if Hesperians had not found aerial vessels possible among so many triumphs. He turned toward me and, looking behind me, smiled as he answered:

"I will leave Phyris to tell you that; I must go elsewhere."

I was pleased at this new event, yet shyness at once asserted itself, and though vexed at this fact, my vexation seemed only to increase my timidity. Taking, as I supposed, no notice of this shyness, she said:

"We rarely go, except we go astrally. We seldom care to avail ourselves of our aerial vessels; but we have them. It may be that thou, or shall I say 'you' to lessen thy—your—shyness of me?" and Phyris bent a pair of laughing eyes upon me, a gaze that, while it gave most delicious pleasure, had the effect of confusing me, past recovery, I feared.

"Perhaps," she continued, after gently laughing at my piteous abashment, "perhaps you think we Hesperians can transport our physical bodies here and there by some occult process, or other. For instance, as all forms of matter are but divine ideas clothed in the One Substance, it is possible to disintegrate the material form, but preserve the psychic idea and transport that as other thoughts move, by effort of will, then rehabilitate it in matter. Thus it is, articles can be brought from the earth here to us. But if you think we can do this by our own bodies you are wrong, for ourselves are the ideas embodied. Truly we can emerge from these bodies, and travel in one brief instant from one to any other star. But we cannot have two corporeal bodies at once. If we leave the one we have, we can, by putting it in a cataleptic trance, leave it in fit state to reoccupy upon our return. But if we leave it and make around ourselves a new one, like in all respects to the other, and abide in it, the deserted temple will perish. We could do it; but we have no need to, and consequently do not. All about you is matter, every breath is matter, differing only from iron in its molecular speed. The air is matter; electricity is matter. I will show you. See, I wish a plate, several plates, cups, saucers, knives and forks, so I image them (imagio, I create) in the mental or psychic form. Do you see them? Eyes of Earth could not; you have for a time Hesperian vision."

Before me was a pile of delicate tableware, with the pattern upon each piece of a different kind.

"These articles are really only thought forms; no eye unable to perceive a thought could see them. But now look, I gather to myself the higher rate of speed, the extra force which makes air of the One Substance, and the force which I leave is just that of the various minerals of which I desire my ware to be 'made.' Observe that one plate is a ruby, the real crystal aluminum; and another is a pearl, others are of various gem stones, as that cup and saucer, crystal carbon, diamond each one. On the Earth those dishes would be valued into the millions of dollars, yet here they are valued for their uses and their beauty only. Do you see, Phylos, I know the terms of your language and what ideas are conveyed by your words. But now I, like Sohma, must go, for I have a dinner to get, a use for my plates, cups and saucers, which I have made, as well as more yet to make. Quite like an ordinary mortal, you say? Indeed, and why not? Do you think an occultist is always rapt in obscure speculations? You are mistaken, Phylos, you are mistaken, indeed. You may go into the library, where you may find something to interest you." To the library, therefore, I went, and if you will, you may go with me, in a mental way, and see something of it. Do not object that these Hesperian objects were unreal, just because I have said that no one with ordinary terrestrial eyes could see any evidences of life on Venus. Reality does not necessarily imply earthly solidity.

At least forty thousand volumes lined the shelves; many of them were plainly, but some richly, bound. On my first introduction to this apartment I had found that the books on the shelves were all in the phonetic print of Hesper. But I saw on a table one whose cover bore in Anglo-Saxon in gilt letters the title and name of the publishers, and as I looked, for a brief time the memory power of Earth returned. The inscription was:

"A THOUSAND MILES UP THE NILE" By Miss A. B. Edwards Published by Longmans & Co. 1876

That volume had been brought all the many millions of miles across interplanetary space along the "currents," just as Phyris had done when she "made" the tableware, only in the case of this book she had not created the thoughts in the book, but had disintegrated the matter, preserving the astral, the only reality about an object, and after bringing it from Earth to Hesper, had re-clothed it in matter after its journey. I looked about, and found other volumes, one entitled:

"THE ROSICRUCIANS" By Hargrave Jennings.

I found copies of Milton's works, of Tennyson's earlier poems, of Moore, and a pile several feet high of other standard works; on top of all lay the "Essays of Emerson," upon which, as I gazed, appeared a piece of white paper, and as I looked, the words seemed to form as if precipitated from the air, "Phylos, these books I have brought for you from the distant earth. I did so that you might contrast them with our Hesperian works. Finally, consider this: that we who are illumined by the Spirit of the Creator do little with books or such crude methods of learning, caring only for them as specimens of the work of souls on certain planes. To read them we have no need, no desire, they serve only as texts, for when we would learn, we retire within our souls and listen to the All Knowing Spirit."

That message was signed by Phyris. It was written in English. Written? No, precipitated, and as soon as I had read it, it disappeared as it had appeared, with no hand to remove it, no person save myself in the room. With its disappearance I also ceased to retain memories of the world from which I came. As I stood, considering what to do next, Phyris came in and said:

"Horo is an invention by Sohma which will render your delight greater; I know it is always great where books abound."

She picked up a book from Earth, Shakespeare, and placed it in an instrument which turned the pages automatically, and a strong electric light being cast on the visible pages, its beams reflected upon a metallic plate. Unseen wheels revolved within a case, and a voice issued from a funnel-shaped mouthpiece. To my pleasure I heard the reading of page after page of the great English literary gem, in appropriate tones for the various characters. While I listened, absorbed, Phyris withdrew, and it was some time before I noticed her absence. I think I should then have gone in search of her, or of Sohma—Mol Lang had gone to a distance, on duty bent, leaving his body asleep in his room— but as I was about to go out of the library, a hand—a woman's hand, reached over my shoulder, and a soft voice said:

"Put these over your eyes."

It was Phyris, who gave me a seeming pair of spectacles. They were indeed spectacles which all the fortunes of earth could not obtain. How thoughtful she was of my pleasure! As I put them on, all the shelves of books disappeared, and a book being placed in my hand, as I know from retrospection, for I did not know then, I found myself seemingly amid scenes of most familiar appearance. All the mental pictures conjured up by vivid perusal of Scott's famous poem, "The Lady of the Lake," all the voices of its characters became seen and heard, as if I were on the spot where all was said to have transpired. For the time I was transported by means of those magical eyes-pieces into the mental world of Walter Scott, which, while he wrote,

"Lay around him like a cloud, A world he could not see."

Except with the vision of the creative imagination.

The Secrets Of Mount Shasta And A Dweller On Two Planets

The whole was presented in a few moments, for thought is swifter than the senses, and when the King threw his golden chains over Malcom's neck and laid the chain in fair Ellen's hand, without waiting for the rest Phyris withdrew the wonderful spectacles from my eyes and said:

"These would banish material surroundings, and let the reader directly into the author's realms of imagery, whatever the book, but not whoever the reader, for only fine, developing human senses, none that are controlled by the animal, can enjoy the use of them. And this is because they are a species of sensitive magnet, linking psychic facts but not material things. But there, I do not know much more about them, and you must ask father of them if you would learn more. I am only a girl, and must learn to be more before I can assume to teach. And I should dislike to fail in offering you an explanation. Your good opinion of me would lessen, and that would be mortifying, for I treasure it—I, well, never mind," she said, as a delicate flush spread over her face, "Come with me; I think it is well not to be too long a time among any one set of influences, as literary surroundings."

Much, aye, most that I saw in Hesper had been unfamiliar. But that delicate blush—it set me thinking, my own ideas meantime in a confused, ecstatic whirl. What did it mean? Did it denote reciprocal affection?

"It does in truth," she said, in reply to my unspoken question. "But the significance of it is beyond my knowledge. Thou, nay, you, see me a maid of not many years. Your love shall behold me a woman. Do I speak a riddle? Only time can solve it. You are with me, and I with you, and our ages differ not greatly. You have little understanding; I have more; both are imperfect, yet the Spirit shall make us whole. If I asked you now, 'What is will power?' you could not answer it truly. Yet I tell you, and my words shall sink deep, and guide you to me. I said erroneously that you are with me, and behold, you are so only in the sight of our Father in the beginning, but not now. Yet one day shall come, and when I shall ask, 'What is will?' you shall say of your own knowledge: 'Will is the command of consciousness.' If it is the will of the animal soul, its result will be only a subjective thought which shall energize muscles to do an objective reality conforming to the subjective plan. If it is of the human soul, it will be of greater intensity and nobler, but still the brain, and through it the muscles, must render its directive into material form. But if the will be the authority of our Spirits, and trained, we shall say to any material force, 'Obey me,' and it shall obey. Because our Spirits are of our Father and one with Him, and the Will of the Spirit shall need no intervening brain nor muscle, but shall find every natural power its direct servant, and this is the faith whereof Jesus spoke. So, Phylos, my own, I have told you, and yet you, hearing, hear not. Why not? Because our Father is not yet manifest in you. But when you, having heard, understand, then shall we who are separated be one, for it is so written in the Book of Life."

As she ceased speaking we came into a plot of ground wherein grew the fruits for table use. Of these she gathered some, but of others desired, none were growing. Stooping, she drew on the soil a figure which looked familiar, although I could not tell where I had seen it previously. The reader will remember that it is the same that I described the Tchin as making when he caused the Vita Mundi to flame as he stood within it. It was also creative fire in Phyris' hands, though it had not been so as exhibited by Quong. In the space Phyris planted seeds, and then, completing the symbol, the flames rose above the area sown.

"Behold, Phylos! If I have but the seed, the herb shall come forth after its kind. ₁ But if I have not the seed, my poor, human soul wisdom could not make that herb grow. Mol Lang could, being transfigured. Having seed, I can bring God's Viviant Fire to aid its germination— see! It sprouts; and again watch it—it grows visibly."

I was astonished to see, mounting up as fast as evening shadows lengthen, green tendrils, and buds unfolding even as the flowers of primula spring forth, flowers, blossoming, blossomed; seed scarps forming, formed; and the matured fruit hanging in clusters in the radiant flame of the Vita Mundi, as high as my head from the ground, where before there had been only vacant soil. And this girl, who declared herself not a grown woman, exercising such magic as this and thinking it only ordinary! This was an inherent power of the Human Principle, my friends, and will be common to you also when you become developed in the Human. Earthly man is still only in the first stages of his humanity in a few favored cases, but is very largely in his animal-like state. Most of mankind is merely animal, not human, except by grace. Yet the dawn of the glorious new era is at hand, and in its fullness of days Christ shall come again to it and enter into the hearts of his own; and it shall be the Father that shall enter, and by Messias. You must then be prepared for the coming of the Spirit, for no man knows the day nor the hour thereof.

Footnotes

322:1 Luke xxi; 34, 35, 36.

322:2 Mark xiii, 26.

329:1 John xvi; 13.

329:2 Rev. xx; 13, 15.

330:1 Rev. xx, 13-15.

337:1 Genesis, i, 12.

CHAPTER VII. "THE DESERT IS BEFORE THY FEET"

So the days passed. It was over two weeks of the local time that I had been in the Hesperian environment. And during this interval the longing for the past life grew; the few occasions when Mol Lang, Sohma or Phyris had recalled the vivid memories of Earth had been seized upon by my Pertozian astral, and thus each such event renewed the certainty of my having had a place in which all my surroundings had been familiar. It saddened Phyris to know that every time I was left alone my thoughts I yearned with increased longing for that past. At times a strong effort of my own will would successfully bring it before me, bring, in fact, my earthly astral from Earth to me, that astral which was the sum of my experiences and memories of Earth. Then, being in Venus, I still knew myself a man of Earth, and a stranger, and my yearning grew strong for America, my "ain countree." That was home to me, oh! So much more home, although I had no relatives living, all gone to devachan's rest, and no friends comparable to those I had so strangely found in Hesper. My friend, it is the soul that is chained, not the body of man. Unchain your souls, oh, brethren, and seek to know the things of heaven, of the high life with God, and everything else shall be added to you, yea, even the ability to explore the stars in person. Mine was bound to Earth by love of home and native land. Then these moments of knowledge of Earth would cease, because my will power was not strong enough to hold the astral when it was summoned, and it gravitated to its own level, which was the world. Again I would be left unconscious of the Earth life and brooding over the puzzle, until some of the family banished the mental state producing it! No, I was a soul not at home except on Earth; I was here on a higher plane; I might be born after devachan into the level of the Hesperian, but the fact continually interfered with increased emphasis that as yet I had not been so born.

It was a pleasure to me to sit at table when my friends took their simple meals, for though I could not eat, nor indeed did I need food, it was agreeable to be with them when they gathered together this way.

The next day after I had seen Phyris grow the fruits to eat, I was at supper with the family when Mol Lang, speaking to his son, said: "Sohma, is it wise to tell our guest so much philosophy as you said your sister has done and to contemplate doing it even more?"

"Why keep secret the truth, my father?"

"Because, son, Phylos must return to Earth; it is so fated. He cannot know these things, for hearing is not knowing, nor is seeing. He has no faculties developed with which to know them, and neither you nor I cannot permanently enter our knowledge into his soul. Jesus of Nazareth, unless He entered into the souls of His hearers as into a temple, could tell them nothing. Caiaphas, the High Priest, and all the Israelites heard the Savior with their ears and saw His doings, but were blind and deaf and did not understand. But to those who were His disciples and followers He entered, and they saw and heard and profited. That was the Spirit which the Master awakened in them and they followed the Word, even as Jesus followed it. But the world has had to read the printed Word for these many centuries, and though many have believed, yet none, no, not one, has been illuminated by the Spirit like unto Paul. What you would say to Phylos will come to him in astral form when he begins to yearn for Hesperus, even as his astral of Earth now comes to him as he yearns for Earth. And, having forgotten Pertoz, forgotten us, still he will utter these bits of occult lore, and will suffer because of it. Suffer, because some hearers will be mystified, others scornful, and none, himself included, will be able to explain or understand."

"Yes, my parent, you speak wisely. Yet let me say, he will utter truth. Truth is mighty and will prevail. If, at the time, it be misunderstood, it still must cause some act in both speaker and hearer. I need not say thoughts are things, for all things are thoughts. Even a stone is a thought concept of the Eternal Spirit, and the stone seen by ordinary eyes is but the externalization of the idea. If, then, Phylos shall think, and his hearers think on his utterances, that is an action, making the actor responsible. If a small thought, then a small hot; it will doubtless finish its karma in the life of its utterance. But if it is a great thought, or deed, it will make its doer his or her own inheritor, and then? I speak to you also now, Phylos —the inheritor of his own actions shall find the deed becomes part of the great karma of the human race, and is himself responsible for its fruition, because, 'Till heaven and earth pass, one jot or one tittle shall in no wise pass from the law till all be fulfilled.' ₁ Only thus can Phylos ever come to us again."

"Well spoken, my son!" was Mol Lang's sole comment.

Sohma then said to me: "Phylos, my brother, there is no man or woman who has not, in some past as well as present life, done grievous evil to one or more fellow beings, man or animal. Whatsoever a man sows, that shall he reap. And our Father has ordained that in life, subsequent to the one witnessing the greater sins, he that did them must also requite them, and must do so by setting against the evil counterbalancing good. In no other way shall any one come into the Kingdom. This is the law of karma."

On leaving the table I went with Sohma, into his own rooms to see a painting which adorned his wall. Its size was three and a half feet by six feet, and it was framed with rubies, sapphires, diamonds, pearls and other gems set in cement, precious stones which on Earth would be each valued into three periods of figures. Not so in Hesperus, for they were produced as Phyris produced the jewel-dishes. But the picture exceeded the frame, a production of art magic which all the wealth of the world could not buy.

I saw a view of a boundless ocean, the billows lashed in tempestuous fury, seabirds skimming the crests or flitting through the air above. It seemed a sunset on the great waters, for the red beams shone through breaking clouds, lighting the aftermath of the storm with a great glory. Close at hand, so close that one could see the anxious intensity of mingling emotions on their faces, two men and a boy clung to a floating pole. One of the men was held by his mates as he wildly waved his arms to a ship that lay, an acute silhouette against the monstrous disc, right in the very middle of the bright red sun. "Such a scene could not be worth so great a sum as I named?"

Truly, it was useless to attach a figure to what no money could buy. But what do you think when I say that the pictured billows rose and fell as real water does? And the wind scudding along caught the combing, breaking billows and hurled spray and spume for what seemed hundreds of feet. The seabirds and gulls dipping their feet in the water left a momentary ripple as they rose again. Clouds flitted across the horizon, and coming across the great sun were lit by its crimson, while, even as I looked, the blazing orb sank its lower edge beneath the waters. The tall ship had sailed to the edge of the shield and, looking, I saw a flag raised and lowered as if in answer to the men on the pole. Then a boat, a mere dot in the distance, was launched. But the castaways were too near the level to see these things and, as the sun sank completely from view, one of them raised his arms in wild despair and slipped from the pole to his grave in the depths. After a time the light of the full moon replaced that of the set sun, the clouds cleared away, and in the pale, silvery light I saw the approaching boat, seeking the castaways. I saw them, having now floated to one side of the canvas, but the searchers at first did not. They rowed here and there, and finally were successful. Lifting the perishing man and the boy into the boat, they pulled away to where the lights of their ship gleamed in the night. Then the watery waste was left lifeless as the boat disappeared in the gloom towards the ship, which, as I looked, sailed out at one side of the picture, as if the whole scene was one beheld through an open window, and the vessel had sailed behind the window casement. The canvas slowly whitened, and presently was perfectly blank of color or figures.

While I still gazed, out from the side on the right of the frame appeared a black point, coming slowly into view, and tossing up and down. Waves grew in green sullenness across the whole canvas, and Sohma said:

The Secrets Of Mount Shasta And A Dweller On Two Planets

"See, it is about to repeat itself. By watching you shall see the whole thing again. It is a scene of a shipwreck on the Atlantic Ocean, on the distant Earth. As soon as it is all completed it turns white, and then is repeated. It is another example of the power of an occult mind over matter; the artist's will changes the speed of the color, and either reduces or raises it so that the vibrations making red are increased and range up through all degrees of color-force, always exactly in harmony with the astral image put on the canvas by the creative power of the occult artist. 'Who painted this, you ask?' Phyris. She painted it before you came to Hesperus, when you rescued a woman from a life of shame. This scene is prophetic. It is of a time coming on Earth, when that rescued woman shall be lost at sea, years from now. But look at the picture."

I looked, and saw that though the storm was yet only a menace, it was surely coming and would overtake the proud vessel that now had appeared in full perspective, half a mile over the waters from me, as it seemed. At the mainmast floated the Stars and Stripes, Flag of the Union. The sight brought my astral to me, and memories of Earth and homeland filled my eyes with tears. But Sohma put away the sad feeling, leaving me only partially conscious of the past. I could see a sailor go to the ship's bell and ring "eight bells," see, but of course not hear, four o'clock in the afternoon. The sailor had hardly struck the time when a man came on deck and seemed to give orders to "close reef." The men swarmed into the rigging and obeyed; it was from their actions that I knew what the orders had been. Then coming back on deck, they battened down the hatches and put everything safe for storm. Not a moment too soon. First a cloud overcast the sun; then a black pall in the north, obscuring the view. I could dimly see that things on shipboard began to flap in the wind, and soon the noble vessel careened far over to starboard under the white-topped rush of frightful billows. Then the fugitive craft, with its mainmast hanging over the side, began to flee before the demon of the storm. I could see it as it rose and sank in the maddened swirl, while it seemed as if the vessel was in rapid motion, giving the effect of flight. Presently a squad of seamen made a rush across the decks for the pumps, at which they worked with the energy of despair. A woman came from the one hatch left open for passage below decks, and winding the cordage of the stump of the mainmast about her slight form, cheered the men in their desperate toil. The foremast now snapped, and was cut adrift. The vessel was filling faster than the men could pump out the leakage, and a jump for the boats was made. One by one these were lost, swamped as they touched the water, till only one remained. Into this the captain ordered his men. Two more men than there was possible room for in the boat; and the captain with his mate and the woman, whom he held in his arms, stayed. The boat was not seemingly a hundred feet distant when the gallant ship pitched forward, prow first, and went down. A pole floating by the lone boat was the salvation of some of those in the frail shell, which I saw overturned by the heavy waves. A moment later I saw white faces, for the boat was near in the foreground. I saw the woman's face as she sank, and she was near enough so that I saw, not terror, but a peaceful smile depicted on her features. Then I saw two men and a boy, clinging to a pole, and the scene had come to the point of repetition, for on that pole, when two days had elapsed (in seeming), I saw them as at the beginning of this description. "In seeming?" Yes, because the canvas depicted that night's blackness, the next day's somber light, another night and the second day. The whole scene took about two actual hours for its performance.

Sohma said no more concerning occult wisdom. He knew that my mind, ignorant of the philosophy of this higher life, was not in touch with its significance, and that I wearied of it as a child does of studies at school; obscure occupations presenting to its limited comprehension no actual connection with the facts of its little world.

Mol Lang still taught me one thing more there in Hesper, saying it was for my guidance, and that I would not forget it at any time. We were beside the great river which flowed past his home at a few hundred yards distant. I sat on the gravel of the shore; Mol Lang sat above me on the bank, close enough to touch me. He planted a seed, and held his hands over it, palms downward. It grew fast, and soon stood mature at the height of his head. Banana-like fruit hung amongst its broad leaves. He plucked some of the fruit and ate it.

The Secrets Of Mount Shasta And A Dweller On Two Planets

"See, Phylos, such is plant life. You have said: 'Why not take animal life to nourish our bodies,' and 'If it is wrong to take life of animals is it not wrong to take that of vegetable growths?' My son, where any form, mineral, plant or animal, exists, there also is an entity created by the Spirit; the matter-form is nothing but clothing to the astral, and this to the soul. Now there are plant souls, animal souls, human souls, all children of our Father, but they are not transformed one into the other in any given period of planetary activity; but all progress towards the Creator as plants draw sunward. No man can make even a plant soul exist; but if he knows the law, he can find a plant soul and give it a body of plant shape, if the body is a higher type than it had before. He can— I can incarnate such a plant soul. It is a simple experience; it begins by the sprouting of seed, by the growth of the young plant body, by maturity, budding, flowering, fruiting and ripening more seeds, seven simple actions. I can hurry these, and crowd them all into a few minutes. Then I have given the plant soul its little experience. Left alone it would have no others, but would die, the last experience in its incarnation. Very well; I take its body, but cut off no needed process. It is as virtually my body as my own flesh, for I made it and loaned it to the plant soul. Out of me went the strength to do it. Reverse the process, eat the plant, my strength returns into me. But no man could foresee the experiences which each day, hour and minute bring to an animal soul, each and every one necessary, for it is growing toward the Eternal, and each experience is a responsible link, making it a karma which shall bring its animal soul into a next incarnate life. Kill it, and you cannot compensate it for its opportunities; but to a plant you may do so. Compensation is God's law. If you do a thing and cannot compensate for it, that is sin; but if you are able to make proper balance, it is no sin. So the Master of Nazareth did no sin in the matter of filling the fisherman's net; but you would have sinned in doing likewise, for in you the manifest Spirit is not made One with you. Because you cannot repay an animal soul for its bodily life, you sin in killing it. And the flesh is accursed by reason of that sin. Behold, I say truly, if you do such a sin, you shall reap the penalty; no butcher can see God in His Kingdom: he must cease to be a butcher before he can have hope of knowing the occult realm which is His Kingdom."

The Secrets Of Mount Shasta And A Dweller On Two Planets

Mol Lang arose, and I did also. He put his arm around me and said:

"My son, the desert is before your feet. Its hot sands will scorch their soles, yet listen to your own intuition ₁ which reveals God to your soul, and you shall come out of that desert. Be you faithful unto death, and you shall have a crown of life from our Father. God be with you and keep you; I, also, will guard you."

My friends, years elapsed before I saw Mol Lang again, weary years of sorrow and trial. He left me there by the river, and there Phyris found me not long after.

Other people soon gathered about us, mostly young persons, even some children. In Hesper, the Seventh Principle has a fair beginning of growth, while as for their physical perfection, any Hesperian has an almost godlike beauty and grace. But to illustrate how great is the height of that plane above anything earthly, and how many seemingly miraculous powers have there become characteristic of humanity, so as to be common inheritance of every ego incarnate there, there is this example: A little child, only four years of age, but very mature in demeanor, while essentially childlike in many things, came and stood beside me. Though the little one laughed and chatted with me, if I had at first been disposed to think her babyish, I soon regarded her differently. Young as she was, and of course unacquainted with any deep occult laws, still as a child of a branch of humanity advanced to the perfect human plane, and upon the threshold of the spiritual, she herself was fitted to be there by untold, previous incarnations. As the heritage of these many lives the little maid possessed astonishing powers which earthly men and women must acquire by the slow process of study through years.

Study first to conquer the animal nature, then meditate on the principles which, for those who have the will to know, are in these pages. Do only as they teach. Follow the Way. One shall guide all who earnestly ask Him, even before the Day of Man.

Apparently satisfied regarding my appearance, remember that I should have been invisible to non-clairvoyant eyes, but was not so to her inherited psychic sight, the little one remarked in sweet confidence:

"My father has often told me of a numerous branch of the human race, compared to which we Pertozians are as the leaves of a single tree to those of a forest. He has pointed out the planet where these lower humans dwell; I have never seen any of these lower human beings until I see you now. Is it not strange? And they tell me, too, that neither you, nor the mass of people have come to have knowledge of the karma yet, nor other occult powers that you foolishly scoff at, indeed. It is strange. Still you, and the others also, will grow in knowledge. God demands it. Then your personal appearance will become more pleasing." (!)

I was completely ashamed. To hear a mere child talk this way, and conclude with the remark that I would grow, well, grow to grace, was most astonishing. It was pleasing, too, for though it showed the vast gap between the Earthly man and the spirituality of Hesper, it still showed the vista of human possibilities with a clarity which nothing else had done. Man needs comparisons to enable him to judge between relative values. St. Peter's Church at Rome is the greatest building the world now knows. But these vast buildings must be compared with others, themselves large, to enable the human mind to comprehend how vast they are. So with spiritual truths: until this little child revealed it, I had not had anything but a vague conception of the exalted truths I had heard. Mol Lang's marvelous actions, those of Sohma and Phyris even, had impressed me as acts of a superior being, whose side I could never gain as an equal. Truly, Mol Lang said he came there by study and, further, faith in the Father. But my eyes saw not his progress; they only saw his attainment; neither had I seen this child acquire her position, but my soul could recognize the fact of her growth being still in progress. In place of vague desires, I began to feel the thrill of hope and a knowledge that I also might grow. Until that moment I had accepted the statements of my friends that I could grow up to them. Faith was now replaced by knowledge. Through this little one my life was lifted and linked to the higher life of Pertoz, that of man perfect. I was ready to say in earnestness, "Of such is the kingdom of heaven."

The Secrets Of Mount Shasta And A Dweller On Two Planets

The dozen or more friends present asked me to tell my life story, in order that hearing the living voice, they might study me as I spoke. I complied. At last I finished. I had told of my hopes in life, and they were lofty, noble hopes, like those which crowd the heart, subduing the animal nature, when one listens to music whose chords thrill the soul to do and dare for the high reward of hearing Him say: "Well done, thou good and faithful servant."

Then Phyris spoke to me, slowly, but how sweetly only one can know who puts away all that spoils the human soul. I noted that she no longer used the ordinary personal pronouns, but in this last conversation reverted to the solemn style though using the familiar English language.

"Phylos, you have related all that you know about your life. I know much more, and I will tell you also, even though you go to Earth, forgetting us, forgetting me."

"Phyris, don't say that. I can never forget you!" I said sadly.

"Yea, Phylos, you will forget me, because only your Hesperian memory knows me, and it must yield to your Earthly astral when you have returned there. Yet it will only sleep, not perish, until the time comes again for it to govern your life. When the years of karma are flown, you will come here once more, and then you will yearn for Earth no more, as now. My twin, I would happily keep you here; I cannot, for karma is set against me, and karma is the Christ law, saying, 'Whatsoever a man sows, that shall he also reap.' Though forgetting Hesper, you shall still have an astral record, and it will at times come to you, even as your earthly record comes here, disturbing you, and it will be a strange thing, for it will seem like yourself, yet you shall not recognize its words as your own history, so it shall also seem to be someone else.

"You have told the story of your life so far as you know it; but back of it you have heard that you have had myriad other lives. And in these I have been involved. Naturally so, for my spirit is also your spirit, though our souls are not now near together as they have been in other times. I could tell you much concerning this eternity past, which you have had and known, but forgotten page by page as the Angel of Death turned the leaves of your book of life. But I will not tell you, Phylos, though I could remember it from that living, eternal record of cause and effect, of the mutual action and reaction of the forms of life and of matter; it is the astral record, the Father's 'Book of Life.' Memory is but the power of the soul to read this great astral record. I have that power; you do not; but I will not tell you, but leave you to find all this yourself; to know this past from your own coming wisdom. Then you shall know me as one with yourself. And I will in that time write the long history of our lives from the remote days when you and I lived in old Lemuria, days before the Earth had known the continent of Atlantis, or the glacial epoch of geologists— it was the golden age. But we will know farther back than that, even to the time when Earth did not exist, nor Venus nor Mars, neither the sun nor any star. But of this I will not try to tell the world all, not that it might not be told, but no reader could comprehend that state wherein Man that is, was a race not become Man as yet. When I say Man I say also all associate animals, for every sort of being that lives on the Earth is Man, there being men and animals, lesser men. No, they who heard the words could in no way comprehend beings neither animal, plant nor mineral, which nevertheless lived. I will therefore deal solely with the later time which came before the last glacial epoch, and still later with the time of Zailm, and when of him, of yourself, for my Phylos is but Zailm reincarnate, returned from devachan."

I raised my head, which I had kept bowed while Phyris talked. We were alone, the others of our party having withdrawn. Phyris continued:

"I will write of Anzimee, and so of myself; and I will write of others also. But now I speak of ourselves.

"When Man was born into the earth from Mars, as he is eventually to be born from the Earth into Hesper, that was the basis of the allegory of Adam and Eve, but before them came all their lesser brethren, the animals of land, sea and air. And back of the race birth were the race lives on Man, and before then lives on two other planets, neither of which are of matter which the Earthly eye could perceive. There is in them now no life process, for these world souls are resting, and so also is

Mars. Thus I have spoken of four of the seven planets of which the human race makes cyclic visits, going from One to Two, to Three, to Four (which is the Earth), to Five (Hesper), to the one to which Man will go after his years on Hesper, and from there to the Seventh or Sabbatic world. These last two, like the first two, are imperceptible to the eyes of man on Earth. There are seven worlds, and seven times the race of Man circles them; three times already Man has circled the series and arrived en masse at the fourth of the number in this, his fourth round. So, Phylos, I speak of all these many race-lives; of Earth, of Hesper, of Mars, and all other human planets, after the ordinary sense. But whoever wants to may go with our Great Master, escaping the Rounds, and of that Life, no words can tell. But such determination is rare, and there are few that find that Way. Yet here are some of the signs along that Path; hear them, heed, and thus find—me. Use all things as abusing none. Drugs, as drugs; food, as not gluttonously; drinks, as not excessively; society, as a study; marriage ₁ as a Way, but restraint as His Highway. Most of our race must go by the lower path, for the Cliff-brow Way is too dizzy; none can walk it, unless He holds their hands, and there are few that manage to let Him, for desires tempt them. But they that refuse that Life now, how shall they find it again? They will not, and so shall cease with the world. Then that which is written will come true, 'There shall be time, and times and half a time.' Alas that it should be so. You shall deliver a message of this judgment in a day not afar off. Being in the middle of its journey upon the Earth, the race is half through an experience of life that has engaged it for a period of time too vast for your real comprehension."

"Will you not tell me?" I inquired. "I am curious."

"Tell you? Yes, and in words you can understand, yet the figures can convey only vaguely to you, who know not what all the period has seen transpire. These are the figures," and Phyris solemnly counted a period of time which my mind confronted as one helpless, lost in thought. "But see you convey to none other this knowledge, until our atonement has recurred. Such is the lapse of Time since the Universe was without form and void, and darkness was upon the face of the deep. Each man we see, except those who have been transfigured, is but a semi-ego, and each woman the same, two of these having one spirit. When the perfection time comes, all the halves shall unite, each with its own, and lo! This is the marriage made in heaven. But first comes the Trial, the Crisis of Transfiguration."

"And if," I asked, "if a soul pass not, why not, and what will happen, and if one half, one mate, shall fall, shall the other also?"

"Oh, my twin! If a soul pass not, it will be because the waywardness of its many lives has clipped the wings of its strength so that it cannot fly above the concentrated temptations of that trial. Such a fate is the portion of all failures in this most supreme trial. And lastly, personally, if you do fail? Your soul shall go into the Second Death, and because of that, so also shall mine, for we, and all egoic mates, fight this last fight with our combined strength. Your eternal life depends on me; my hope rests on you; but upon the Spirit rests all our hope. And we cannot find It if we do not follow the Path shown to us by Christ; if we seek It not, It will not seek us. Unless Christ is ours, and in us, we will fail in that fearful trial. But come, Phylos, and see the Earth as it was in the days of Zailm and Anzimee, and seeing that time, behold it now."

Speaking this way, she arose and touched me, and I perceived for the first time that she, like myself, was in astral form. I seemed to sleep momentarily, yet was conscious of motion, the sort of motion that one experiences when passing from deep sleep to full wakefulness at once. This was the passage from Hesperus to Earth. The sensation was due to the fact that my present astral was in some sort material; as I had not even an astral when coming from the Earth, and so nothing material, therefore I could not be conscious of that transition. The sleeping unconsciousness was now due to Phyris, who wished to draw my attention from her words and—herself.

————

Once more all the scenes of Earth appeared. I saw the broad waters of the Atlantic. Phyris said:

"Names are appropriate; see here is the Atlantic Ocean where was the Atlantean Continent. And now we descend into it; above are its waters, and around us. They do not harm us, for our psychicality is superior to their psychicality. Behold the psychic record of the past, the concrete history of the world, imperishable until time shall be no more. Do you want to read of a first destruction of Poseid? Seek it in your Bible, and find it as the Noachian deluge. This was before the age of Zailm, or of history which they knew, many thousands of years. Would you like to learn of the destruction of Lemorus, that great people who were in the Earth before the Age of Ice, when the world knew no cold, nor snow, nor frost; who preceded Poseid by countless ages? Turn to the book of Job and read of how the 'deep boiled like a pot,' and reading, you shall learn that Lemuria perished of fire from out the interplanetary depths. So one cycle of mankind died of fire, and the next of water. And again, the next dies of fire. The races of Earth today shall come, afar off as that day still is, to perish of fire, and the Earth shall be blasted and rolled together as a scroll, you find this prophecy in the second Book of Peter III: 10. Yet knowledge of all this is not from my telling. I have spoken. And now, my other self, I take you awhile to fulfill the law and the prophets and your karma. And I will await your coming again to me; we part, see, here is the Sagum, there Mendocus. Aye, beloved, we part, but it is for a little while, and then for eternity we shall be one together. Let some dim perception of me awaken in your mind, and sweeten your life, and lead you ever upward. My peace, so much as it is such, will be with you, and keep you!"

She put her arms around me, and held me long, while our eyes looked into each other's souls. Then her lips met mine in one ecstatic throb, and—she was gone!

Footnotes

340:1 Matthew, v. 18.

345:1 St. John, xvi, 13.

350:1 Cor. vii; 1 to 9; also 29, 31, 32, 36, 37 and 38.

CHAPTER VIII. OLD TEACHERS TAUGHT OF GOD

I awoke. The place was in one of the smallest rooms of the Sagum; it seemed not unfamiliar, although I had until then been only in the greater apartment. Mendocus sat by my side. There was a sense of having lost something; I knew not what, but the loss made me inexpressibly sad. I felt hampered, as if my freedom had contracted. Otherwise, too, I felt weak, as if long ill. But Mendocus put his hand over my eyes, and I slept.

The next conscious moment came, and the weariness was gone, but not wholly so the sense of loss, of restricted freedom. It was one thing to lose comprehension of memory and events; to have entirely forgotten Hesperus and Phyris, and Mol Lang and Sohma, as I had done; but it was a wholly different and impossible thing to forget or in any way put away the growth of my soul during my five weeks of absence from the Earth. Yes, five weeks, for despite the seeming months in devachan, and the time in Pertoz, all but one part in a thousand of my time of absence had been spent in Hesperus. Five weeks of Earth time.

It would have been impossible for me to have remained in Pertoz and been happy. It would be impossible for you, my friends. Why? Because it was a plane of soul life so exalted above our familiar Earth that only growth can introduce the soul there, long, slow, often painful, but growth. To me, then, or to you now, irrevocable transference to such a high plane of life would be fearful punishment; all our ordinary powers of life, all our present selves put away, and an entirely different set of sensibilities and a new, unknown, untried self in their place, knowledge in the use of all which, amidst wholly strange phenomena and unlearned laws, the misplaced soul would have to acquire through long, unhappy years. It is a divine blessing to humanity that sudden transition from one plane to a higher is as impossible as is any real retrogression.

I sat up, and then stood up, Mendocus assisting me, for I was weak and dizzy. I remained at the Sach until several days had elapsed, learning of various occurrences and making various decisions and resolutions. Asking for Quong, I was told he was dead, and knowing now nothing of the past five weeks, I accepted the news with intense regret.

Mendocus told me that I was a man still possessed of earthly appetites and passions, although I had lately been where humanity was of the heavenly order, as measured by terrestrial standards, where no sensuality ever invaded, although the people were not grim, nor was life there devoid of pleasure.

I agreed for the sake of courtesy, without knowing anything of whom or what he spoke, more than an untraveled commoner of a great city knows of interior Africa. He saw my ignorance and became silent.

His remarks about social sin I did not feel applied to myself, for although I mingled with the people of this world, I did not sin in the meaning of the term as he used it. Perhaps from environment I was not free, but free of these errors I was, and without any pharisaical self-praise.

Speaking of the fallen, however, where was the really sweet noble girl I had tried to raise, and who, agreeing to my efforts, had gone to Melbourne? Life interests were again claiming me. The animal soul was reasserting itself, and warring as strongly as its feeble selfhood allowed with the human soul and the stirring spirit which cannot sin nor err, because it is one with the Over Soul, and so always draws the human soul upward, while the animal pulls it downward.

Then Mendocus said to me:

"Mr. Pierson, the sins that you condemn in your fellow-creatures were once yours, and, if you shall condemn the doer, may become yours again. That which you judge, you are not past the danger of committing.

"Judge not, lest you be judged. But a light has been placed in your inner soul these past five weeks, a lamp from God. Hide it not, but let it so shine that it gives light to the Sinful who have no light. Pity them, deplore their error, but if you condemn them you will not follow Him who said 'neither do I condemn you; go and sin no more.'"

Mol Lang had set a proper estimate on my powers in refusing to make irrevocable my ascent to the Hesperian plane. I had stood ready with the torch of desire to fire my earthly ships. If I could have known of my escape I would have felt thankful. As it was, Hesper was become an unmeaning name, and the ships were not burned. Pleased as a child I had gone to the devachanic plane, where all things that the child in experience desired, although it wished never so foolishly, seemed to occur. Now the child, having confronted the sober fact that inexorable laws govern all the reign of being, had become stricken, brokenhearted at his failure; had returned to his own sphere, and, blessed mercy, was enabled to forget it all until such time as the five weeks' leaven had leavened the whole, and return was possible in the circumstances of one coming to his own. Friend, never assume the attitude of childishness toward the sublime—you may not escape as lightly as I did. Count the cost, or else plod along with the commonplace masses. Both roads lead to the goal, one short but inexpressibly severe, the other long, and, alas! quite severe enough. It is no paradox to say that the shortest road is the longest; life is not always measured by years—some lives are but a few short years—but oh, the bitternesses and not impossibly, sweets, too, crowded in them would require a thousand years of other and less marked lives to essay.

Before I left the Sagum, Mendocus laid down esoteric rules for my guidance in the days to come, days when sole dependence must be governed by my knowledge of these rules, since no esoterist would be near to counsel me,

"Mr. Pierson," said the grand old sage, "I have here a Bible. Lo! I have read it, the Old Testament, eighty-seven times; the New, even more times. Yet I always see new beauties in the Book. I have here the Books of Manu, and also the Vedas. All are authorized by the Christ-Spirit, under different human names, truly, and in different ages. All are more or less allegorical; all require His Light to interpret; without it, serious errors may arise as they have arisen before in the world with sad frequency and fearfully long lived persistency.

"I will therefore declare to you a guidance from them. Knock, and it shall be opened to you. But see that you knock with the will of the Spirit, for although the mind knocks, forever, the Way shall not be opened.

"Ask, and it shall be given. But although the animal man ask forever, no answer shall be given, for this also means that unless the request is made by the Spirit in you for the Truths of God, and not for earthly things; these last follow as shade the sun. Whatsoever is asked of the Father in the Christ's name, that shall He grant. But consider that asking in the name of the Christ is asking for the things of His Kingdom. With the gift of these things all lesser things shall be added, food, clothing and everything else the body needs. This is hard for the natural mind to comprehend. He will not let you perish even though you die of hunger.

"Whatsoever a man sows that shall he also reap. This is karma and the law, and every jot of it must be fulfilled. Man is a creature of many incarnations, each earth life one personality, strung on the unbreakable string of his egoic individuality, which reaches from everlasting to everlasting, from the East to the West.

"No demand of karma may be ignored; all must be paid in the course of the lives.

"Then 'do unto others as you would be done by,' and remember, as you do unto the least of your fellow creatures, in that manner and measure is it done unto our Savior, and unto the Father, and shall be done unto you again.

"Keep all the commandments; you shall in this way come to the everlasting, where is all wisdom."

That evening I went out of the sacred precincts and back to the town.

The Secrets Of Mount Shasta And A Dweller On Two Planets

There I learned of various things. My mining partners were now willing to buy my share without further discussion. From that sale I received approaching three hundred thousand dollars, paid in installments, seven quarterly payments of nearly forty-three thousand dollars gold coin, each one.

Tho arrangomont having been made for depositing these sums, as they fell due, with my bankers in Washington, D. C., I was overcome with a desire to travel; this and my ability to gratify it took me to nearly every civilized land. Yet no object except unrest prompted this wandering.

———————————

Almost two years had passed since I left ——————— City, the scene of my esoteric experiences. I was in Norway, away from the wide, wide world, in a little hamlet close to a celebrated fjord, where I had arrived the previous day. My guide and general utility man spoke English sufficiently well to make himself readily intelligible. He proved to have been a sailor on the ship in which I took my first voyage, and had returned to his native land to minister to the wants of travelers, in which service his knowledge of Anglo-Saxon did him good stead. He was delighted to see me, a feeling which I reciprocated. His name? Certainly, Hans Christison.

Hans said that four or five other summer travelers were staying in the village, "One ish ein young leddy; she haf a crazy for paint und brushes—ish ein nardist, I think so."

A week elapsed before I met this "purty leddy," and meantime Hans guided me, equipped with gun and fish rod, he rowing our light skiff. One afternoon I took the skiff and went off alone to a rock jutting out of the fjord, whereon grew several birch trees of graceful beauty. I tied the skiff, and then climbed out and sat down to read the letters forwarded to me from New York.

While reading these I heard a little sound behind me as of some other person on the tiny island. Turning my head I saw a woman, and then I laid down my paper and sprang to my feet. I was too much surprised to raise my cap or even to speak, and she seemed equally astonished. Then I said the one word:

"Lizzie!"

"Mr. Pierson!" she replied.

"How came you here?" was our next exchange. I told her of my aimless wanderings, and she related her life since we parted in —————— —— City. From Melbourne she had gone to New York and then to Washington. There she bought a residence and established an art studio, assuming the name of Harland. People were told little and learned less of her past, and were allowed to suppose that she was a young Australian widow of moderate wealth. Each of the two summers after her advent to life at the capital had been spent abroad, and this, the third summer, she was spending in Norway. Her pictures had sold well, and she had made up the entire sum which she had used from what she called my "loan." This she insisted on giving back to me, but I laughed, and tentatively agreed, saying, "Before I leave, if you insist." I stayed there four weeks, stayed until I learned from a chance remark that she was going away in a few days for a little stay among the Scottish lakes. Then without saying anything to Mrs. Harland, I had Hans take me by night to the steamer which visited the little port once a fortnight, and was then due, and going on board, paid Hans, adding a tip. As the ropes were being cast off, I said:

"Hans, let the 'young leddy' know that I am gone; tell her, if she asks, I am going to St. Petersburg. Good bye, Hans."

To the Capital of the Czar I went, and was there a week.

Then back to Paris, then to London, and in another week I sailed for New York, then to Washington.

A year passed. One afternoon as I strolled up Pennsylvania Avenue, I came face to face with Elizabeth Harland. We stopped, spoke, and then I turned and walked with her. The old times surged over us; I remembered the days in California; then more tenderly, the peaceful month in Norway, when I had come to really believe I loved this girl, not only for her radiant beauty and sedately sweet womanhood, but for her tremendous effort to triumph over error, and her success, how she had come forth from the fire, pure gold.

Before we parted I learned her address, and resolved to call as soon as an opportunity offered.

Next evening a bank messenger came to my apartments, and left a packet. It held two hundred bank notes of the value of one hundred dollars each, and a letter. This I opened hastily and read:

Sept. 3rd, 1869.

"Mr. Walter Pierson:

"Enclosed find the sum of my indebtedness to you, and accept my heartfelt gratitude for the same. And we will be friends; you are ever welcome to come to the home of

Your sincere friend,

Elizabeth Harland."

I pondered the situation, and when the moment of decision came made up my mind very suddenly. The money which she had returned I put into my pocketbook, took my hat and, being in proper attire, went down the street until I found a cab. Entering this, I gave directions to the driver to take me to No. —, ———— Street.

It was a pretty place. When I rang the bell it was answered by Mrs. Harland herself. Her manner was cordial, but I thought somewhat reserved.

On the wall of the parlor hung a picture of rare merit. A man, whose face and general air was as expressive of divinity as it lies in the power of paint and brush to depict, stood looking on a woman whose face was hidden by her hands. In the dust at his feet characters were written. The environment was that of the architecture of the Holy Land. Under the painting, which was half life size, were the words, "St. John, VII: 11."

I sat down in a proffered chair, and for a moment silence reigned. My hostess broke this, saying:

"You received the money, Mr. Pierson?"

"Yes." I drew it out of my pocket and following my resolve, and waiving all opening remarks, I said:

"Unless you give me yourself with this money, I will not take it out of the house. Will you be my wife, Elizabeth?" I asked as I knelt by her side.

Her eyes gazed into mine a moment, and she said.

"For myself, because you love me, and cover the past with the success of the present?" tears in her eyes, tears in her voice as she spoke.

"Yes, darling!"

With a convulsive sob she rested in my arms, and cried as if her heart would break. At length she said, tremulously.

"All the world is worth less than this true love."

Our wedding was quiet, and after it we went for a brief trip abroad, going only to England, and in a short time returned home.

CHAPTER IX. THEY WHO HEED HAVE PEACE

Once during the wanderings before my marriage, and while I was in Hindustan, I met an old man of unappealing appearance, whose faded eyes no sooner rested on me than he said:

"You are the one Mendocus told me about, and ordered me, saying 'tell him certain things for me.' This I will do. Young man, your life shall be sad and bitter on Earth, but sweet after that. Things will happen because of which your animal soul shall embrace itself and say, 'This is joy.' But immediately the still voice of the human soul in you shall say, 'This joy is but a Sodom apple,' and in that moment you will know that it is so. From that point onward, you will continually have a war between your animal soul, which is innate depravity, and your spirit, which is of God, Brahma, the One. See in it the allegory of Adam and original sin; it pulls your human soul down to death; the other, the Spirit, draws the human upward. Listen then to its sayings; I will illustrate them for you:

"Before your eyes can see God they must be incapable of shedding tears for any suffering of your own. Before your ears can hear, they must have lost sensitiveness. Your voice may not speak eternal wisdom until it has no power to wound. Before your self can stand in the presence of the Eternal, its feet must have been bathed in the blood of suffering, penance, restitution. Then kill the ambition to excel in the poor paths of Fame. Cease to regard this life as your best possession.

"Then work for God as earnestly as others work for Mammon; and respect your life as those respect life who treasure it most, and be happy as those who live for happiness. In the hearts of all is the source of all error, in disciple as well as in the man of desire. Study a plant of mustard, witness it grow and bud. But if you shall cut it down so that it never bears seed, behold a strange thing, it will sprout again and grow through the years, if it never bears. And this although it is only a material form. Now, therefore, if a human soul shall not be cut down, yet shall not enter into life as a creator by reason that it wills not, then the Spirit of life everlasting shall go into it, and it shall contain itself, and therefore live forever. Study the truth of mustard life. Only the strong in God can act upon this teaching and hold the lower nature. The weak must wait its maturity and then will come their struggle. It will strive to keep the feet from the Path; and may succeed. But if once all its power be wiped out; if once you do the will of the Father earnestly, as His obedient child, that is the atonement, for it shall give strength to do every work of the Creator of Being. It will seem to take your very life. That is because it takes the animal soul and throttles it. But the human soul will recover, and the Spirit will come into it. This is the time of the Silence of the Soul. Then it shall be clear to you how dark are the lives of those who are around you and have no goal of union with the Spirit towards which to race. And you will see and know karma. Also you will see that because of your past incarnations your karma is inextricably interwoven with the karma of the world. This is that saying which the Nazarene answered when it was asked of Him, 'Who is my neighbor?' If, Walter Pierson, you shall once be able to know the Peace of Silence, you shall then learn of all things about you, for the Earth is Brahm's, and all in it teaches His works."

I was surprised at being called by name, and also of being told of Mendocus. The old man said further:

"If your soul once knows this Peace, no storm of sin or of sorrow can ever more drive you far aside from the Path, for its knowledge is an abiding wisdom. Heed also the words of Mendocus, read your Bible, read the Vedas, read Manu; and study. It shall all be a staff to your hand and a lamp to your feet. Peace be with you."

"And to you, peace," I replied as he turned and walked away into the crowd, for we had stood by a public drinking fountain. Now that Elizabeth was found and was my wife, I pondered deeply these things I had heard of the occult lore. Not that she had connection with it. But because, as the years went by, I found she knew and cared little about these obscure studies, which I did. So our lives drew apart. But she was oblivious of this fact, and I was glad because she was. She had her church work and I aided her in all her sweet charities. To us came two lovely little daughters, the greatest treasures of our lives, and oh, so carefully taught regarding life and shielded from its dangers. So long as these little ones were with us, I was content. And yet I felt, in an ill-defined sorrow, that Earth's experiences were but Sodom apples.

Sometimes I found my lonelier hours disturbed by a strange voice which whispered to my inner consciousness. As time passed it grew stronger, and one day it appeared before my sight as a ghost. The Shape talked. What it said made me eager to hear more, so I cultivated it. From that time on, it became a regular visitor, and from that to being always present when I was otherwise alone was but a step. It spoke of having been on a distant planet which it called "Pertoz," sometimes "Hesperus," again "Venus." It spoke of persons whose names were strange, calling one "Mol Lang", another "Sohma" and a third "Phyris." Then it described these people, and I listened eagerly. Who were they, and what human soul was this which had gone to Venus? The ghost looked marvelously like myself. But my slumbers at night were as sound as if it visited me not.

I called it my ghost. How unconsciously true It told of everything related to my being with Mol Lang, and in Venus; it drew my mind's eye to the psychic scene in the bed of the Atlantic. It told of a visit to the sun with Sohma, of which I neglected mention in sequence. Briefly, Sohma went with me to the sun, and showed me that it was a vibrant body of less size than astronomers believe, but of enormous density. I saw its oceans—they were heavier than Mercury. But it had no life forms which I took as such. Yet life of some sort there is everywhere. Perhaps, indeed, not animal, nor vegetable, but from the high standpoint of those who know much of the works of the All-Father, forms that no earthly man would call life are such, nevertheless. But the sun is a force of such fearful vibrative pulsing that even my subtle astral body was not unaffected. Sohma said of it:

"See the immediate center of our solar system. You would call it a dynamo, the great dynamo of the system. You would be right, and wrong also. The attempt to define the sun as an analogue to a dynamo-electric machine has much to support it. But to define it as identical is erroneous. The trouble with that theory is the trouble which lies at the root of and weakens all other theories to account for sun-heat and sunlight. It is that science does not assign a sufficiently high value to the sun. The combustion theory is invalid; the solar mass contraction theory is but partially tenable and meteoric showers do not account better than the first two. Neither does the electric-dynamo theory. Truly, the latter explains how sun-heat and sunlight may coexist and not be inharmonious with the awful degree of cold between earth, the planets and the sun. It explains that which denies the simple combustion theory so completely, viz. that the farther one goes from the earth center, either in a balloon or on a high mountain, the colder and darker the air gets, so that interstellar space is several hundred degrees below zero, and black as midnight, with the sun a luminous disc, without rays. But the dynamo theory does not explain the solar spectrum, nor the bands of spectra, nor coronal 'flames,' nor 'sun spots,' nor solar nor lunar eclipses."

The above statements were made by Sohma, as will be remembered by the reader, while I was still in the Hesperian astral state and for the time was unconscious of a previous earthly existence. I had therefore no memory of the mundane knowledge and was unbiased in my judgment of the remarks of my friend. He had ceased to speak after uttering the word "eclipses." I waited for him to continue, but as he did not, I finally asked, "Well, what does explain all? What is the truth?" Thus questioned, he resumed:

"I have said that the value accorded by astronomers is too small. Seeing a fire, they would seek to explain by its means the sun. Finding this unworkable, and aware that a contracting mass gives off heat, they next attempt an explanation on that hypothesis. But this will not do, nor will meteoric showers, nor any hypothesis based on facts now known, all are too low in aim; the Infinite cannot be explained by the finite, nor will less explain greater; fire is energy, and electricity is energy, and God is energy. But fire will not solve the query, 'What is electricity?' nor will electricity answer 'What is God?' but God will explain both the others, for the sum of the parts is equal to the whole. But a man does not know the full number of the parts; the partial sum he does know will not explain God."

Sohma ceased again. But I, filled with some vagrant earth memory, allowed no time of pause; I was too eager to wait, and I said:

"But this does not tell me what the solar puzzle is."

"You are impatient, my brother; know then, what was at one time known upon the earth, but is now for ages forgotten; that Nature has a dual aspect, is double, is positive and negative; that the great positive side is the side known to mundane science, while the other or negative, or 'Night Side,' or, as it was once known in the earth by the men of Atlantis, 'Navaz,' is a side all unknown, and scarcely guessed in the most exceeding flights of speculation, left un-broached, secretly kept by a few, who know not that they entertain an angel, an angelic wisdom that in a century more, yea, less time! shall overturn much of the face of earthly things, shall bestow aerial vessels, and everything else once known to those men of Atlantis of whom I spoke. Do you not yet understand?"

I said that I did not; that I thought he referred to some domain of the physical forces not yet known; but what had this to do with the sun? "This: the suns of systems are centers of forces of the Night Side of Nature whereof I spoke, and are force, and matter of a higher value than are planets and satellites, just as water above a cataract is water, truly, but being above and mobile, flows over and down, developing energy. In other words, out of the cold, dark, negative side, or 'night side,' force emerges, drawn to the positive polarity which constitutes in its outgoing flow that termed Nature, and develops in its *fall*, magnetism, electricity, light, color, heat and sound, in order of descent, and lastly solid matter, for this latter is a child of energy, not its parent. When the Navaz forces drop to light, if the light waves enter a spectroscope, they will emerge as colors; these correspond to the various spectrum bands, and will, as the descent progresses, give the noted fines of the solar spectrum, as the great 'B' line of oxygen, the conspicuous '1474' line, and the brilliant 'H' and 'K' violet bands."

I thought I now saw the truth; but I saw only a part; a grand vista was yet to open. I saw it when my companion resumed:

"Thus the evidence of flames, and metals on fire, and all that leads astronomers to think sun and stars flaming hells. But their 'fires' will not decrease, for the Father is immanent, and the forces of 'Navaz' are perpetually fed by Him. The graphic picture of a 'burned-out sun' is a dream, never to be fulfilled. A day will come again in the earth when instruments will be made which Atlantis once well knew, when the prismatic rays from a spectroscope will be found to be a source of heat, and of sound, so that the so-called 'flames' of the sun, and of the stars, will produce music, harmonies divine. ₁ Yea, further, for going on down, the dark green solar spectrum of iron will be made to yield iron for use in the arts, and so with the other bands and lines, the intense greens, blues, and blue-greens that give copper, lead, antimony and so on. It is by these Navaz currents that the circulation in the universe is kept up, as blood in a man's arteries. The suns are the systemic hearts. But you are tired, my brother, or I would explain yet more, that the planets which receive all these currents must return their equivalent. And thus would another vast field open before your sight. This last would explain that which so worries science on earth, the molten earthly interior. That also is something of an error. All the phenomena which seem to declare the earth to be in a melted condition inside do not prove it so in truth; all point to the return currents, the positive; all exhibit the veins/currents of our universe, back to its hearts."

Sohma concluded with an apostrophe to the leading minds of the Earth which was beautiful indeed:

"O Science of Earth, in you is the hope of the world, when you shall become handmaiden of God. Look up, value His works highly, and you shall read clearly many things which now puzzle you sadly. You are the Joseph, and Religion the Mary, and you two shall show forth the Light of

Life. You are blessed."

When my "ghost" retold me this conversation I seized my hat and went out to look sunwards and marvel if all were true, and astounded, reflect again, "Who is this Sohma?"

The puzzle grew, and my discontent with life grew; the lump was becoming leavened. The more I studied the truth of the mustard plant, the clearer grew my perceptions, and I knew that never in my present body could I achieve much progress, for in our union Elizabeth and I had passed by the mustard unheeding, writing another karmic chapter.

For a time my "ghost" was agreeable to my wishes as regarded its comings and goings; but it now seemed to have entered in and coalesced with me. I no longer heard or saw it, but instead was often one with it, and saw and heard its visions and perceptions as if they were my own; and indeed, as you know, this was a fact. It was in truth the record of my visit to Pertoz, and was a true rendering in all ways of my life there.

Often my soul was torn by faithfulness to the duty of life as pointed out by Mendocus. And then my only escape from trouble was to allow myself to rest in the Hesperian astral to the exclusion of that of Earth. At such times I was living again the life with Phyris and the loved ones of Pertoz. Elizabeth was saddened by this lapse, as she thought it; and my blessed little daughters grew to regard "papa" as "funny" and I was held in awe. Not a pleasant experience, my friends. My wife would look at me sadly and I know she wept when alone because I often absently called her "Phyris." Indeed, Elizabeth was my closest realization of the Phyris of whom I knew but could not find on Earth. Under all this I grew thin and pale, and aimlessly wandered about possessed of a huge disgust for worldly interests or amusements, filled with sorrow for the sorrow I saw the world held, and yearning for the high plane which I at last knew was not a fantasy, and where Phyris was, and Sohma, and Mol Lang. But I could not get there; and they did not come to me; therefore I studied the rules of the Path, because I was torn with crazed regret when the lower nature triumphed and I fell in sinful error. But although

The Secrets Of Mount Shasta And A Dweller On Two Planets

I fell, I rose again. Then the effect this had on my sweet, loving wife came home to me. Was this doing as I would be done by? No. So I set my will in firm resolve and subdued my own sorrows, and made my nature a tool for my soul, not a master over me.

Then once again I smiled, and the color and flesh came back to me. So Elizabeth was happy once more; and I? I had found the true Path at last. Service. I no longer wept for myself; my ears were no more sensitive, my tongue no longer wounded any one with its morose utterances; the greatest triumph of all, my feet were bathed in the life blood of the animal nature, so that I lived unselfishly, my whole being bent on doing my best, living as happily as if solely for happiness, as earnestly as if for ambitious motives. Then it was that the Peace of the Silence came, and I waited for the Savior to take me and fight in me and do His work with my hands. The Holy Spirit had come into my life.

It was a sad blow when my little daughters died of epidemic scarlet fever in the year 1878. Thereafter I used my life to comfort the sweet woman whose vital breath nearly died in that cruel loss. I think Elizabeth never cared for anything in life after that, except my loving devotion. And I gave it, for I knew Phyris would have me do so, and I waited on Earth now only to make it tolerable for the woman I had sworn to cherish. She waited in anticipation of rejoining her children in heaven, and meanwhile devoted all her time and energy, with feverish application, to doing all the good she could, using our unlimited money for the purpose. How joyful I was that the money was drawn from the gravel of the mines, and did not come to me from harassed debtors.

It was less than two years after Dora and Maydie, our two little girls, had gone to the Summerland, before Elizabeth followed after them.

I felt the need of a radical change in living methods for the sake of my health, and so, under an assumed name, secured a situation as mate on an American ship, a splendid vessel. My purpose was to expose myself to the toil of a sea life for a season in the idea of recuperation coming from active duty.

Nothing would satisfy Elizabeth, except going as a passenger on the same vessel; she refused to leave me out of her care. The captain knew her relation to me, so did the crew, so that her being a passenger was natural.

Near the Bermudas a terrible storm came up, and I ordered the sails close reefed; then the squall struck, the mainmast went over, the vessel sprang a leak, the pumps were inadequate, and the boats were swamped, all but one, as fast as they were lowered. Into that went the crew, and I would have put Elizabeth in, but the men, seeing the boat full, pushed off and left her, Captain Washburne and me to our fate. Hardly five minutes elapsed when our noble vessel pitched bows on under the engulfing waves, carrying us with it.

I had lashed myself to the deck cleats to avoid being washed overboard. So now I was doomed to die—and was glad. As the waters swept overhead, I called out in my soul: "Phyris! At last! At last I come!" I saw Mendocus as I lost consciousness, and when I next came to knowledge, I found myself in the Sagum in California. Yet my body drowned off Bermuda's coast! Here was Phyris, and—yes! Mol Lang. It was not long before I again bade Mendocus farewell, and with Phyris and Mol Lang went home to Pertoz, home now, my own attained plane, and "Earth with its dark and dreadful ills" left behind forever, but not Earth with its mighty secrets of life. Yes, Terre, is, if insignificant, a point from where the Human soul reaches out into the boundless sidereal universe and formulates its laws, knows them, and is greater than all. I was now to leave the Earth, where so many incarnations had known me.

"It was a time for memory and for tears. Within the deep still chambers of the heart a specter dim, Whose voice was like the wizard tones of Time, Heard from the Tomb of Ages, points its cold and solemn finger to the beautiful and holy visions that have passed away, And left no shadow of their loveliness on the dead waste of life. That specter lifts the coffin lid of Hope and Joy and Love."

O Earth! A point in the heavens, yet type of all the stellar universe.

Shall I descend a moment to figures? Shall I speak numbers almost inconceivable? I will. Just for a moment think of what we have come to know in the schools of Earth, think of our human civilization that permits us new comprehensions, see the parallel of how we measure time

404

and distance compared to the Indian, who measures one by "moons" and the other by "looks," one being the interval between one full, or new moon and the next; the other being how far he can look and distinguish a man. Civilized man measures by years and by miles, and science by "light years." How much is a light year? In the time of one second light travels one hundred and ninety-two thousand miles, approximately. In one year there are thirty-one million, five hundred and fifty-six thousand, nine hundred and twenty-nine seconds; hence the distance of a light year is the multiplied product of one figure by the other, briefly, the inconceivable distance of sixty trillion, five hundred and fifty-three billion, ten hundred and fifty thousand miles. All that, and yet we see a star in the northern heavens said to be one hundred and eighty-one light years distant from the earth around which our own sun revolves, one of its satellites, as the moon is satellite to the earth. Such is the material universe, an infinitude, one of God's Works, but only one, and yet it is a comprehensible mechanism, not, from the material point of view, comparable to the value of one soul of Man. Why do I thus digress?

Friends, to let you know what a proud place Man occupies. Think of all that nearly interminable distance to Arcturus, and then reflect that that bright member of the constellation Bootes is only a little way out in the boundless universe! That vast bulk of matter, capable of being seen nearly one hundred and twenty million times farther than the distance between the earth and the sun. How great is that bulk? Estimated by comparison it is more than half a thousand million times larger than the combined mass of the Earth, Venus, Mars, Saturn, Neptune and Mercury. And yet the human mind reaches into this almost infinite thing called the universe and grapples understandingly with its problems of matter, force, time, space, eternity, infinity! Laus Deo! Thus Arcturus is our yardstick in the sidereal universe, which in itself is in the House of our Father only one mansion! Beside it are "many mansions," and, friends, there is one mansion of the many to which I have called your attention, that of the Soul. The Soul is not material, and one loved one who shall go away out of your home into the "Unknown Country" is farther away from you than Arcturus, for it is in another condition of

405

being. Wondrous privilege. You stand on the threshold, for you are embodied children of the Creator. You can learn His Ways, and go to the loved ones gone before; or you can leave matter behind and go into the psychic mansion, and reenter matter wherever you wish; be in the World one instant, in the astral the next and in Arcturus the next. I speak no idle tales—whoever has ears to hear, let him hear.

———————

Now I had left the world for a new life, a new vantage point. So far I had lived a life purely of sacrifice and sad duty to Elizabeth, all the later while knowing myself, through my other astral, to be far from home and Phyris and knowledge. And now the release had come; my sacrifice to Elizabeth was completed, my charity had covered a multitude of sins, oh! many more than I knew at the time of the completed sacrifice. And yet, I had not quite atoned for all the weary errors of past incarnations. Almost free, however, almost free!

While yet living with Elizabeth, my obedience to the rules of which I have spoken and others of which I have not spoken, all from Mol Lang and Mendocus, had given me insight into some of the past. Thus I had learned a little of the dead personality known to the reader as Zailm of Poseid. I knew that Zailm's spirit, human soul, his individuality, were also mine; that I, Pierson, had been Zailm. I was able to form a fair remembering of Zailm's life, and of its events and his friends. I knew that the acts he did and the sins he committed were my inheritance and that I was responsible for them, because though his personality was not my personality, his individuality was, and is, mine. Although I knew not who Lolix was, or that she lived, yet for Zailm's (my) sin with her and for her tragic death, I must atone. To whom? Anybody in the Earth whom I could serve as CHRIST had said in declaring, "Even unto the least of these." I served with the sacrifice of my living happiness the duty I contracted to Elizabeth, by living for her, and dying on my ship that she might have the chance to escape. I had rescued her from a nameless sin of life in ————— City, and brought her to saving faith in JESUS, THE CHRIST. If as Zailm, I, the Me, had tripped with Lolix, I, as Walter Pierson, had arisen with another (?) soul to salvation. So karma balanced there. Karma, self-made fate, binds the soul to make reparation in some life or lives for its sins in others. It bound me; I paid the debt. It binds you for debts contracted sometime, somewhere, and will you not follow the Path, and after paying the debt, be with the free forever more? Charity is great: its least worthy aspect alms giving, for although I give all my goods to feed the poor, and have not (that) charity (which is love) it profits me nothing.

I have said that my wife, Elizabeth, cared little for my esoteric studies. But to infer that she cared nothing would be wrong. She once found me in my library, using an occult needle. This was a steel bar seven inches long, square, and one-third of an inch thick, pointed quadramidally, with gold tips. It swung in a glass case suspended by a hair over the symbol.

Could you have been gifted with clairvoyant sight, and have looked upon me as Elizabeth found me, you would have seen that needle hanging motionless, and all about it a golden light or aura. From either end went a beam of this poetic luminosity—one to me, and one to a distance. Looking along the latter you could have seen at its end a man, standing beside a dining room sideboard; in his hand a glass of brandy. That man was a dear friend of mine, with but one grave fault, drunkenness. As he poised the cup to drink I said firmly:

"No! 'Touch not, taste not, handle not!' Neither now nor from now on! Heed my voice, or you shall not enter the Kingdom of Heaven."

Willis Murchison, the would-be drinker, let the glass fall to the floor, where it broke to fragments. A day or so later I met him, and he related that he had had a vision, and heard a voice from God, saying that he should no more drink lest he lose his chance of heaven. He never did touch liquor again. He heard the mysterious voice and heeded; yet he had not heeded his friends. By the occult secret of that glowing tipped needle whose power enlisted the service of spirits not human, I held mesmeric power over him. Herein is the peril of letting the masses know these things, for had I been unscrupulous, lawless, a sorcerer, I could as easily have moved Murchison to any crime. Elizabeth asked what I was doing there in the dark. Having achieved my purpose with my friend, I said to my wife, "Let me tell you certain things." I told her of the law of karma, and much besides. When nearly through, I willed the gold pointed needle to connect her mind psychically with mine. Between us the line of light was established. I whispered then:

"Look! See your past life on earth, and know it. Then tell me, and don't forget what you learn."

She was silent for a few moments, then her breath came as in sleep. Presently she said:

"A noble, wonderful man is guiding me. I see him seemingly uncover a remote age of the world; it is the day of a mighty nation, who sail the air in what they call 'Vailx.' A splendid city is about me. Now I am in a vast temple; the interior of it is ornamented with real stalactites. I stand by a large cube of crystal quartz, and on this is a strange flame which burns without fuel. I see a young couple whom a grave, priestly man is uniting in marriage. Ah, it seems as if I loved the one to be wed better than I love life! I beg the one in the gathering who seems to be a ruler of the nation to prohibit the wedding. Then the priest turns to me, now he looks at me, and, oh! My God! His look chills me in death! I seem to rise above the scene and yet my body still stands in a stony, petrified rigidity. Now it seems some time elapses, and I see the young man who was to be wed. I see the Monarch, too, and they are both in the temple. Now the young man lifts the—my body of stone, and lets it drop into the Light on the great quartz cube, and it disappears instantly. But a foot was broken off, and the young man hides it in his cloak and carries it away. It seems all this was due to some evil done by him, and by me through love of him. I—ah-h-h!"

Elizabeth sighed and then awoke to her surroundings. I lighted the study-lamp, and she watched me curiously. Suddenly she said:

"Why, husband, that young man I saw was—was you! Oh, I believe now in all these things you have told, but which I never believed till now I have seen this." This experience had a great effect on her, so that she looked more and more into the strange learning, and as a result redoubled her efforts to do good in the world. Thus did she observe the Scripture, "Be you doers of the word, not hearers only," for strange though this learning seems, it is not so to Christian Esoterists, but only to mere hearers, and to a lesser degree to doers on the exterior plane of Christian service. Thus had I, who led Lolix astray, led Elizabeth back into His deeper Path. But I first had to travel in it somewhat myself, before I could guide her. This occurred only a few months before her last voyage with me, the Bermuda trip. But she had learned enough to know we were both doomed on the occasion of the wreck, and when I would have placed her in the boat, she said:

"Husband! Walter! I will not go into that boat, for out of the past I know that now we change. I have come to know that in esoterically doing His word, and not hearing it only, is there alone Life. Now I see again into a past age. And you and I are together, and a little babe is before us, wailing to us. You take it bleeding, into your arms, and you also clasp me. Then you ask God for mercy. Generously you took all the blame; yet I, too, having broken the law, had to share the penalty. Then said One who was truly the Christ, although then we knew it not. Therefore, in a far off day, you shall gather a sorrowful harvest of woe, and repay all that you are indebted. When you have come again, and she has also come with you, and you are again ready to go into Navazzamin, you will find yourselves free of Earth forever: My dear, dear friend, it must be that we both die now; I fear not, for we will of necessity meet again. Farewell, my love, till then; kiss me. Is not my karma paid in full, so far as Lolix's error is? More even, possibly? And Christ, shall He not receive me now?"

And I said: "Yes, dear wife, it must be! Goodbye, and God bless you, for we will truly meet again, beyond the great deep River, with Him." And so in death I held her close.

Do you continue to marvel at her contented smile in the photographically true picture of the death scene executed by Phyris? And I, friend? Was not the special crime of Zailm atoned for, in that I brought her to know God's law, karma, and in making my life a living sacrifice for, and at the last dying in an effort to save her to happiness and enlightenment, was that score not requited, fulfilled, and Jesus the Christ obeyed?

The Secrets Of Mount Shasta And A Dweller On Two Planets

Sins, evil deeds, lies, thefts, adulteries, murders even, are in themselves only the shadows of lives turned to face away from God into outer darkness; they are weak places in the chain of character; unsymmetrical places in what Christ our Lord would have perfect, even as He is perfect. For in Him, the Perfect One, are none of these things, nor shadow of turning. He beseeches us, saying, "Be you likewise perfect." "Come unto Me, all you who are weary, and I will give you rest." So, in His divine love He proposes Himself to take all these (to Him) shadows that to us are so horribly real. Of ourselves we can do nothing, for as we undo through the lapse of ages, we also do fresh evil. Not shadows to us. But He is the Light of the world. So the glooms we see while we look from His way will cease to be if we turn to His following. If we have kept the laws from youth upwards, yet, that is but doing no sin of commission. Behind is an unrequited eternity. And, brethren, friends, the time is short (Cor. vii: 29.) He will take these sins, and it shall be to us as if we took a boxful of shadow from a cellar and opened it out in the noontide rays of the sun. But while the sins are all by Him atoned; while when the days mount to years, the one robbed or tied about, or otherwise injured, finds the Father's laws have made it up to him, if he only also knows that Father too, still we have a work. Jesus, the Great Master, took all when we, weary, asked him. But we, while doing these crimes, walked in darkness. The tree of our lives could grow nothing but sickly growths, pale leaves, dwarfed buds, blighted fruits, in that darkness of the soul. We may have always seemed righteous to others; may have even cried "Lord, Lord" with our lips. But if our deeds knew Him not we were growing our life-tree with fair bark, but decayed wood. So, after He has taken on Himself our sins, and they are ceased, yet, with our faces toward Him, we see our tree of character, pale, sickly, with few leaves, and no fruit, standing in God's karmic light. Will we work to make green leaves, and fruit in plenty? If we follow Him, yes. For He always said in language unmistakable to those having ears to hear, that only those who obeyed the Father's law, God's Will, could hope to win salvation. He will remove our burdens; will mediate and atone, but we must undo the errors with the strength He gives; we must each take our cross and follow Him, and He, the Good Shepherd, will lead us Home, to the immortal heights, where there is no more death, nor sin, nor suffering, neither parting. In Him we have, all of us, time, strength, opportunity to undo, after He has atoned and shown us the way. He is that Way. And we, letting Him dwell in us, make our life the Path. There can be no home-going till, in Him, we become our own Path. If there was another way, I would tell you. For I have come before His second coming. It is near. Beware, lest night find you idle. Say not I knew Him not, either as Zailm, or as Pierson. To know Him by lip service is one; to know Him by life lived as He bade us, is another. Having lived, now I speak. Be you doers of the Word, not hearers only.

Footnotes

365:1 Job xxxviii, 7.

CHAPTER X. AFTER THE YEARS, RETURN

Sparing details, what was the appearance of Phyris after the flight of the years? When I left she was a bright, beautiful maiden, in the budding days of womanhood, having the divine, spiritual glory which characterizes the higher race of the perfect Human grade. How did she look now? Different only in the maturity of rounded womanhood, the prime which in Venus withers not with age, because there the animal is subdued, and there are no excesses, indulgences, nor any of that feverish grasping after unattainable things which the "children of a larger growth" who dwell in the human-animal plane of Earth pursue today. Phyris, the dark-haired, starry-eyed girl who was yet more than a girl, was a woman divinely fair, was again before me. Again I beheld the sweetly natural, dignified air that reminded me of the first time I ever saw Mol Lang, that air of quiet, but marvelous power. Enhanced by this appearance, as is a gem by its setting, her sweet, pure selfhood shone forth, that sweet spirit which in Phyris was divine, yet had lost none of the human characteristics which have rendered Jesus so dear to mankind. The spirit was there, the perfect human, also, but the animal, the nature of Man on Earth, was reduced to its place of servitude. When I met the fair, beautiful woman I was embarrassed. At that moment the tide of the years overflowed my soul and awed me. Sometimes I had known of Phyris when the Hesperian astral controlled me. But far more often in later years, the years of duty, this astral did not come, and then I knew Phyris only as an ideal, and with the attributes of that ideal I tried to endue Elizabeth, and the failure was agony to me.

Wonderingly, wholly delighted, I looked on Phyris now. I did not deem it a lack of social appropriateness that she should kiss me and whisper, "Home again," her eyes lighted with the peaceful joy reflected from my gaze.

No passion was in me, no prompting to be sentimental—no, that was gone with Earth's feverish dream.

How familiar all things appeared when at last I had come home. For six Hesperian months ₁ I did nothing but wander in my psychic form in this Elysium, this stellar garden of the Hesperides. In the other time most of my visit was spent in the company of Sohma or Mol Lang. But now Sohma was otherwise engaged. Mol Lang, too, was occupied in the work that attracted him, that of guiding, teaching and helping mankind, en masse, as well as individually; that portion of our race yet on Earth. Unconscious of his efforts, or of how, with others equally great, Mol Lang was influencing the affairs of men, these men on Earth went on with their doings, fondly thinking that they themselves were doing everything. How little humanity on Earth knows that it is guided this way. Yet our Father gives it to His occult children to lead their lesser brethren, just as He gave it to Jesus, one of the Sons of Light, higher than any other, who was an incarnation of the Christ. Perhaps human acts were not, are not, guided individually, as a rule, although exceptions exist. But just as shot, running in grooves, is checked by the leaden pellets before and behind, so the acts of one man depend on the acts of others; these on others still, until finally it appears that the mass is influenced in the whole, and every individual in the mass has his or her acts unconsciously controlled by what are termed circumstances, fates, adverse or favorable, inexorable, the grooves in which they run. That is to say, humanity is ordered in its action by what may be named the Universal Karma. So long as men grope in the dark, ignorant of occult laws, so long must they produce this inexorable karma. It is fate, self-made, running from life to life, incarnation after incarnation, unavoidable, for it is born of the infraction of the laws of the Creator. Even Mol Lang, before he passed and triumphed at the Crisis, to which I was soon to come, and which he experienced a century ago, was controlled by the great, Universal Karma. But in passing that ordeal he passed from finite life to everlasting, and became a law unto himself. And then,

413

free of karma, he returned to minister to those bound by circumstances. Mol Lang had become more than man. He had taken of the Tree of Knowledge, also of the Tree of Life. ₁ As such he utilized the elementals, those nonhuman, non-embodied powers of the air. They find in mankind the tendency to sin, and use it, so that the erring ones climb the ladder on rungs, each of which is a conquered fault. The great religious movements, wars, and the fields of commerce, all furnish experiences for mankind. Do some seem cruel, evil? Yet each is a part of the scheme of the Creator, each is a tool in the hands of His ministers, and all teach that except a man, as part of the Eternal Whole, works for that Whole, subduing the selfish animal in himself, he can in no way come to the Father.

"Except by My Path," says the Savior.

If Sohma and Mol Lang could no longer be with me as companions, who then could? Phyris. She became my tutor, my guide, and led me farther on towards the point where soon I must take the Key and enter alone on the dread struggle, with only my faith in God to sustain me.

One day Mol Lang said, "Phylos, come with me."

I went to his special apartments. There he said:

"Until now, you have only an astral body, but now you need a physical body as a base of action, for now you must learn about your own self. Sleep, so that I can gather material atoms around your astral."

I immediately slept, as I lay on the couch where he had told me to recline. When I awoke he was regarding me, and, for a moment forgetful, I sat up.

"Arise," said Mol Lang. I obeyed, and found myself clothed in flesh. Thus I became a Hesperite. I was now of the same apparent age as Phyris, and was thereby seemingly dispossessed of some twenty-five years. Soon there came to shine in me somewhat of the Spirit-nature, and as the same ego shone in Phyris, so therefore we grew to resemble each other. Because of this indwelling Spirit, Nature had become an open book, and occult wisdom addressed me from all sides. Soon I could leave the body at will. Other steps followed, and I grew quickly to know many of the minor things reserved by our Father for His aspiring children.

Now a Voice was abiding with me, 1 and as it demanded of me, I answered and knew. It said:

"What is heredity?"

And I answered from my spirit, knowing this thing:

"Heredity is the sum of experience which the souls of men carry from one life through devachan into reincarnation. It is in no way transmitted from parent to child, but its leading trait is attracted by the like trait in the parents. The lesser traits are brought about by cultivation, or else lie dormant, according to environment."

Again the Voice said:

"It is not well; you who have reaped, must now sow. I am the Eternal Spirit in you; obey me. You are now able to stand in my presence; able to see; able to hear; able to speak; conqueror of desire, attainer of self-knowledge. You have seen your soul in its bloom and heard the voice of Peace. Go and read my writing in the Hall of Learning, which is My Works. Read.

"To stand—is to have confidence. To hear—is to have opened the door of your soul. To see is to have attained perception of My Works. To speak—is to have gotten the power of helping others. To have conquered desire is to have acquired control of self. To have self-knowledge is to have come unto Me, where you are able impartially to view the personal man that was yourself. To have seen your soul in its bloom is to have had a momentary glimpse of that transfiguration which shall eventually make you more than a Man.

"Stand aside in the coming battle, and though you fight, do not be the warrior. Look for Me, and let Me fight in you. Obey My orders for battle. Obey Me as if I were yourself. My orders are your desires—for I am yourself, yet infinitely more than you. Look for Me, lest in the fever of battle you pass Me. I will not know you if you don't know Me. If your cry comes to Me, lo! I will fight in you and will fill the void in you. Then you shall be unwearied. Without Me you shall fall; with Me you cannot fall, for I am the Spirit.

"Listen now to the song of life in your heart. Do not say, 'It is not there.' Listen deeper. This song is in every breast; it may be obscure, yet it is there. It is in even the most wretched outcast, for all are children of the Father, which is I. Listen to My Song, for while you are still only a man, I shall not speak continually, and your strength must sometimes be in memory of Me. Inquire now of the Earth-matter; of the air, of the water, the wind; and seek the treasurers of the snow. My Peace I give to you."

At last I saw; I heard; and, my friend who reads this, I speak. My words go to the multiplication by types, and then by myriad copies through the world, to be known by those that "seeing, see and comprehend." And with each copy shall go my love and greater, my eye shall note each hungry seeker for the truth, and, be it in the palace, or cottage, there, too, will I be, not figuratively, but my Spirit.

I had gone into a lonely mountain spot to hear this Voice, and now as I walked, a Being not Man joined me. Its presence was one of light and glory and goodness. With it came Mol Lang, saying:

"This is one of the Beings of Good. Behold, Phylos, our Father's House has many Mansions, and in these are Beings created by Him, and endowed with the ability to choose, like as Man, yet they are not human, never were, nor ever will be. Man shall be perfect when the Spirit of the Father enters him. Then he shall know all things, and be perfect. What is perfection? Absolute harmony with His Infinite Creation. So there may be perfect men; also perfect Beings which are not Men, as this one with us. This is a Good Being. But there is an opposite in the Things of the Creation. There are perfect Evil Beings, which likewise are not, never were, nor ever will be human. What are these? They are in perfect harmony with the laws of their existence, but those laws and their conditions are absolutely opposed to ours, and to good. Because of this, such are hostile to our life and so, evil. Yet this sort seek us not, nor we them. In the scheme of Creation evil and good are evenly balanced. What disturbs harmony with us, therefore, disturbs them by disadjustment of balance. Therefore, they seek not our harm. But Satan, do you know him? He was an Angel of Light, fallen, and come to so much the greater fall in that his height was so lofty. ₁ He is a rebel, and out of harmony.

"Life, Phylos, is limited, for it is but the action in the Mansion of Human environment. But existence is not limited, because this Good Being with us is not of Life, but of Existence. See, It goes. This is Its symbol, and the name of Its Mansion And when your trials are at their worst, draw around you on the ground that figure and stand in it; do not go out, but call on the Father. He will send His Beings to help you. Peace go with you."

Mol Lang disappeared, and I was alone.

Men dread most those insidious diseases, which attack not openly, but at the weakest and most unguarded point. So, in the last, final Trial of the Crisis, I would also be insidiously attacked by the Satanic hosts. Earth has tried me during many lives; now was to come a trial greater than Earth. The attacks of mere human error differ from that of the well-organized, intelligent assault of those to whom evil has become natural, to Lucifer and his fellow-rebels.

Of what nature is this Trial of the Crisis? ₁ It is the deciding whether in the long series of incarnate lives the soul has improved its opportunities for good; if it, in the main, followed the Path which Jesus pointed. If so, it has or will have strength to cope with the best efforts of the Satanic foe. If not, it must fall and die the second death. ₂ His incarnate life made the soul forgiving of all wrongs, forgetful of selfish interests, helpful to those having less light, more gloom, misery and sin to encounter, a self-contained nature? Has it become like the Man of Sorrows, full of faith, hope and charity? Then it has heard the Voice, and will not fail. But if the soul is not like that, then, although it has the prophetic sight, and knows all things, though it has faith sufficient to removing mountains, yet shall it be only the more like Satan, and the worse its fate.

"Go into the Holy Place." ₃

And I, knowing obedience, went into a room built of stone, apart from the house. Then I was in the Presence where I had been as Zailm when Priest Mainin was blasted: It was the Presence of the living Christ. It was Man, yet more, for it was the Spirit; as much more than Man as the sun is more than a glowworm. Then a wondrous Voice said:

"Be not afraid; it is I."

Around that Holy Place were forms of fire. Ink and paper can give little idea of the semblance. Yet look at the picture and try, with my aid, to see. The bolt blazed as a thing of flame, so also the Great Star and all the lesser ones. The Leaf was as life, and the cross the open Way, to the House thereof, while the Ring, I knew, symbolized the Eternal One, endless, beginningless. The Book was the Word, and it blazed with flashing, crimson flame. But over all, a Personified Presence was the Eye, the Eternal, sleepless, omnipotent omniscient Supervisor. So I stood in the presence of the Father, made manifest for me. As I remained, I knew all things of His Works, for the Spirit entered in. But not to stay, for the Trial had still not come to pass.

For weeks I stayed in the Holy Place, and did not come out to eat or drink, for I was wholly sustained by the Spirit. At the day of the Great Peace this Spirit must enter in and I be in It and It be in me forever more. But no guide could exist, no law for the Trial, except my strength of ages. Even the Spirit would be veiled in that ordeal.

Footnotes

377:1 About 112 terrestrial days. The solar you of Venus is 224.7 earthly days.

378:1 Revelations xxii; 14.

379:1 St. John xvi; 13.

381:1 St. Lake xii; 48.

382:1 St. Luke: xx. 35-36.

382:2 Rev.: xx. 15.

382:3 St. Luke: iv, 2.

CHAPTER XI. TEXT: ST. MATTHEW IV

"To be, or not to be: that is the question."
—HAMLET.

That was indeed the question when I arose one morning and knew that the event of the Crisis would that day decide whether or not I had Eternal Life, whether I was for the Spirit, or the Second Death.

I arose and went forth into the wilderness of the mountains, accompanied only by a pet animal, somewhat resembling a fawn, which went with me everywhere. In a woodland mountain meadow I traced with my staff the symbol and it instantly became crimson fire, which leaped and rose and fell, unbroken, continuously. I was inside, the pet animal grazed on the meadow. After making the symbol the Good Being introduced to my knowledge by Mol Lang was with me, and it spoke much to me, and I to It. It said.

"Lo! Your time comes when I must leave you, although I would do for you, but it is so that no being can endure for another the fierce Trial, neither help them in its midst. Yet I say to you, I believe you will win, for have I not known you, lo! many ages? But now is that Trial come for you, when your past, in all days and lives you have ever had, shall rise up and you shall be judged thereby, whether you shall become perfect, and your name be Phylos, or whether you shall fail, and have again all the bitterness of life to go through during ages to come. The Father says through the Spirit, 'Every idle word that men speak, they shall give an account thereof.' How much more then of their actions?"

I listened mutely, for what record was against me? It might be evil, or good, or, worse, that lukewarmness which the Spirit will not entertain, but rather heat or coldness of nature.

"Fear not," said Ovias, "for you have not lived in vain. Do not expect a record written concerning you. For know this: that the principles impressed on the mind by the Christ-Spirit, which outshone Buddha and all the mightiest of the Earth, incarnating in each, and Itself being Son of God, not they, until by union of It they became Sons of God—know that if you have made these principles both warp and woof of your character, you have no need to fear. For this sort of fabric is strong, and was that which Jesus meant when He said, and says forever, Timeless One that He is, "Lo, I am with you always even until the end of the world." Not one individual act shall be brought forth to accuse you, but each, all and every greatest thought, and least, and word or deed, in all your many incarnations—these have formed your character. Is that character, then, woven of the woof provided by Christ, and shown forth in the Divine personality of Jesus, and illuminating Buddha, and Zoroaster, Moses, Manu and other Saviors? If that is the cloth, then indeed you shall prevail, though no one sustains your arm. But if not that weaving, lo! You shall fail, and not even I could save you. I go. Be brave, and may the Comforter be in you. Peace."

All that day I stood there and was not weary. Night came. Around the midnight hour, my pet cried out in terror and came leaping toward me. As it came I warded it from the flame, and it stood outside, trembling. But I saw nothing to alarm it, except Mol Lang, who was approaching over the level around me. He did not hesitate, but seemed about to cross the line of fire, as *he* could, but mindful of my perilous position I said:

"Stop! If you are Mol Lang, then come. But if you are only a tempting shape, woe to you if you shall cross that line, for It shall punish you as only an immortal can punish."

He did not come; instead he ceased to appear as Mol Lang, and was another sort. This tempter said:

"If you are proof against me, who so seemed to be your loved teacher that you really did not know, then you are a conqueror over death and sin. I have no power over you, and you are free to enter eternal life, wherein shall no more incarnations occur. I go."

This Shape withdrew, but the Voice in my soul whispered:

"Beware awhile longer."

I stayed on unmolested until I caught myself napping, and knowing this to be the fatigue of the flesh, I regretted that I had not met the Trial in astral form.

"Not so," whispered the Voice, "all your elements, both physical and psychic, must be with you here."

But again I dozed, and quickly aroused myself, for the scene all around me had changed. The mountain meadow was gone, and in place of night seemed day. I gazed, seemingly, on a scene where all the races of men and immortals were gathered under the sweep of my prescient eye. I seemed to have taken over this realm, and a fair, godlike being in appearance was my guide. Yet, in caution, I sheathed myself from head to foot in the flame as in an armor, at which my guide smiled, but said nothing. He took me with the speed of thought, so that we seemed to go from star to star, now crossing vast interstellar spaces, now come on fresh realms. All these realms were inhabited by creatures of human shape, or at least they had human attributes. Before me they all bowed and worshipped, for my guide said to them: "See your master." Otherwise they were all engaged in pursuit of pleasure. The multitude of passions of man on Earth was indulged without fear of penalty. My fair guide said:

"These are souls in whom I created certain passions and appetites, and shall I punish them for indulging, without stint, traits I have given? Now, tell me, why should all creation not have free license to get pleasure as it may? My creatures do. There is no sort of restraint placed by me on their free pursuit of carnal things, lusts, appetites. See, they are happy! For a time I am giving you control of them. Through indulgence of their passions they create a sort of vital magnetism, and as their present ruler, it thrills you like new wine."

As my guide said, the sight and sensing of all this license did thrill me ecstatically, and was affecting me with a delirious, carnal joy. I put it away and refused to feel. At that, the beautiful Being said:

"Oh! You are blind! Behold, you shall have these realms for your own, and have absolute authority, so your word shall be life or death to these people, if you wish. Here, too, into this eternal joy, you may bring Phyris, and lo! You shall do your will with her forever, and hers, and no penalty be exacted. Will you take this gift of supremacy? It is free; I ask no return for it all. Only take it."

Oh! Where was my knowledge, gained from the many lives, and from the Voice? Gone! Gone, or else I would have known at once not to accept the alluring gift. I was offered all this for free, thereby violating the divine law, which never allows something for nothing. But I gathered my armor around me, in case this Being, who seemed so fair and good, was not so, and if not good, its touch might be fatal. Then I said:

"It must be that you are clothed in the uniform of heaven to serve Satan better. Demon, you offer that which subordinates all other beings in these realms to my will. This realm is governed by pleasure, passion, appetite, lust, all selfish; and no penalty set upon wild license. These carnalities would conquer me, too, if I accepted; me, who is instead about to become immortal, more than Man, karma-less. These are selfish. Pleasure so gotten is the essence of selfishness. Truly, you must be the creator of it all, since it is selfish. It is yours. It could be mine? Yes, but only because you would reign over me. I am not now your subject; nor will I ever be. Only the Unknown God is my Master. Get away from here, behind me!"

The scene slowly faded, like mist in the sunlight. There came a lull, and I hoped the battle was over, for I was weary. But I stood on the meadow again, with the fire leaping, quivering in crimson pulses around the lines. Nothing could break that guardian flame, for it was a symbol of the perfect state of being of another, but nonhuman, race. Only perfection could avail against it. Perfection of good might; so, too, perfection of evil might; but the latter had not yet come against it. I even doubted the existence of any perfection of evil. What offer, after all, had been made but of the things which were mine by reason of the divine Sonship? God gives his children control over each other for good, and for evil also, through mental influence. What more absolute authority is there than love, exercised as He hath ordained. None. While I reflected, a soft and lovely vision came, and lo, Phyris stood before me.

"Are you Phyris?" I asked.

"Could anyone but Phyris disregard the flame around you?" she replied, penetrating the barrier, and sinking by my side. This seemed to be true, for Ovias was a perfect being of Its own condition. Only perfection can stand with perfection. At last I heard her sigh softly, sadly. Her eyes brimmed with tears.

"Why this sorrow, Phyris?"

"Phylos, you ask? I reply. Because of my confession to make. I, too, am on trial as you are. A sad story of sin is mine. Woe is me if you should reject me for it." She hesitated.

"Speak," I answered, apprehensively.

"This, then. In a long ago Poseid day, when I had a personality called Anzimee, and you had one called Zailm, you know the day? Aye, and with sorrow even yet! When you had gone in your vailx, fleeing from the memory of Lolix, I sorrowed intensely. And I did not know your location then. When you did not return, crazed, I went to Mainin the Incalix. He marveled at my frenzy; then said:

"'Do you love Zailm, Rainu?'

"'As my own soul, Incalix.'

"'I marvel at that. But never mind. Help you to find him? What if I love you, I who am a vowed celibate? What if, in my ability, I say Zailm shall no more come back?'

"Then, Phylos, I begged for you as for my own life! I implored his mercy. At last the stern lines of his face relaxed, and he kindly said: 'I would not keep you apart; I was only testing your love for him. Yet my aid must receive compensation. Not money, nor jewels, nor power; these have I in abundance. Only one thing you can give will I have;

listen: in other days, when I came to knowledge of Nature's deeper secrets, I was curious to experiment, and I sought the aid, all confident of my power to subdue my servant, of the host of Satan, one demon. But I overestimated my power and I was subdued, a victim. So one day in the future my soul must be forfeited to Lucifer to pay my debt and its ever growing size. There is only one way I can prevent this, by delivering another, although less experienced soul, in place of mine. Before this night a maiden and her lover will seek me at the hour of worship, that I may solemnize their marriage already long announced. But I shall be gone, purposely. You will be there, and except for you, only those two. Now, they are weak, but have never sinned.

"Their natures incline to error. All I ask of you is that when they ask for me, tell them I am gone, but say, 'You have come here to be wed?' then smile and say, again, 'Only the simple folk make their matings public; the wise are never wedded, yet are wedded in truth.' Say no more. If they take that mild hint, they will sin, and lose their souls, but I, the great Incalix, shall be saved. I will in any event bring Zailm to you again, for perhaps your hint will not be acted upon.'

"Mainin ceased speaking. I recoiled in horror. Yet even as I was about to refuse, he said, 'Remember, only you can save Zailm.'

"I thought him a fiend. Then I thought it is only natural for him to wish to save his own soul, even at another's cost. And oh! I so desired the return of my Zailm! Tearfully bobbing, my soul whispering the wrong of it, but my heart pleading me to be blind for that once to wrong or right, I yielded and said, 'Even as you require, so will I do.'

"I did so. But false to Incal, Mainin was false to me, and he did not bring Zailm back. When Rai Gwauxln told me of Zailm's death, I, too, died of shame and a broken heart. The man and woman took my hint, and died after years of well-concealed, terrible crime. But I Phylos? In my consent to Mainin's will, I sold my soul to the Arch Fiend, Mainin's master. So my life is forfeit unless I can be helped. Forfeit, though I know much, and hard as I have tried to do right and atone, all in vain! Yet, my twin soul, you are able to save me. If you do not save me, then the Eternal Law shall cause me to die the second death. My soul will be annihilated, my Spirit, which was unable to unite with my soul, shall go back to the Source, our Father. And then, being a soul, but your Spirit also my Spirit, you must also perish. Save yourself then as well as me."

"How?" I asked, soul-sick to the depths, and suffering such intensity of misery as almost of itself to cut off my life. Sick, because I felt Phyris, my other self, my pure angel, to be in mortal danger, herself in a fatal mire, and threatened with soul death. And because she was, I was also, for our Spirit was the same.

"How?" I asked again, whispered.

"This way! The man whom, as Anzimee, I led astray, has incarnated several times since then, each time worse and worse, until now, a man on Earth, he is about to confront a temptation which, if he fall, will aim his course from that time forever for evil, and the final death of his soul. If he does not yield now, he may or may not at last escape, but the delay will put him beyond use to us, and we shall surely die, whether he does or not. Aye! We shall if you do not act now. If his soul is now made forfeit, we shall surely escape; so says Mainin, who is blasted and in outer darkness, yet owns me; it is the only, though slender hope. O Phylos, think! Think!! On the one hand eternal life, brightness, and a chance to atone for all our sins, perhaps even rescue this man at last, but on the other, death, blasting into outer darkness and eternal demonhood."

In the calm night she stood before me and begged me to act for her, her hands clasped, her eyes streaming, her agony fearful to see. Act for her whom I loved better than life, and for myself; save our lives that all might be well. How? By using my occult power to whisper to a man, already sin-sodden, on a distant planet, a man who might not conquer his temper even though I withheld my influence. Do what? Influence him to sign his name as Governor of a great state to a denial of pardon to two men about to die for murder. Yet they were innocent. I knew it; the Governor knew it, because he had already sinned horribly in using his office, money and power to weave a net of circumstantial evidence which would hang his two enemies for a murder committed by his own hand. He would, in an hour more, sign or not sign the fateful paper, for at the last his courage was faltering. All I needed to do was to occultly encourage him. Already so sinful, was it likely he would ever turn from evil ways to good? Barely possible. But I was to psychologically influence him to pass this opportunity and complete his double murder, in order to save Phyris, whom I so loved, whose Spirit was my Spirit, whose soul's destruction meant my soul's destruction also. It was so easy to do!

All crimes are easy. But while the agony of despair numbed me, a ray of hope came, and the question arose, would this act save us? Had not God said, "Thou shalt not kill"; and would not the double murder be on me as much as on the Governor? Then I arose, and said, calmly,— Oh! how frightfully, despairingly calm!

"Lo, then. If we shall both die into outer darkness, still I will never do this thing. You, who are more precious than my own life, must not ask this! Says not our Father: 'Whoever does evil, of him will be exacted the penalty, of some thirty, some sixty, some one hundredfold'? And if I, we, shall consign a soul to darkness, do you think, oh! my spirit mate, that we shall not the more surely go there ourselves? Then, although these words seal your death, and mine, still I will refuse to sin. I will not do your will. I have not sinned so much that I cannot put forth my hand and, by the aid of the Christ-Spirit, cut off the progress of your sin, and you may go back to the time, the place, where your soul was before your error, and be reborn on Earth so often as is needed to expunge and atone this sinful act. And I will wait for you where my soul has now arrived, during the years, though they be tens of thousands, until pure, you may rejoin me. I will guide you, so that you will sin no more during the atonement. Aye, except that I must stay here to guide you, I would go again into the life of Earth with you; but I must stay here so that my light remains clear. All this I will do, or if atonement for someone else was a possibility in the Universe, I would go for you, and let you stay. But condemn the man on Earth, and ourselves with him, no! I cannot sin in this way."

With a convulsive shudder, and a despair in her starry eyes that struck me so that I cried aloud to God in my agony, Phyris said in a mournful wail, as of a lost soul:

"O Phylos, think well; for it might be that you are protectively surrounded with that sort of righteousness that makes the Angels weep and the Fiend smile!"

"Phyris, beloved, I have spoken! I will not change it."

She moved away with her hands covering her agonized face, sobbing in her intensity of despair. When she came to the fire she said:

"Phylos, I could enter. My power is gone, and I cannot go out; put it aside."

I looked from where I lay, almost dying in my pain of an immortal hurt, and found that I also was too weak to lower the barrier. Then I looked within my being, and I saw that no more was the Light of the Spirit within me, but it was gone. And then I knew what that awful appeal of Jesus of Nazareth meant, that He, too, in the fearful strain of his Human trial of the Crisis had beheld the Spirit in Him wane, when He cried out: "Eloi, Eloi, Lama Sabacthani." Like Him I cried out to the Father, and in that instant the Light returned, and with a roll as of mighty thunder the darkness broke, and the night which had been around me fled, so I saw that the sun was high in the heavens, and I alone had been in a local gloom. The flame paled, and "Phyris" knelt before me and implored mercy. Then I knew that Phyris had not been near. I knew that God the Father was entered in me to dwell forever, and that the perfection of evil had failed in its last, most subtle, horrible and insidious attack, its last attempt to open the door to downwardness for me. My strength out of all the lives had withstood, and, all fainting, I was come unto Christ. All the weary way of woe I had journeyed, atoning as I came. And now my karma I had blotted out, and in me was Life Everlasting. Gloria in Excelsis! Laus Deo! The song I heard was the song of the starry hosts of God.

Then the Voice spoke: "Your trial is over; I am well pleased. It is written in sacred Scripture, 'You must be born again, of water and of the Spirit.' Even so, you have been born now. Of water, which is the world of matter. And of the Spirit, which is I entered in. But the death of

428

the carnal body, and rebirth in the new, is but night after day, and day after night. To these successive days and nights of the soul, that Scripture refers not. You have been born in the Earth many times, and each time your carnal body has died. But the rebirth was not that rebirth of the waters and of me. Those incarnations only prepared you to come out of the waters of materiality for Me. But now you are born of that and of Me, and have become a Son of Light, and at one with the All-Father, and like unto the Nazarene. Carry My Word to all men, that all may come likewise to Me who will, even as you, following the first Man who came to Me, have yourself also come."

Now when I saw that Phyris had come, I knew that it was truly she. She, too, had had her Trial, and equal temptations had been offered her, and been withstood, ninety centuries of years before, however. How do you say: "I thought twin souls must fight the final fight together, and now you say nine thousand years were between?" Behold, friend, time is but the measure of energy exerted. We worked the same work, so we were together. Is Paul more saved than the latest restored soul? Yet Paul knew Jesus Christ near two thousand years earlier. It had seemed to us both that the Great Crisis had occupied centuries. To us, as we stood clasping each other, a glorious vision came, and the Voice spoke, saying:

"Behold. Look back over the mighty past. And when you have done so, look on Earth, and see how there to effect the work of giving the people of Earth your life history. That shall take but a moment for you, but that moment shall seem like years to your agents on Earth. Then again, look; I am your Voice and your Spirit. Your souls shall unite. Behold, you shall now hereafter have two bodies no more, but only one, and it will be your Spirit body. Mine, for without Me you are nothing. Peace is yours forevermore."

Friend, you may have trouble in understanding this strange union. Yet, ponder it deeply, for it is to be your experience someday if you are true to your Savior and follow Him, drinking of the cup which He drank, and triumphing at the Critical Ordeal.

End of Book Second

BOOK THE THIRD

Chapter I. Ye Shall Reap As Ye Have Sown.

The Perception

Suppose the struggle had proven me wanting, and the verdict had been, "Mene Mene Tekel Upharsin"? Then my—our—fate would have been that of Mainin of Caiphul. To me who knows the dread meaning of this fate, it is more utterly frightful to contemplate than it can be to you. It means being a brother to devils, and subjection to Satan, who could so cunningly, awfully tempt as we were tempted, and when successful, make a servant of the victim, forever to pile up fresh karma. And such karma as Satan's service makes is worse in a moment than the wickedest man could pile up in a long lifetime. It means such servitude until— when? Forever? Until the end of material things. Then, when the heavens are rolled as a scroll and melt in fervent heat, Satan (Lucifer) shall, with his minions, be cast into that lake of fire which is the second death: which means that the force, the energy of the rebels, that which has made them distinct, potent souls through all the past, shall become depersonalized, and dis-individualized, cast into the sum of the Fire of Elements, which form the forces of Nature, the winds, odic and magnetic and electric forces.

But there is no annihilation, there is no death, though there is such a change as constitutes the destruction of the union between soul and Spirit, the return of the first to the great impersonal Vis Natura, the re-

430

turn of the other to Him who created life. Then, after millions of years, the Father will gather the glowingly hot elements into nebulae, star-plasm, worlds, suns, systems, and a "new heaven and a new earth" shall come forth. Then the depersonalized rebel host will begin to reincarnate in protoplasmic life, and from there evolutionize up, up, up along the myriad incarnations until, after an eternity of matter, they come once more to human conditions, to another Crisis, to win or fail, and either, like Sisyphus, run again the weary course, or else inherit hard-won entrance to unconditional being. There is not, nor can there be, any death of the Spirit, but of the individuality only. Study this well, my friend, for such is the fate of evildoers who sell to Satan, because such is Satan's portion.

Our Father has provided a Way. It is the sharp, knife-edge Path, on which all things so evenly balance that there is turning neither to the right nor left, but only a steady, even pursuit of the Path, wherein all who travel that way contain themselves in all things, in eating and drinking, in sleeping and all those things which cause the cares of this world. Those who shall be accounted worthy, without further incarnation, to obtain the resurrection from the body of materiality neither marry nor are given in marriage, but must receive the Kingdom of God even as if still little children. Yet whoever does not do so, it shall not be eternally counted against them, but only till another incarnation. It must be that the things of sensation which are an offense to the Spirit occur, but karmic woe will stay with the offender until he finds the Path and travels upon it. Hear, if hearing and understanding are in you, for these are the words of the Master.

———————

CHAPTER II. JOB xxxviii:7

Contemplating the victory in us of the Father, we chanted a song in answer to that of the Sons of God who were our fellows. Perfect at last, in rapport with all the law fulfilled, karma-less, immortal, beside Jesus, no more need to incarnate. Life was ended, but Being had just commenced. Paradoxical? In all the eons of time we had Life, but Being, which has no beginning, neither any end, and is not under the dominion of Time, every ego has forever from the Father. But Life has beginning, so also it must have end; it has an end. If its conditions are strong enough to chain someone, then the soul is diverted from its ego to the tracks of Life, and is then the recipient of death. Only if a soul does not forfeit Life its hold on Being then its ego shall not die. Sin is the error of turning from Being to Life, and thus to the shadow of death. The soul that sins and does not turn away from finite life and its conditions shall die.

Down all the realms of light echoed the jubilant expressions of praise, as when the "Morning stars sang together and the Sons of God shouted for joy."

CHAPTER III. "Fair forms and hoary seers of ages put, an in one mighty sepulcher."

For a little while yet Phyris and I were not wholly one entity. But we had come to a point of remembering. With arms clasping each other, we walked slowly onward, till by the banks of the babbling brook we seated ourselves. Then I said:

"My twin, let us scan the past; let us draw aside the curtain of by-gone ages, and see the record of the Book of Life, mirror of all events, sights, sounds, shapes, all things. We can do this, because we are karma-less, deathless, and are at one with the Father of Being, seeing, knowing as he knows, because He is in us."

We pondered the scenes of our Atlantean life, lives, and I saw ill-fated, sweet Princess Lolix, to whom I had been her ideal. Where had her sad soul gone when Mainin petrified its clay? In the imperishable record we saw where her lifeline crossed ours. In her Poseid devachan she had found her dream of life seemingly realized. Reborn into activity, again her lifeline crossed mine, her heritage pursued her, and she conquered it, for Lolix's individuality was Elizabeth's (my wife). Her crime in Poseid was atoned for, and so, too, was mine. Karma was fulfilled there. 1

Man's course upward to God is so blind, so untaught, instinctively like the sunward turning vine. I had so confidently, in the Sagum, taken an irrevocable step, except for Mendocus; and then had fallen again into blind darkness, despair, but instinctively true to law and to Elizabeth, the object of my efforts—so upward, till at last I had gained the immortal heights. So had my alter ago, Phyris. Down below were the deserts of life, and fair appearing fruits, apples of Sodom. These ashes are good, for they cause the soul to test the heights.

Poseid, and all the lives, had given us a large share of gall fruit, but our errors required it, and Karma is a sure paymaster.

Sin created karma and karma had exacted pay. Thus had I, for I am not relating Phyris' history, given up hopes, happiness, as one gives his open veins in the Sahara to quench the thirst of his friend. ₂By this neglect of duty I had lost my life and found it again. Karma, as the long record showed, was not always requiring pay; for every good act I had ever done I saw that I had been fully paid in kind my every jot. These were the good judgments and endowments of life. There is no accident in life; it is possible that a man may die "by accident" and no man could be sure whether the coming night might not find the earth dropping into, or else away from, the sun; or, seeing the sun set, could feel sure it would rise again. All things, small or great, are ordered. Not always from any preexistent incarnation; sometimes from one's last year's or yesterday's action the fruit springs. In short, I, we, saw that the lesson of life was, "whatsoever a man sows, that shall he also reap," cause and effect. There are those who will make a trivial argument, contending that "accident does exist, and all is not order." I do not argue, for "they that have ears to hear" will understand. One cannot see over a mountain range unless he stands on a taller peak. To the greater vision, accident is but an arc of design, and disorder is but an arc of order.

Footnotes

397:1 St. Matthew v: 17-18.

397:2 St. John xv: 13.

CHAPTER IV. THE FALL OF ATLANTIS

Again we looked over Atlantis, and saw many other things. The Zailm time possessed a peculiar interest. I saw that dim, distant past, a past old in the earth and ancient when Earth was still a babe in the cradle of time. Atlantis, foremost of the prehistoric races, numbering at home in Poseid, and abroad in the colonies, almost three hundred millions of souls; Atlantis, known through the olden earth as "Atlantis, Queen of the Seas," and her people as "Children of Incal," i. e., "Of the Sun," and as the "Sons of God." How the mighty are fallen! For now I behold her ancient site as part of the bed of the restless sea, covered with ocean ooze and slime, and to be known as the haunt of man only through the clear vision of the perfected eyes which scan astral records. Again the scene was presented so that we saw it as the eyes of my poor, weak, and pitifully mortal personality of Zailm had seen it.

There was stately Caiphul, the Royal; and there, far away, and not so stately, Marzeus, its towers and turrets and chimneystacks and lofty buildings marking where had stood the greatest of Atlantean manufacturing centers, where the machine shops and the mills had been which supplied Poseid with vailx, and naims, and all sorts of machines and instruments; with the products of the looms, the cereals and endless articles of use, and of art.

Over a million artisans there by day, but by night scarce fifty thousand, all gone by car or vailx to their homes anywhere from fifty to a hundred miles away, a few minutes' ride. And all this to perish because

435

of man's iniquity, a few short hundreds of years later. Here and there I caught glimpses of canals, distributing either natural rivers or streams, or the product of aqua-aerial generators, such as Zailm had a small model of in his last days in Umaur. We saw the world as Zailm saw it: Suern, with its millions of people; Necropan, with its ninety-odd millions; Europe, then a barbarian land, only about one-sixth its present area; and Asia, not so large in extent then as now, but containing over a half million of souls. But the sparkling, brilliant civilization which was more than the equal of even proud today, that was glorious Atlantis! Eleven hundred millions of people, civilized or only semi-civilized, and as many more scattered over the continent and islands of the seas who were utter barbarians—such was the world of Zailm, generally viewed. The numbers of the human race, and especially their increase during several generations, has appalled the pessimists. But the greatest of pessimists, Malthus, need have felt no alarm had he only known. Because:

"The world goes up and the world goes down, And the sunshine follows the rain."

There are a varying number of people always in the world; now more, now less; for as a soul comes to Earth (having been in devachan) a soul passes from Earth into devachan. But now two come while one goes, or two go while one comes, relatively. Which is why the world is apparently intruding upon the sources of supply, or again why the supply of all things exceeds demand. But only a fixed number of Human Rays went forth from the Father, and only so many have Life, or ever will have. But these come and go as the tides ebb and flow, now on Earth, now in Heaven. Malthusians need not fear.

Zailm had been my personality.

Thirty centuries later, approximately, we saw this land again. But how it had changed. Caiphul had lost something now. Not the tangible matter visible to earthly men — no, this was not gone. But the men we saw were not the high, lofty, noble-souled men known to Zailm and to Anzimee. And when manhood suffers decadence, degradation, all nature with which he has to do also sensibly alters for the worse. Marzeus, the city of manufacturing arts, was no more; it had gone down before corruption. Art had not suffered so much as had science. But the science which drew upon the mysterious forces of Nature, the "navaz"— this had so far disappeared that airships were forgotten, or at most were semi-mythical history. So were many other instruments which Zailm had known—the naima, those wonderful, wireless, combined telephonic and photographic image transmitters. And the vocaligrapha, the clairvoyant instruments and the water-generators, all were lost in the night of time. But the men of the twentieth century shall find them all again. Twenty-eight decades of centuries has now continued here, and soon it shall be proclaimed,

"The evening and the morning are the seventh day." You who hear all my message are the men and the women of this new day, and shall inherit all things from our Father forever. And the full eventide of that day which comes shall behold you caught up "into the heavens" to escape the end of all things, when the earth also, and the works that are contained in it, shall be burned up. 1

But I should deal with the past, not with the future. The seeds of corruption sown in the hearts of men by the Evil One, master over Mainin, germinated and thrived, and then began, some centuries after the time of Gwauxln and Zailm, a long, steadily downward course which weakened the self-respect, manhood and womanhood of Poseid, a loss revealed in countless ways, culminating in national depravity and ruin.

It was upon one of these phases of ruin that we gazed next. We saw a woman upon whose face rested a light almost divine in the power of its transfiguring beauty. Her slight figure seemed not so much of Earth as of Heaven. The loose robe of gray which she wore fluttered in the breeze, the long tresses of brown hair, unrestrained, swept back from the glorious face, on which sat pity and despair, yet mingled with a wonderful radiance of appealing, entreating, agonized hope that some might hear and turn away from the course they were following. Her appeal assumed that most perilous form, for the champion, which an appeal can assume, that of sharp denunciation. She denounced the hideous system of blood-sacrifice in religion as being in diametrical opposition to right, to God, to man, and was responsible for the corruption of the people. At this, the priests among the crowd uttered hoarse cries of rage. In a voice, the astral record of which still rings, and will forever, for those who have ears to hear such psychic tones, she cried, from her high place on the pedestal of the monument, twenty feet from the ground and the upturned faces below:

"Oh, you! Do you think that Incal will accept the blood of innocent animals for your crimes? Whoever says this does lie! Incal, God, will never take the blood of anything, nor any symbol of any sort which places an innocent in a guilty one's stead! And the Incalithlon, and the Holy Seat, and the Maxin Light are dishonored whenever a priest lays an animal on the Teo Stone, and strikes a knife to its heart, tears it out and tosses it as sacrifice into the Unfed Light. Yes, the Unfed Light does truly destroy it instantly. But do you think that because of this that merciful Incal is pleased? O you brood of vipers, you priests that are charlatans and sorcerers?"

An angry Incali stooped as she uttered this, and picked up a jagged bit of stoneware. In front of him was a litter borne by sad-faced slaves. On this, reclining amidst soft silken cushions, was a woman of dreamy beauty, the very impersonation of shameless abandon. In the warm, tropical atmosphere she lay, without any covering, except that the heavy waves of the hair of her beautiful, if wicked, head partially concealed her nakedness. The shameless sight did not attract notice because of its shamelessness; the only attention bestowed by the dense and wrathful crowd around her was that of sensual admiration from one or another. Such sights were all too common in these last days of Atlantis. Seeing the priest pick up the shard, this woman said:

"What will you do with it?"

"Nothing," answered the priest.

"Nothing, indeed! I know you would throw it at yonder blasphemer, if you had the courage!"

"I do not lack the courage," was the sullen reply.

A voice in the surging crowd now called out that the blasphemer of religion ought to be sacrificed on the Teo Stone, and her heart given to the Maxin. "Listen to that! The people and the Incali would be with you," said the lascivious woman. "Throw the piece, and see if maybe you might not reach the target."

The ecclesiastic raised his hand back, and poised the missile, while the crowd nearest him gazed with eager eyes. Then the cruel bit of pottery hurtled through the air towards the fair speaker overhead. Her temple was exposed, and the missile she might have avoided had she realized it was coming, struck full on the dainty mark. With a cry of pain she threw up her hands, reeled, and then fell outwards, down-wards, the twenty feet to the hard pavement below. The crowd, which had hushed an instant, now uttered fierce growls, and those nearest ran to the victim of the coward priest. Several of the priestly caste picked the poor body up, and carrying it by the feet, arms and hair, quite as if the assault had been prearranged, instead of being the work of one miserable fiend, started off to the Incalithlon, whose vast pyramid loomed not far away.

"See!" said Phyris, "the first human sacrifice in Caiphul! Me, even me, they slew, for trying to stem the tide of depravity and ecclesiastical criminality. I repeated to them the prophecy of the Maxin, and they did not listen, but slew me. For that woman was my personality when I reincarnated, three thousand years after you, as Zailm, left me, as Anzimee."

With a strange delight in crime, the priests, scarcely pausing an instant, placed the still unconscious victim on the Teo. Then the chief priest, still called the Incalix, stepped from the Holy Seat, as it once had truly been. By the side of the victim he stopped and profaned not God, but Man, by a prayer to God; for no man can injure God except through injuring Man. Then he threw open the gray robe and bared the white breast. Swiftly he raised aloft the keen edged knife, then struck. A shudder shook the reviving victim, who was close to recovering consciousness. The murderer then tore out the quivering heart and cast it into the Unfed Light, where it disappeared and made no sign. Then the flesh was divided piecemeal amongst the murderous crowd, together with the bloodstained garments. But most of the blood had run into a depression in the Teo, made for sacrificial blood. To this the priests added liquor, and in a maddened frenzy heartily drank the mixture from golden goblets. The scene was sickening, and I felt my very being revolt! And that poor murdered woman, a virgin—who had given her life to rescue her nation from sin—that was she, who had long centuries before been Anzimee, and now was Phyris, part of myself, and I part of her being, for our Spirit was one reunited. I could forgive the crime I looked back upon, for the criminals knew not what they did. And they have suffered for it, and shall still suffer, for it is their karma. When Death, the conqueror of all mortals, garnered his harvest in Atlantis, these souls, which had sown sin and grown tares, were reaped by the Great Reaper, and the tares were sown with the good wheat when next those souls reincarnated. And they have had to glean and uproot as they could, and so must continue to tear up the evil weeds till every one be uprooted. Then they will have atoned unto God. There is time enough, lives enough, but O friends, none to waste!

After this human sacrifice the thirst for blood which the people manifested became unappeasable. They demanded the life of the priest who struck down the woman, for they were not yet accustomed to the rights the Incali had so newly decreed without proper authority, those of human sacrifice. They claimed that he had really murdered the woman, that they were unprepared to go so far, that therefore he who threw the missile must die. The tumult became so violent, and insurrection seemed so imminent, that the wretched priest was dragged out and offered by his fellows as the woman had been. But now the denouement came. When the high priest turned to cast the heart of the last victim into the Maxin, he staggered as if struck, his hand fell by his side, the heart dropped on the pavement, and the stricken man fell forward unconscious! The tall taper of the Unfed Light was gone; the Maxin book was gone! In its place stood a human form, that of a Son of the Solitude. In his left hand was a sword, in his right a pen.

"Behold, the day of destruction is at hand which was foretold ages ago! Atlantis shall now be no more seen by the sun in his whole course for the sea shall swallow you all! Pay attention!"

The Secrets Of Mount Shasta And A Dweller On Two Planets

Then the dread apparition vanished. But the Unfed Light did not return. The people fled, shrieking, leaving the priest who had fainted lying on the floor. It was just as well, for when those willing to take the risk came into the Incalithlon many days later, he still lay as he fell, for he was dead. In his greater knowledge, for although he was wicked he was still the chief, he knew, sorcerer that he was, that there really was a power of right which was destined to bring the corruption of Poseid low and uproot the hideous mockery of sin enslaving the nation. And in his knowledge his soul had gone forth from his body in desperate fear, to return no more.

But the stupid sensuality of the masses, finding that after a few years nothing terrible occurred, gradually lapsed till they were worse than before, for human sacrifices became common, lust, gluttony and drunkenness ran riot, and the moral night's deep darkness closed in yet more blackly.

One man and his family who lived apart did not partake of the general wickedness. True, he and his mate, like the ordinary people about him, were not married, save as the higher animals monogamize. Nor were his sons and their wives any better. But blood sacrifice neither he nor they would do. And when the monarch proclaimed that all must worship according to the new standard, and sacrifice babes and women, these men, giants in stature, and far superior, any one of them, to a dozen of the corrupt slaves of the Rai, refused to obey the mandate. Fruits and treasure they offered, but not blood. In his seclusion the father, Nepth, had a revelation. It came from the Sons of the Solitude, who had in no way changed from the ancient high standard, but Nepth thought it direct from God. The revelation was but a repetition of the prophecy of doom, but the knowledge of that prophecy having been neglected for centuries, bore to Nepth all the force of a new revelation. So he came to know of the coming destruction of Atlantis, he and his sons. And they considered how to escape. Vailx were unknown. Nepth and his sons were unskilled builders. But they received instructions from the befriending Sons of the Solitude, who came to them in astral shape. And so these better men of Atlantis began to build a great vessel. It was clumsy, but secure, and had room to receive several of all kinds of useful animals found in Atlantis, and to simple ignorant Nepth these constituted every animal on earth, for he knew nothing of other lands across the seas, scarcely knew of the provinces in Incalia or Umaur, for in these last days communication was not closely kept up. His neighbors and friends jeered and reviled him as a blasphemer, and he and his sons as crazy men. But the years lapsed, and the great ark of refuge grew, until one day it was complete. Then Nepth and his sons provided it with ample supplies, and they took the animals from the pens in which they had been placed after they had captured them in years past. Indeed, most of these animals had been born in captivity and were tame, so long had Nepth carried on all works together, not knowing just when the dread prophecy was to be fulfilled. The final preparations were none too soon completed. Only a few days elapsed before the earth shook and trembled in a frightful manner. Rivers left their beds, or sank through vast crevices in the earth; mountains shook till they were left as hills, and "Bowed their tall heads to the plain."

A narrow crack opened close by the vessel of refuge, and the river which, half a mile wide, had flowed past to the ocean, fifty miles away, now poured with a mighty roar into the opening. For three days this awful turmoil continued. A man came, begging to be let in. But Nepth said: "No, you would never believe in other days. I told you then this land would sink under the seas, and you abused me verbally. Now go your way and tell everyone you meet that 'Nepth spoke truly.'"

Three days of horror, and three nights. Death stalked through the land, for the mountains fell on the plains and floods swept unrestrained. But the worst was to come. On the morning of the fourth day it seemed as if the rains of heaven would drown all, yet the thundering and turmoil was not lessened. The gates of heaven and of the great deep were yet to be broken, and the continent, yea, much also of the world to be drowned. The people not yet destroyed were myriad, and were gathered in the high places. Suddenly it seemed as if the foundations of the world were withdrawn, for by one frightful, universal motion the lands left unflooded began to sink. With never a pause to the hideous, sickening sensation, all things sank, down, down, down—one, two, a dozen feet! Then a period of rest. The rains, which came in sheets, instead of drops; the wild blasts of furious wind; the sinking motion, all ceased while men might count a score. One score, two, three, yet no resumption. The wretched people, hidden in such poor shelter as they could find and dared avail themselves of, began to breathe easier—perhaps the fearful ruin had at last stopped! But, no! A slight tremble, scarcely noticeable after the mad three days, and then with one swift leap down to death the great continent of Atlantis sank as a stone sinks in water! Not a mere dozen feet, nor even a hundred, but almost a mile it sunk in one horrible bound!

Nepth? In the middle of the third day his vessel of refuge had floated to the ocean on an outgoing rush of the floods, and there the winds had carried him until, when Atlantis sped down to death, he and his storm-beaten ark were a couple of hundred miles away. A very few other people had been similarly forced seawards, and these, after weary weeks, at last came around the southern promontory of Africa, and drifted northeasterly, to land on the west coast of Umaur. Here, too, the destruction had left but a few miserable survivors. But the few hundreds thus left founded the race which, repopulating that land, was found by Pizarro after many centuries upon centuries had elapsed. And a few thus became many. They would not permit blood sacrifice, but yet, like Nepth, offered fruits to Incal, and retained the name, slightly modified, so as to be Inca, a name bestowed upon their rulers. A few survivors landed further north, and repopulated the land conquered by Cortez, the Spaniard, a few short centuries ago. But these did not heed the lesson, for no sooner were they landed on the desolated shores than they slew a woman as a thanksgiving for their escape. But Nepth? For many days his vessel drifted over the silent seas, with only the ceaseless roar of rain upon the roof to break the stillness. At last the vessel grounded. He did not know where he was, for he was an ignorant man. But the face of things was completely changed. When at last he descended, and let loose his living freight, though he knew it not, he was in Asia. This land had not suffered as other lands, but still the floods had covered all the western part of Asia. The eastern portions, and what there was of Europe and America, had not remained inundated after the quick subsidence of the enormous tidal-wave, which, thirteen hundred feet in height, swept outward from Atlantis' site upon the recoil of the engulfing ocean. Thus the scene closed for us; the great deluge was over.

Then Phyris and I turned to other phases of the mysterious past. These, though not less interesting, may not enter these pages. Rai Gwauxln had come to be Mendocus, while Rai Ernon of Suern was with us now, as Mol Lang. Sohma was that Son of the Solitude whom I took on my vailx when I was Zailm, away from Suern. So we saw the interweaving of the life lines. Then we saw the course of the lost soul, Mainin, from remote ages when Atlantis was not known in the earth, a sin-laden man then, until we found him, serving Satan, an outcast from human ranks, blasted from that time by that Son of God, "first fruit of them that (had reincarnated) slept."

Looking, we saw that early Rai of Poseid, him of the Maxin Stone and the Unfed Light, the Lawgiver. We knew him for the Christ, illuminating man then, and later as Buddha, and again over-shining that greater than Buddha, the Nazarene. "Before Abraham was, I am." Whoever the Christ-Spirit enters into and abides in, becomes a Son of God, and an equal with Gautama; but into no one will it enter who does not travel the Path. That mighty One blasted Mainin. Yet we saw that because Mainin had crossed our life then, I was thereby made the instrument of mercy to him by Christ, and that occasion was yet to come. Before the time of Zailm we gazed upon a scene on the great continent of Lemuria, or Lemorus. We saw a great house built of stone, standing on a grassy plain, over which roamed herds of cattle, and queer little horses, having three toes to each foot and high shoulders. Far to the east was a blue mountain range, beyond that a great ocean. But a silvery lake flashed between the large house and mountains.

Within the house were many people, all servants to two people, a woman and her son. Gloom covered all their faces, the gloom of blood. To a chief among subordinates the son gave orders. This slave, grim, ferocious, a very incarnation of cruelty, attracted my notice. His brown skin was dark, his hands claw-like. Only a breechcloth clothed him. Receiving his orders, he disappeared, but soon came again, pushing two handcuffed people, plainly of a different race from anyone else there. One was a youth, lithe, erect, with a rather haughty air, his hair brown, his features symmetrical; that individuality of twenty-three thousand years ago is now Sohma. The other captive was a fair girl, sister to the youth, it seemed. Her beauty was delicate, but voluptuous. The fierce, cruel eyes, gleaming like live coals from under the shaggy brows of the master of the house, lighted with admiration as he saw the girl. His heavy-set figure, his coarse jaw, thick neck, and round, shaven head, all fitted him to be master of the brutish crowd around him. This man extended his hand as if to touch the captive maiden. She shrank away, and drew her figure erect in a queenly scorn.

"Ha! Stubborn as ever!" said the master. "We shall see."

First Sacrifice Of Self For Love Of Another

He nodded to the chief slave, who threw the captive boy on a sort of altar beside him. He bound him. But the victim said firmly: "Sister, do not surrender; die first." Her eyes shone with an awful light of horror.

"Stop his voice," exclaimed the master; and the slave, without reluctance, cut out the poor boy's tongue!

"Beast!" hissed the girl to the master.

"Ha!" he replied, "I will prove that true," and he struck the bared breast of the tongueless lad with his own dagger, and tearing out the heart, threw it at the sister's feet. A goblet of the blood was caught and the master's mother, a priestess, who stood by the block, took it and gazed into it. Then she said:

"The gods say that the girl also must die."

"Do they say so? By all the powers I will not obey," shouted the master. "Not though my troops of war fail, and the King fails!"

"My son," said the priestess, "you may not avoid this sacrifice and live, say the gods."

"No? Then the gods be served. Give me that knife." He felt its keen edge, and then asked, without taking his eyes from the weapon, "Do the gods still say so?"

"They still do," said the priestess.

"Bind the maid," and his orders were obeyed, though the girl had fainted. The executioner laid his ear to her breast; a faint smile relaxed his features, and he said in his soul, "She is dead." He laid his hand on her breast, stood erect and said:

"Accept, you gods, this sacrifice."

The knife glittered overhead for an instant, then the next moment he buried it in his own heart. So had the heart that knew no mercy yielded to love; the stern warrior was dead. The gods must have blood, he thought, but he gave his own. What personality was he, was the girl, dead from horror? Myself! And Phyris!

Footnotes

400:1 II. Peter iii: 10.

CHAPTER V. "MAN'S INHUMANITY TO MAN"

Again the dead past revealed another scene. I saw myself in the person of an ill-fed, ill-treated slave, ever hungry, wretched, too much so to feel resentment. I died hungry, and then had a devachan of seeming realization of my wants. Then again rebirth, and through a karma not to be explained here, the new man had ease, wealth, plenty. But a physical karma pursued, and he was always hungry in the midst of plenty, and lazy when action was necessary. This state caused disease, and as the product of (in his previous life) "man's inhumanity to man," he was afflicted with cancer of the stomach. This killed the ferocious appetite, and the seeker of physical comfort, free of this, set to work to cure himself. Finding he must fail, he sought comfort in religion, and went forth to the wilderness to become a religious hermit. Now, a hermit's life is one of uselessness to mankind. In that lone state my individuality lost opportunities to cultivate moral strength by worldly contact, and behold, after death I came to life again as Zailm, weak enough to sin with Lolix and create then a karma that lasted, with newly gained strength, till only a few years ago, punishing me more bitterly than death, as you know. If Zailm had sorrow, you know he also had joy. So every life-karma is made up of sunshine and shadow. "A tooth for a tooth?" Yes! But also "for a kiss a kiss."

CHAPTER VI. WHY ATLANTIS PERISHED

Looking along the line of life's yesterdays, the reason became apparent why all the wondrous attainments of Poseid had ceased and left no sign, why Atlantis, which metaphorically held aloft the world into the light of science, had sunk beneath the waters and gone down into deep, mysterious caverns, to be hidden in an ignorance greater than that which shadowed Pompeii and Herculaneum from subsequent centuries.

Natural decadence tells the story. As the centuries following the time of the great Rai Gwauxln passed, ten, fifteen, twenty and more, the nation came to a greater glory of mechanics, of science, and of Physical condition than even Gwauxln's time had known. One by one the scholars found that those things which had always been possible only through mechanical gadgets were more easily accomplished by purely psychic means; they learned it was possible to remove themselves from the flesh, and in astral body go wherever they wanted and appear, instant as the electric current, at any distance. They learned that they could perform material actions when they had thus projected themselves. Then the cruder methods, vailx and naim, and all similar things, were allowed to lapse into that semi-forgetfulness of the Suerni; and exactly as they, so the mass of Poseidi depended on the priesthood for all these things. For only the few exalted minds could thus reach out into the deeper nightside of Nature; the many must remain in the lesser places. Inevitably then came corruption of power; the few were masters, and the many had no one to help them, because the master of psychics is invulnerable to the laws of physicality when wielded by men less than he.

Then, indeed, the day came when ripeness was on the land and on the people. The ripe pear cannot keep perfect, but at the heart begins a decay that spreads from core to cortex, and lo, the end. So in Poseid, at the core began the outward-spreading rot. That core was the education of the people. Whenever earth's nations shall cease to educate the coming generation, decay shall begin for the people. In Poseid the few had attained such exalted knowledge of natural forces that the many could not hope to overtake them. Then, discontented with the comparatively poor education they had, they permitted all its marvels to wane. Thus, before thirty centuries after Gwauxln, the Poseid race was as Suern, but more corrupt, and lust, appetite, passion and power had laid a fatal hold on the proudest people the earth has ever known. How little do you realize when you read in Hebrew Scriptures of the destruction of the cities of the Plain that it is the account of the doom of Marzeus and Terna, destroyed by the Navaz forces they had forgotten how to control That destruction heralded that of the continent, nine centuries later. Ah, you! Poseid rose to an altitude which the wildest dreams of science have not predicted for the modern world; arose, flourished and decayed, in the fullness of cyclic times. And America is Poseid come again, reincarnated, and shall see its scientific people repeat, but on a higher plane, the attainments of Atlantis. As the centuries pass it shall see those souls return in sequence and be made flesh, souls which in Atlantis made that land proud, prouder, proudest. But it shall do even more, for America has developed that soul-element which, when her people were Poseidi, was first faintly traced. So, though repeating, it shall do more—it shall have all Atlantis' marvels wedded to the glorious soul foreseen for mankind by Him of Nazareth. It shall flourish so, and then, in the fullness of its time, decay. But that shall not be for four and a half centurial decades.

CHAPTER VII. THE TRANSFIGURATION

I might give many more life scenes. Let these suffice. Turn now to our present.

The reunion of the semi-egos is one in which, after the mighty ordeal of the Great Crisis, the souls of the feminine and masculine elements become on the same plane; both are perfect. This is the marriage made in heaven. Become so that each thinks, wills and expresses itself the same in all ways simultaneously, the two alter egos are then one, having a feminine, negative, and a masculine, positive, aspect. Then these two potentials unite and receive the Spirit, or I AM, which was always undivided, and which illuminated each soul of its pair equally. So is this last union. Thus Phyris is me, living, being, immanent, and speaks this message with me; is I, and yet, mysterious truth, is herself! Likewise I am her and yet again, myself. I speak, and it is she; she speaks and it is I; for we are one being, one spirit, androgyne, perfect.

Yet not perfect as our Father is, for He is perfect as Condition-less Being, but our perfection is that of a part, because we are all of God, but not He of any one of us. Indeed, were this not true, then our attainment of perfection, Jesus' attainment of it, or any child of the Father, would find in its realization annihilation. But only the soul that sins is cast into the second death, fated to the Sisyphic round till it does succeed. Perfection may be condition-less in all respects save that it is not that of the whole. And because we each are parts, therefore we are forever attracted to the Father, who is sum of all parts, and this attraction is to onward Being. And we are forever attracted to the other parts, both those which are equal and those which are less. It is because the part is forever drawn to the sum that there is no death, except in defying and abandoning all hold on the Whole. Perfection of a part only draws it nearer to the Whole, and perfection of the Whole compels It to depend on each of Its parts. There may be change; there is no death. And there may be extinction of personality, the sinning soul may perish, and itself and its deeds be annihilated, but the Spirit from the Father does not die. If for your soul you would have eternal life; if you would not see your soul, that product of untold ages of time, lost in the second Death, and yourself, oh Spirit, child of our Father, doomed to recreate another soul to lay as acceptable offering before our Lord, then subdue it, subdue your soul, atone it to God through Jesus Christ our Lord, by recognizing that it is His, given Him by God, made by you to serve the Creator. If you make your soul serve you in His service, you have it eternally. But if you serve it you shall lose it and have to make another during coming eons.

Will you follow the Path, even as I have pointed out to you that it leads to the Kingdom? Be sure of yourself before you embrace occult learning, lest it prove a veritable Bridge of Mirzah, full of fatal pitfalls for your feet. Better to shun the Secret Wisdom than fail, for straight is the gate and narrow is the way that leads to Being, and there are few that find it.

Do you know me? A good tree cannot bring forth evil fruit, but a corrupt tree. Will you cut me down and cast me into the fire, who testifies concerning the Spirit? "Not every one that says Lord, Lord, shall enter into Heaven," but he that does the will of my Father in Heaven. The time is brief.

I have spoken. Peace be with you.

The End

The Secrets Of Mount Shasta And A Dweller On Two Planets

GLOSSARY.

Note:—Readers of "A Dweller on Two Planets" will please remember that in the Atlantean or Poseid language the word-terminations conveyed grammatical number and gender. Thus the singular was indicated by the equivalent for "a," the plural by "i," feminine by "u," while the absence of this terminal indicated masculinity.

Aphaisism—equivalent for mesmerism, but not hypnotism.

Astika—a prince.

Bazix—the name of one of the weeks of the year.

Devachan—the life after death.

Ene—terminal signifying study or student.

Espeid—Eden, Edenic.

Incal—the sun; also the Supreme God.

Incaliz, or Incalix—High Priest.

Inclut—first, or Sunday (also Incalon).

Inithlon—college devoted to religious learning.

Ithlon—any building, like a house.

Incalithlon—the great Temple.

Lemurinus, Lemuria or Lemorus—a continent of which Australia is the largest remnant today.

Karma—consequences growing out of one's actions in former lives.

Maxin—the Unfed Light.

Mo—to thee.

Murus—Boreas.

Naim—combined telephone and telephote.

Navaz—the night; also Goddess of the Night; also secret forces of Nature.

Navazzimin—the country of departed souls.

Ni—to.

Navamaxa—cremation furnaces for dead bodies.

Nosses—the moon.

Nossinithlon—insane asylum; [lit. a home for moon-struck persons.]

Nossura—mocking bird.

Pitach—a mountain peak.

Rai—Emperor or monarch, as Rai Gwauxln, pronounced Wallun.

Raina—a land governed; as the Raina of Gwauxln-Poseid.

Rainu [also Astiku]—a princess.

Su—be is gone.

Sattamun—desert, or wasted land.

Suernota—the Asian Continent.

Surada—to sing, or I sing.

Teka, or Teki—Poseid gold coin, value about $2.67.

Vailx—an aerial ship.

Ven—a linear unit of about a mile.

Xanatithlon—conservatory for flowers.

Xio, or Xioq—science.

Xiorain—the self-government board of Xioqua.

Xioqene—science student.

Ystranavu—the star of evening; also, when used astronomically Phyristunar.

Zo—personal pronoun, possessive my or mine.

The Secrets Of Mount Shasta And A Dweller On Two Planets

POST OFFICE BOX 753
NEW BRUNSWICK, NJ 08903

EXPLORE UNSPOKEN MYSTERIES AND EXAMINE THE EERIE PLANET WE LIVE ON!!

ALL ARE LARGE FORMAT BOOKS – FOR TRUTH SEEKERS ONLY!

MAN, BEAST, GODS OF AGHARTA: DISCOVERING THE MYSTERIOUS LOST KINGDOM OF THE INNER EARTH AND THE HOME OF THE KING OF THE WORLD—Does a secret subterranean paradise exist beneath the earth? Does its vast libraries house the wisdom of ALL AGES? Why is its very existence kept a secret under penalty of death? Contributor Dr Raymond Bernard was the first to popularize the concept of life inside our globe. This book's primarily author Ferdnand Ossendowski (one of the most spellbinding writers we have encountered) experienced compatible findings while trekking the frozen tundra of Russia. Speaking with monks and lamas he was told him about a subterranean "holy land." Millions of Buddhists worldwide accept the reality of Agharta and its benevolent ruler, though some say that it actually exists on the "edge of reality," in a "parallel universe," Hitler once sent a team of anthropologists to Tibet to seek out the kingdom. They hoped to make a pact with the King of the World who would not meet with the outsiders. Some of those who have ventured into this remote territory have never returned. No bodies have been found, leading to speculation that they eventually found the land that has been lost to time. ,This may be one of the most important books you ever read on the way to spiritual enlightenment. **Order: MAN, BEAST, GODS OF AGHARTA - $20.00**

OCCULT, WITCHCRAFT AND THE DEVIL'S FEAST IN OLD MOTHER RUSSIA
Those interested in the works of Madame Blavatsky, Nicholas Roerich, amd T. Lobsang Rampa will find this greatly expanded updated work to be a most rewarding venture into a frozen land of mystery and intrigue which has just started to thaw. The atheistic government of Russia did not want to be associated with these throwbacks occultists, they saw as practicing primitive paganism. Sorcerers were thought of as being older people who possessed the secret science of curing men and animals of diseases, of appeasing demons whenever they waxed into a great fury, of staunching blood, freeing insect-infested dwellings of vermin, de-haunting houses, tracking horse thieves, invoking the souls of the dead, foretelling the future and discovering hidden underground treasures. The Wizards, Witches, Shamans, and Hags were performing what seemed like "miracles," and so noted Polish-born scientist Ferdinandi Ossendowski activist and explorer, who had gained a reputation as a believer in reincarnation and cloistered underground cities like Agharta, went on a quest throughout Mother Russia to ascertain the truth about all matters supernatural and mysticism. **Order: OCCULT AND WITCHCRAFT IN RUSSIA - $20.00**

OUR ALIEN PLANET-THIS EERIE EARTH: ENTER DOORWAYS TO OTHER DIMENSIONS:— One of the most valuable resources on the Ultra-Terrestrial "Invasion" and on the Sky People! This work and companion audio CD reveals the stunning truth about: ** Ghost Lights & Glowing Orbs. ** Energy Fields. ** Interdimensional Life Forms.. ** Time Warps. ** Crop Circles. ** Ley Lines. ** Invisible Phantoms of Myth and Illusion. ** Mysterious Messages From the Soul of the Planet Conveyed In Signs and Symbols and Freaky Weather Phenomenon. OUR WORLD IS A SPOOKY PLACE — FIND OUT FOR YOURSELF! Here are documented tales of fairies, leprechauns, goblins and ghosts, to say nothing of unicorns, Mothman, flying Thunderbirds and an assortment of out of place forest and land dwellers. Authors Sean Casteel and Tim Beckley tell where "doorways" and "windows" exist on key junctions of a mysterious global grid system. Learn how earth itself possesses a superior intelligence and is capable of dramatic — and often violent — mood swings. You will learn what it is trying to say and how it goes about conveying messages to us planetary dwellers. **Order OUR ALIEN PLANET (book and CD) — $20.00**

TWILIGHT: HIDDEN CHAMBERS BENEATH THE EARTH—"There are," says T. Lobsang Rampa, "certain places in the Earth where it is possible for the Initiate to travel down into the center of the Earth and meet representatives of that inner civilization, and among quite a number of people there is a definite knowledge that people from the inner world do come out to converse with those of the surface. Then there are the tunnels from Tibet to the inner world and tunnels from Brazil to the inner world...and one tunnel beneath the greater Pyramids."In addition to a belief in the Inner Earth reality, Rampa explores UFOs, Astral Projection, the Laws of Kharma, Hypnotism and tells readers how to cope with modern day life. Rampa always considered this among his most vital works and it was his wish to share Twilight with as large an audience as possible. **Order TWILIGHT: HIDDEN CHAMBERS BENEATH EARTH - $20.00**

Note: If you want to learn more we suggest Rampa "companion volume" CAVE OF THE ANCIENTS which describes the Hall of Records and additional fascinating underworld factors, add $20 to total order. SUPER SPECIAL – Four books and one bonus audio CD as described just $64.00 + $8 S/H. Note: Add $20 if you wish the Cave of the Ancient book as well.

Timothy Beckley, Box 753, New Brunswick, NJ 08903

MAGICAL POWERS ONCE ENTRUSTED TO ONLY A FEW CAN NOW BE BESTOWED UPON YOU AT ONCE!

THE LATEST PSYCHIC TOOLS FROM REV. WILLIAM ALEXANDER ORIBELLO, DRAGONSTAR AND OTHERS

DIVINE BIBLE SPELLS: LIVING A PROSPEROUS AND HAPPY LIFE BY UNDERSTANDING THE SECRETS OF THE HOLY BOOK

There are many secrets in the Bible that you can flourish from – but first you must know where AND HOW to look. Let this work by William Alexander Oribello and Dragonstar operate as your personal guidebook.

YOU'VE HEARD IT SAID A THOUSAND TIMES . . . *WITH GOD ALL THINGS ARE POSSIBLE!* HERE ARE LINKS TO HIDDEN MYSTICAL MEANINGS IN THE BIBLE THAT YOU WERE NEVER TAUGHT IN CHURCH! DISCOVER WHAT ONLY A FEW "TRUTH SEEKERS" REALIZE — THAT A SECRET CODE HAS BEEN EMBEDDED WITHIN THE SCRIPTURES THAT COULD MAKE YOU PROSPEROUS ALMOST OVERNIGHT. Among The Many Things You Will Learn Are: ** Magick and Metaphysics are NOT of the Devil, but were always a major part of Christianity until such teachings were denounced during the Middle Ages. ** That the burning of colored candles at specific times and on specific dates plays a significant role in a program of Biblical illumination that can lead an individual to riches. ** There is a reason why the Three Wise Men arrived in Bethlehem with a variety of types of incense, including Frankincense and Myrrh. Burning incense while repeating certain verses from the Bible can triple the manifestations of your desires. ** That money is NOT the root of all evil, but is our GOD GIVEN right! No one needs to be poor. Abundance is part of the natural flow of God's Universe. TAKE CONTROL OF YOUR LIFE! PUT THESE DIVINE BIBLE SPELLS TO WORK FOR YOU NOW! (Some of this material was originally published in Divine Money Spells).

ORDER: DIVINE BIBLE SPELLS for just $22.00

WANT MORE INFORMATION ON THE SAME TOPIC? - Read the original BIBLE SPELLS as well as CANDLE BURNING WITH THE PSALMS by Wm Oribello. —$22 each – all 3 of these titles - $55.00 + $6 S/H

THE MEDIUMSHIP OF SPIRIT: THE ASCENSION OF WILLIAM ALEXANDER ORIBELLO

Authored by William Alexander Oribello, Abridged by Aurora Thyme, Designed by Tim R. Swartz

AN IMPORTANT SPIRITUAL MESSAGE TO HIS STUDENTS, FRIENDS AND ASSOCIATES — "Though I am in spirit, I am NOT dead! I am still here to assist in your needs."

"It is funny that one really never stops to consider what life is all about until it is over," declares the late metaphysician and occult adept from his new home in the spiritual realm. "We should come to accept help from the Ascended Masters whose mission is to bring the Great Wisdom of God the Creator to Planet Earth and usher us back to the Golden Age of Mankind that has eluded us for so long."

The CONTENTS of this masterful book include: ** **LIFE THE GREAT MYSTERY ** RETURNING HOME ** TO YOUR GOOD HEALTH ** LEAVING IT ALL BEHIND ** MAKE YOUR WISHES COME TRUE ** THE CHOICE IS UP TO YOU! ** THE SPIRIT OF ABUNDANCE ** GUIDING OTHERS ALONG THE PATH ** SO YOU WANT TO LIVE FOREVER? ** THOUGHTS MADE REAL ** THOUGHT ENERGY AND HOW TO USE IT ** LISTEN TO WHAT THE UNIVERSE IS TELLING YOU ** FIVE GREAT SECRETS YOU MUST KNOW!**

ORDER: THE MEDIUMSHIP OF SPIRIT (Expanded Edition) for just $20.00

WANT TO LEARN MORE ON THIS TOPIC? We highly recommend ( ) THE SEALED MAGICAL BOOK OF MOSES and ( ) SACRED MAGIC REVISED – ADD $20 EACH TO YOUR TOTAL ORDER

TIMOTHY BECKLEY, BOX 753, NEW BRUNSWICK, NJ 08903

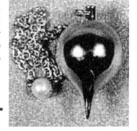

MARIA D'ANDREA PRESENTS

MYTHICAL, MAGICKAL BEASTS AND BEINGS

They Are All Around Us. Whether We Can See Them Or Not!From Our "Unordinary" Pets to Interdimensional Beings, Ancient Gods and Goddesses, Elementals, Dragons, Mermaids— and Yes, *Even Vampires!*

Come explore the supernatural side of man's best – and worst – "friends" as related in the strangest stories involving beasties of all sorts – seen and unseen. And uppermost learn how to get them to assist in our lives in a positive way.

HERE IS PROOF OF A PSYCHIC – OCCULT – PARANORMAL CONNECTION BETWEEN HUMANS AND EVERY MANNER OF BEAST AND BEING...FOR INDEED THERE ARE AS MANY ANIMAL PHANTOMS AS THERE ARE HUMAN SPECTERS!

Master Psychic and Spiritual Teacher, Maria D' Andrea tells us that, "Mythological and magical creatures have been with us in mythological stories, in religions, as well as in art forms. Dating back to the cave drawings, we can see pictographs of beasts, aliens and amazing figures. Heroes, Gods, Goddesses, objects and customs (some form the basis of our civilization)."

The author of **Heaven Sent Money Spells** and TV host states further, "These stories can give us hope, expectancy, lessons, teachings, intrigue and motivation. They let us know there are things out there that we can connect to, which help make our lives easier, help us to improve our lives and work with the elemental kingdoms, spiritual planes of existence and the unseen inter-dimensional beings that have been with us for centuries."

In her latest work, **MYTHICAL, MAGICKAL BEASTS AND BEINGS,** Maria notes that some of these beings come from our deepest imagination, our visions, from psychic "seeing." These beings are thought forms we create with the power of our minds, and they can be beneficial as well. We can, in essence, call upon them from within the deepness of our souls when "the time is right."

MAGICKAL BEINGS INCLUDES:
** Mermaids Of The Deep. ** Dragons. ** Elves And Manos Of The Ancients. ** Crystal Beings. ** Undines. ** Astral Beings.

In addition, natural intuitive **Penny Melios** reveals the true nature of the Elemental Kingdom and the best times to approach for communications purposes and for assistance when needed the most.

Not to be outdone, **Sean Casteel** says that some animals even have the gift of speech, and that according to the Bible, a talking donkey caused a wicked man to repent, while in the 1930's England a talking Mongoose moved in with a farm family and became a terrifying member of the household.

Charles Fort, a British researcher and collector of "nature's oddities," dug up hundreds of cases in which it literally rained a multitude of species from the sky. With no explanation of course!

Elliott O' Donnell recognizes the fact that some "animals" operate in the great unseen. There are, he reports, countless incidents in which phantom horses have been heard and seen, and even wild animals have put in "physical" appearances even though they might not have been there to begin with.

This work of NON FICTION will enthrall and thrill. If you enjoy the works of **Ripley's Believe It Or Not** and are able to open your minds to incredible possibilities...

☐ **Order MYTHICAL AND MAGICKAL BEASTS AND BEINGS for just $18.00 + $5 S/H**

TIMOTHY BECKLEY · BOX 753 · NEW BRUNSWICK, NJ 08903

OTHER BENEFICIAL TITLES BY MARIA D'ANDREA

☐*HEAVEN SENT MONEY SPELLS - $20.00*
☐*YOUR PERSONAL MEGA POWER SPELLS - $25.00*
☐*OCCULT GRIMOIRE AND MAGICAL FORMULARY - $25.00*
☐ *SECRET MAGICKAL ELIXIRS OF LIFE - $25.00*
☐ *OCCULT GALLERY AND SPELL CASTING FORMULARY - $24.00*
BONUS DVD WITH ORDER

460

461

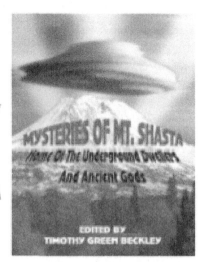

Printed in Great Britain
by Amazon

29293902R00262